Twentieth Century Art
Painting and Sculpture in the Ludwig Museum

Karl Ruhrberg
Twentieth Century Art
Painting and Sculpture in the Ludwig Museum

RIZZOLI NEW YORK

This selective catalogue was published on
the occasion of the opening of the new
Ludwig Museum, Cologne, September 1986

Translated by Michael Robinson, London
Edited by Ian Robson, Leeds and Stuttgart
Designed by Rolf Brenner, Michael Maegraith

Jacket subject: Max Beckmann, *Two Women,* 1940

First published in the United States of America in
1986 by Rizzoli International Publications, Inc.
597 Fifth Avenue, New York, NY 10017

© 1986 Museen der Stadt Köln (Museum Ludwig)
and Ernst Klett Verlage GmbH und Co. KG,
Stuttgart.
Verlagsgemeinschaft Ernst Klett –
J. G. Cotta'sche Buchhandlung Nachfolger GmbH,
Stuttgart
ISBN 0-8478-0755-X
LC 86-42724
Printed and bound in the Federal Republic of
Germany

Contents

Dedicated to
Dr. Kurt Hackenberg,
Head of the Cultural Administration of Cologne,
1955–79

Twentieth Century Art

There is a commonly held but erroneous view that 20th century art started at a zero point, and therefore has no past and no historical perspective. Views of this kind have been encouraged by our chronological closeness to turbulent, inherently artistic revolutions and counter-revolutions, to an alienation of artist and public which has its roots in the 19th century; they are also encouraged by the lack of a uniting and binding "style" and the confluence or clash of conflicting currents and tendencies caused by that lack. Other factors have been: revolt against the academic and the conventional, rejection of direct succession in protest against anaemic historicism, polemics by artists and their poetic and critical friends aiming to conquer and defend a position of their own, and finally a general resistance to regimentation and restoration. Thus, the too hasty conclusion is understandable, but does not stand up in the face of reality.

The art of our century, so-called Modern Art, does have its traditions and a long prehistory. The distinguished art historian and theoretician Werner Hofmann, Director of the Hamburg Kunsthalle, has traced the "incubation period" back to the Middle Ages. Coming to terms with the artistic past is motivated in ways fundamentally different from those which used to apply, different from the relationship of Renaissance artists to a much-admired antiquity, above all different from the historical understanding of the academic and salon art of the 19th century. Artists have turned uncompromisingly against the uncritical worship of things classical prevalent in this period, which, it is recognized, can only lead to potentially crippling historicism in a classical mould. Thus, the classical period is ignored in favour of others which have hitherto been neglected (like the Pre-Raphaelite Quattrocento, or Mannerism). A radically new and unconventional choice is being made. Even more important is the fact that the "Moderns" do not see the art of antiquity as a model, but more as a stimulus. They no longer imitate, they seek inspiration, and then handle ideas and forms freely, and bend them to their own expressive will and ideas of form. Besides – and this again we owe to systematic historical analysis – time and space are more at our disposal than ever, as can be seen simply by considering the complete œuvre of an artist like Picasso. The influence of the Far East is clear in the "Japonnaiserie" of the Impressionists and their successors, and quasi-Romantic interest in "exotic" art and "primitives" inside and outside European culture (black Africa, Oceania) is constantly on the increase – not least as part of the search for a new "originality." This is the source of the "anti-traditionalism" of the early Moderns. In the case of Gauguin, who wanted anti-historical art, it grew from an essential hostility to history, but this is not true of all the artists concerned.

Dictionaries define the adjective "modern" as: of today, new, of the most recent times, or timely. In this sense the definition is inapplicable to many, if not most, artistic periods in our century. Something which yesterday was "up-to-date" and "contemporary" can today be "yesterday's work" and "not in step with the times." The law of exponential acceleration which governs the scientific, political, social and economic processes of our age, the enormous wear and tear to which ideas are subjected, has affected the field of art as well, sometimes with continuing power to shock. Impressionism and Symbolism, Cubism and Futurism, Constructivism and Surrealism, Art Nouveau, and abstract art as a world language, have passed into history; these movements and the artists who represented them have either entered the pantheon or have been sent to the bottom of their particular historical class. This does not mean that another turn of the spiral might not bring them back to the front again.

This is true in our times of the early Fauve painters around Matisse, and of the German Expressionists of the "heroic" period, who have influenced many of the anti-heroic "New Savages" of our own day. This is part of the late historical effect of expressive painting, which is not always synchronized with the history of its early days. A historical example of the opposite kind is the rediscovery and revaluation by the Surrealists of Mannerism, which was long felt to be a kind of decadent Renaissance.

Art Is Always Contemporary

Art, traditional as well as modern, is always subjected to changing judgements, it only exists to the extent that it is seen. But we see it, just as previous generations did, with the eyes of our particular present. We can no longer look at Rembrandt through 17th century eyes; the Italians of the Quattrocento, at the latest since the time of the Pre-Raphaelites, are no longer brilliant "primitives" paving the way for the perfection of classical art in the High Renaissance, the view taken of them in the 19th century. A biological view of art as something which develops in a straight line through youth, maturity, age and decay is now no more than a historical curiosity, and the progress theory too has now been dismissed; it was loosely based on Hegel and made the artist the "manager of the mind" – you could say, of the contemporary mind – a critic and apologist but also someone who points to a better future.

Even the conservative Jakob Burckhardt suggested: "Life is only in movement, however painful it be." The static and the motionless produce stagnation, numbness and death. The notion of a straight line of development to an ideal goal under the banner of Hegel's metaphysical optimism – parallel to the movement from a static to a dynamic concept in science – has been replaced by the more pragmatic perception that Burckhardt's "movement" means endless open-ended change. As a consequence of this the history of the art of the century which is drawing to its close must, like that of the art of the past, be continually rewritten and interpreted, and discussed publicly by means of critical and analytical examination and exhibitions. Only this continuing dialogue, the ceaseless questioning of works of art, the exchange of views on and insights into past and present, will keep art alive, beyond day-to-day polemics. This is why museums constantly rearrange their collections and alter their emphases, and also resist the temptation to discard items which seem to have become valueless or temporarily without relevance. For example, what would have happened to all the works of 19th century art which could not be seen as forerunners of classical Modern Art when, in Germany in particular after 1945, the revision course on "degenerate art" was running full speed ahead, if everybody had given in completely to this temptation? We would be the poorer by many important works today, when we see more clearly that the artistic problems of the 20th century, like many others, have their roots in the 19th.

It cannot be denied that there has been a break with an epoch which lasted for more than four hundred years, beginning at the end of the Middle Ages with the Italian Renaissance, or that Modern Art occupies an exceptional position when we undertake its long-overdue

Gustave Courbet, *Beach,* c. 1866

integration into history, an integration which does not exclude either mutations and leaps, or the contrast between "continuity and contradiction" (Laszlo Glozer); nor does this integration exclude Daumier's and Courbet's categoric demand "Il faut être de son temps" ("One must be of one's time"). Our way of seeing has altered radically; without a binding style tendencies and currents change at a pace which is sometimes breathtaking.

The Break

The break came in the last third of the 19th century, when cracks began to appear beneath the surface of European optimism, beneath the surface of belief in the blessings of technology and in our ability to organize the world; it began to seem less certain that "wonderful times" of prosperity and ever-increasing mobility lay ahead, and not only in the Imperial Germany of

Camille Corot, *Ville d'Avray,* undated

the Gründerjahre (the 1870s). Doubt, in the later stages of development often close to despair, is reflected in the work of artists whose sensitivity and gift for accurate observation caused them – consciously or unconsciously – to react at an early stage to the change in the era's awareness of life. The temptation from our present perspective to make this a reason to see them all as highly-stylized "prophets" of the future should be resisted, however. Even though they are diagnostically way ahead of their more coarsely-programmed contemporaries, who lack a sense of future events with seeds in the present, they remain children of their own time, even the Expressionists, whose distortions present a world which is about to fall apart.

This is already clear if one considers Impressionism. On the one hand, these colourful and glowing paintings are a manifestation of the "last hour of European happiness," as the poet Emil Barth put it after a visit to the "Jeu de Paume", the climax and the last link in the glorious chain which leads from the early Renaissance almost to the end of the 19th century. Illusionistic art celebrates its latter triumph in the pictures of Renoir, Manet, Pissarro, Sisley, Degas and above all Monet, and in the sculpture of Rodin. The Impressionists also exploit pictorially the last fragment of reality, drawing

Pierre Auguste Renoir, *The Oarsmen's Breakfast,* 1881

on the newly-won freshness of Barbizon school open-air painting, on "père" Corot, Charles Daubigny and Théodore Rousseau, on liberation from academic regimentation and idealized revelation in the filtered light of the studio, and also on Courbet's powerful realism. They give permanence to the fleeting moment, and do not simply portray reality as it is, but also the permanent process of change to which their subjects are exposed. In Impressionist pictures, being is replaced by becoming, as Carl Einstein, the first important interpreter of art in the 20th century, put it in 1926.

The other side of these painters' entirely earthly conception of reality is the pleasure they take in portraying the everyday, their courage in choosing banal subjects. An "Oarsmen's Breakfast" (Renoir), the "Gare Saint Lazare" (Monet) and a "Bundle of Asparagus" become subjects worthy of being painted. "A cabbage can be just as beautiful as a Madonna," as Max Liebermann was to say later. One thing these stylistically very dissimilar works have in common is their avoidance of

Pierre Auguste Renoir, *The Sisleys,* 1868

Edouard Manet, *Bundle of Asparagus,* 1880

Claude Monet, *Nymphéas (Water Lilies),* c. 1914–1917

dominant formal organization, of academic perspective, of the principles of classical picture composition, but their most important characteristic is that colour is made autonomous and taken for granted as an emanation of light. Parallel to this is the lively surface of Rodin's sculpture with its bumps and hollows and vigorous play of light and shade.

We have thus established a basic theme of the art of our century, which has maintained its relevance through many variations and dialectical reversals via Van Gogh and the Expressionists, the abstract Impressionism of Bazaine, "informal" art, American "action painting" and colour field painting, down to the "violent" or "wild" pictures of today.

It should be remembered at this point that some of the most important Impressionists not only experienced the subsequent "artistic revolution" brought about by the Fauves, Expressionists, Cubists, Futurists, Dadaists and Surrealists, but also acted as influences upon it through their openness to change, and certainly survived it. Monet's "Haystack" and his magnificent series of water-lily paintings were a source of inspiration to scores of abstract painters, from Kandinsky to the Informalists of the fifties. Lovis Corinth's important late works also belong to this period. Bonnard, the last great master of light-painting, only duly appreciated in our times, died in 1947, seven years before Henri Matisse, who was at the same time a "Revolutionary" and a classicist, and whom we consider to be the best, or at least the most cultivated, painter of the century – alongside the dramatic Picasso. He was only two years younger than Bonnard.

Lovis Corinth, *Lake Walchen, Panorama,* 1924

The simultaneity of opposites is a long-neglected theme which would be worthy of thorough examination. The example of Bonnard–Matisse is enough to show that the phenomenology of art resists chronological arrangement, the handicap of the historian. This perception should prevent layman and expert alike from looking with one eye at "the latest and most up-to-date the world has to offer" and closing the other to something which may be from the past, especially the most recent past, but which is assertively of the present because of its undiminished artistic substance and effect, and the vigour with which it progresses from stage to stage. Nothing is more idle than to quarrel about whether a twenties picture by Otto Dix, George Grosz or Max Beckmann is "more modern" than one from Monet's late "Nymphéas" (Water Lilies) series, painted at about the same time.

tionally apart from each other, without any overlapping. Parallel to this, their strict and scientifically-minded system led back to form, to motionless pictorial architecture in a classical, or one might almost say classicistic, mould.

This pictorial design is also emphatically present in the more brittle, incorporeal black and white of the drawings, again most strikingly in the drawings of that genius of pictorial architecture Georges Seurat, who, as becomes increasingly clear with the passage of time, despite his early death, so far surpasses his more immediately appealing comrade and successor Paul Signac, who stuck more closely to nature. The impersonal, stylized appearance of Seurat's figures ("La Grande Jatte", "Le Chahut") is – independently of the form of the particular picture – stamped with an inner monumental quality of archaic style in its striking simplicity

The Culmination

If Impressionist painting and – as we see more clearly again today than we did a few years ago – Rodin's sculpture stand fairly precisely at the break point between art since the Renaissance and Modern Art, then Neo-Impressionism, or better still Pointillisme, shows how a movement which dominates its period can culminate in turning into its opposite. The Pointillistes, with the incomparable Seurat at their head, took the Impressionists' principle of autonomous colour, their loose network of commas of paint, to an absolute extreme by making the commas into dots and placing their pure, unmingling dabs of paint systematically and unemo-

Georges Seurat, *A Sunday Afternoon on the Island of La Grande Jatte,* 1884–86

Pierre Bonnard, *Nude in the Mirror*, 1910

and the silence of the arrested movement. The Impressionists' "Dionysiac" dissolution of form, their open pictorial construction in the tradition of Ruskin's "confused modes of execution" is transformed into its "Apollonian" counterpart by scientifically developed Impressionistic means, on a basis of old and new theories of colour and colour analysis. The inherently fragmentary, selective nature of Impressionist pictures once more becomes integrated form. At the turn of the 18th century Schiller stated: "The difficult operation is the reduction of empirical form to aesthetic form." The Pointillistes, and above all Seurat, performed this operation successfully. His coolly-distanced, positivistic scientific approach, which took him further from his natural models than Signac, marks the point at which rationalism entered the art of our time.

Thus, it was before the end of the nineteenth century, very close to the period of Impressionism and Neo-Impressionism, that the signposts to the two principal routes of 20th century art were set. One leads via Van Gogh to the Expressionists, early Kandinsky, European Informel and American-style Abstract Expressionism (action painting), and finally to the uninhibitedly neo-expressive, backward-referring art of the eighties. The other begins with Cézanne and continues via Cubism, western and eastern Constructivism, the austere rhythms of late Mondrian, the platonistic abstraction of Josef Albers' "Homage to the Squares", and Barnett Newman's silent coloured fields. This route also ends in the immediate present.

Paul Gauguin, whose adventure-filled life and exotic themes have long distorted our view of the way in which his painting points to the future, renounced perspective and the illusion of space even more decisively than the Impressionists. The key factor in his art is not a wealthy man's Romantic flight from civilization to Tahiti, however symptomatic that may be of the search for untapped originality, nor is it the unsuccessful attempt to make a new "synthetic" mythology by uniting the heathen and the Christian; it is much more his unequivocal commitment to the two-dimensional and – regardless of the subject – to abstraction. "Let us remember", wrote that pious Symbolist Maurice Denis, who had been a follower of Gauguin in the early Breton years, in his famous essay of 1890, "that a picture, before it becomes a warhorse, a naked woman or any story you choose, is in essence a flat surface covered with a particular arrangement of paint."

Gauguin's approach to painting transforms this programmatic thesis into pictures. Their hallmark is the richly contrasting harmony of horizontal and vertical organization, of free-flowing line and pure colour. Also, the synaesthetic notion of "music in colour," the understanding of colouring as sound, later to be so important for Kandinsky, are characteristic of Gau-

14

Paul Gauguin, *Riders on the Shore, Tahiti,* 1902

guin's understanding of art. There is no doubt that – despite his vehement attacks on Delacroix's diametrically opposed and conservative counterpart Ingres – there is an underlying yet cryptic classicism within him. It is the counterpoint to Gauguin's lifelong search for new sources of inspiration beyond old Europe and his weariness of the old civilizations. The idea of "pure painting," independent of its subject, is heralded in the works of this adventurer, who was anything but a "naif." Daniel-Henry Kahnweiler, the friend and discoverer of Picasso and the Cubists, reproached Gauguin with the fact that his pictures were too decorative, there was nothing to "read" in them.

Anyone who, like Kahnweiler, sees painting as writing, is probably bound to come to that conclusion. But Gauguin, unlike the Cubists, was a potential wall painter: "There must always be a sense of the surface, the wall, tapestries do not need perspective," he said, and commended to his colleagues "every object in silhouette form." His work falls between two periods: it shows the influence of past European and non-European cultures from Java to India, from the Aztecs to the Japanese, from the Parthenon frieze to the sculpture of the South Seas, from Breton folk art to the early Italians, from Islamic ceramics to Christian stained glass. But Gauguin was also influenced by his contemporaries, the much older classicist Puvis de Chavannes, Manet in his pre-Impressionist period and Edgar Degas. Without him the arabesques of Toulouse-Lautrec and Art Nouveau are unthinkable, and so are the Japonnaiserie of Bonnard and Vuillard, the glowing colours of Henri Matisse, the colour tone of Kandinsky. A mere glance at the work and development of this pioneer of the art of our century (Gauguin died in 1903) clearly shows the multiplicity of the roots of "modern" art. Recourse to the treasures of the "imaginary

museum" (André Malraux), which was not possible to this extent until history was understood in a new way, already points to a connection with history and a revaluation of non-European cultures, avoiding the "classical" epochs of European art, which had been discredited by imitators and academic regimentation.

Despite Gauguin's flight from Europe it can be established that what follows is not a rejection of history, but a decisive about-turn from the uncreative, lifeless weakness-after-greatness of "historicism", to use Karl Popper's phrase. None of those who paved the way for Modern Art advocated total rejection of the history of art; they only made different selections, to avoid being caught in the shackles of rigid rules.

On the other hand, tendencies can be identified which have moulded extensive fields of modern art right up to the present time: a visible commitment to the two-dimensional surface (to which Gauguin did not always keep), which makes the picture itself an abstract idea, or pictorial architecture, but also a commitment to pure, unmixed colour. Two opposing principles, construction and the dissolution of form under the dominance of living, flowing colour (to be known as "couleur vivante" in the fifties) are the poles between which the richly contrasting practices in the field of Modern Art unfold in a multiplicity of variations and mixtures, similar to the contrasts between Poussin and Rubens, Ingres and Delacroix in the past.

Set against this, Gauguin's personal fate has only anecdotal significance. He came to grief in the attempt to escape from civilization and discover paradise on earth, like generations of artists after him. Think of all those attempts to withdraw into ivory towers outside reality, the neo-Romantic "individual mythologies" of the seventies: the inner way also proved to be a cul-de-sac.

Setting out to change the world by radical criticism and the rejection of all traditional values, including artistic ones, failed as early as the Dadaists, who were finally thrown back upon themselves. The group among the Surrealists which was politically active and engaged in agitation for a time could not prevent new wars and new misery. In the last resort this is also true of the mass student movements of the sixties and seventies.

Art and Revolt

"Contrary to the hopes of many present-day artists," wrote Eberhard Roters as early as 1970, "it is impossible to give too low an estimate of the social relevance of fine art." This judgement is particularly welcome in the case of militant futurists, who usually place themselves at the service of fascism. It is however less wel-

Vincent van Gogh, *The Church at Auvers,* 1890

come in the case of the Dadaists or the moral rigour of the youth of '68 and particularly in the light of the partially conforming and affirmative profit-orientated artistic practices of the eighties. This does not in any way alter the sobering realization that the effectiveness outside artistic circles of the "Modern Art revolution" was and to a certain extent still is overestimated by its enemies as well as its supporters. This is true of a conservative historian like Hans Sedlmayr, whose polemics mourned the "loss of the middle ground" as a result of artistic revolutions, under the unspoken Koestler motto "God's throne is empty," and equally true of the apologists of the avant-garde at any point. Many of them believe, as we read in the catalogue of the Basel exhibition "Everything, and a Lot More Besides," that even today art, and only art, can help to avoid a nuclear war. They have all failed to recognize the limited possibilities of a revolt against tradition. The effect of revolt remained, as becomes increasingly clear with hindsight, limited to fields in which art is inherent. The critical artists' prophecies of doom went unheard, the powers-that-be did not act upon their designs for "possible worlds" (Paul Klee), or ignored them altogether. Arrival at this conclusion marks the beginning of the illusion-free "New" or "Second Modern" period in the forties, which coincides almost exactly with the beginning of the Second World War. "Do not saddle the poor poets with a mission!" demand-

ed Gottfried Benn, half cynically, half in resignation. A painter or a sculptor could have said the same thing, or something very similar. The command "Change the world!" was replaced by the more modest theme of the preservation of freedom, of the "incorruptible space," which Theodor W. Adorno demanded for the arts in one of his late essays, a last reservation for the humanist, a space without ideology, a space in which you cannot get your hands dirty.

In this context the life and death of Vincent van Gogh acquire exemplary significance. Unlike Gauguin, Van Gogh, the first Northerner among the leading artistic figures of our century, did not try to flee from the civilized world, but to change it. But as the Grand Inquisitor firmly rejected Christ come again in Dostoevsky's novel "The Brothers Karamazov", so the institutionalized church rejected the curate Van Gogh, who tried to practise original Christianity in a godless age; and those he loved turned from him too.

Because he had failed as a preacher and reformer, Van Gogh became a painter. He operated alone, outside the society which had rejected him, outside what is now known as the artistic scene or, more sloppily, the art business. The one-man show which is his life demonstrates most depressingly the depth of the gulf between artist and public, how since the Romantic period it has become impossible to understand contemporaries other than through inherited clichés. The British painter Francis Bacon, our contemporary, painted a series of pictures showing the Dutchman's isolation with all the empathy of a kindred spirit, and with a mastery entirely suited to the task. The pictures, like Stations of the Cross inspired by Vincent's own representation, show the lonely Dutchman in Provence on his way to work, his painting equipment on his shoulders as if it were the Cross.

Today, when contemporary art receives more publicity than ever before, when even fashionable magazines occasionally put their pages at the disposal of young star painters, the question is whether this benevolent embrace might make artists just as harmless as did the social ostracism of the past. This question is implicit when one considers the new relevance which Van Gogh's expressive, blazing line and the luminosity of his paint, applied to the canvas thickly and violently, have acquired through Expressionism and action painting. It is not only his flamboyant cypresses, the shuddering contours of his trees and churches, the glowing light of the "Midi" over his landscapes, or the exciting drama of his brushwork which mark the beginning of one of the two principal routes leading to the art of the immediate present: his subjects are revolutionary as well. An abandoned chair, a pair of worn-out shoes, the poverty-stricken feel of his bedroom in Arles, the sinister atmosphere of dim night-clubs, soup

Vincent van Gogh, *The Drawbridge*, 1888

kitchens, hostels – and of course the asylum in which he was treated – are equally worthy subjects for pictures as the poor potato-eaters of the early works. There is no longer a sense of transfiguring Romanticism, as in Spitzweg's "The Poor Poet", no likeable-untidy genre work as in Jan Steen, in whose pictures the ordinary people are always in a good mood, no erotic exoticism as in the work of Gauguin. Misery is taken seriously, the most banal things are worth portraying: the hierarchy of subject matter is broken.

Van Gogh's pictorial world points far into the future, not only to the socially revolutionary art of the Expressionists and – under quite different stylistic conditions – to the post-war Realism of the twenties, but also to essential aspects of the complex work of an artist like Joseph Beuys. Van Gogh's "Yellow Chair" and Beuys' fat chair are related across the years, not in style, but in the attitude which they express.

Vincent van Gogh, *Van Gogh's Bedroom in Arles*, 1888

Paul Cézanne, *Mont Sainte-Victoire,* 1904–1906

The Classicists of Modern Art

The second principal route taken by the art of our century leads via Cubism, Constructivism, De Stijl and Geometric Abstraction to the threshold of our own times; it begins with Paul Cézanne, the lonely painter from Aix-en-Provence, considered by those around him to be a crank and a madman, whose death was scarcely regretted in his home town, even though fame had caught up with him by the end of his life.

In Cézanne's early days no-one could have imagined that he was to become one of the great classical modern artists, the painting "constructor" of a colourful pictorial world "parallel to nature." He started his career with violent, "wild" pictures in the manner of Delacroix and Monticelli, which were turbulent and chaotic in an almost baroque way. Unrest, murder, rape and extravagant sexual fantasies were among his sometimes quite brutally treated subjects before he was rejected by the Academy and turned to Impressionism under the guiding hand of Camille Pissarro,

who as the Impressionists' father-figure had never abandoned a stabilizing pictorial framework. Cézanne made Impressionism, as he intended, into "something solid and lasting, like art in museums." The Venetians Tintoretto and Veronese, but above all Nicolas Poussin, the "painters' painter," with his great understanding of art, were his models. What he found interesting in the work of Tintoretto was not the unclassically open design, or the manneristic stretching of figures and the spiralling crookedness of their movements, but the way the colours were put together, the dense structure of forms mingling one with another. Cézanne went beyond the Venetian he so admired and was well ahead of his own time in grasping colour as form, a theme which is still relevant in our own times, as even a fleeting glance at the work of such different artists as Nay, Graubner or Morris Louis will show. The way the brush strokes mingle – "My canvas holds hands with itself," said Cézanne – resulted in a dense web of strictly two-dimensional colour. The painter, unlike the Impressionists, was not concerned with portraying the fleeting

18

moment, but with permanence, not with the appearance, but with the essence of objects and figures.

In contrast with Van Gogh, Cézanne was nothing but a painter. Drawing interested him as the first stage of painting, not as an artistic medium in its own right – he was suspicious of limiting fields of colour by outline. For him, art was not there to criticize its times and improve the world, an attitude which finally led him to lose the friendship of the socially critical writer Emile Zola. Cézanne wanted to do nothing less than make visible the "eternity" of nature. For him, a picture was an autonomous creation, the artist's reply to reality while suppressing himself as an individual (whom he saw as a medium).

Cézanne's ideal of a classicism unfettered by its time is broken by the vibrato below the surface of his paint structures, which in their multiplicity and liveliness point to the fact that emergent essence finds form in the pictures of the man from Provence. As was later the case in the decomposition of form without perspective of the Cubists, the movement of the colours protects Cézanne's classicism from the danger of academic paralysis, despite its strictly systematic nature, a danger which his late successors, the quasi-platonic Abstract Geometricists like Magnelli, Mortensen, Dewasne, and even Herbin and Vasarély, did not avoid: even in 1955 Werner Haftmann felt the need to warn them against an "Abstract Academy".

The First "Fauves"

Cézanne died in 1906. A year before this the Paris Salon d'Automne exhibited work by that group of artists who have gone into history under the misleading name "Les Fauves" – the wild ones. The name was invented by the critic Louis Vauxcelles, incidentally not with malicious, but rather with ironic intention. The harmlessly classicist small-scale sculpture of the now forgotten Marquet was swamped by the provocation of pure unrestricted colour, exceeding the boldness of the Impressionists and Pointillistes, exceeding Gauguin and even Cézanne. "Donatello parmi les fauves!" ("Donatello among the wild beasts") Vauxcelles is said to have exclaimed.

Matisse and Marquet had first trodden this path seven years earlier, but Matisse is the only one who explored it to the very end with undiminished creative energy throughout his very full life – with never-ending creative variations right through to the "papiers découpés," the scissor works of the master in his old age – thus becoming the actual classic among the moderns. After him the greatest talent is the contemplative, spiritual Georges Braque, who combined Cartesian "clarté" with intensity and later, together with Picasso, became the father of Cubist pictorial architecture, with its programmatically subdued colour. Georges Rouault, the darkest, most sinister of the Fauves, changed from being the accuser of unjust judges and the partisan of victims, the debased and the abused into the icon painter of a new and expressive religiosity in heavy, thickly-applied black-outlined colour, which had nothing to do with the "wildness" of earlier years in either subject, colour or form.

The Fauves wanted to revolutionize art, but not to change the world. Their art is "culinary," to use Brecht's famous formulation. The very title of Matisse's key picture demonstrating the transition from Pointillisme to pure colour in its final, liberated form shows this quite clearly: "Luxe, calme et volupté" ("Luxury, Peace and Pleasure"). The vigour of the early days did not persist. Maurice Vlaminck remained the only "wild man"; he could be called the Fauve Expressionist, but without the supportive base of the group his pictures lost substance in the course of the years. Derain withdrew to classicality suffused with Gothic form, Marquet's colour became more and more gentle, Dufy became a charming illustrator. Matisse himself, however, to whom Moreau once prophesied: "You will simplify painting," became the classical painter of "joie de vivre". What he brought into being through all the stages and transformations of his work was, in Maurice Denis' fine formulation, "painting with all the chance elements removed, essential painting, pure painting," but also "the quintessential search for the absolute" through artistic thinking. The older he became, the further he moved away from the ideology of progress in art, which was only a reflection of the academic and political thinking of the period. Matisse did not see himself as avant-garde: "The artist," he said, "simply sees old truths in a new light, because there are no new truths."

Henri Matisse, *Luxe, Calme et Volupté*
(Luxury, Peace and Pleasure), 1904

Henri Matisse, *The Blue Window,* 1911

German Expressionism was a completely different matter; the great Italian art historian and former Mayor of Rome Giulio Carlo Argan said of it: "Here for the first time art foresees and foretells an imminent and monstrous historical catastrophe." What was neeeded for that were diagnostic rather than prophetic abilities, which were lacking in contemporaries blind to fate in the same way as they were in the generation before the Second World War. As we know, they have not developed much further today, under the shadow of a total global threat. The philosopher Günther Anders has pointed out that lack of imagination is mankind's real downfall, above all for those in positions of power who cannot imagine the consequences of their actions and therefore conjure up catastrophe after catastrophe. From this he derives the demand that we should "also interpret" the "change" in the world which is taking place before our eyes almost every day – and after three industrial revolutions at an ever more breathtaking pace. "And indeed change this (that is, the change itself). So that the world does not change any more of its own accord, without us."

The imagination invoked by Anders is possessed by artists to a large extent, and they also have the ability to interpret. This is what makes them different from their less sensitive contemporaries. This is the root of their "prophetic" gifts and their "political" importance beyond all ideology and daily polemic. This is true of the German Expressionists, independently of the drama of their age. Unlike their contemporary French colleagues, but more like the great Norwegian Edvard Munch, they interpreted not only art, but also the world and society. Their idea was collective solidarity for all mankind, but also the freedom of the individual: squaring the circle. They did not want only to paint, they wanted to give the industrial world a new ethos. A prerequisite of this was criticism of the world in which they lived, and also the old dream of "new men." They wanted to smash the world to pieces to build a new one from its ruins. The war destroyed their utopian hopes, which the greatest of them, Ernst Ludwig Kirchner, was later resignedly to call "youthful folly." But the pictures, above all the early ones, have outlived this disillusionment.

Unlike the art of the Fauves, which started with Cézanne and the Pointillistes, Expressionism, which at first made substantial borrowings from the French (Kirchner predated some of his pictures to conceal this), was not only art, but also a way of looking at the world, however undefined its political concepts may have remained. Its roots are in Romanticism, its ideal is not perfection in the finite, but openness to the infinite. Taking up and continuing Van Gogh's blazing entanglement of line, it shows the subjectivity of the hand as a means of expressing elemental sensations. Even

Edvard Munch, *Four Girls on the Bridge,* 1905

Kirchner's nervy, splintered hieroglyphics could become a "psychogram"; Kandinsky was to complete the process.

The distortion of objects and figures also enhances their expressiveness. Colour, however much it may be influenced by the French at first, is applied symbolically, to heighten reality, to make the representation of landscape, figure or still life or pictorial parable. This spontaneity of drawing or painting points ahead – in its subjectivity as well as its vehemence – to the ecstasies of the "Informel" and above all of "action painting," and also to the "écriture automatique" (automatic handwriting) of the Surrealist painters and writers around André Masson. This agitated picture writing is not just the application of an artistic ideology, but also a sign of existential bewilderment.

The Calm After the Colour Storm

Cubism, the actual classical art of this century, is very different from the work of the pre-1914 "Young Fauves." The bases of this school of painting are extreme discipline in the place of ecstasy, a high degree of objectivity in the place of unrestrained "expression," deep reflection in the place of emotion-charged spontaneity. At first glance this may be surprising, as one of the two founders of the school, Georges Braque, had been a major figure among the Fauves, along with Matisse, but above all because the other was called Picasso, the great source of unrest and the expressive dramatist among the painters and sculptors of this century. In fact the picture which is the key to Cubism, the "Demoiselles d'Avignon", does have some thoroughly

Pablo Picasso, *Les Demoiselles d'Avignon,* 1906–07

expressive features alongside hints of hard Spanish-Catalan realism. The decisive factor however is the formal boldness of Cubism: the figures are forced into a surface without perspective; the negro masks of the women in the right half of the picture are also logically made two-dimensional by means of long parallel brush strokes. The impression of corporeal mass is as strong as the contrast between light and dark. Georges Braque, who found the surprisingly radical quality of the picture as disquieting as most of Picasso's other admirers, when he saw it came up with the vivid suggestion that Picasso wanted "to make the public drink petroleum."

But the very next year he himself was submitting works for the Paris Salon d'Automne which did not have the exotic radicalism of the "Demoiselles", but in which the crooked lines and "petits cubes" (little cubes) made a structural – one could even say constructive – framework for the Fauve colours. Behind all this is Cézanne's famous observation that all natural shapes can be reduced to the sphere, the cone and the cylinder. But we should not forget that for him it was colour which gave the picture its structure, and made his canvas "hold hands with itself."

The Cubists, too, wanted to make their art "something solid and lasting," but their artistic medium is not colour, which they tone down radically in favour of the construction of the picture, restricting themselves to grey, ochre, brown and a dark and resonant green: a scale in which an accent is only occasionally set by a stronger red. The movement of the Fauves becomes a calm which is almost that of a still life, organic growth is replaced by the constructed, nature is replaced by

pictorial organization. Behind this is an uncompromising, almost fanatical will to truthfulness, a rejection of all beautiful deceptions. Anti-illusionism is driven as far as it will go, nothing is atmospheric any more. The world of the picture is closed within itself and faces the outside world autonomously.

It should not be forgotten, however, that the first goal of all Cubist exercises was a higher degree of reality. "We all thought of ourselves as realists," said Picasso later. With the assistance of painterly analysis, by moving around the subject of the picture, by "total representation" of it from various points of view, by adding what they knew about things to what they could see of them (everybody sees what he knows, as well as what he has before his eyes), they arrived at the simultaneous representation of one and the same thing at various times and from various sides. Thus, time becomes part of the static world of the picture, of the "cadence of tectonic surface forms" (Carl Einstein), a phenomenon of which the Futurists took advantage.

The intention was, therefore, to move away from the "lie" of optical illusion to the "truth" of definition, to concretize the essence of a thing and not its appearance. "To define a thing means: to replace it with the definition," said Georges Braque. This early declaration is not all that far removed from the more recent demand of the philosopher Anders not primarily to change the world, which is changing anyway, "unconsciously", but rather to analyze it thoroughly first of all. The Cubists sometimes added fragments of reality to their pictures and collages, as did the artists of the Middle Ages, however they did not use costly materials which transcend themselves and become immaterial, but everyday objects; these give the picture the character of an object and thus raise its degree of reality, make it into a "thing in itself." Behind this is a remarkable, almost Kantian rigour, and also a conscious renunciation of spectacular effects of breadth which hardly seems credible today. It is above all the analytic Cubism of the years after 1910 which – for the sake of greater "legibility" – was transformed under the influence of Juan Gris into the more readily decipherable, clearer, synthetic Cubism, which bears the stamp of secret, unsensual puritanism. It requires of the observer that he reflectively complete the picture by "reading" it associatively and with care, as Kahnweiler, practitioner and interpreter of Cubism, demanded uncompromisingly throughout his life.

This demand was later made more radical by the Conceptual artists, who hermetically denied sensuous vividness by supplying only the idea and leaving the observer to make it real by means of his own thought and imagination. Cubism, which saw itself in the first place as rigorously realistic, did not just inspire the practitioners of Geometric Abstract Art by emphasis on the two-dimensional quality of the picture, by its constructive elements and its quasi-platonic intention of letting the "idea" shine through behind the representation of the subject; Cubism is not only the classical art of this century, it is also (but not only) the Conceptual Art of the first half of the century.

If one bears in mind that the artists who have produced the most profound and certainly some of the most beautiful pictures and sculptures of the modern period nevertheless broke free from their self-imposed restrictions in order to make their work comprehensible to the public again, then it is hardly surprising that the rigid idealism of the radical "Conceptual Art" of the seventies had to reduce its demands on the observer in order to make art acceptable again.

Reaction in the form of the accentuatedly sensuous art of the eighties and finally, at its most extreme, the proclamation of the "dilettante as genius" (Walter Bachauer in the catalogue of the Berlin "Zeitgeist" exhibition) were not unexpected logical consequences.

Social Utopia

It was Fernand Léger, the grandson of Normandy peasants, who transformed the other, realistic component of Cubism into pictures, logically and with impressive vitality. He did not distrust the reality of the visible world. His painting is the art of accepting technical existence under the machine. In time his particular form of Cubism – jokingly christened "Tubism" (Tubisme) because of Léger's predilection for tubes – became his own "Nouveau Réalisme", a realism which has nothing to do with the realism created in the sixties in Paris by Yves Klein, Armand, César, Christo, Spoerri and others. It is an art of social and human engagement, and becomes increasingly representational; it is concerned above all with the anonymous "little men" in mass society, with whom Léger identified very strongly as a result of being a soldier in the First World War. "I left intellectual circles," he said, "Apollinaire, Jacob and the others, to find myself back with the farmers, navvies, miners and sailors. But I was just as strong as them, I wasn't afraid of them. I soon became their mate."

The simplicity of his later figures, construction workers and artists, their everyday and Sunday world, is in tune with the powerful simplicity of his pictorial design, in which art and nature, nature and technology are more in harmony than in the work of his friends. The strong colour, influenced in his later years by his experience of America, is also in tune with this. Léger never went along with the elimination of colour of the early Cubists, and felt himself closer to the glowing

"Orphism" of an artist like Robert Delaunay than to the contemplative renunciation of colour of the "analysts." The terse force of his reduced, broadly contoured designs, monumentalizing nature, technology and figures, does not suffer from this. He sets materialistic optimism against the metaphysical pessimism of his colleagues. In his pictorial world there is no distinction between person and thing, Sunday and weekday. If a brotherly "social realism" of solidarity and optimism were to exist beyond sweetly sentimental or pseudo-heroic glorification of an everyday world far from reality, then its paradigm would be the late work of Léger: a utopia which has lost none of its power to convince, however far it may be from realization in either the capitalist or the socialist society of our times.

This look at Léger and Robert Delaunay's glowing world of light and colour, which also started with Cubism, and which so deeply impressed the artists of the Munich "Blaue Reiter" – Marc, Macke, and to an extent Kandinsky as well – shows the whole span of Cubism from Realism to Conceptualism, and also the inexhaustible nature of this art, which still affects us today. It opened up artistic ground upon which we still move. It was "innovative" in the sense of Thomas Mann's definition of genius, because it made visible what before was not thinkable in that form until it was actually realized; but it was never intentionally "avant-garde" in the literal sense – and above all not in the political sense. Braque, along with Picasso the great innovator at the enthronement of "analytic" Cubism, said of himself: "I am not a revolutionary painter, I am not looking for hypertension, tension is enough for me." So the "revolutionary" of the early Fauve and Cubist years became one of the great "conservative" painters of the century.

Storming the Museums

The Italian Futurists were really "progressive," obsessed with a belief in progress. They and the Dadaists are the two movements in the art of the century which really did make a violent attack on tradition. But the museum stormers who surrounded the poet Filippo Tommaso Marinetti, living as they did in the classic country of museums, which so frustrated them with its artistic conservatism, soon ended up, and quite rightly, in museums themselves. It is more important to wonder, taking the example of such excellent artists as Boccioni, Ballà or Severini, where unreflecting political anarchy, lack of historical perspective, naive belief in progress and uncontrolled dynamism for its own sake might lead – in fact to the "dynamism" of a "movement," in this case to fascism: Prampolini, most important as a stage designer, glorified Mussolini's blackshirts in an artistically excellent picture, and the less gifted Soffici also succumbed to the fascination of the Duce. This is not surprising in the face of the glorification of war and violence in the work of their spokesman Marinetti, but one should examine other areas of his acutely mystifying and ritualizing thought in terms of its claim to be progressive. It is soon clear that the greater part of the writing is rigidly reactionary. On the one hand we find

Giorgio de Chirico, *The Disquieting Muses,* 1916

Umberto Boccioni, *Dynamism of a Soccer Player,* 1913

the famous maxim, "A racing-car is more beautiful than the Nike of Samothrace," which may appeal to us more than it did to Marinetti's contemporaries, as we are perfectly prepared to put an elegant Bugatti in a museum. It is well known that even Lenin could not manage without a Rolls-Royce from the home of Manchester capitalism, and thus helped the car to museum status. On the other hand, Marinetti shows chauvinism to a quite sinister degree, and rigorously rejects equal rights for women. We have long been aware – and painfully so – that political "progressives" are often among the most culturally conservative; the converse should also be noted, however: "progressive" artists can be political and philosophical "reactionaries." The rejection of history (including art history) and certainty about the future in terms of "belief in progress" do not on their own guarantee a better world, either in life or in art.

Critical reflections of this kind do not make the pictures of artists like Boccioni, Carrà (who later, under the influence of de Chirico, turned to the markedly history-oriented "pittura metafisica"), Ballà or Severini any worse, but they should make us a little more careful about the use of big words like "avant-garde" and

"progress", and indeed today, when everyone is talking about the "crisis of the avant-garde," we should not immediately come up with new catchwords, whether it be "Post-Modernist" or "Trans-Avant-Garde", often invented by the same people for whom not long ago things could not be "avant-garde" or innovative enough.

The Futurists' role in the history of art was to make possible the portrayal of sequences of movement in painting and sculpture, thus – as "primitives of the new way" – starting a development which was later taken up and continued by the film, which has a great deal to thank them for. The restlessness, the rush, the nervous dynamism of "modern" city life was first convincingly depicted in artistic and pictorial form by them. Boccioni's famous picture "The Street Enters the House" is a key work in this respect. Music and the theatre also benefited from Futurism. "Brutisme" paved the way for the "musique concrète" of the second half of the century. In the field of stage design Futurism produced solutions which have been fruitful even in our times. Finally, the short but intensive flowering of Russian revolutionary art was emphatically encouraged by the Italian pioneers.

After the fall of the Tsars in Russia, the search for new directions and optimistic visions of future collective happiness were social prerequisites, before everything sank back into petit-bourgeois pseudo-socialist mediocrity as a result of Lenin's artistic and political move to "Social Realism" in 1923 and Stalin's brutal repression of artistic development. But the futurist ideology of the Italian artists who, "standing on the summit of the world [...]," wanted "to hurl our challenge at the stars once more," declined into the First World War and finally into the fascism of Mussolini.

The Spiritual Element in Art

The Cubists were less concerned with revolutionizing the world than with revolutionizing art, but their work, opening up as it did hitherto unknown territory for painting, had more far-reaching consequences than the Futurists' attacks on tradition and history. This is also true of the artistic and theoretical activities of Vassily Kandinsky. There could hardly be a starker contrast than that between Kandinsky's almost elitist and esoteric theories on pictures and art and the Dresden "Brücke" Expressionists, whose cloudy, socially utopian commitedness was suspect to the "Munich" artists of the "Blaue Reiter" group. They were concerned with "the spiritual in art," as the title of Kandinsky's work on artistic theory has it. "It is pure art," wrote his friend Franz Marc, "which thinks so little of the 'other', is so little motivated by 'the purpose of uniting people', as Tolstoy says, hardly pursues any purpose at all, but is simply a symbolic act of creation, proud and quite 'of itself'." The picture does not have to portray anything, or reflect anything, it is a self-contained, concrete object. To this extent the term "abstract" is misleading. Kandinsky was later to accept the term "concrete art" suggested by the Dutch "De Stijl" artist Theo van Doesburg, although he himself earlier defined the only two legitimate, polar possibilities of pictorial creation as the "great abstract" and the "great real," as manifested for him above all in the "naive" painting of Douanier Rousseau.

The "great abstract" stands for the spiritual aspect of art, which is set against the positivist-materialist thinking of the age; it is not concerned with the real, but with the spiritual world, in which such everyday, "material" – i. e. earthly – feelings like love, pleasure and fear have no place. It is the empire of pure spirit into which many friends of Kandinsky and Marc, including Erbslöh, Kanoldt, and finally August Macke as well, did not wish to enter. This art is a phenomenon because spiritual ideas, perceptions of the soul, can be made accessible to experience, and even the "non-representational" visions of Kandinsky the artist are subjugated to

rational control by Kandinsky the scientist. The way had been prepared by the Fauves and Robert Delaunay's "Orphism," the doctrine of simultaneous contrasts by the analysis of light. Colour is understood synaesthetically by Kandinsky as sound. (Apollinaire had already seen poetic and musical games in the painting of Kupka.) For Kandinsky, the line has its own energy and its own meaning. It should cause related reactions in the person of the observer: horizontal – peace; downward – mourning; upward – joy. Swelling or becoming thinner also causes psychic reactions. The same is true of shapes, round or square, upright or lying on their sides.

Kandinsky expected that the public would learn to read the vocabulary needed to understand his and his friends' works, rather like Kahnweiler with the works of the Cubists. Kandinsky, too, saw painting as writing, even though his premises were more Romantic than rational. The picture itself becomes the "world inner picture," human sensibilities are projected outwards. Freud and the psychoanalysts are naturally involved in this, as are the increasingly abstract formulae of science, the discovery of the fourth dimension and the splitting of the atom, which impressed Kandinsky so deeply that for him "everything (became) transparent, without strength or certainty."

Outer reality lost its power to support, became merely an illusion created by the imagination. Despite this, Kandinsky never succumbed to the misunderstanding of art as an analogue of science, in contrast with many of his lesser successors, who, especially after the Second World War, tried to grasp the world in abstract signs and symbols corresponding to the formulae of the scientists. Only the more naive Franz Marc was convinced that the art of the future would be "our scientific condition made concrete." For Kandinsky, on the other hand, art was an absolute. He was quite confident that one day he would achieve "absolute painting," painting which revealed inner sensations and at the same time encoded them as the painter set them down: this too is a suggestion that Kandinsky the intellectual Romantic kept his visions under control. The more constructive symbols of the ensuing Bauhaus years, up to their late, colourfully folky, almost desperately happy dissolution in the emigration years, are scarcely conceivable without a knowledge of the pictures, sculpture and models of the early Russian "avant-garde". The Suprematist members of the movement had made a principle of the "supremacy of pure sensation" as opposed to the visible world, and the Constructivists rated technology more highly than nature, set the engineer above the traditional artist. Kandinsky broadened the possibilities of painting almost beyond its bounds. Many who came after him lost their way in all this space. The protagonists of the international abstract movement of the post-war period, which dominated the art of the fifties, principally from Paris, never reached the heights of Kandinsky's art, which pointed the way for them; in retrospect they seem at best eclectic, at worst a pale shadow of what had come before.

Universal Harmony

The strict, rectangular arrangements of the Dutch "De Stijl" group, above all in the work of the pioneer Piet Mondrian, are diametrically opposed to the expressive line and colour of early Kandinsky. Despite its basis in mysticism, their utopia is more brittle and at the same time to a certain extent more robust, more "worldly," than that of the Russian émigré. For Mondrian and his circle, particularly Theo van Doesberg, did intend to change the real world. It was not by chance that Georg Schmidt, the important Swiss art historian and museum director, called Mondrian the greatest realist of the century; for the Dutchman's ideas, despite their philosophical origins in the thinking of the anthroposophical mathematician Schoenmaeker, were not distanced from reality, but related directly to the world in which we live; they were intended to be realized here and now – and of course finally only in the future. The "De Stijl" ideology is a concrete utopia. For Mondrian, art was the realization of "universal harmony," a design for earthly happiness. He did not simply see himself as a prophet, rather, as the "De Stijl" interpreter Hans Jaffé has said, he devoted his whole life to this utopia, and lived in it.

It is not just coincidence that the majority of the group's pioneers, not just the enthusiastic Mondrian but also the more sober Van Doesberg, who by founding the magazine "De Stijl" gave the movement its name, and also Bart van der Leck, the sculptor Vantongerloo, the influential architects Rietvield, Oud, Van Esteren and Van t'Hoff came from Calvinist families. What they wanted was art which would be for everyone, removed from nature, and certainly not "parallel" to it. The new aesthetic of the right-angle and the programmatic restriction of the palette to the basic colours red, yellow and blue and the "non-colours" black and white (occasionally tending to grey) places a man-made order, expressing his striving for harmony, against the uncontrolled luxuriance of nature. For this reason the natural colour green is still strictly excluded from the work of Mondrian worshippers like the sculptor Nicolas Schoeffer, for example. The "universal harmony" inspired by Platonic thought, with the picture as its meditative centre, strives for collective happiness, and is set schematically against European individualism. In this it is connected with Suprematism –

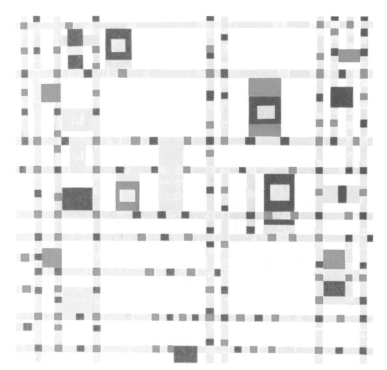

Piet Mondrian, *Broadway Boogie-Woogie,* 1942–43

which it must be admitted is still dominated by Romantic longings for eternity – and above all with the Constructivism of the early Russians.

Mondrian was the great painter of "De Stijl". His artistic development moved quite logically from a harmonious, already somewhat architectural naturalism of Dutch origin via Impressionism and analytic Cubism to the bleak, rectangular arrangements of his later years. Piet Mondrian was the visionary enthusiast, Theo van Doesberg the intellectual, the propagandist and the driving force of the movement. The fact that he later became an architect had enormous influence on the Bauhaus, and was a factor in its philosophical rejection of the drama of its beginnings in favour of greater objectivity; his move to architecture was a logical consequence of a will to change the world, which actually happened in the urban field from Gropius via Mies van der Rohe, Le Corbusier, Oud and their disciples down to the monotonous "walls with holes" of unimaginative imitators. "An artist like Mondrian," wrote the museum director Johannes Cladders, "sat (…) in an aesthetic cage. There he played his glass bead game of Constructivism (…). What at first made little impact on society now determines aesthetic categories in architecture, in interior design, in almost all areas of our lives. It was precisely his glass bead game which degenerated under such an embrace into what we now see as the brutality of the present. To this extent Mondrian (and, one must add, Van Doesberg – Author) was more relevant to our times and to society as a whole than someone like Käthe Kollwitz, who was working at the same time." The reaction which has since set in as "Post-Modern" architecture, the revolt of a nostalgic new generation against their "progressive" fathers, confirms Cladders' statement.

De Stijl had an enormous influence on painting and sculpture. Almost all artists who met the provocative flood of advertising and the new media, of optical environmental pollution, with sensitive, purist pictures or the stark structures of an anti-baroque, almost architectural sculpture without pedestal (Minimalism), were inspired by De Stijl. This is almost true of Barnett Newman, the leading light among America's "colourfield" painters, for whom the right-angle in the pictures of his European father-figure Mondrian was still too "naturalistic," because it also occurs in nature. He replaced it with the "zip", a strip without a beginning or an end running through the picture.

Art for the Collective

In post-revolutionary Russia art, encouraged at first by Lenin, aimed at collective happiness by changing the environment and consciousness. For the Suprematists around Malevich and for the politically and ideologically programmed Constructivists and Productivists the models of fine art led – as with the exponents of De Stijl – to its assimilation into architecture. "Organic growth is unambiguous," wrote Malevich uncompromisingly ("Building. Architecture"). The bourgeois concept of "fine art," of the beauty of pictures and sculptures with no purpose, was dismissed, and replaced by an anti-individualist, purposeful, normative collective art without hierarchies. It is intended to affect life, whether through pictures, sculptures, design or typography: in other words, using means which had to be at the service of architecture, which crowned and subsumed everything.

In contrast with the Dutchman, Malevich set his pictorial forms in front of endless backgrounds. His architectural models reach out into metaphysical, spheric spaces, while those of the Constructivists, under the diametrically opposed influence of Tatlin, fascinated by technology, related their projects to concrete reality. One could simplify by calling the Suprematism of Malevich and his supporters Suetin, Kljun, Puni, Mansurov, Popova, etc., the beginning of the "Romantic" variant. The Constructivist version initiated by Tatlin and taken up by Rodchenko and above all by El Lissitzky can be seen – as Georg Schmidt has it – as the "realistic" current within the Russian avant-garde of the period. What they all had in common was the stimulus of the Cubists, above all their early "material pictures" and Picasso's spatial collages. Others, like Alexandra Exter, were influenced by Futurism and developed "Cubofuturism".

Not everything created by the painters and sculptors was lost as a result of Lenin's verdict, some of it was preserved in the field of so-called applied art. Thus Lissitzky, who with his "Abstract Cabinet" had in Hanover created the model for a "Living Museum" (A. Dorner) of the future, was allowed in 1927 to design the Soviet pavilion for the Cologne "Pressa" of 1928. Then influence shifted away from the isolated Soviet Union to Poland, and to Western and Central Europe, and persists even into our times, not least because of the effect of Russian emigrants like Kandinsky and Chagall. Malevich's "Black Square on a White Background" is the prototype of those "last pictures" of which so many were to be painted in our century, documenting an endless sequence of borderline situations. Ad Reinhardt, Yves Klein, Robert Ryman, Clyfford Still, Raimund Girke: all benefited from Malevich's aesthetic radicalism. Tatlin's constructions had a marked influence on the brothers Gabo and Pevsner, the Hungarian Bauhaus master Moholy-Nagy, and later the kinetics of artists like Calder, Tinguely or Schoeffer, to say nothing of far-reaching effects on the abstract film, design and photography.

But Russian architecture, which set out with such high hopes and such excellent achievements, the intended crown of all creative work, was overrun in the most devastating fashion by the pompously crushing, empty monumentalism of the Stalin era.

The notion of the "Gesamtkunstwerk" was – and still is – a potent force in the history of twentieth century art, and has progressed far beyond Richard Wagner's limited and vague ideas, which he never formulated completely and certainly never realized. It leads to the cen-

Kasimir Malevich, *Black Square on a White Background,* 1913

27

turies-old dream of life as a work of art, which not only determines the creativity of an artist like Joseph Beuys, but will be with artists to the end of time.

Social Obligation

The great idea of art with social obligations led to the foundation of the Weimar, later Dessau, Bauhaus. Here, as in the thinking of the Russians and De Stijl, architecture was allotted the decisive role or rather – to use the Bauhaus terminology inspired by the American architectural pioneer Sullivan – the decisive "function." The founder of this new-style non-academic school of art, Walter Gropius, had enough insight and was liberal enough, however, to allow fine art the space which was its due, particularly in the case of painting. In Weimar, too, hierarchies were dismantled, there was no distinction in rank between "fine" and "applied" art, and here too one of the aims was to make a better world, and a world which worked better. Of course, the vision of an environment full of beauty for a classless society had been adopted, and this was driven to extremes and ideologically narrowed in the final phases after Gropius' resignation in 1928 by the last director of the Bauhaus but one, the architect Hannes Meyer. We are aware today that total "functionalism", the break with history, the utopian longing for something which had never been there before, were the great weaknesses of Bauhaus ideology in the architectural sphere. "Global world civilization," said Wolf Jobst Siedler, "(…) has become brittle." In the twenties the swing against history was still dominant.

The connection with De Stijl and the Russian avant-garde was intensified by personal exchange of ideas during visits by Van Doesburg, Lissitzky, Gabo and also Malevich. Paul Klee, in charge of stained glass and weaving, in whose work the constructive is so incomparably combined with the imaginative, wrote his "Paedagogic Sketchbook" here, which throughout the period of Conceptual Art and down to the present day has remained one of the finest pieces of theoretical writing by a fine artist. Kandinsky was able to continue and develop his academic work and his painting here under ideal conditions, Oskar Schlemmer was able to try out his great subject "figure in space" in pictures and on the stage, the Hungarian Moholy-Nagy – also an emigrant – was able to continue his Constructivist studies experimentally. These experiments – in the field of fine art – have maintained their relevance down the years to the light-art of the international Zero groups, to Kineticism, to the "democratic" mass editions of "ars multiplicata" and not least to photography and the photorealist painters, to the work of artists like Chuck Close and also Gerhard Richter.

In Weimar the young Josef Albers, impressed by De Stijl, made important contributions to industrial design, and even at the heart of the work of the secret Romantic Lyonel Feininger – in its synthesis of Cubist and Bauhaus principles – we find "a passionate longing for the strict shaping of space," and indeed "without painterly passion," as the American-German added. Mies van der Rohe, the successor of the dogmatic Meyer, was not able to rescue the Bauhaus from its fatal crisis; the Nazi Bilderstürmer made this impossible. But the very name of this important architect points us towards America. In the Chicago "New Bauhaus", where Moholy-Nagy worked in his second emigration, and in Black Mountain College, where Albers taught, the doctrine of the Bauhaus was taken up and continued, with great influence on the language of world architecture and the artistic scene in the New World, which was slowly emancipating itself from Europe. The attempt in the fifties, at first under the direction of the important Swiss painter, sculptor, architect and designer Max Bill, to link the Ulm Hochschule für Gestaltung (College of Design) directly to Bauhaus doctrine – brought up to date in terms of highly developed technology – never came to fruition. However, despite grinding conflicts which led to Bill's resignation in 1956, it has been a considerable influence on the struggle for good design in the industrial age.

Between the Wars

If one considers the artistic scene in Europe in the period after the Bauhaus crisis, which began at the end of the twenties, that is to say, the scene in the thirties up to the beginning of the Second World War, one could accept the well-known assertion that the significant revolutionary arguments of Modern Art were present without exception before the First World War, and that everything which followed was just variations on a theme. For it was not only the period of the Bildersturm, no longer restricted to the East but moving to Central Europe and present in Germany in the final phase of the Weimar Republic, which crippled creative powers, but also the depressing feeling, all too soon to be brutally confirmed, that one was not living in a time of peace, but in a time between wars. This state of affairs was bitterly criticized by realists like Grosz, Dix and many others in Europe, and in America by artists like Ben Shan. In the work of the incomparable Max Beckmann it reached the level of mythic tragedy. Others dedicated themselves reflectively to subject matter which was presented retrospectively in an instructive exhibition in Cologne in 1965, under the title "Dream – Sign – Space".

The end of the Classical Modern period with its blue-

Otto Dix, *The Trench*, 1920–23

prints which, despite astringent criticism, were based on a belief in the possibility of changing the world, was at hand. This crisis-ridden consciousness is also reflected in the work of living classicists, as the first section of another Cologne exhibition "Art of the West" made so penetratingly clear in 1981.

Even anarchic and non-ideological Dada with its furious revolt against "the stupid swinishness of war" (Max Ernst), with its attacks on the sacred cows of the West, on nationalistic thinking and pious aesthetic doctrines, was essentially idealistic to the extent that – unpolitical as it was – it always implied a hope in the possibility of changing the world. Nothing could therefore be more foolish than to lump these loosely connected Dada groups in Cologne and Paris, in Budapest or New York, together as "cultural Bolshevists"; they represent an international movement made up of marked individualists in a Western mould and of mainly middle-class origin, whose offshoots and friends in the East never had a serious chance. Unlike the early Russians, the De Stijl group and also the Bauhaus, the Dadaists were just as suspicious of a perfectly functioning world as they were of belief in progress, which they were convinced had experienced its final fiasco in the First World War. Dada was not an artistic movement, it was – with the exception of the solidly political and politically active Berlin group – an individual and anarchic protest, an anti-artistic revolt by artists who were filled with rage, but also with joie de vivre and irrational hope.

Dada could never become a mass movement; it was far too intellectual for that. "The cynicism of the Dadaists is a mask," said one of them, the sculptor and poet Hans Arp. We can believe him. In the last resort Dada anti-art became art again, particularly in the work of Hans Arp and Kurt Schwitters, an art which has an ironically broken, poetic quality which is among the finest manifestations of artistic and literary sensitiveness of the twentieth century. It is significant that these are the two exponents of Dada whose work is still influential today. To see this clearly we only have to look at the work of Robert Rauschenberg, the material collages of many other contemporaries, and the images of early English and American Pop Art, including the early happening.

Dream and Intoxication

Dadamax Ernst soon directed his energies elsewhere, or rather he allowed his teeming imagination and caustic wit to provide him with new solutions to his artistic problems, and thus became one of the most important Surrealist painters. His person and his work incontrovertibly show the connection between Dada and Surrealism, which the group around André Breton, the author, spokesman of the movement, were not eager to acknowledge. The famous picture "Au rendezvous des amis" ("Rendezvous of the Friends"), painted shortly after his arrival in Paris, confirms the connection simply by the people who are in it: apart from Max Ernst himself, sitting on Dostoevsky's knee, with Giorgio de Chirico, the forerunner of Surrealism, and the literary spokesmen Breton, Aragon and Eluard, the Dadaists Hans Arp and Johannes Baargeld are to be seen.

The concept of reality was broadened by the Surrealists, not uninfluenced by psychoanalysis, to include the categories of dreams, intoxication, madness and the irrational. With the authority of the Marquis de Sade, violence, libertinism, murder and satanism were also included. The historical ancestors were: Hieronymus Bosch, in fact deeply religious, Brueghel, the Piranese of the "carceri" and labyrinths, the Prague court painter Arcimboldi, Füssli, Blake, Odilon Redon, Douanier Rousseau and the Symbolist Gustave Moreau, not to forget James Ensor with his ghostlike world of masks ("Skeleton Looking at Chinese Pictures"). Other influences were certain early works of Chagall and Léger, and not least the sign world of Paul Klee. Acceptable literary figures were the French "poètes maudits" Arthur Rimbaud and Charles Baudelaire. The unconscious, hidden away in man, was placed on a level with conscious life. In their invocation of the fantastic, the world beyond reality ("surreal"), they quoted the authority of science, rejected the "myth" of the creative artist out of hand, but accepted trances and automatism ("écriture automatique"). Adorno speaks of lost childhood memories made visible, and feels that this is one of the most

James Ensor, *Skeleton Looking at the Chinese Curios,* 1885

also André Masson's work produced in exile in America, proved that the obituaries had been written too soon. What is clear is that in the case of the Chilean, the Cuban and the Frenchman we are not dealing with the paranoid genius and mannerist <u>immoralism</u> of a Dalí, but with artists who were made to suffer by their perception of the absurd and the imperfect development of mankind, its cruelty, its atavistic and <u>aggressive</u> "eye for an eye, tooth for a tooth" mentality, the fact that

Salvador Dali, *Autumn Cannibalism,* 1936–37

important reasons for the fascination which Surrealism still holds – think of the overcrowded Dalí exhibitions of recent years – for young people.

What this does not explain, however, is the fact that Max Ernst, the most important and the most intelligent Surrealist, has still not become comparably popular, perhaps because his pictorial riddles require too much thought and effort. Unlike the fantasies of the Spaniard Salvador Dalí they are never entirely decipherable, and always retain some elements of impenetrable mystery. In this respect Surrealism is entirely comparable with Dada, essentially anarchic, and without any hope of possible change. This is confirmed by the fact that there was only a temporary flirtation with the radical political left. The lack of a political point of view, which is characteristic of most Surrealists, shows most irritatingly and extremely in the fascination which first Hitler and then Franco held for Dalí.

For a long time it was generally believed that Surrealism ended with the Second World War. Feeble imitators in various European countries, including the Federal Republic, seemed to confirm this, until the Latin Americans Roberto Sebastián Matta and Wilfredo Lam, and

everybody was fighting everybody else, and who attacked these things. "Even those who are bound in a high degree to the clear world of the spirit," formulated Masson, "have to make extensive expeditions into the world of violence and <u>lust</u>."

Surrealism has had <u>legitimate</u> and independent successors right up to our day, particularly in its intellectual form, significantly influenced by the ex-Dada Marcel Duchamp. The way leads via the Belgian René Magritte, who was always more important in the field of philosophical and literary pictorial ideas than for their painterly realization, to his pupil Marcel Broodthaers, who was a poet for ten years before he became an artist for ten years, and then died relatively young. In Broodthaers the doubt of contemporary man over and above Nietzsche became a creative force. His radical questioning of history and museums, always tinged with philanthropic humour, his ambiguous, ironically fragmented symbols, are manifestations of a late "Alexandrian" culture. With their inscrutable, melancholy scepticism they belong to the illusion-free world of "New Modern Art", which began in the early forties in Europe and America, under the shadow of a catastrophe which was not only continuing, but expanding exponentially – the Second World War. To have no hope and yet "to exist in the dark, and do what we can:" this quotation from the late work of Gottfried Benn, completely cured of his errors, could stand as motto for the work of the Belgian.

The Great Refuser

The most "up-to-date" artist of the early modern period is Marcel Duchamp, who still has the most influence today. Originally, after starting in the circle of the Impressionists, Seurat and the Fauves, he became an interesting Cubist painter with a dash of Futurism (although he insisted that he was influenced in his dynamic early pictures not by the Italians, but by photographic studies of movement), and was then the leader of the New York Dada group. He was an early prophet of the end of the European tradition and the emancipation of American art. He was a victim of Baudelaire's "ennui," the boredom of the late-born, educated European confronted with endless repetition. From 1918 onwards he renounced painting, to devote himself to intellectual games, including, for ten years, chess, played at international competition level.

It is however not unreasonable to suppose that this "anti-artist" and ostensible iconoclast was not disgusted by art itself, but by the mendacious abuse of art, on the one hand as a substitute for religion, on the other as an object of speculation. He hated repetition, he was disgusted by the mass production of art for commercial reasons. "I am interested in ideas, not in visual results," he said. No further comment is needed on the shattering effect of this statement right up to the present day.

Duchamp went in for pictorial thinking without pictures, he produced, in the words of W. Hofmann, referring to a quotation from the English reformer Ruskin, "facts without art." As early as the "Chocolate Mill" string was built into the picture, something real from the everyday world, in the manner of Cubist collages, to enhance the reality, the "factualness" of the work. From this point the way is clear to the "readymades," to the urinal signed "R. Mutt" and called "Fountain", to the totally crude bottle-rack, and to the bicycle wheel on a stool: objects which Duchamp, in a momentous, programmatically ironic gesture, placed in an "artistic" environment completely foreign to them. The fragmentary "Large Glass", which could never be quite deciphered, and on which he worked for ten years, the "bachelor machine" with the literary title "The Bride Stripped Bare by Her Bachelors, Even", are manifestations of his last farewell to painting, but certainly not, as was believed for a long time, to art. For in secret

Marcel Duchamp, *The Bride Stripped Bare by Her Bachelors, Even,* 1912

Duchamp was working on the culmination of his œuvre, the environment which can be seen through two peepholes in the Philadelphia Museum "Etant donnés: 1. La Chute d'Eau, 2. Le Gaz d'Eclairage" ("Contains: 1. The Waterfall, 2. The Gaslight"). It consists of a naked woman without pubic hair, holding a gas burner. Her arm is covered with twigs, the background is a wooded landscape with lake and waterfall. This apparently naturalistic pictorial work is rich in allusions and ciphers, and even harder to penetrate than the "Large Glass". It expresses by various means (of which the clearest are the little peepholes) Duchamp's firm view that if there is to be intensive communication, there should be "visual coitus" between picture and observer: a clear pointer to the latent eroticism in the work of the Frenchman.

Duchamp's work and thinking opened up many paths. With him begins the epoch of art which crosses boundaries, the removal of barren distinctions between the genres painting, sculpture, organized space ("environment") and concrete object ("readymade"); but also the inclusion of the literary, of artistic theory and richly allusive philosophical thinking within the bounds of fine art. The great refuser did not just reject but also – and this is in the last resort where his importance lies – stimulated generations of artists to look for new possibilities for art beyond outworn models. His influence extends via the pictorial world of Magritte to Pop Art (Richard Hamilton is one of Duchamp's best interpreters), to Conceptual Art and to Beuys, despite the latter's provocative pronouncement: "Marcel Duchamp's silence is overestimated."

America Conquers Europe

The indirect effect of Duchamp the great refuser is more all-embracing. No thinking artist of our time can avoid coming to terms with his ideas. His remorseless questioning of reality, his doubt without illusions, the cool sincerity of his diagnoses have created the most important prerequisites for the – post-Nietzschean – insistent "backward questioning" of the relationship between art and reality by a thinking artist in our times. It was also he who not only foresaw at an early stage, but also didactically demanded, a leading role for America, the shifting of the balance from Paris to New York, soon after the Second World War. "If only America would realize," he said in his early Dada years in New York, before his temporary return to France in 1921, "that European art is dead – and that America is the artistic land of the future."

Two decades later it had happened. From the mid-fifties on, even the Europeans had to admit it – more precisely, from the time of the Brussels World Fair in 1958. What was seen there was not just a magnificent collection of the European Modern Art of the first half of the century, but also and most strikingly an impressive documentation of the enormously vital American scene of the previous few years, completely emancipated from Europe. This experience bowled over expert and layman alike, and the second "Documenta" a year later had exactly the same effect. Subsequently, not only did New York become the centre of the artistic world, but for many years European art fell under the influence of the partly inspiring, partly crippling effect of the great Americans.

Prior to this we had seen the triumphs of the international abstract Ecole de Paris, which led many people to the serious belief that from now on abstract painting was going to be produced to the end of time, despite the late work of Fernand Léger and other important representational artists. In those days these triumphs were just an alibi, a way of proving one's own impartiality.

Many of the great names from that period have been forgotten, and we realized long ago how weak and modish was much of the work at that time considered the "dernier cri," a new golden age of cultivated painting in the "tradition française". Certainly, in retrospect we are now just as quick to condemn work which was greeted with rapture thirty years ago; artists like Riopelle, the early Hans Hartung, Bazaine and others are as unjustly treated in this context as the Germans who set the standard, who – like Baumeister or Nay – came to the forefront again after the war and won back West Germany's right to move on the international plane. People have always shouted "Hosannah!" and "Crucify him!". History will make a more just choice.

More important than the sensations of the day, than the cosmopolitan signs and symbols of the offical abstract international movement, which thought that it was at one with up-to-date scientific knowledge of the kind that could only be grasped in terms of abstract formulae, were the shock-waves caused by a new way of seeing which – at first almost unnoticed by the public – had their anonymous effect in Europe as well.

Art, whether it is representational or abstract, realistic or conceptual, is always a response to reality, although the concept of reality must not be so narrow as only to include what everybody can see, superficial appearance. Between 1939 and 1945 this reality altered radically, the history of old Europe came to an end in those six years. The traditional religious, ethical and philosophical values of the "Occident" are from then on not only questionable, they are completely without force. The basic structures of civilization are destroyed, the world is divided into an eastern and a western hemisphere, the deadly threat to all mankind has become a daily experience. The crisis which began with the first industrial revolution did not end with the Second World War. Belief in the possibility of changing the world, even of improving it, has suffered – to put it mildly – a severe shock, the conflict between capitalism and socialism is part of the structure, there is no solution in sight. How can this conflict not affect art which, if it is to be taken seriously, is always concerned with reality?

The crisis of artistic consciousness was, as we have already seen, a feature of the artistic production of the thirties. "The spirit of the age forces modern art onto the defensive," wrote the young art historian Peter Barth with reference to this period. These problems came right to the forefront in the forties. The idealistic notion of world citizenship of the western post-war international movement, held up against the social realism of the East as a symbol of freedom, has proved itself to be a beautiful delusion. National conflicts, which only occur nowadays – often controlled and provoked by the great powers – in the Third World, have been replaced by global ideological confrontation. The movements of Classical Modern Art – even when, like Dada, they were determinedly at odds with the existing system – had idealism as an implicit element, as they at least thought that change was possible. All hopes of this kind have finally been dismissed since the end of the fascist National Socialist nightmare and the illusory blossoming of cosmopolitan ideas in the years immediately after the war. World improvement is no longer the artist's motive, but has been replaced by self-affirmation in the context of a tragic freedom, as formulated by the post-war Existentialists. In a absurd world – according to Albert Camus – only the individual "thrown" into being can hold out as "a human being in revolt." "We must prefer ourselves to eternity or immerse ourselves in God – this is the tragedy in which we must assert ourselves." Thus Camus in his famous essay, "The Myth of Sisyphus". Camus, together with his more ideological, Marxist-critical opposite number Jean-Paul Sartre, determined the thinking of the period, particularly for young people. The last sentence of the essay reads: "We must consider Sisyphus a happy man."

Prelude to New Modern Art

The work of the artist who begins the illusion-free period of New Modern Art was similarly shot through with a brave but pessimistic understanding of existence: Wolfgang Schulze-Battmann, known as Wols, a late "peintre maudit", a German painter in Paris, whom few people knew, but whose friends included Miró, Max Ernst, the ex-Dadaist Tristran Tzara, Calder, Simone de Beauvoir, but above all her life-long companion Jean-Paul Sartre. The writer-philosopher not only looked after Wols – until his early death – but also made a wider public aware of his work.

Wols was a quiet, withdrawn man, who lived out his life in private, a wandering scholar, a "person without a home." He was thrown upon himself, without contact with the artistic movements of the period, and – as he considered it immoral to sell pictures – without a gallery or even a museum to take an interest in him. In private he prepared the ground for the most far-reaching revolutionary movement in European art in the middle years of the century. His starting point was Surrealism; he first of all drew on Paul Klee but, sceptical that Klee's notion of "design for possible worlds" could be realized, he then smashed the mould completely. Painterly execution and his own existentialist situation are present in his gestures, the one interpreting the other. All traditional criteria are null and void if applied to his pictures. Wols produced a "creatio ex nihilo", a creation from nothing, art without any reference to any past aesthetic, not reforming or presenting variations, but developing new criteria from within itself, without any preconceptions.

This way of painting, which with its basic existentialist mood and its spiritual attitude is clearly related to the sculpture of Giacometti, who was also an important painter and close to the "Hostage" ("Otage") pictures of Jean Fautrier, started the movement which has become known as "Tachisme" or "Informal Art". Its history also started with a roll on the drums: the first Tachist was the greatest, as happened with Kandinsky in the case of the abstract painters and Max Ernst in the case of the Surrealists. Only the works of artists who were dominant from the beginning have, through many transformations, survived beyond the end of this "Other Art" (Michel Tapié), including above all the Spaniard Antoni Tàpies, with his solemn, silent panels, and the Germans Emil Schumacher and Bernard Schulze. Apart from these there are Walter Stöhrer, long underestimated, and the important Austrian loner Arnulf Rainer, although from his early "overpaintings" to the late death masks he was never quite part of a prevalent tendency.

Jean Dubuffet's provocative "art brut", inspired by the art of lunatics, the scribblings of children and users of urinals, is the expression of "disgust with the culture of the West" (Laszlo Glozer); he renewed Baudelaire's aesthetic of the ugly on a plane of crisis-consciousness which was entirely in tune with the times. The Danish-Belgian-Dutch group Cobra (Copenhagen, Brussels, Amsterdam), among whom the outstanding figure was the Dane Asger Jorn, made a quite different contribution with their abstract Expressionism.

At the same time as Wols, in his cramped quarters, was anticipating informal painting, which did not become an international movement until after his death (and then became fashionable and trite), America, in an admirable feat of strength, finally overcame the dependence on Europe so criticized by Marcel Duchamp and the isolation of the "American scene," of which the outstanding figures are Edward Hopper and the late Georgia O'Keeffe.

The American Wols is Jackson Pollock. Common to both artists, in other ways so different, is the lack of historical and aesthetic preconceptions in their mature work. Even though Wols smashed the traditional mould, he expresses typically European sensitivity and apocalyptic melancholy in relatively small formats, while Pollock's canvases and abstract Expressionism, despite hints of Surrealism and the visible influence of Jungian psychoanalysis, are much more open and more vehement. Pollock's "action painting" is thematically primarily a representation of the painting process itself, the direct subjective expression of his own personality and inner feelings. The painter himself said that he did not want to describe feelings, but to express them, without reference to aesthetic doctrines and refined techniques. Like Van Gogh he wanted to "forget" technique. The philosopher John Dewey formulated this painterly pragmatism in his influential book "Art as Experience" even before it existed in practice. Artistic work needs no justification for Dewey, it carries its meaning within it, construction and expression are at the same time action and result, the artist thinks "through the material" and "without transcendence." There is no longer any sign of the European search for "deeper meaning."

In comparison with Wols' morbid chamber music Pollock's action painting is more explosive, more vital and – despite all its civilization neuroses – much more self-confident. This self-confidence also breaks impressive new ground in the pictures of the other great "action painters," who were decisively influenced by the German emigrant Hans Hofmann: the direct drama of Franz Kline's vehement brushwork, the intellectual control of Robert Motherwell, the painter of the "Spanish Elegies", whose early work was in the European mould, and not least the work of Willem de Kooning, a Dutchman by birth. Perhaps he is the greatest of the action painters, even including Pollock, certainly so in his thematic breadth and the multilayered quality of his work – from the eerie idols that were his early female figures to the freely surging colour design of the late period.

Clyfford Still, who occupies a linking position between the Abstract Expressionists and the meditative colour-field painters Rothko and Newman, also expresses the new pragmatic and anti-traditional ethos of the Americans: "We are now committed to action without presuppositions, not to the illustration of worn-out myths or contemporary alibis." The observer – and this is diametrically opposed to Duchamp's "visual coitus" – should not see the picture as a mirror of his problems, but as a creation sui generis, without reference to the external world.

Counterpositions

The opposite pole to "Abstract Expressionism", which experienced a literary and philosophical variation on a high intellectual plane in the mysteriously encoded, richly allusive pictures of Cy Twombly, is the art of the colour-field painters Mark Rothko and Barnett Newman, from Eastern Jewish families. In their meditative painting the picture itself becomes a coloured myth unrelated to the world of European imagination, which they both subdued after their Surrealist beginnings. Rothko's pictures, with their soaring coloured shapes against limitless backgrounds, can still invoke monumental "abstract icons" and temples, whereas Newman's huge formats, to which the observer should stand very close, make colour itself into a de facto

space for meditation, in which one should allow oneself to be embraced, should lose and forget oneself. The contrast between the spontaneous gestures of action art and the new myths of colour-field painting allows us to measure the whole span of American art, which freed itself from European tutelage by an unprecedented demonstration of strength. This is also true, though to a more limited extent and with a smaller number of brilliant exponents, of sculpture, with the outstanding figures of Alexander Calder, commuting between America and Europe, and the lively David Smith at the top of the pyramid. Both have digested European influences, but both have found an unmistakable form of expression of their own. Calder's popularity as the creator of cheerful and wilful, gracious "mobiles", unthinkable without some stimulus from a specifically European spirituality, still to some extent distorts the view of his totems and "stabiles", with their almost monstrous massiveness. Smith came to iron sculpture via Picasso and Gonzalez, but lent a hitherto unknown quality to American practice with his inventive "Voltri" and monumental "Cubi". His work is char-

Richard Serra, *Terminal,* 1975–77

acterized by its range of pictorial ideas, mass and boldness of form, acrobatic and confusing statics, and gigantic format. In our days the angular Richard Serra has created monumental sculpture; he is perhaps the most important exponent of "Minimal Art", with no debt to Europe, but with comparable force and radical reduction of the arsenal of shapes. In their uncompromising hardness, in the contrast of slabs weighing tons with their fragile balance, calculated to a nicety, his works represent the poles of technical existence. Eduard Trier, the leading interpreter of the sculpture of this century, drawing on conceptual references and technical problems, has referred to Serra's work as the "equestrian statues" of our day (e. g. "Terminal", 1975–77). The heavy, silent seriousness and the aggressiveness of these works are an insistent and often provocative counterpoint to the architectural triviality with which we are surrounded. No wonder that uncompromising work like this meets resistance in a world of conformers, but how appalling that this artist should become the first victim of a new variation on the Bildersturm in the immediate present. Serra's sculpture "Tilted Arc", commissioned by the government for the only federal building in New York, and perfectly related to the site, had to be removed because "public decency", something better known in Germany since the dark days of dictatorship than on the other side of the Atlantic, presented a welcome excuse to do this. This incident, unique in post-war American history, shows how threatened art's "incorruptible space" still is today, even in America, which was said by Marius de Zaya in the legendary periodical "291", many years before the breakthrough to artistic independence, to have "the same complex mentality as the true modern artist."

The long-standing hatred of orthodox minds for works of art not open to absorption into their ideology is clearly at work in this alarming incident. No distinction is made between openly critical and abstract art. The brutality with which the tyrants of our time persecuted "abstract" artists in East and West is still a bitter memory; it is the corollary of our fear of the wordless message of a silent picture. One is tempted to think in terms of a return to belief in pictorial magic and spells, the revival of the notion of "effective reality" and effective power in pictures. But in our day something else is involved, something which can be described in a more concrete way, which Jakob Burckhardt noticed: the fear of criticism of a status quo when it is no longer adequate to one's needs. According to the great Swiss historian, culture "never ceases to modify and dissolve the two permanent forms of life (state and religion). It is their critic, it is the clock which strikes the hour at which form and object no longer correspond." Even if one cannot quite accept Burckhardt's – to a certain extent optimistic – argument that in the last resort it is

culture which actually shapes society by flying in the face of state and religion, the unease of conservatives when confronted with art which questions and does not conform is nevertheless always with us. This conflict is not always tolerated, even in a democracy. Therefore art must continue to fight for its freedom, which in our age is also its legitimation. These problems became of burning significance in the changed social and cultural conditions of the stormy seventies, in stark contrast with the superficial bustle of a hectic art market with ever-changing heroes and record prices.

The Optimism of the Kennedy Era

Even today it is difficult to imagine that shortly before this, at the time of the second surge of so-called Modern Art, it looked as though the freedom of art was not only secured once and for all, but also that it was possible for political and artistic intelligence to be in harmony; a dream which quickly vanished along with the extravagant hopes of the Kennedy era. It was the period of British and American Pop Art, which had a built-in optimism about the future which showed in the title of the early London exhibition "This Is Tomorrow"; this optimism became tinged with scepticism in Britain sooner than in the USA. Trivia – from a refrigerator to a comic strip – became fit subjects for pictures, the passionate was trivialized.

Striking examples of this development are Richard Hamilton's collage "Just What Is It That Makes Today's Homes So Different, So Appealing?", the "Flags" and "Targets" of Jasper Johns, which he used, as the American critic Max Kozloff pointed out, to relieve abstract forms of the meanings which they had been given by consent of society, thus taking away their social function. Claes Oldenburg's partially realized suggestions for the raising of the banal to the level of memorials and monuments (clothes pegs, umbrella, toothpaste tube, shovel) transform everyday things into ideas and symbols. Things which we handle daily without really noticing them become magical objects, monuments to set against loss of unity of thought and feeling as our understanding of the world becomes increasingly abstract. Roy Lichtenstein, inspired by the "Proletarian Olympus" of the late Léger, and certainly more of an eclectic aesthete than the more complex Oldenburg, tried to do something similar with blow-ups of comic strips, whose terse simplicity had put its stamp on a visually trivial culture.

The justification of the banal and the involvement of the trivial in the previously sacred world of the picture took over from the dramatic blows struck for freedom by the Abstract Expressionists and the new mythology of the colour-field painters. The pioneers of this development in the United States, Jasper Johns and his friend Robert Rauschenberg, who originally drew his inspiration from Schwitters, both based in Abstract Expressionism, are not Pop Artists in the strictest sense, but rather paved the way for it; they gave artistic legitimation to the democratization of art which the Pop Artists were attempting. "And I think a picture is more like the real world when it's made out of the real world," said Rauschenberg. The inclusion of objects and prefabricated components in pictures is an attempt, as in the case of the Cubists' collages, to achieve a higher degree of reality for a work of art while at the same time allowing immaterial components to be part of the picture, and thus transcending reality: dialectic of this kind – whether intentionally or not – makes apparent the relationship of this apparently trivial, but in fact highly artificial and intellectually multifaceted art, to historical art, going back as far as sacred and feudal art in the Middle Ages. Even Pop Art, which never became as popular as its initiators would have liked, is not sealed off from history.

Realism – Idealism

Working with and manufacturing real everyday things is the leitmotiv of Nouveau Réalisme, the Paris movement grouped around Yves Klein. Its protagonists transcend their beginnings in Pop Art and Johns' and Rauschenberg's "Combines", which linked painting and object art. John Chamberlain's colourful sculptures made of parts of scrapped cars are nearer to European principles, but colour and form still carry meaning, as they did for the painters of Abstract Expressionism, and thus point to content beyond their real appearance. Sculpture from the scrap of civilization is a "memento mori".

The works of the New Realists are less ambiguous, more concrete. Arman "accumulates" everyday objects in series and without compositional interference: alarm clocks, spectacle frames, paint tubes, jugs. César "compromises" objects, even including the racing car, i.e. he presses them together, or he makes a monumental sculpture out of a cast of his thumb. Hains does not stick coloured paper together, but rips it down from hoardings and sets the technique of "décollage" against that of collage. Jean Tinguely's mobile sculptures ironize the perfection of technology to the point of self-destruction in the most inscrutable fashion, but they also make ceaseless movement visible as a sign of a constantly changing life. Daniel Spoerri's "trap pictures" set a trap for chance and transience by shamelessly fixing everday objects, e.g. remains of working materials, leftover food and cigarette ends, onto plates,

in all their banal shabbiness. In this way he perpetuates the traces of the presence of those now absent and gives a lasting quality to a recent departed second of life between life and death. Christo, who was on the fringes of the group, at an early stage alienated everyday objects by packaging ("empaquetage").

The connection between material and immaterial shows most clearly in the work of Yves Klein ("Yves le Monochrome"), who only uses a single colour in his meditative pictures (above all ultramarine, but also red and gold) and makes it possible to experience its spiritual and physiological existence. This principle becomes more concrete in his "Anthropomorphia", blue imprints of living bodies on paper and canvas, the "Spurensicherung" of living existence ("looking for lost traces of our steps in the dust, the sand, the ashes" – Nancy Graves), and finally in the use of sponges for his picture panels, or in his blue objects and figures. On the other hand, his exhibition of emptiness in a white gallery or the exchange of the intangible for gold leaf, half of which he threw in the Seine and half of which he used for a gold picture, are references to the metaphysical component of his œuvre. The judo master's meditative attitude is influenced by the philosophy of the Far East and the mythology of the Rosicrucians. Yves Klein was not just the pioneer of "New Realism", but also – with Lucio Fontana, who punched a hole in his canvas to let space into the picture – the leading figure of the international Zero movement; he encouraged the idealization of light which dominated its early stages. Colour was celebrated as an emanation of light. Mack and Uecker, citing their Polish predecessors Stazevski and Strzemiński as authority, emancipated themselves from the flat, the illusionistic and the two-dimensional and from representational pictorial content. They made the surface of the picture vibrate: Mack at first by the serial organization of coloured shapes of equal value, later with the assistance of reflecting light on metal plates and objects; Uecker with his particular medium, the nail, which he first of all used as a material among others, as a painter would use colour. As his work developed, Uecker's nail became increasingly a device for creating a sensitive, pictorially structured interplay of light and shade, dematerialized by white, which contains all colours within itself. In the mature work of this artist the nail becomes a fetish, at the same time both instrument, and vehicle for ideas.

The Zero ideologist Otto Piene – under the influence not only of Yves Klein, but also of the Munich "Zen" group, formed at the end of the forties, with Rupprecht Geiger as the outstanding figure – was the first to make serious use of monochrome. He and Uecker are connected by a mutual inclination to pictorial structuralism, to equality of the elements within a picture, and serial organization. They used "égalité", in tune with the long-departed optimism of the period, as an encapsulation of hoped-for social changes; their goal was a society of men with equal rights, joyfully anticipating the future. "Yes, I dream of a better world," said Otto Piene straightforwardly. He and his friends thought that art should produce antitypes of the existing real world, and surrender to the transparent moment, the happiness of here and now, rather than be like the "Tachistes" and brood over the catastrophes of the past, hoping for an illusory eternity.

The international impact of this Düsseldorf group shows how much optimistic futurology was in tune with the times. The Dutch "Nul" association, the "gruppo t" in Italy, and the French "Groupe de la Recherche d'Art Visuel", and parallel movements even in Japan, would not have existed without them. The frontiers of the genres were constantly being breached by "Zero" and like-minded artistic groupings, pictures were turning into sculptures and objects. Action and demonstrations – from Piene's light-ballets, his rainbow over the Munich Olympic site to Mack's Sahara project – were effective illustrations of the Zero ideology and met with great response from the public. It is by observing Uecker's powerful, thoughtful work in subsequent years that we see clearly how the shining optimism of the early days became more and more tinged with scepticism. Gotthard Graubner, who for a time was classified as a "Zero" associate because of his ostensible "Monochromie", which is in fact "Polychromie", richly-graded and multi-coloured, had quite other aims in his painting, inspired by Caspar David Friedrich and William Turner. His subject is coloured space.

Revolt Against Tradition

The revolt against tradition, against compositional and social hierarchies with implications for art, was radicalized by Minimal Art, again imported from America. Nevertheless, there is also a historical source, European Constructivism, particularly in its Russian version, which – differently from Dada and part of the Bauhaus movement – wanted to do away completely with the purpose-free aesthetic and inherited social order of art in its traditional form. The reduced works of the colour-field painters Rothko and Newman, Ad Reinhardt's silent black panels and David Smith's sculptures are also part of this movement; Smith, according to the neo-conservative American critic Hilton Kramer, subordinated the rhetoric of the Paris school to the specialist language of the American machine trade; the early, almost monochrome pictures of the young Frank Stella also belong here. These artists were a

powerful influence – in contrast to the name given to the movement – on the mostly monumental, radically simplified architectural sculptures without plinth of Tony Smith, Ronald Bladen, Robert Grosvenor, Don Judd, Robert Morris and Robert Smithson, but also on Dan Flavin's space-oriented neon tube assemblies, Carl André's steel plate arrangements and Sol LeWitt's geometrical structures. "We simply cannot go back," Frank Stella had said right at the beginning of the sixties. If something is used up, abandoned, over, why then still bother with it? In Minimal Art, more aptly called "Primary Structures" by the American art writer Lucy R. Lippard, playing with pictorial elements is replaced by an unambiguous striving for a new spatial completeness for objects, with a complete disregard for detail and distinctive processing of materials. The seemingly archaic, roughly monumental quality of much of the work of the Minimalists is modelled on the pyramids of Egypt and the stone constructions of ancient history. Elimination of the slightest trace of individual "handwriting," mechanical preparation and – in the case of André, Judd and Flavin – the serial arrangement of the individual elements are evidence of a clear commitment to contemporary scientific and technical thinking and its extension into the immediate future.

Against Cultural Colonialism

Like Minimal Art, early Russian Constructivism-Productivism in the first half of the century and – working from other premises and with quite different artistic results – the vehement expressiveness of American action painting in the second half of the century are in the last resort signs of a revolt against domination by old Europe and "cultural colonialism."

Minimalist sculpture defines space. In the open air it is a counterpoint to the surrounding architecture. Unlike the work of Henry Moore, it does not intend to enter into a dialogue with the landscape and become a piece of nature. Tony Smith, for example, wants his work to dominate nature, as man dominates it. The organic elements of his work do not derive from nature, instead they are closely related to chemical and geological modular structures.

In Minimal Art, strict rejection of tradition, history and the history of art are demonstrated not so much by aggressive manifestos as by the works themselves. With an exclusiveness of a kind which has never been seen before – and certainly not in the "Classical Modern" period – newness is a quality in its own right, and art coolly proclaims that it is exclusive to its own age, and uses technological means. It is quite a different matter that occasionally an undertow of pathos, a hidden "Romanticism", creeps in – as it were by the back door. An important role is played by the idea of refusal to be consumed, resistance to being taken over by museums, even if, as one might have foreseen, it could not be kept up in practice. This thought is developed logically in the subsequent "Land Art" and "Earth Art" movements, and in Conceptual Art, which is to a large extent present in embryo in Minimal Art. Robert Smithson, who was the victim at an early age of an air crash when flying over one of his works, was one of the most important and thoughtful of the Minimal Artists before he later became interested in Land Art. In the late sixties he was involved in the development of the huge Dallas-Fort Worth airport. His artistic contribution "Earthworks, or grid-type frameworks close to ground level," which he called "Aerial Art", was never realized. The design, however, by a dialectical connection of the visible to the invisible, of space to nonspace, points to spiritual proximity to Minimal, Land and Conceptual Art. "The world seen from the air," wrote Smithson, "is abstract and illusive. From the window of an airplane one can see drastic changes of scale, as one ascends and descends. The effect takes one from the dazzling to the monotonous in a short space of time – from the shrinking terminal to the obstructing clouds." Aerial Art, through its concentration in "invisible" space and "invisible" time, was able to develop an aesthetic "based on the airport as an idea, and not simply as a mode of transportation."

Sol LeWitt had stated that "the idea becomes the machine that makes the art," and that the craft and technique used in carrying it out are insignificant. (He followed this through by having his wall drawings executed by assistants.) It was only a step from here to the statement that the idea was more important than the visible work.

Breaking out of the Museum

Land Art and Earth Art are the moment of breaking out of the museum. They place artistic markers for man and his creativity in the untouched landscape and far out into the desert. Land Art alters the landscape and has the concept of transience built into it. At the basis of it is the grandiose attempt to withdraw art from commercial consumption, from the rapid wearing out of styles, and from museum-worthiness and the embrace of benevolence, i.e. the defusing of its conceptual explosive force by the fact that it is purchased. The work of Michael Heizer, the son of a geologist (e.g. "City One/City", 1972–74), the "Lightning Field" of the metaphysician Walter de Maria, James Turrel's desert projects, are impressive examples of art which is precisely related to the place in which it is realized, which "wished to bring about a primeval state, in order

Michael Heizer, *Complex One/City,* 1972–76

to ask basic questions about existence and to find new answers to them" (E. Weiss). These artists were never able to resolve the contradiction to this pure idea contained in the fact that works, like this, withdrawn from the everyday and the art business, are dependent on wealthy sponsors, and that only very few of the people interested in them ever have an opportunity to see such artistic landmarks. Documentation, even if it is defined as part of the work of art, is only an imperfect compensation for the limited accessibility of the work. Sketches and plans, but also completed work, cannot escape the collector, commerce and the museum, not even an impressive and intelligent work like De Maria's "Broken Kilometer". A similar fate awaited Richard Long's pseudo-archaic stone arrangements, the documentation of his wanderings, or the data tables and telegrams ("I'm still alive") of the philosophizing Japanese Ori Kawara, intended as thought monuments and fixed points in his wanderings in time and space. Only De Maria's kilometer-deep hole in the earth at the Kassel "documenta VI/1977", originally proposed for the Munich Olympics in 1972, escapes from the consumer because – an unrepeatable work between Land Art and Conceptual Art, with a meditative cast of mind only partially understood even today – it can only be reconstructed, "rethought," in the mind of the observer. The removal of boundaries between the genres, concretely and symbolically, was taken to extremes in works like this; the burial of objects (by Claes Oldenburg for example) was a conceptual forerunner.

The works of Christo, which only have a transient existence, are a model and uniquely special case, specific to Land Art, of an expansive artistic activity related to landscape, town and history, and beyond convention. The wrapping up of a section of Australian coastline, the "Valley-Curtain" in Colorado, the 42 kilometer "Running Fence" in California, the "Surrounded Islands" in Florida, the wrapping up of the Pont-Neuf in Paris and the planned draping of the Reichstag building in Berlin, on the border between East and West, as a symbol of the division not only of Germany but of the entire world, are undisputedly an exceptional pheno-menon in the history of art and in the history of our century. This is true both of the enormous number of people involved, of whom many are directly confront-ed with artistic ideas and their realization for the first time, and of the financing of the projects without the use of taxpayers' or sponsors' money. (Christo is his own sponsor; the most he does is to take out credit for a limited period of time until he can pay it back by the sale of drawings, collages, models and photographs related to the project.) In his case, too, thorough retro-spective documentation as a substitute for experience for those who cannot be there is important. The fact that Christo mobilizes the population of entire coun-tries and cities and makes them confront artistic ideas, regardless of education or social status, makes them agree or disagree, makes them take part in discussion and involves them actively in the project, this is the most significant fact for the future, particularly at a time when many people still believe that the art of this century confronts them with insoluble riddles, even though the pictorial worlds of Picasso, Mondrian, Kan-dinsky and their successors are certainly not more dif-ficult to decipher than the symbolic world of a mediae-val Madonna or Watteau's "Embarquement pour Cythère".

For Christo, too, the idea is a primary factor, as expressed from the outset by the choice of the place for the event. It does not hinder him in the realization of his expansive projects, but drives him irresistibly towards it.

Concept and Reality

Conceptual Art is no different in this respect. It does not just show an essential scepticism vis-à-vis tradi-tion, it is more an almost excessively lucid demonstra-tion of Duchamp's doubt, sometimes even despair, over the possibility of artistic creation and the ability to communicate it. There is no longer belief in "art for all," or in the possibility of integrating art and environ-ment. The impotence of art in the face of repression and wars, which have persisted from 1945 to the pres-ent day, and of the geographical and ideological divi-sion of the world between the great powers and the countries dependent upon them, put a definite stop to the optimism of the sixties, at the latest at the climax of the Vietnam war, which struck a blow at American self-confidence. A withdrawal from superficial perfection-ism under the banner of new technology was evident in the Italian "arte povera" of the sixties, with its pro-grammatic turning to "poor" materials. It took up a mystical position in the space productions of an artist like Jannis Kounellis and in the Fibonacci theories, which derived from a mediaeval mathematician.

"Individual Mythologies", as presented in concentrated form by Harald Szeemann at "documenta V/1972" – including the conceptual "recherche du temps perdu" of the Frenchman Christian Boltanski, the obsessive "Diaries" of the German Hanne Darboven to the hippy art of the American Paul Thek – signalled a withdrawal into the private sphere, into new ivory towers, which can be penetrated only by an observer prepared to complete the artists' ideas in his own mind ("live in your head"). It is obvious that only a small section of the public, privileged by education or gifted with espe-cial powers of imagination, will be able to meet these demands. Despite its attempt to activate the observer by appealing to his own (re)creative qualities, this brittle art is made elitist by its very requirements and lack of vivid pictorial qualities. It never stood a chance of becoming popular.

Art's doubt in itself and in its ability to influence or even change the world and mankind, as expressed in Conceptual Art, has never been so radically formulat-ed, particularly not in the early modern period, and not even by Marcel Duchamp, who did leave behind a late work ("Etant Donnés") which was complex and richly allusive, even if it was still a little mysterious, a little unwilling to subject itself to definitive interpretation. This kind of self-doubting awareness of crisis, the corollary of which is intellectual pride, a not unknown phenomenon, would not have been possible in the first half of the century, for all its astringent criticism of the status quo and traditional values.

Diametrically opposed to this radical scepticism we find attempts to use art as a weapon in the day-to-day political struggle. Such attempts have only been suc-cessful when they used a suitable medium, for example Klaus Staeck's mass editions of posters and postcards, which took over where John Heartfield left off and developed his ideas in an independent way suit-ed to the times and to changed political and social con-ditions. The slogans of the revolts of '68, which brought art into the streets – Lautréament's famous dictum, later taken over by Karl Marx, "Poetry must be made by all," or "Power to imagination" – could only have a transient effect in the context of the moment; they then became interesting documents in contem-porary history, with no further effective power. Corre-sponding attempts in painting and sculpture landed up, as was to be expected, in the ideological cul-de-sac of agitating propaganda art ("agitprop"), as most artists failed to show direct political commitment in their work. Exceptions, like the sculptor Siegfried Neuen-hausen and his work with prisoners or Hans Haacke with his provocative works, prove the rule.

Thus it was no wonder that in those turbulent years painting and sculpture were didactically and prematu-rely pronounced dead, even though in the seventies another movement took up an unambiguously opposed position: this was the so-called Neo-Realism, in all its forms from Photo- or Hyperrealism to "Relative Realism"; even today Neo-Realism is still undervalued, although it produced much which is significant, and was by no means uniform or superficial; in fact it was simply ignored into oblivion. Debate about realistic and veristic tendencies in post-war art, about the artistic movement which was brought into the public eye in 1970 by the "22 Realists" exhibition in the New York Whitney Museum, still suffers from a lack of distinction and a superficiality which are as astonishing as they are regrettable. It is true that there was a Realism section in "documenta V/1972", but it was decidedly in the shadow of the "Individual Mythologies", These are to be understood as the first stage of Harald Szeemann's "Museum of Obsessions", a visionary idea which led to three exhibitions impressive both in their success and in their partial failure, "Bachelor Machine", "Monte Verità" and "The Tendency to the Gesamtkunstwerk".

In contrast to this, Neo-Realistic movements show a deficiency in the formulation of theory which has still not been made up. Instead of defining the considerable differences in the works of apparently or genuinely realistic painters and sculptors, their works, which are in form and content totally different from each other, are all dealt with in exactly the same way, that is, if anyone bothers to deal with them at all. But what do the hard, monumental portraits of the American Chuck Close have to do with the painterly sensibilities of the European Franz Gertsch, what has the mirror world of Richard Estes, reflective both pictorially and intellectually, to do with the classicistic-manneristic figures of an artist like Philip Pearlstein? How could one relate Gerhard Richter's early and middle photographic overpaintings to the archetypal everyday situations of the Canadian Alex Colville? Colville insists that the "mythology of the everyday" is not the especial preserve of writers of the calibre of James Joyce, but that contemporary painters could use it as well. "The inexpressible really exists," said Ludwig Wittgenstein, and the Viennese philosopher continued: "This is obvious." This has seldom been recognized in the work of the high-quality Realists of our time, far removed from Naturalism, either in the fetishized everyday objects taken out of their contexts (shoes, buttons, jackets) in the work of the Italian Domenico Gnoli, or the breathless, hyperreal "figure world" of the American Duane Hanson, in which concrete situations in life become existential ciphers. This is a state of affairs which is not contradicted by the enigmatic humour used in the portrayal of an American tourist couple.

Neo-Realism has never been as unanimously accepted as the "wild" Neo-Expressionist movements of the eighties. On reflection, the reason for this is that "depth hidden on the surface" is the key to the best Neo-Realist works, and many observers have not yet discovered this.

The short period in which Neo-Realism flourished was at the same time the moment of a kind of "analytical" or "conceptual" painting which was as sensitive as it was intelligent. It spread in an astonishing range and variety from New York to London, from Düsseldorf to the Kunsthochschule in Berlin, a city steeped in Realism and Expressionism both in the past and now, in which bleak purist art always had difficulty in making itself felt, or indeed in making any impact at all. The subtle, reflective works of Robert Ryman, the brooding analyst, and Brice Marden, the mystic of chromatic abstraction, "Blinky" Palermo and "Imi" Knoebel, pupils of Beuys, Gotthard Graubner, the colour-space painter and Raimund Girke, whose pictures are created from the interplay of monochrome and structure, the American Jerry Zeniuk and the Englishman Alan Green, the Italians Calderara and Zappettini, mark important stages in the development of unassertive, gentle art; their work has certainly not gone unnoticed. Despite this it took courage in 1973, though probably not a high degree of inspiration, to dedicate the Düsseldorf avant-garde exhibition "Prospect 73" to "Painting", and thus to face up to the omniscient prophets and to predictions that the traditional artistic genres were finished. These predictions even included "environments," those pictorially organized spaces which had only found an enduring place as an art form in Europe in the sixties and early seventies, principally through the works of the Americans George Segal and Edward Kienholz, whose guest appearances in Stockholm, Amsterdam, Düsseldorf and Zürich unleashed a "shock for Europe," as Werner Spies wrote at the time.

Pluralism in the Seventies

It was also in the seventies that Joseph Beuys, still the most discussed artist of our time, finally made his breakthrough. His profoundly melancholy, very complex and very German work, with roots which can be traced back via Romanticism to the apocalyptic visions of the late Gothic period, includes drawing and collage, sculpture and environment, happening and political action. Beuys is not only striving for the complete work of art. The utopian goal of his work is much more the realization of the old dream of uniting life and art in a world freed from political pressures and social taboos: a world in which each person is not just a nameless member of an amorphous mass society, but a creative, self-determined individual in a free community.

Beuys' anti-real, visionary art and the magic glow of his personality, somehow reminiscent of Dostoevsky, have exerted a lasting influence on his many German and foreign pupils and colleagues, and affected the image of the German artist throughout the world. To that extent he prepared the way for those who came after him. It took the rest of the world decades to discover Expressionism and the international success of contemporary German artists working in this tradition, from the "founding fathers" Baselitz and Penck to Immendorff, Hödicke, Lüpertz, Kiefer and the younger ones, was to an extent also due to Beuys, however different their artistic ambitions might be from those of the great youth idol of the sixties and seventies.

This statement looks forward to the eighties. The artists of the seventies – more pronouncedly than their predecessors in the previous decade – still bore the stamp of "Conceptual Art", and above all exhibited a multiplicity of contradictory tendencies and trends bewildering to expert and layman alike, and all – rightly or wrongly – asking to be labelled with the smart adjective "progressive." This did not prevent, as the critic Horst Richter pointed out, "their representatives and spokesmen from asserting their own movements to be the true avant-garde," although there was no dominant tendency or even style comparable with Classical Modernism or the art of the sixties. The phenomenon of the contemporaneity of the contradictory manifested itself almost to the point of chaos. For the uninvolved observer the "avant-garditis" of this period was clear proof of the deep crisis which the militant concept of the avant-garde had reached, after being the war-cry of the Classical Modern period. It was based on a comparatively naive belief in progress, which had long been rejected by science and philosophy, and which no longer had an effective function. Of course, many of the leading figures in the changing history of twentieth century art had never seen themselves as avant-garde in the narrow, "progressive" sense. Others, who felt themselves to be the standard-bearers of art for tomorrow and the day after, certain members of the international abstract movement for example, for a time produced work of limited originality. On the other hand, the work of an alleged eclectic like Francis Bacon has stood up to the visual wear and tear of the decades; his extraordinary visionary strength only achieved due recognition, after considerable delay and a few trial runs in the late fifties and early sixties, after the major exhibition of 1972 in Paris and Düsseldorf.

The seventies were also the period of "Expanded Arts", Joseph Beuys' "Erweiterter Kunstbegriff", the age of the new media: Video Art with Nam Jun Paik as the outstanding exponent; the partly masochistic, partly narcissistic "Body Art", a radical questioning of one's own existence; Process Art; instructions for "Using Objects," given by Franz Erhard Walther in a manner which was as intelligent as it was thoughtful. It was also the era of spontaneous art in the "happening," of the "fluxus" as a living collage or artistic-sculptural spontaneous theatre and the "performance" which developed from it, of the artists' film and – belatedly catching up with America – of the recognition of artistic photography as an independent genre. The wheat has since been separated from the chaff even in these new fields. Those who pronounced eager dilettantism, lack of knowledge and wretched craftsmanship to be the hallmark of genius no longer cut any ice. The new terrain set broader limits for the classical artistic genres painting, sculpture and graphics and opened up numerous new possibilities of artistic creation and involvement of the observer in the completion of works of art. "Spurensicherung", with interesting and contrasting exponents like Charles Simonds, the Poiriers, Nikolaus Lang and Lothar Baumgarten, anchors its criticism of civilization and its humane utopias in a historical or imagined past, or in nature, which has no history. Following Lévi-Strauss' "Sad Tropics", it presents with penetrating clarity the problems of forgotten peoples, landscapes and cultures threatened with extinction. None of this has anything to do with flag-waving quasi-academic avant-gardism raised to the status of a programme, but it has a great deal to do with artistic creation at the high level of knowledge of a late culture, which knows no boundaries be they of thought or of geography, and for which the past too has become accessible and available.

The End of "Modernism"

The English critic Edward Lucie-Smith wrote: "It is now possible to speak of the end of Modernism," in the introduction to his book "Art in the Seventies", which appeared in 1980. But the end of the avant-garde ideology of the seventies does not mean the end of art. What actually happened was that painting, which had been pronounced dead, celebrated some vital triumphs in the first half of the decade. It even put all the other genres in the shade after the interlude of the largely ornamental "Pattern Art", at least in the expressive form which originated in Italy, Germany and also America, and all the more so as many Neo-Expressionists followed the example of their forefathers and created sculpture as well, albeit with varying degrees of success. The international success of the "Transavantgarde" in Italy, the "New Savages" in Germany, Switzerland, Austria, Denmark, Great Britain, France and the Netherlands, and "New Image Painting" in the USA is no surprise after the thirsty years of an intellectually supercooled art of ideas without sensuous visual qualities. Artistic asceticism was followed by a new and spontaneous sensuality; the rejection of subjective "handwriting" was replaced by the enthronement of emphatic, impulsive and generally uninhibitedly highly-coloured painting in the wake of the German Expressionists of the first half of the century and the American abstract expressionists of the second half. Van Gogh and the late Corinth also provided stimuli. Even a less famous nineteenth century artist, the markedly pictorial-realist Ferdinand von Rayski – born 38 years before the great Wilhelm Leibl, influenced the early work of an artist like Georg Baselitz.

And so it is hardly surprising that "Dramatic Realism" was the banner under which Baselitz and his friend Eugen Schönebeck – who moved from East to West Berlin and had more than a nodding acquaintance with Social Realism – mounted their first exhibition "1 Pandämonium": radical and critical painting of taboo-breaking vitality, dismissed by Baselitz when he was an established figure as "puberty slime," just as Ernst Ludwig Kirchner had denounced his own early work as "youthful folly." At the same time these pictures, which so alarmed the police of the Affluent Republic, probably had more explosive force than the mature and successful artist's subsequent practice of standing his beautifully painted pictures on their heads, in order to demonstrate his perception, certainly correct but hardly new, that painting is to a large extent independent of its subject and also looks good upside-down.

A. R. Penck, alias Ralf Winkler, also came to West Germany from the GDR, though much later than Baselitz and Schönebeck. A "Friendship Picture", painted in expressive colours and showing the documentary film-maker Böttcher, the singer Wolf Biermann, Georg Baselitz and Penck himself as a child but with the head of the adult Picasso, is the preliminary step towards the later "system pictures," in which Penck used the formal methods of prehistoric art to capture possible cybernetic models and systems pictorially: "What I have in mind is a kind of physics of human society, or society as a physical body." Little sympathy for this notion was to be expected in the GDR. Baselitz, alias Georg Kern, important not only as a painter but also particularly so for his drawing, and A. R. Penck are, although still relatively young and operating at the height of their powers, the fathers of "violent" German painting. It was first introduced to the public with this description by Thomas Kempas in 1980, and restricted to Berlin before Wolfgang Becker invented the effective title "New Savages" for his more broadly based, historically comparative show in Aachen. Markus Lüpertz, Bernd Koberling and above all Horst Hödicke provided stimulus or instruction for the ebullient young artists. Despite their highly individual choice of large formats

and uninhibited handling of paint, this Neo-Expressive art is undeniably linked with the art of the past, in just the same way as the painting of leading GDR exponents Bernhard Heisig, Willi Sitte, Wolfgang Mattheuer or Werner Tübke, although in conception and realization, especially in comparison with the mannered coarseness of Sitte and Tübke, it is less conventional and more open.

Beyond the Avant-garde

"Transavantgarde", also known as "Arte cifra", was proclaimed in Italy; the critic Achille Bonita Oliva was its most indefatigable promoter and prophet. His doctrine was: "Transavantgarde allows art to move in all directions, and this includes the past." The movement wanted to free painting from intellectual calculation and "good taste," to make it unafraid of historicizing quotation, and able to make uninhibited use of the whole range of materials which the "Imaginary Museum" has to offer, from all ages and zones; this long-suppressed desire breaks through violently, though with considerable differences in quality, in the work of the exponents of this richly allusive new painting for a late culture – the artists are Chia, Cicchi, Clemente, Paladino, etc. Old myths are quoted – sometimes in depth, sometimes not – and made topical. The late work of modern classicists like de Chirico, Chagall and even Picasso, hitherto despised (or undervalued), is glorified by quotation and stylistic imitation.

In West Germany as well as Italy expressive painting avenged itself for the decades of contempt which it had suffered at the hands of various practitioners and apologists of the avant-garde. It did not just rehearse the uprising – whether it was in the Moritzplatz in Berlin, the Mülheimer Freiheit in Cologne or the Hamburg enclave of the Oehlen and Büttners brothers – it performed it with such vehemence that awareness of the contemporaneity of opposites was pushed into the background again, and as far into the background as the up-to-date avant-garde of any particular moment had managed to push it by means of didactic promises. There can be no doubt that the spiritual in art is being forced to take a back seat by the affirmation of a long-suppressed expressiveness, of an unconcerned, narcissistic subjectivity, of self-expression with exhibitionistic traits, of the irrational, of the visionary, or even of lack of style as a way of life, as practised by the roguish Jiri Dokupil in various masterly guises. And all this happens, encouraged of course by business interests, with the same lack of either inhibition or justice with which figurative art, especially in its expressive version, was treated for a number of years.

Faced with this new sensuousness, more restrained

and intellectually disciplined artists are not having an easy time in making their presence felt. One of the apologists of the new wave, Robert Rosenblum, calmly proclaims "liberation from the repressive constraints of the intellect, which has dominated the art of the last decade." Marcel Duchamp would not have been pleased to read this. Under the circumstances, the balance should be restored and an unduly limited view avoided by pointing out not only the existence of but the need for "intelligent art," as demanded by Duchamp.

There are various reasons for the triumph of "violent", "wild" or merely ebullient painting in Italy and Germany, in Switzerland and Austria, but also in the less romantic, more pragmatic world of America. There, Jonathan Borofsky breaks down boundaries of genre and also readily admits the influence of Dalí and Fellini on the one hand, and Walt Disney on the other, but also speaks of art as the "tool of his craft," with which he wants to open up the personal for the sake of the global self of mankind.

One of the reasons for the success of these artistic movements has already been mentioned: exhaustion as a result of a "progressiveness" threatened with sterility and leading to absurdity, opposition to the "remorseless pressure of artistic innovation" which has never been as great as it has been in the twentieth century, and particularly in the second half. Another reason, not unconnected with the first, is the reassessment of historical German Expressionism with its emphatically emotional, quasi-Romantic approach. For a long time it had been considered outside Central Europe as a "Gothic" aberration, as "bad painting," and this included the work of the outstanding Max Beckmann; indeed one could see why some of the "New Savages" made "bad painting" their trademark. The Expressionist exhibitions of the last few years, not least in America, have led to a far-reaching change of mind. Dismissive indifference has given way to unanimous, almost uncritical admiration.

Art and Its Times

A third reason was put forward by Hilton Kramer, a rigorous "hawk" and leading contributor to the New York periodical "New Criterion", the magazine of the affirmative, neo-conservative American intelligentsia. He pointed out that art has hardly reacted to the general protest against the traditional bourgeois way of life, to far-reaching cultural changes like the sexual revolution, drug culture, women's movements, etc., which were key factors from the socio-politically hyperactive late sixties right up to the threshold of our own decade. This is only half right, as Kramer simply

brackets out the political scene in art and also overlooks the – admittedly largely non-polemical – presentation of the young scene in Pop Art or in the pictures of Neo-Realists like Franz Gertsch ("Marina making up Luciano", "Medici", "Irène"). The political art of those years, to the extent that it was not street art and action-based, overwhelmingly used traditional models and had no artistic originality. Minimal, Conceptual and Land Art did not come to terms with everyday experience in the sixties and seventies. For this reason, according to Kramer, the private "cultural revolution" was not granted access to art, art did not concern itself with the world as it was. The Expressionist blueprint was reserved for life, not valid for art.

It is to some extent ironic that a writer anxious to restore the old order of things should make a statement that art does not always reflect the spirit of the times, in an essay in the catalogue of the Berlin "Zeitgeist" exhibition, of all places.

It was not until the revolutionary impetus had died down and the neo-conservative wave under the leadership of the Americans had swept through the Western world that taboo subjects began to appear; previously they had only cropped up in a few places in the works of the Post-Moderns – for example in the early Baselitz pictures – and had caused a scandal. In contrast with the turmoil of the preceding years they hardly gave offence and were accepted by collectors and indeed the wider world public without any moralizing or protest; an example is Salomé's painted declaration of his homosexuality. Irreversible changes in our way of life were at last expressed in the politically relatively reticent pictures of the Neo-Expressives. Even petit-bourgeois morality which – with a tragic climax in the 1937 "Decadent Art" action – tended to take on iconoclastic tendencies when its need for peace and quiet was disturbed, either by criticism of the status quo or radical alterations of artistic forms, restrained itself to an astonishing extent. The "violent," "wild" directness and spontaneity of the new pictures apparently do not have the power to disturb the apostles of morality – unlike the works of artists like Picasso, Mondrian or Barnett Newman when they first appeared; and this is true even when the self-satisfied satiety of the affluent society and its sacred values are questioned in a more or less provocative manner by artists like Immendorff, Bruce MacLean or Eric Fischl. In any event, attacks like these are accepted much more calmly than the intellectual formalism and radicalism of the avant-garde generation, now suddenly relegated to history, whose departure – at least for the time being – from the scene seems to be greeted with something approaching relief.

Unexpectedly, this almost brings up to date the thesis, over a quarter of a century old, of the conservative

43

sociologist Arnold Gehlen, that art should perform an "easing" function, particularly as it is accepted in essence even by the theoreticians of the Transavantgarde. The thorn in the ample flesh of affluence is blunted. The character, somewhat conservative in both style and content, despite violent presentation, of many works referring to history and myth has certainly contributed to this. History and myth are also clearly visible in the exuberant formal quotations across the range of Post-Modern architecture. Repetition, variation and unhibited historical allusions, even to the most recent past, of the kind found particularly in the problematical works of as brilliant a painter as Anselm Kiefer, broaden into reminiscences of blood-and-soil mythology which in their excessive empathy could become irritatingly close to Romantic idealization, even though this cannot be the artist's intention, as he wishes his work to be seen rather as mourning for and "coming to terms with the past."

These areas of thought are the hallmarks of an art which can also been seen in the context of the general wave of resigned nostalgia which, after their unsuccessful revolt, has seized even young people. The "hunger for pictures," to use the apt title of Wolfgang Max Faust's book, has for the time being stilled fear of the wordless power to convince of silent images, which has manifested itself again and again in the long series of furious protests against the arts which our century has seen. Despite the violence of their gestures, despite the pleasure they take in breaking strict moral taboos, in comparison with the works of the "Classicists", but above all with those of the post-war Modernists, the new expressive pictures seem more familiar and less strange. This is even true in cases where for once there is socio-political content, or where the pictures are to a large extent existentialist ciphers, as in the highly individual works of the Austrian Maria Lassnig or – in a quite different, more emotional way – in the works of the Swiss Martin Disler.

It is understandable that a business with an eye on turnover requires general goodwill, but this blurs marked differences in artistic quality and spiritual substance. In the mid-eighties this perception seems gradually to be getting the upper hand over the undiscriminating enthusiasm shown at the beginning of the "New Wave".

Powerful new collectors like the Saatchis in London, whose activities affect not only the art market and market values, but also the production of contemporary art, have started to look critically at their collections, to prune and to make additions. Virtuosi like Julian Schnabel, however, who made "violent" painting elegant and fit for the drawing-room, are certainly not affected by this procedure, at any rate for the time being. For the present, Schnabel remains for the upper

middle class of the twentieth century with an interest in art what Hans Makart, the prince of painters, was for the public of the "belle époque" in nineteenth century imperial Vienna. "We need him to show us what to feel," wrote an enraptured lady collector: the star had become an idol.

But there are artists with a firm place among the chosen few who represent other points of view: the Americans Cy Twombly, Brice Marden and Andy Warhol, the intelligent cynic. It was he who commented ironically on German and Italian dominance of the Transavantgarde movement by quoting fascist architectural features, which themselves of course were now "Post-Modern", though with quite different implications. Another member of the inner circle is certainly the wittiest and most enigmatic of the younger contemporary painters, Sigmar Polke, whose work takes its cue from "Capitalist Realism", Pop Art and the trivial mythology of the mass media.

Looking Ahead

But it is not only that the arbiters of taste among the dealers and collectors are broadening their range. It is much more the case that there is a general awareness that the dictatorship of a particular movement, whether it is revisionary or revolutionary, avant-garde or Transavantgarde, is bound to lead to artistic sterility. The Neo-Expressive artists themselves, like all their predecessors, are increasingly inclined to leave the warmth of the group nest, to develop their own individuality. Figures who up till now have been influential but have kept a low profile, like the master of the Berlin "Violents" Karl Horst Hödicke, are emerging from the background into the public eye. Those whose artistic substance is too slight for the long march through the world of consumerism are lagging behind.

The passage of time allows us to see things in perspective, and this is gradually becoming true in the emotionally charged world of the Transavantgarde. In principle, this process works in the same way now as it always has done. However, like every other development, it is subject to the law of the age, the law of exponential acceleration, which from time to time is concrete proof of Andy Warhol's ironic remark that anyone can be famous for a quarter of an hour. Despite all this, the critical confrontation which is starting, however hesitantly, is broadening the horizon and permitting us to see, beyond the squabbles about the "latest and most up-to-date from all over the world," the variety which there is even in the artistic landscape of the present day. Mammoth exhibitions like the tourist-slanted Paris Biennale of 1985 failed to take note of this, which led to an unfocused one-sidedness which was much to their disadvantage. Serious artists have never taken this limited view of life. Jonathan Borofsky, for example, the American painter and mixed media artist already mentioned, concerned himself just as intensively with the Minimal Art of Brancusi through to Sol LeWitt and Carl André as he did with his childhood and the painting of the Surrealists, before he found his own way. The influence of the Minimalists "was too extreme, and one extreme calls forth another," he said in an interview, "…I began to keep both the conceptual and the other side – the side of intuition, of dreams, the inner world."

High-quality European Transavantgarde has never denied its sources: De Chirico, Picasso, Nolde, the "Brücke" painters, Dix, Grosz and even Paul Klee. Bernd Zimmer, with Salomé, Fetting and Middendorf one of the first four Berlin "Savages", even talks of a "return of the object, but with abstract techniques": a remark which could have been made by Juan Gris. Zimmer is also happy to express his high regard for the colour-field painters Rothko and Newman.

Gerhard Richter takes a very different line, and tries to tackle the problem of capturing reality in a picture by trying out a sequence of new artistic techniques between Purism and ironized Romanticism, Photorealism and Expressiveness. The strong colour gestures of his new abstract pictures do not mean to him what they would mean to the Transavantgarde: "Abstract pictures," he wrote in the catalogue of "documenta VII/ 1982", "are fictitious models, because they reveal a reality which we can neither see nor describe, but which we can conclude to exist."

In art, as in all things, freedom is the freedom to think differently. This maxim tends to be forgotten when people who are always right quarrel about the only road to happiness, even though, after the end of all utopian hopes in the second half of the century, there is, as Giulio Carlo Argan says, no longer an "a priori" in art; this forgetfulness has left a lot of damage in its wake. The end of naive and ideological belief in progress could lead to a time of reflection and a new beginning – with the proviso that the return of images does not lure us into flight into the opposite extreme of stagnant, historicizing conservatism. In art – we should have learned this lesson – there can be no dogma, no eternal verities. Art does not live on progress, but on perpetual transformations. This process is going on before our eyes at breakneck speed. Ideas have never been tried out, then cast aside once and for all, as rapidly as they are today, when there are no more binding standards and no fixed criteria. What is important is that art should not come under the law of the market place and become a consumer commodity intended – "Quick, next please!" – for rapid consumption.

It looks increasingly as though the abundant possibilities of pictorial expressiveness between the sensuous and the spiritual, between expression and construction, between sculpture, painting and the new media are once more penetrating more deeply into our consciousness. No-one can know where the journey will take us. To ask whether art has the strength to live is the same as to ask the unanswered question of whether our threatened culture has the strength to survive.

Of Collectors and Collections

A Short Chronicle of the Ludwig Museum

The history of the Ludwig Museum is brief. It began on February 23 1976, when its benefactors Peter and Irene Ludwig of Aachen signed a momentous contract with the city of Cologne. Seven and a half years previously, on October 30 1968, Gert von der Osten, then Director of Museums in Cologne, had opened negotiations with the collectors about the possibility of their wide-ranging collection of contemporary art being placed at the disposal of the Wallraf-Richartz Museum for an indefinite period. Contemporary art at the time of these discussions meant "the art of the sixties," and this was the title of Wolf Vostell's finely designed catalogue, which first appeared early in 1969. The five subsequent editions, each considerably expanded, have been out of print for years and are now rarities in antiquarian bookshops, seen as works of art in their own right.

"This was the collector's reaction," wrote Von der Osten in his "Editorial" to the fifth edition in 1971, on the subject of the suggestions made in Cologne. "He wouldn't hear of a special exhibition, and he would also prefer to avoid an official opening. He didn't want any special attention, and indeed would prefer the collection to be integrated into the existing departments of the museum. Nothing like that had ever happened to me before," continued the distinguished Director of Museums, "even though the museum had been much helped by private individuals and public funds. It was a unique act of generosity."

This discussion held in 1968 was to be historically significant not just for the Cologne museums, but for the artistic scene in Germany and the whole of Europe. At that time the collection consisted, according to the first edition of the catalogue, of 90 pictures, sculptures and other objects, and also 50 items of graphics. When the fifth and final edition appeared, in other words no more than three years later, the number of works of art had already doubled: there were 216 important exhibits, not counting the graphics.

Even at that time it was not just a Pop Art collection, as many people have suggested, although Peter Ludwig had been fascinated by the art of the Kennedy era on

The artists and pictures mentioned in the "Chronicle" are treated more thoroughly in their art-historical context in subsequent chapters. In case of doubt please consult the index.

Andy Warhol, *Portrait of Peter Ludwig,* 1980

his visits to America, and this had been the deciding factor in his all-important decision to concentrate on collecting 20th century art in future.

The 1971 catalogue lists (not including drawings and graphics) 91 artists, of whom only 25 were figures from the New York Pop Art scene or from "swinging London," as it was then known. Another 66, including 36 Europeans and 30 Americans, never had anything to do with Pop Art. The great Jasper Johns and his friend and kindred spirit Robert Rauschenberg, who in terms of quality and quantity are more impressively represented in the Ludwig Museum than in any other art gallery in the world, are both classified under Pop Art, although this is a rather generous interpretation of the concept, as they both, along with the great sculptor Claes Oldenburg, started as abstract Expressionists, as "action painters," and only later became the "founding fathers" of Pop Art. The dominant, genuine American Pop Artists are equally impressively represented by Roy Lichtenstein, James Rosenquist, Tom Wesselman and Jim Dine.

The impressive groups of works by these artists, in whose orbit the works of the pioneers of the London Pop scene, Richard Hamilton, Ronald B. Kitaj, Eduardo Paolozzi and David Hockney also belong, are the heart of the Ludwig Collection, and its raison d'être. But even in the early stages the collection contained comparable numbers of important works of very high quality by many other American and European painters, sculptors and other artists of first rank: Yves Klein, Antoni Tàpies, Jean Dubuffet, Wols, Jean Tinguely, Richard Serra, Joseph Beuys, Morris Louis, Frank Stella, Gerhard Richter, Konrad Klapheck, and the supreme master, Pablo Picasso.

This array of high-calibre works is the basis of the collection acquired by the city of Cologne, first on permanent loan, and then, on that day in late February 1976, as a gift. The condition for the handing over of the private collection as it then existed to the city was that a new museum should be built by 1985; this was to be a new home for the Wallraf-Richartz Museum and was also to provide suitable accomodation for the newly-founded Ludwig Museum. (The opening date was later moved to 1986.)

variations), continues the architectural rhythm of the Minorite church and was derided by Konrad Adenauer, Mayor of Cologne and later Federal Chancellor, as the "factory" of the "Wallraf-Richartz Works"; he recommended that it be "pulled down" at once. It is now considered one of the best examples of post-war German architecture: a rarity in the fifties, when buildings went up at a furious pace but with no particular regard for taste, and when the highest good was "a city fit for the motor car."

Schwarz had conceived the building as a treasury of traditional art, expressly including the 19th century. It was always intended, long before the negotiations with the Aachen industrialist Ludwig, that there should be a building opposite to house the modern collection. As so often happens, the money ran out. Thus the city of Cologne and the Ludwigs had a common interest in the demand for a new building which would meet all the technical and spatial needs of a

Ewald Mataré, *The Stefan Lochner Fountain,* inner courtyard of the old Wallraf Richartz Museum, 1955/56

Dani Karavan, *Model, design for the square of the Wallraf Richartz Museum/Museum Ludwig, Cologne*

The "Wallrafianum", built by Rudolf Schwarz adjacent to the Gothic Minorite church, had long been outgrown, and anyway the architect had not intended it to house 20th century art. This plain brick building, adopting mediaeval principles (with contemporary

modern museum, and do justice to the museum's explosively expanding collections, particularly in the field of modern art. The new building by the Cologne architects Busmann and Haberer, who surprisingly won the competition to build the new Wallraf-Richartz/Ludwig Museum against rivals of the highest calibre, not only met the conditions of the contract, but also filled one of the most sensitive gaps in the cultural landscape of Cologne, on one of the most distinguished sites in Europe, in the shadow of Cologne Cathedral. The complex includes a spacious concert hall and an austere but handsome piazza (to be known as Heinrich-Böll-Platz, in front of the new Wallraf-Richartz/Ludwig Museum building); Israeli artist Dani Karavan was commissioned to design the layout of the piazza (architects: Peter Busmann and Gotfryd Haberer). Karavan's Minimalist sculpture in various materials is a striking focal point, related in scale both to the architecture and the surroundings. This Israeli is one of the few contemporary artists able to combine sculptural design with overall town-planning concepts.

As well as Gert von der Osten, Kurt Hackenberg, Head of the Department of Culture at the time, who stimulated the cultural life of the city for almost a quarter of a century, was a significant force behind the completion of the ambitious project. From the start Wolfgang Hahn, Head Conservator of the Wallraf-Richartz Museum and the Ludwig Museum, gave the Ludwigs constant support and expert advice; he was himself an enthusiastic collector of contemporary art and his own collection has now found a home in Vienna.

The first phase of the history of the Cologne "Ludwig Museum (Modern Gallery)", as it is described in the published text, began immediately after the Second World War. When Peter and Irene Ludwig joined the ranks of important benefactors, the modern art department of the Wallraf-Richartz Museum already had an oustanding reputation. The Aachen collectors would never have considered concentrating their activities on Cologne without this excellent basis. The high standard reached in the years immediately following the war is due to Josef Haubrich, the man after whom the Städtiche Kunsthalle is now named. A comparable event to Peter and Irene Ludwig's choice of Cologne was the agreement signed by this lawyer with his home town shortly after the catastrophe of 1945. In 1946 he left the greater part of his modern art collection, with the emphasis on "German Expressionism and Realism", to the city of Cologne. Three years later it was on show in the court of honour of the Kunstmuseum in Düsseldorf – Cologne's old museum buildings were in ruins. This exhibition was an inspiration to the whole of the post-war German cultural world. It showed that despite the Nazis' Bildersturm, from which the Wallraf-Richartz Museum had not been spared, all contact had

Gerhard Marcks, *Josef Haubrich,* 1953

not been lost with international developments; this was also true in the field of art collection. Haubrich had not only protected the items of "decadent art" in his collection from confiscation and destruction, but had also had the courage to buy additional works by the proscribed artists: pictures and sculptures by Liebermann, Corinth, Kirchner, Heckel, Schmidt-Rottluff, Kokoschka, Macke, Hofer, Lehmbruck, Kollwitz and Barlach, and also works by Van Gogh, Vlaminck and Utrillo. The foreword to the catalogue for the 1949 Düsseldorf exhibition rightly stated that the "Haubrich collection, presented to the Wallraf-Richartz Museum in 1946," not only made up for losses in the Nazi period, but "far surpassed" the original modern art collection.

A comparison of the catalogue, now more than 35 years old, with the list of works confiscated in 1937 shows that this was no exaggeration, although it lists painful losses such as Picasso's "Soler Family" (now in the Musée des Beaux Arts in Liège), Gauguin's "Rider on the Beach" (now in the collection of the shipowner Niarchos), Otto Dix' portrait of his parents (now in the Basel Kunsthalle), Kokoschka's "Portrait of the Actor Etlinger" (now in the Karlsruhe Kunsthalle) and Edvard Munch's lost "Field".

Like Peter and Irene Ludwig, Josef Haubrich never

stopped collecting. Ludwig often cited this powerful personality as his model. This is consistent with his conviction that private collections should not only be shown to the public as frequently as possible, they should finally belong to it.

Thus the Ludwigs collected not just for themselves, but always for the museum as well, which in the famous saying of art historian Gustav Pauli is "the most democratic of all educational institutions," and in the formulation of Jürgen Habermas "a meeting place of people with equal rights." Many benefactors in and around Cologne have lived up to this perception. Günther and Carola Peill, and also Lilly von Schnitzler-Malinckrodt, may stand as representatives of many; some patrons prefer to remain anonymous.

Max Beckmann, *Lilly von Schnitzler-Mallinckrodt,* 1928–29

The fact that the Cologne collection expanded so rapidly in quality and size is not due to the example of committed private individuals alone. The city itself, in many cases with the support of the Land Nordrhein-Westfalen, has made a significant purchasing contribution, and many men and women involved with the museum encouraged the systematic build-up of its collections. These include museum directors Leopold Reidemeister, Otto H. Förster, Gert von der Osten, Gerhard Bott and Hugo Borger, then those directly responsible for the Wallraf-Richartz Museum, first Helmut May, and then above all Horst Keller with his eighteen years of service, and many other colleagues who worked with them. The Ludwig Museum in its present form could not exist or have become as important as it is without their efforts and expertise.

The collection has grown considerably in the ten years since the Ludwig Museum became independent. Expressionism and Pop Art remained focal points, but other fields have been explored. First among these is avant-garde art from early post-revolutionary Russia, a collection hardly surpassed in any Western museum,

despite the magnificent Malevich collection in the Stedelijk Museum in Amsterdam. Other artists particularly well represented are Max Beckmann, with ten impressive new pictures added from the Schnitzler bequest, and not least Pablo Picasso, with significant works from various periods acquired by Peter Ludwig. Even metaphysical painting (pittura metafisica) and Italian Futurism, entirely absent in Cologne ten years ago, are excellently represented, thanks to the generosity of an anonymous donor, by pictures by De Chirico, Carrà, Ballà, Severini, Sironi and Morandi. Dada and Surrealism boast fine additional works by Picabia, Man Ray, Hans Arp, Dalí and Giacometti, and the Max Ernst collection, which was always impressive, was recently enriched by the acquisition of an important twenties work ("Virgin Smacking the Christ Child"), a programmatic early work which caused a scandal at an exhibition in Cologne in 1928. This picture is an authentic illustration of one of the artist's creative periods hitherto completely unrepresented in the museum. Fernand Léger's "Proletarian Olympus" is now part of the collection, along with some late Matisse and Henri Laurens' Cubist period. The art of the fifties was considerably supplemented by a key Informel picture which had already made history, Wols' "Blue Phantom", and also by pictures by Asger Jorn, the "Cobra" pioneer, and works by Emil Schumacher and Bernhard Schultze. There are at long last pictures by the master of the American action painters, Hans Hofmann, and the group of calmly monumental works by Clyfford Still, Mark Rothko and Barnett Newman found congenial neighbours in a "black painting" of the "Black Monk" by Ad Reinhardt, and a picture by Brice Marden. The significance of the American sculpture collection, which already had fine works by Richard Serra, Walter de Maria, Michael Heizer and Carl André, was further enhanced by two sculptures by the great David Smith and an important work by Mark di Suvero. The field of "Nouveau Réalisme" is supplemented by the "Compression" of a prize-winning racing car by César Baldaccini, who was hitherto entirely unrepresented. Concept Art and "Spurensicherung" found welcome additions in works by James Lee Byars and Anne and Patrick Poirier respectively.

Additions to the classical and recent modern art collections are entirely true to the character of the Ludwig Museum, which does not see itself as a defined and finite collection, but as a "musée infini", a living institution without a final full stop, with no areas disregarded, but completely receptive to the art of the immediate present and the future.

The city of Cologne was never a royal seat, it was always a city of proud and self-confident burghers. For this reason the history of Cologne's museums does not

Günther und Carola Peill

worthy of note for his place of birth." The poet called for the building of a Wallraf Museum even then: "It is therefore to be desired, that this treasure be acquired with all possible speed for the common weal, so that the years still granted to their worthy owner might be used to order these costly objects meticulously, to make them open to enjoyment and use. All this, however, presupposes an adequate accommodation, which in all probability could be found in this extensive city." The unselfishness which Goethe praised so highly, the civic sense of a "citoyen", not a "bourgeois", a sense of social responsibility, caused more and more great collectors and benefactors to place their private treasures at the disposal of the people. In this they are all the same: Wallraf the canon, Richartz the merchant, Haubrich the lawyer, Peill the manufacturer and his wife Carola, and also the art historian and industrialist Peter Ludwig and his wife Irene. Their motivation is strikingly encapsulated in a short sentence by the English writer and historian H. G. Wells, incidentally a socialist: "Deep within mankind is a resistance to transient deeds." Public recognition of what they have done, "public happiness" as the philosopher Hannah Arendt put it, may be the reward of these people in their lifetime. What they also hope is that their name and their work will survive. "My dust scattered, my memory shines on like a star," wrote the poet Arno Holz. Why should what is true for a poet not come true for these benefactors?

begin with the presentation of curiosities and wonders to the people by enlightened princes. It begins with the "collection of Canon Professor Wallraf" who, as Goethe reported in his notes on his Rhein-Neckar journey of 1814–15, "passionately possessed of his native town, used his whole life, means and goods, indeed even denied himself the first necessities, to keep all that was

Artists and Artistic Movements
in the Present Century

1. Pictures and Objects
in the Ludwig Museum

Luminous Colour – Purity of Line
The "Fauves" in Paris

The artistic revolution began just after the turn of the century. The key date is autumn 1905, when Henri Matisse and his group unleashed a scandal at the Paris "Salon d'Automne" which if anything was even more intense than the uproar caused by the first Impressionist exhibition of 1874, held in the house of the famous photographer Nadar in the Rue des Capucines. "A pot of paint thrown in the spectator's face!" was the outraged reaction. As so often in the subsequent history of art in this century, it was not just aesthetic ideals which seemed threatened, but morality and public order as well.

"The world is there, it would be pointless to repeat it," as Kasimir Edschmid, the apologist of the German Expressionists, was later to say; they owe a lot to the "wild" French, the Fauves around Matisse. The revolutionaries of the Salon d'Automne would certainly have put their names to this statement, because it also describes their relationship with the visible world and naturalism in art. For them, pure, glowing colour was the instrument of expression, pure form the pictorial medium in its own right, and pure, pared-down line the tool of pictorial architecture. Art no longer ran "parallel with nature," as it had done for Cézanne, but was contrasted with it as an autonomous creation. The world of art now had its own reality. The fleeting world of appearances, which had so fascinated the Impressionists, was transformed into a unique pictorial emblem. The Fauves brought to a logical conclusion what the Impressionists, Cézanne, Van Gogh and above all the "surface painter" Gauguin had started to create. This was the birth of "pure" painting, and the beginning of "Modern Art" – only a few years before the first phase of Cubism. It is also the beginning of the Ludwig

---

Editorial Note

All the works of art illustrated in this volume are alluded to in the text, with their titles in inverted commas; some are discussed more thoroughly. To assist the reader, individual pictures and the text relating to them have been placed as close together as possible. There are some slight displacements for technical or contextual reasons.

In the case of some artists, additional works are mentioned for reasons of clarity, even though they are not illustrated or do not figure in the Ludwig Museum collection.

Museum's collection, although on a modest scale in comparison with other movements.

When the Modern department of the Wallraf-Richartz Museum became independent a decision had to be reached about where the break should be made. After a good deal of thought, the year 1900 was chosen as a "dividing line," particularly as there was no doubt that visitors to both institutions would have access to excellent examples of the background history of "Modern" art. To this extent there is no clear break between these two museums under the same roof. Works by Cézanne, Van Gogh, Gauguin, Bonnard, Munch, Corinth and a fine late water-lily picture by Monet (1905) allow an almost seamless transition from the Wallraf-Richartz Museum to the Ludwig Museum. Only the Pointillistes are not represented.

The earliest and finest piece of Fauve painting in the Cologne Museum of 20th Century Art is a small picture, Henri Matisse's "Girl Seated" of 1909, by which time the clash with the Neo-Impressionists Cézanne and Gauguin was long since over and reticent "Expressionism" in the French style fully developed. The artistic chamber music of this magical figure picture is based on the contrasting complementary colours red and green, their cold and warm tones reconciled by the white-ochre of the body, set on the diagonal. Pictorial space is created by colour; Cézanne and Van Gogh provided the stimulus for this. The young girl's relaxed, reflective pose and the melancholy in her face give the intimate scene a lyrical note, a reticent musicality.

At first sight the scissor cuts of the old Matisse, whose physical condition in 1948 no longer allowed him to wield a paintbrush, have little in common with his work as a painter. This first impression is wrong, however. His mastery in handling patches of colour, his unfailing security in compositional, space-creating division of the surface, his incomparable ability to concentrate form by reduction, and his rejection of anecdotal detail all come to a late flowering in the work of his last four years. He first developed the technique of "papiers découpés" when preparing his pictures. Between 1943 and 1950 it became an independent method beyond painting.

The composition "Women and Monkeys" (1952) was originally in two parts. Matisse, living at the time in a hotel in Nice, created it for himself. The group of seated

Henri Matisse, *Girl Seated,* c. 1909

Henri Matisse, *Women and Monkeys,* 1952

women came first, then the monkeys which surround them. Finally the artist – after a few corrections – placed the two parts in the harmonious and decorative arrangement which is the hallmark of his later years. The rhythm of the picture, its wave movement, beginning on the left and breaking on the right, is conveyed directly to the onlooker. Objective reality and abstraction are perfectly balanced: the figures and objects become independent pictorial ciphers, but remain clearly recognizable. The formal decorative elements, balanced with sovereign skill, nevertheless allow the mythological background of the "earthly paradise" to shine through; that paradise which informed the iconography of Matisse in his latter years with such joy and serenity: a world in which man, animals and plants live together harmoniously and without problems.

At the opposite pole to the latent classicality which shows clearly even in the early work of Matisse is the impetuous Maurice Vlaminck, who earned his living by cycle racing and playing the violin before he finally opted for painting. He could be called the Fauve Expressionist, the "wildest of the wild," with his instinctive, uninhibited vitality. That his instinct and exaggerated self-confidence – "I am Fauvism," he once said – did not always guarantee impeccable taste did not become clear until the leading spirit of the group could no longer support him. His "Still Life with Flowers and Fruit" dates from his good period, however (1911). It is an outstanding composition, as well as resonant in its colouring, and is painted with a reticence which could not always be taken for granted; Vlaminck liked to see paint spurt out of a tube.

Gert von der Osten wrote an excellent description of this picture: "The table rises, indeed practically tips itself towards us. The delicate, transient trivia upon it emit a fiery glow. If the goal of still life painting is to express quiet beauty and transience, to express the vanity of the world, then it has achieved that here, flaring to the highest and final peak of radiance, with scarcely no repose remaining, nowhere the eye can rest. Silence and tenderness have found a voice. We can see shades of blue, white and ochre which just capture the beautiful trivia, like an epilogue for the world they

inhabit, whether landscapes, buildings or texture. Thus, in the last resort, what at first seemed random can be seen to be highly structured. Vlaminck has brought his exuberant colour under control – thanks to the determining power of Cézanne."

André Derain was a close friend of Vlaminck, but artistically they are diametrically opposed: Derain was a contemplative, knowledgeable man, who had concerned himself intensively throughout his life with the art of the past – perhaps at times a little more than was good for his imagination. Derrain painted some of the most beautiful, glowing and uncompromising Fauve pictures, but kept closer to natural models than did some of his contemporaries; round about 1908, however, under the influence of Cézanne and the Cubists, he returned to a more constructive, more "structured" way of painting, with calmer tonality. The "View of Saint-Paul-de-Vence", though still set in the French Midi, shows this very clearly.

Albert Marquet's painting stands comparison with Matisse's in terms of culture, if not in power and richness of imagination; they met at an early stage and Marquet shared Matisse's studio for a few years. Marquet seems to have been the first of the Fauves to deal seriously with painting in "pure tones." As early as the turn of the century, between 1898 and 1901, he was making his first experiments with this style. He, Raoul Dufy and Henri Manguin belonged to the July 14th group of painters, named after the French revolutionary holiday. Their representations of streets decked in flags (dating from 1906) are reminiscent of treatments of the same subject by Monet (1878) and Van Gogh (1887), which were themselves aglow with colour. Although Marquet visited Morocco with Matisse in 1913, he grew further and further away from Fauve directness of colour and form. His pictures are bathed in a quasi-Impressionist light. The colours become more restrained, the dominant and quiet tone is a richly graded, colourful grey. The architecture of the 1935 "portrait" of the Moroccan town of Rabat, called "Fond Memory," is still generous and free, but formally very much more differentiated and smaller in its parts than the orchestral glow of his earlier sheets of colour.

Maurice de Vlaminck, *Still Life with Flowers and Fruit,* 1911

André Derain, *View of St. Paul-de-Vence,* 1910

Many of Marquet's subtle pictures have that silver shimmer which from time immemorial has been the hallmark of the master painter.

Raoul Dufy, a pupil of the great colourist Bonnard, is the least problematical of the Fauves. His serene and cheerful pictures have been compared with the music of Mozart: perhaps Rossini would have been a better choice. Dufy's art is light, sketch-like and illustrative, for which reason he is sometimes known as the Fauve Impressionist. In the middle phase of his life he tried in his own way to "liberate" colour by banishing any element of drawing from his pictures, so that the "sound" of the colour should not be disturbed. The sketch "The Harbour" (c. 1925) dates from this period; it seems to be connected with Dufy's work on a larger picture, "Festival of Ships in the Harbour".

In the twenties and thirties the Dutch portraitist Kees van Dongen was the star of the chic society of the period, and that did not do his work any good. In the preceding years he had been one of the Fauves, origi-

Albert Marquet, *Fond Memory, Rabat*, 1935

Kees van Dongen, *Portrait of Ana,* c. 1905/06

nally influenced by Toulouse-Lautrec and Van Gogh. In this period he painted outstanding portraits and pictures of figures in strong, glowing colours applied straight from the tube to the canvas, but he, in contrast to his friends, soon began to mix them. The rich "Portrait of Ana" dates from the pioneering days of the Fauves (1905/06). Van Dongen, too, treats colour as an element in the creation of form; but, despite the spontaneous painting of the only Fauve who was not a Frenchman, even in these early days of "striving genius" one cannot overlook a certain reticence and mellowing of the strong colours.

Several German painters had gathered around Matisse in Paris. Their meeting place was the Café du Dôme. Hans Purrmann was particularly close to the Fauve leader, and under his influence he abandoned Impressionism, travelled with Matisse and organized the day-to-day running of the Académie Matisse. Purrmann's still life "Flowers and Fruit" dates from 1949, long after the crucial years in Paris, but colouring and background still show Fauve influence. However, the handling of line is less decisive and the areas of colour dissolve into differentiated textures. Purrmann is again more concerned with detail and mutes the purity of his colour with more subdued tones.

Rudolf Levy, who died in Auschwitz in 1944, was a member of the same circle. His "Naked Female Back" (1921) is moderated Fauvism, lightened by atmosphere, while the "Portrait of the Painter Purrmann" expresses the unusually strong, uncompromising personality of the man by means of tight, concentrated presentation.

Oskar Moll was the lyric poet among the bohemians of the Café du Dôme. His 1916 "Landscape by the Grunewald Lake" combines Fauve and Expressionist elements. One cannot overlook a certain closeness to the

Rudolf Levy, *Portrait of the Painter Purrmann,* 1931

55

Hans Purrmann, *Flowers and Fruits,* 1949

serene pictures of August Macke, who had been killed in the war two years previously, although, one could say, in a minor key, informed with gentle melancholy. A peaceful idyll, streaming with light, is set against the horrors of war.

Art as an Expression of Its Times
The Dresden "Brücke" Painters

German Expressionism drew on different historical sources from those of the more cosmopolitan French. The prelude was played in North Germany, among the moors and heaths around the artists' village of Worpswede, near Bremen. There Paula Becker, who was born in Dresden, married the painter Otto Modersohn, an exponent of withdrawn, quiet, natural lyricism, which he had developed in the North under the influence of Jugendstil (the German Art Nouveau). Paula Modersohn-Becker's early work also showed similar tendencies in its light-toned but already slightly expressive

colourfulness. But then, about the turn of the century, she went to Paris and was deeply impressed by Millet, whose work first of all reinforced her slightly Romantic lyricism, but then by Van Gogh's expressive force and above all by the structure of Paul Cézanne's pictures. Like him, she tried to combine precise observation of detail with broad formal scope, as demonstrated in her beautiful "Still Life with Pumpkin" of 1905. Her application of paint is less light and fluent than that of her mentor. She applies thick strokes of grainy material. Her inclination to monumentalize by simplification and by capturing the essential element of appearance shows more clearly in her self-portrait of 1906, the year before her early death, than in the picture of the "Blind Little Sister" (1905), painted with maternal tenderness and involvement.

The painting of the Dresden cultural association "Die Brücke" is a far cry from the fine-toned reticence of Modersohn-Becker. The group was founded in 1905, the year of the Fauves' succès de scandale in Paris, by four students from the Technische Hochschule: Ernst

Paula Modersohn-Becker, *Still Life with Pumpkin,* 1905

Ludwig Kirchner, Erich Heckel, Karl Schmidt-Rottluff and Fritz Bleyl, and dissolved again in 1918 because of basic differences of opinion. Other artists had joined in the meantime, however: the Swiss Cuno Amiet, Emil Nolde (until 1907), Max Pechstein (excluded in 1912) and Otto Mueller. In 1911 they left provincial Dresden for Berlin, already the home of Pechstein and Mueller. The foundation date marked the beginning of the "wave of Expressionism," which had spread throughout Europe by 1907. Eighty years later, the catalogue of the London exhibition "German Art in the Twentieth Century", clearly referring to the Neo-Expressionist modern German "New Savages" and their circle, maintained that the striving of German artists for a cosmopolitan, international reputation after 1945 had no effect beyond the borders, and remained provincial. Today, "now that German artists have decided to take up their own tradition and speak their own language again," German art has been internationally successful to an extent which none of them would have dared to hope for in his early years." Against this one must set the fact that the Expressionists of the first half of the

century were denied success, just as the very German "Informel" movement was denied it later. Their "own language" and also a relationship to their "own tradition," to the Middle Ages for example, as seen above all in Expressionist graphics, was dismissed for more than half a century as a typically German aberration, as cultural irrationalism with no sense of form. German expressive artists did not make a breakthrough until decades later than their French kindred spirits, the Fauves, with whom they tried to establish a relationship at an early stage. In 1908 Vlaminck, Marquet and Van Dongen (who had been invited as early as 1906) had pictures in the "Brücke" annual exhibition. Matisse held himself aloof.

Their affinity with the French cannot be overlooked. The Germans also detached themselves radically from the principles of Naturalism and Realism, at first under the influence of the Pointillistes and Van Gogh. They also liberated colour from the constraints of nature, but it carried more symbolic weight and was more subjective than it was for the Fauves. The Expressionists also emancipated form, but not for the sake of "presta-

Paula Modersohn-Becker, *Self-Portrait,* 1906

Others used hieroglyphics in their handling of line, and in the early years of the "Brücke" Kirchner was also influenced by his friends, by Erich Heckel in Berlin for example, whose crystalline, crisply cold "Canal" of 1912, devoid of human figures, evinced a clear response in the work of Kirchner. But the excited spontaneity, the feverish line, always at a high voltage and in the last resort "Gothic", are the psychogram of an artistic personality of the first water, and of the highly vulnerable sensibility of a human being under permanent existential threat. After his flight to Switzerland and the idyllic world of the mountains he finally became the political victim of the barbarians who had driven him out of Germany.

In its colour and – comparatively awkward – form Kirchner's earliest significant work is clearly influenced by the Fauves, as is confirmed by a detailed look at a picture like "Girl under a Japanese Parasol" dating from 1909 (Kirchner predated it 1906) in the Düsseldorf Kunstsammlung Nordrhein-Westfalen. The earliest picture by Kirchner in the Ludwig Museum, the "Half-Nude Woman with Hat" (1911), a portrait of his girlfriend Dodo, also shows this link. Like the more restrained, noble full-figure picture of the "Russian Woman" (1912), it is a comparatively elegant work by a man of the world. The naked figure is like "a well-dressed woman undressed," in Donald E. Gordon's formulation. A classic subject is presented in a new way. The body is not modelled in three dimensions, but melts into the surface of the picture: Kirchner has learned his lesson from the Fauves. In the manner of Matisse the beautifully rounded curves of the body are etched with great euphony of line, the breasts are framed by shoulder and dress to form a triangle balancing the triangle of the neck. Under the broad brim of the hat the upper part of the face shimmers through in a picturesque and unusually charming way. The glowing flesh-tones contrast effectively with the resounding blue sweep of the background. The formal reduction, which sometimes occurs in the work of the French as well, is influenced by the experience of the cult sculpture of Africa and Oceania, which Kirchner had discovered as early as 1904, a few years before Picasso.

The "Still Life with Tulips, Exotics and Hands" is dominated by its exotic subject matter; it was painted a year after the "Dodo". Dancing figures shown as coloured shadows respond to the wooden ritual figure and casket in ecstatic movement which picks up the rhythm of the sculpted feet. The bowing tulips lead to the finely-formed hands holding a snake-like ribbon, the curve of which is echoed by Kirchner's energetic signature. The picture is in Kirchner's typical nervily splintered "handwriting." As the theme demands, the picture was painted rapidly and with a high degree of concentra-

bilized harmony" in an autonomous pictorial world. The problems of the age are made visible, particularly by Kirchner, in an excited pictorial language, in broken forms, and in the tense, splintered lines of Expressionist drawing and graphics.

It is said that German Expressionism wanted to smash the world to pieces and build a new world from those pieces. Such an idea would never have occurred to the French, not even to the "barbarous" Vlaminck. This aggressive idealism tinged with Romanticism remained as alien to them as German Expressionism – persecuted and repressed in its own country by the Nazis – remained to a large extent alien to the rest of the world until very recently.

Ernst Ludwig Kirchner, the most highly individual and most difficult of the "Brücke" painters, is at the same time the most important. For him, form is always symbolic form: "pure form as the carrier of spiritual expression," as Wolf-Dieter Dube, director of the Stiftung Preussischer Kulturbesitz in Berlin put it. Kirchner's famous "hieroglyphics," the X and Y lines, are for him concentrated and abbreviated formulae for the content of "spiritual religions which are to come," as Franz Marc of the Munich "Blaue Reiter" group put it.

Ernst Ludwig Kirchner, *Half-Nude Woman with Hat,* 1911

Ernst Ludwig Kirchner, *Five Women in the Street,* 1913

moment, the arrested movement, and at the same time gives it the quality of a monument. The figures – half goddess, half prostitute – become "representatives." The sharp contrast of the dark, silhouette-like figures – 20th century "foolish virgins" – with the poisonous yellow-green background as a reflection of and symbolic colour for city lighting conjures up ideas of a pictorial sequence from New Babylon, a modern "Hell in the City".

The move to the capital of the Reich was a major turning-point in his work. The human being is still central, not with others, in confident intercourse, but isolated, alienated, left alone, at the mercy of his own haste, his striving for success and the most banal materialism. He has no contact, no companion, like the street girls of the Potsdamer Platz he becomes an object. Many of the most important Kirchner pictures of this period show the collapse of communication and intimate relationships. The consequence of this is loss of self-awareness, of one's own identity. In these pictures the artist shows in the most penetrating fashion the inevitable tension

Ernst Ludwig Kirchner, *The Russian Woman,* 1912

Ernst Ludwig Kirchner, *The Bridge Over the Railway,* 1914

tion, as if in a trance. It dates from the Berlin period. The most important work by this artist in the Ludwig Museum is the Berlin picture "Five Women in the Street" (1913), the first of the famous street scenes. This shows Kirchner at the height of his powers, as in his presentation of the view from his studio window of "The Bridge Over the Railway" of 1914, with its boldly diagonal structure. It also represents the high point of German Expressionism. Kirchner's "hieroglyph" paraphrases the hectic automaton-like quality, the emptiness of a boulevard scene in the excessive "Gothic" elongation of the figures, the ironic monumentalization of the fashionable finery, the partly idol-like, partly grotesquely common characterization of the depersonalized faces. The picture captures a single

between the natural and the unnatural, the collapse caused by guilt and entanglement. These works are documents of the early end of the social utopia of the "Brücke" painters.

Kirchner's optimism, which prompted him to challenge the world in the "Brücke" manifesto, disappeared for good. His problematic nature denied him the opportunity of embracing the glowing serenity of Matisse. His years in Switzerland brought only temporary respite. The shock of exchanging the feverish city for rural peace, the flickering street light for the majesty of the mountains, was at first almost intolerable for this nervous, depressive man. The nervous tension of the early pictures trembles through the striving for full-scale representation of the elemental

Ernst Ludwig Kirchner, *A Fellowship of Artists,* 1925

Erich Heckel, *Canal in Berlin,* 1912

Erich Heckel, *Pheasant Lodge near Moritzburg,* 1910

Alpine landscape. It is true that the flight into an idyll produced some fine landscapes like the "Forest in Winter" (1925/26) with its interplay of towering "Gothic" groupings of trees and the glow of colour under the winter sun, but his failure in artistic confrontation with Picasso and the misery caused by the times would not allow Kirchner to find peace in the last resort.

Nevertheless, he did paint the classical picture with figures "A Fellowship of Artists" (1926) as an echo of a trip to Germany to visit his former "Brücke" friends. The characterization of the personalities is absolutely precise in its laconic simplicity. Behind the open curtain stands the aggressive and melancholy Kirchner, beside him the gentler, almost dreamy figure of Heckel and the belligerent, obstinate Schmidt-Rottluff; seated is the mysterious "Gypsy-Mueller", to whom Gerhard Hauptmann's elder brother Carl erected a literary monument in his artist-novel "Einhart der Lächler". The confusing muddle of arms and legs, which could belong to one person or another, shows that Kirchner was not without humour.

Erich Heckel was the lyricist of the "Brücke" painters. The "Canal in Berlin" which has already been mentioned was an exception among his paintings. His lyricism is at its most marked in the "Pheasant Lodge near Moritzburg" (1910). The blue-black firs balance the glowing colours of the lodge, the figures in niches, the flower beds, the sweep of the lawn and the sulphurous yellow of the sky. Following the principles of the Fauves, there is no perspective. "Mood" is created by the brightness of the colours and the charm of altered form, the objects are subordinated to two-dimensional pictorial organization.

In the twenties Heckel was influenced to an ever-increasing extent by Neue Sachlichkeit. This is shown by the double portrait of the circus artistes "Badini-Taffani", whose reticent, pastel colouring avoids the hard edges of "Magic Realism", while the portrait of the Belgian painter James Ensor has a statuesque, stern quality reminiscent of Otto Dix, who is indeed almost a contemporary.

There are in the collection particularly fine examples of the work of Otto Mueller, whose realism is to a certain extent related to that of early Heckel. But Mueller's world is not bourgeois, and also not militantly anti-bourgeois, but exotic. He felt – as the Düsseldorf artist Otto Pankok was later to be the only other artist to feel – close to a minority of social outcasts and deprived persons: to gypsies, to their culture and natural way of life, which for him seemed to have retained some of the innocence of paradise ("Two Gypsies and Cat", 1926/27). This unassuming "earthly paradise," later smashed to pieces in Germany by the lackeys of the Third Reich, was portrayed by Mueller in pictures painted in distemper on coarse canvas or hessian; pictures full of melancholy and always in free form and stylized figurativeness, particularly girls in untouched nature or in their modest homes: they are mysterious beings with a puzzling, unfathomable charm, as in "Two Nudes" (c. 1919). Mueller's paintings were created with direct sympathy, for he lived with his models and shared their fate. He was not forced to watch their tragic end: he died in 1930.

It was not so much Gothic as the art of the Orient which set its stamp on Mueller's work. It is correct to point to the inspiring example of Egyptian wall reliefs

Otto Mueller, *Two Nudes,* 1919

Otto Mueller, *Two Gypsies and Cat,* 1926/27

Karl Schmidt-Rottluff, *Still Life with Apples and Yellow Flowers,* 1908

Karl Schmidt-Rottluff, *Still Life with Negro Sculpture,* 1913

and the development of certain painting techniques under the influence of mummy portraits. The most vital and belligerent of the "Brücke" painters was Karl Schmidt-Rottluff. He was courageous enough to resign from the Prussian Academy of Arts as soon as the Nazis came to power in 1933. Later he was perverse enough to refuse the Grosses Bundesverdienstkreuz (Order of Merit of the Federal Republic of Germany) because it had earlier been awarded to Gustaf Gründgens, who was "only" a performing artist.

The energy of the brushwork in Schmidt-Rottluff's "Still Life with Apples and Yellow Flowers" shows the influence of Van Gogh, its glowing colours point to the example of the Fauves. The "Still Life with Negro Sculpture", which dates from 1913, the time of a quarrel in the "Brücke" because of something written by Kirchner, is more formally peaceful. The influence of the "expres-

Karl Schmidt-Rottluff, *Greeting to Nolde,* 1936

sive art" of Africa is in evidence, but the composition is calm, almost classical in its harmony. The colour, too, is no longer wild, but full of a muted, inward glow. Free handling of the subject of the picture, avoiding all naturalistic "correctness," is a persisting feature. Schmidt-Rottluff's artistic creed led to the statement that "there is true drawing and there is correct drawing. True drawing distorts certain things and thus cannot be called correct, but it portrays the very core of being of what is seen, and thus gives a more convincing and a more truthful impression." The artist always stood by this, as can be seen in the "Greeting to Nolde" (on the

latter's 70th birthday); a picture which has forsaken Expressionism as a programme in favour of harmonious classicality.

The most successful, because the most comprehensible, "Brücke" painter was Max Pechstein. Like his friends he was impressed at an early stage by African and Oceanian art. He started under the spell of Van Gogh and his feverish application of paint, but later kept closer to his subjects than the others, and distorted them less violently. The strong point of his – sometimes somewhat superficial – work was a talent for forceful, convincing simplification of object and figure, for generous concentration of areas of colour. "The Green Sofa" of 1910, when Pechstein was still a member of the "Brücke", is a clear illustration of this, while the "Two Female Nudes in a Room" (1909) shows the artist's delight in the movement of animally sensuous bodies, also seen in many of his South Sea pictures.

Emil Nolde was a lone wolf. He was a member of the "Brücke" for a short time because he was pleased to have become a painter after long detours as a cabinet-maker and teacher of drawing, and to have been accepted by like-minded younger colleagues. He was very fond of flowers, and developed his sense of pure, glowing colour entirely on his own. The "Red and Yellow Roses" (1907), painted a year after the invitation to join the "Brücke", show a mixture of Impressionist and Fauve tendencies: form is dissolved and the colours shine almost as much as do those of the French. Nolde's reflective North German nature related the fate of flowers to the life of man, in the painter's own words "shooting up, blooming, fading, and finally thrown into the pit" – a melancholy interpretation which would probably never have occurred to the Fauves. Nolde adjusted to the dissolution of form into shimmering colour by statuesque simplification, without giving up his expressive colouring; he was also no stranger to the shadows of night ("After Sunset", 1915). The "Bonnichsen Family" group (of peasants, 1915) more than demonstrates this development, underlined by the stiff and solemn attitude of the subjects.

Alongside the recurrent flowers, which he later, with continuing affection, made the subject of his "Unpainted Pictures" while he was banned from painting, his great theme was Bible stories. For him, understanding was "just a substitute," a substitute for vision and a sense of the immanent, and his inclination to myth, to the inexplicable and unfathomable, was combined with a delight in story-telling and an affection for the grotesque and the innately primitive. These qualities are expressed in his religious pictures, which represent Biblical events as though they had been told by a Germanic bard, with great force and complete lack of concern for the requirements of "good taste." Nolde's version of Susanna in her bath "Young Woman and Men"

Max Pechstein, *The Green Sofa,* 1910

Emil Nolde, *Red and Yellow Roses,* 1907

Emil Nolde, *The Enthusiasts,* 1916

Emil Nolde, *The Bonnichsen Family,* 1915

(1921) is an impressive example of this. Nolde's "programme of contrasts" involving the juxtaposition of wickedness and innocence is strikingly demonstrated by the confrontation of the grotesquely lustful old men with the clarity of Susanna's face.

"The Enthusiasts", painted five years earlier, reveals in its thickly-applied colours the consuming fire with which the painter was filled, the power of the ecstatic visions which befell him as a human being (and sometimes as an artist) and even for a time led him astray politically.

Oskar Kokoschka occupies a special place among the Expressionists; he was a late offshoot of Austrian Baroque. Like Nolde he is represented in the Ludwig Museum by a lavish sequence of major works from almost all the key phases of his creative life. The late works, the portrait of former Federal President Theodor Heuss (1950), but above all the dynamically illus-

trative "View of the City of Cologne from the Exhibition Tower," a work commissioned in 1956, confirm that it is not without reason that he is sometimes called the Expressionist Impressionist.

The young Kokoschka's epoch-making visionary portraits were more important for the development of fundamentally new possibilities of portraiture in the 20th century than the Heuss picture. It is scarcely credible that the portraits of the actress Tilla Durieux and the poet Peter Baum were painted by a twenty-four-year-old (both 1910). These pictures are unequalled in their clear-eyed psychological insight into the personalities portrayed. They seem like artistic parallels to Sigmund Freud's research. The many levels of Durieux's seductive magic are expressed just as clearly in Kokoschka's sensitive, penetrating portrayal as the kindly, sentimental features of the poet, worn with spiritual cares and yet naive; Heerwarth Walden, editor of "Sturm"

Emil Nolde, *Young Woman and Men,* 1919

Oskar Kokoschka, *Portrait of Tilla Durieux,* 1910

and avant-garde gallery owner, described him as a "giant body with a giant soul."

But it was not just Kokoschka's perception which had many levels, but the painting process itself. The pigments are juxtaposed or applied on top of each other; the picture is realized in three layers. Shapes develop from the relatively amorphous, unformed background, and are hesitantly structured. On top of this a third layer is applied in spontaneous, scratching strokes. This procedure reveals that Kokoschka is a drawing painter. There are no first and second versions of his portraits, and no preliminary studies: these are worked into the various levels of the picture.

The second important phase in the artist's work began after his return to Dresden from the war. Here he painted "The Heathens" (1918) (the poet Walter Hasenclever and the actress Käthe Richter), a double portrait realized in excited, exciting, coarse-textured pigment applied with brush and palette knife. The picture is comparable with the "Bride of the Wind" of 1914, the memorial vision of Kokoschka's love for Alma Mahler. In this picture, which is at the same time a variation on and a transposition to the present of the theme of Paolo and Francesca, the artist's Baroque inheritance is clearly in evidence, as it is in the later "Heathens", but so is the threat to pictorial method of the almost complete dissolution of form.

In the subsequent pictures of towns this quasi-Impressionistic melting and mingling is halted by a new technique of picture construction using glowing patches of colour ("Dresden, Neustadt III," c. 1921). Colour is treated as form in a quite different way from that used by the Fauves, and becomes a constituent element of the picture.

In the picture of the "Theatre in Bordeaux", painted four years later, the draughtman's line is more clearly in evidence as a means of structuring the pictorial space, now again using perspective, and achieving a sensitive balance of graphic and painting elements.

Like Kokoschka, the more conservative Carl Hofer was also a lone wolf, and his melancholy œuvre has only a peripheral connection with Expressionism. "I possessed the Romantic; I sought the Classical," he said of himself. Hofer was impressed by the "exotic" works of the early Picasso, and his inclination to the mystical was reinforced by the effects of a journey to India. His classicality comes from Hans von Marées, and his reticent expressiveness is influenced by James Ensor and the "Brücke" painters, probably Schmidt-Rottluff in particular. But Hofer's pictures, the subject of which is lonely and forlorn humanity, are never explosive or "wild."

His tonality is also relatively reticent. The "Masquerade" of 1922, also called "Three Masks", is one of his major works. The artist hides his individuality behind a fool's mask, and understands the world without being able to change it. The "Half-Nude Woman with Basket of Fruit" (1928) allows the artist's suppressed eroticism to show through. But even this self-absorbed girl with her eyes closed remains isolated. The "Great Tessin Landscape" (1925) shows even more than this melancholy figure that Hofer was more a Classicist than an Expressionist.

Oskar Kokoschka, *The Heathens,* 1918

Oskar Kokoschka, *View of the City of Cologne from the Exhibition Tower,* 1956

Oskar Kokoschka, *Dresden, Neustadt III,* 1921

Expressionism in the Rhineland
August Macke and his Friends

The "Rhine Expressionists" have a special place within the Expressionist movement; they first appeared officially in Bonn in 1913, incidentally for a time in association with the "Dadamax" of Cologne, Max Ernst (later to be the high priest of Surrealism) from nearby Brühl. The artistically outstanding figure was the young August Macke, who lost his life at the early age of 27 at the beginning of the First World War. Expressionist painting strikes an unusually cheerful note in his work. This is firstly a result of the artist's happy disposition: he wanted to make the joy of nature shine through the glowing colour of his pictures. The second factor was his experience of French painting on his trips to Paris between 1907 and 1912. The most profound impressions were made by Cézanne's pictorial structure, Henri Matisse's colour forms, creating space and filled with Mediterranean light, and the dynamics of Robert Delaunay's pictures of the Eiffel Tower, influenced by Futurism. August Macke found his own style in uninhibited confrontation with these outstanding figures. He is the most "Latin" of the German painters of the first half of the century, "Ariel among the Expressionists".

Carl Hofer, *Masquerade,* 1922

August Macke, *Man Reading in the Park,* 1914

August Macke, *Lady in a Green Jacket,* 1913

Macke's pictures are filled with quiet life; ludic, formal pictorial construction and glowing colours saturated with light join to make compositions of great beauty and harmony. In 1914 he undertook the famous journey to Tunis with Paul Klee and Lois Moillet, in the course of which Klee at last discovered colour and became a painter rather than a graphic artist. Macke brought back a series of water-colours from this journey which showed a few months before his death that he had reached a premature perfection, while Klee was still at the beginning of his life's work. But even the "Lady in a Green Jacket" (1913) shows Macke at the height of his powers. The orchestral yet richly differentiated colour tones grow on the one hand from the sharp complementary contrast of red and green, on the other from gliding transitions between diffused and related shades. Colour creates the space between the foreground and the background. The assertive yet lucid composition shows the assimilation of Cubist ideas. Macke's sense of the atmospheric, of the dissolution of contours in air and light, of an almost Leonardesque "sfumato", is in evidence in the picture "Man Reading in the Park" (1914) in the most beautiful glow, without becoming in any way diffuse. For Macke, the "organization" of a picture, the seamless connection of painting and constructive elements, was the "highest of high mathematics."

Paul-Adolf Seehaus, *Town in the Mountains*, 1915

Heinrich Nauen's "Good Samaritan" (1914) is cooler and more withdrawn in its colouring, and unusually placed in a winter landscape. The "mannerist" elongation of the figures is reminiscent of El Greco, an important artist for the Expressionists. The "throbbing, splintering" forms are, as the Berlin art historian E. Redslob has said, "entirely characteristic of Nauen's style." Affinities with the Gothic, and with Ottonian book painting, filtered through Cubist experience, are also in evidence. This picture also shows a conscious and programmatic striving for the "spiritualization of man" which is different from anything found in the work of the sensuous Macke.

The pictures of the painter Paul-Adolf Seehaus, who was also a graduate in the history of art, strike an even more serious note. "Town in the Mountains" and the hard "Scottish Landscape with Lighthouse" (1914) have features which are as strongly Cubist as they are Expressionist. The tones are muted: the colours glow, but they no longer shine.

Heinrich Campendonk, who like August Macke was in touch with the "Blaue Reiter" for a time, occupies a special place among the "Rhineland Expressionists" because of his connection with folk art, in particular with rustic glass painting, and because of his marked admiration for Chagall. His verre églomisé picture "Woman with Fish" (1929), a late Expressionist echo of the early years, shows this clearly in its darkly-glowing

Heinrich Nauen, *The Good Samaritan,* 1914

colours, the elemental simplicity of its formal vocabulary, and its construction in ornamental surfaces.

Although he was not an Expressionist, the highly individual works of the Polish-born artist Jankel Adler should be seen in the context of this movement. His pictures bring to life the world of eastern Judaism, a world which delights in story-telling and melancholy, but which, in its awareness of metaphysical safety, is never disconsolate. The partly realistic, partly visionary "Self-Portrait" (1929) is imbued with these qualities. The Constructivist-oriented Cologne "progressives" around Hoerle and Seiwert were important to Adler. They gave his composition a secure framework. The architectural fragments and stylized disc of the sun in the undefined background of "Cats" (1927) are evidence of this influence. On the other hand, Adler's use of unconventional materials such as sand to roughen the surface of his pictures is his own personal artistic contribution. Large exhibitions in the mid-eighties in London, Düsseldorf and Tel Aviv have stimulated interest in the artist's work, although they remained a fragment.

Expressionism in Munich
Kandinsky and "Der Blaue Reiter"

Munich was the second capital of German Expressionism alongside Dresden. In 1911 Vassily Kandinsky and Franz Marc had joined forces there to produce the almanach "Der Blaue Reiter"; it appeared a year later and gave its name to the famous group of artists. In 1911 and 1912 the association's first exhibitions were held; Franz Marc used them to further the work of his Dresden "Brücke" colleagues, the Berlin "Neue Sezession" and his "Blaue Reiter" friends. "Their thinking," wrote

Jankel Adler, *Cats,* 1927

Heinrich Campendonk, *Woman with Fish,* 1929

the former student of theology and philosophy, "has a different goal. They want to use their work to create symbols for their time, to be placed on the altars of the spiritual religion which is to come."

Pronouncements of this kind show that the keynote of the artistic thinking of the Munich group was not a social utopia, making the world a better place, or the concept of a new and uninhibited sensuousness, but rather, as in the title of Kandinsky's theoretical essay, "The Spiritual in Art". Religious and cosmic concepts are involved to a far greater extent than in Dresden or Berlin, particularly in the case of Marc, for whom there could be "no great and pure art without religion" – an attitude of mind which his friend Macke was unable to share. It was not a question of changing the world, but of the "inner necessity," in the phrase used by both Marc and Kandinsky, of creating an alternative world. Paul Klee, who was close to the group without being a member of it, was later to speak of designing "possible worlds."

For Franz Marc animals, regardless of naturalism, were a metaphor of creation. Their purity and innocence express "the divine nature and its rule over all that is" for the painter. His early works are bright nature studies, flooded with light. There are no shadows in this

Franz Marc, *Wild Boars,* 1913

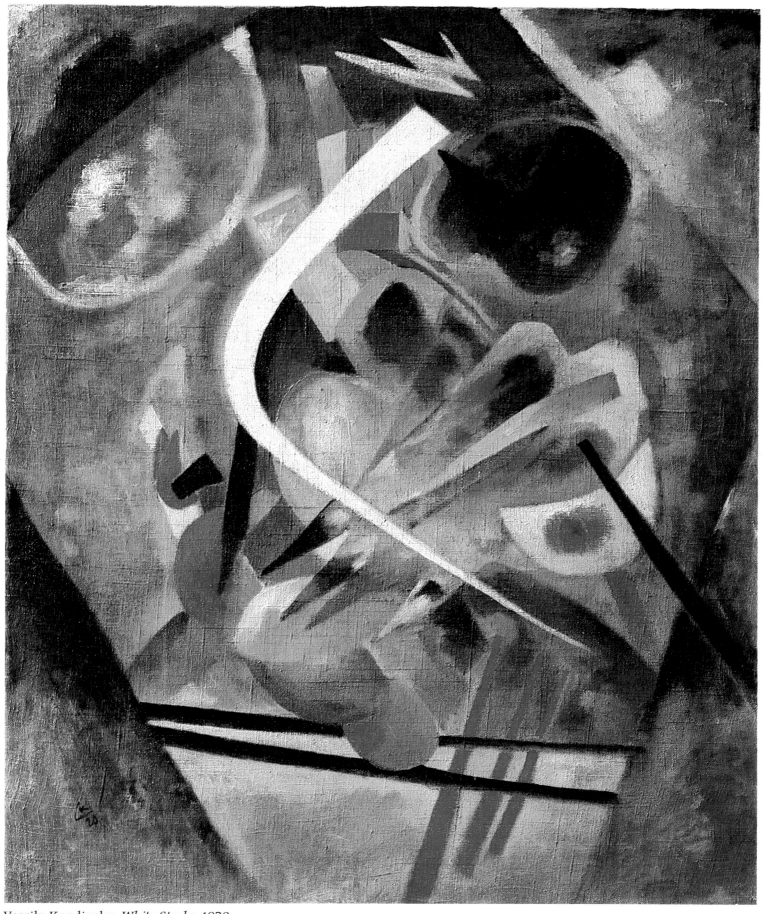

Vassily Kandinsky, *White Stroke,* 1920

Vassily Kandinsky, *Moscow Zubovskiy Square III*, 1916

intact world. But soon colour was to be granted its own value, independent of the real subject of the picture. For Marc, colour is always expressive and symbolic: blue stands for spirituality, yellow communicates, orange raises sensuality to the level of ecstasy, green "rouses" its complementary colour red, "the material," into life. "Green always needs help from blue (the heavens) and yellow (the sun) to impose silence on the material." Thus Marc in a letter to Macke.

The crucial category in Marc's painting after the symbolic value of colour, "essential colour," is rhythm, rhythm as "the formative law of the individual being, as the life order of the species, as the harmony of all creation" (Klaus Lankheit). The colour vibrato, the lucid transparency instilled by Robert Delaunay, the formal movement of circling forms, all these give Marc's pictures a high degree of dynamism. Rational construction based on the works of the Cubists lends a structure of compelling logic to the mingling, sometimes splintered colour forms.

A small masterpiece like the "Cattle" of 1913 and the larger picture of "Wild Boars" dating from the same year are excellent examples of the application of these principles. They are a clear visual demonstration of Marc's striving for pure, crystalline form beyond the material. These animal pictures are in the artist's mind metaphors of his longing "for undivided being," for "freedom from the deceptions of the senses in our ephemeral life." For him the great and Romantic goal of art is "to show an unearthly being, dwelling behind all things." Ideas of this kind led him to the threshold of abstraction and in some works even beyond it. He never achieved the abstract painting of ideas which was his vision. His work remains incomplete.

"White Stroke", his friend Kandinsky's picture painted in 1920, stands intellectually and formally between the artist's theoretical writings "On the Spiritual in Art" (see also: "The Spiritual Element in Art") and "Point and Line to Plane", between the "Blaue Reiter" and the "Bauhaus", to which Kandinsky attached himself in 1922. Some of the dynamism of the early years survived in his formulation of a personal version of abstract Expressionism in an unprecedented explosion of creativity. But the colour tones are already more muted, form is no longer struggling to break its bonds but, despite all the movement, is closing in on itself in increasingly dense compartmentalization. The relationship of point and line to plane is already subject to rigorous examination, though not with the coolly scientific approach of the subsequent Bauhaus years, in which "Shrill-Peaceful Pink" was painted.

Even in his later "period of genius," which started with the first abstract water colour of 1910, and in the turbulent years which followed, Kandinsky continued to paint representational pictures from time to time. He confessed in his early autobiographical writing "Looking Back 1901-13" that the "white-stoned" and "golden-headed" "mother = Moscow" was the source of his artistic endeavours. The picture "Zubovskiy Square III" (c. 1916), with Kandinsky's typically expressive tonality,

Vassily Kandinsky, *Shrill Peaceful Pink,* 1924

Alexei von Javlensky, *Still Life with Vase and Pitcher,* 1909

confirms this. The contrast of light and shade is a reminder that as a young man the artist was much stimulated by Rembrandt's pictures in the Leningrad (then St. Petersburg) Hermitage.

Decidedly more "Expressionistic" than the "White Stroke" are the works of Alexei von Javlensky. His earliest work, the "Olive Grove" (1907), is still completely under the spell of the admired Van Gogh, who with Gauguin gave the final promptings to the former Russian officer who had decided to become a painter in St. Petersburg (Leningrad). The gnarled tree-trunks, the violent brush stabs, the vehement colouring are reminiscent of the great Dutchman. The arabesques of the treetops show the influence of Jugendstil, which was at its height at the turn of the century when Javlensky came to Munich with his friend, the painter Marianne von Verefkin; there he soon met Kandinsky. But only a little later he was painting pictures in which the scope of his formal simplification, an emphatically two-dimensional quality, and celebratory colouring are unmistakably reminiscent of the great Henri Matisse, whom Javlensky met in the year of the birth of Fauve painting (1905) and in whose studio he worked for a time: "Still Life with Blue Jug and Figure" (c. 1908) and "Still Life with Vase and Pitcher" (1909). The stricter "setting" of the objects, their very definite contouring, are signs of "Cloisonnisme", the framing of areas of colour rather in the manner of stained glass windows which Emile Bernard and/or Paul Gauguin introduced into painting.

The "Fairytale Princess with Fan", glowing as if from within, and with its contrast between laconic enclosure of figures and heads in powerfully contoured triangular or almond shapes on the one hand, and the lively

Alexei von Javlensky, *Variation,* c. 1916

Alexei von Javlensky, *Fairytale Princess with Fan,* 1912

František Kupka, *Musical Box,* 1946

interplay of strips of colour and fan decoration on the other, is a clear sign that the artist has come to terms with the painting of the Fauves. But the Romantic emotion in the portrait, the expressive, fairytale look in the large, wide-open eyes, was certainly alien to the less problematic French, their master Matisse, and their worldly and luxurious art. Introspection was not their concern. Javlensky on the other hand was always concerned with the representation of inner, emotional experience. Visible reality was only a motive. This is true of landscape, whether he painted it on a journey or when looking out of his window. But it is above all true of his heads, which he simplified more and more, until he finally reduced then to their "primeval shape."

This radical course of abstraction by means of the simplest formulae – strokes or narrow segments for eyes, nose and mouth, almost as in children's drawings – led to his pictures being called abstract icons, with some justification.

Landscape too was reduced to primaeval form in Javlensky's work: triangle, square, disc and ellipse, in "Variation" (c. 1916), for example, combine in metaphors which continually repeat themselves to form fragments of the landscape which he saw with his inner eye from the window of his Geneva flat. The subject-matter itself becomes increasingly a matter of indifference. Javlensky's pictures are pictures of ardour and absorption, their light comes from within. The expressive gestures of the early days are increasingly removed, and dynamic movement is replaced by peace and withdrawal. The "spiritual in art" and the sensuous glow of colour, which however becomes more and more transparent in Javlensky's later work, mingle to form a beautiful and very personal synthesis in the work of the Russian.

Frantisek Kupka embarked on abstract painting at the same time as Kandinsky, but quite independently of him. His work is rooted in Symbolism and above all Jugendstil, the arabesque lines of which fascinated him. He strove for art which like architecture and music is not derived from nature, but which is freely "created," one could even say, invented. For Kupka, the only artistic reality is the work of art itself: an abstract reality which is not "parallel" to nature but programmatically opposed to it. The Czech aspired, in the tracks of Johann Sebastian Bach, to a kind of "Art of Fugue" in painting. The late work "Musical Box" (1946) shows this in its alternation of large and small and its reference to earlier works, and also its relationship to architecture. "Red and Green" (1913) on the other hand, created directly after the early "Fugue" series, is more pictorial and free, despite the rhythmic play of the climbing segmental shapes.

The Man Who Walked Alone
The Pictures of Max Beckmann

Max Beckmann is the most powerfully expressive German painter of the century. This is clear even in the grandiose and dramatic vision of the early works, forgotten and certainly undervalued until the important exhibition of 1982/83. The baroque and dramatic representations of living and dying, death and resurrection, show clearly that Beckmann was never a Naturalist. "Nature is wonderful chaos," he later taught his pupils, "and it is our task to make order out of this chaos." Beckmann is the painter of the "great world theatre" in our century, an artist of myth-creating force, as shown above all in his impressive series of triptychs. His starting point is always reality, always concrete experience. But he pushes beyond the bounds of reality and makes it into an existential and artistic metaphor. Thus, his work cannot be assigned to any single movement in the art of our century, not to Realism and not even to Expressionism, from which he borrowed some stylistic techniques after its dominant period was over.

The influence of Beckmann continues to increase. The difficulties which the non-German public experienced for a long time with the mysterious ciphers of his mythic, profound presentation of reality, with the drama of his gesture and the uncompanionable hardness of his remorselessly straightforward painting have been overcome. The "Germanness" of his work is now seen in other countries, even in France, the classical home of painting culture ("peinture"), as the expression of an artistic personality which understood painting as an "existential attitude," as Werner Haftmann, the pioneer of 20th century art-historical writing, put it.

From the very beginning Beckmann's technique for mastering reality led him away from mere images to the pictorial symbol. This is true even in his radical and politically critical phase after the First World War, in which his art moved close to that of Otto Dix and George Grosz. His confrontation with French painting led later to his increasing mastery of differentiation in the application of paint. For this reason, the aesthetic quality of his pictures is equal to the work of the great French artists. The Ludwig Museum must consider itself lucky to own 15 pictures by one of the greatest painters of the century.

"The Organ-Grinder" dates from 1935, two years after Beckmann was expelled from the Frankfurt Kunstschule. The picture should definitely be considered alongside the great triptychs, the first of which, with the allusive title "Departure", was painted when Beckmann was already classed as a "decadent artist." It is typical in its combination of a sense of contemporary time and timelessness. Personal fate was the stimulus for the picture, but the development of the theme is much more complex. It gives the picture the visionary force of a metaphor, in which history, a sense of the future, and the present become permeable. Unlike the Expressionists, Beckmann did not allow his own experience of life to possess him completely when he was painting. He kept his distance, even from himself. Leaving aside pictures like the moving "Self-Portrait with a Red Scarf" (1917) and the uncompromising portrayal of murderous brutality in pictures like "Night" (1918/19), Beckmann concealed his own distress behind impenetrable masks. Even "The Organ-Grinder", the only one who can see, a youth in a yellowish-green fantasy uniform looking with wide-open eyes into an apparently desolate future, is an autobiographical mask. The collector Lilly von Schnitzler was not unjustified in calling the picture "Song of Life". But it is not only the "Song of Life" of an ostracized painter, but of an entire epoch, with references to history and myth. "Two women can be made out. The one on the left is half veiled, and holds a little child, apparently newborn, in her arms. The one on the right has a bloody

Max Beckmann, *Landscape with Balloon,* 1917

sword in her hand. Her veil is partly black and partly white, and spattered with blood. It is clear from the pitch-black face with the gleaming white teeth who we are dealing with: this is how Kali, the Indian goddess of death, is portrayed. […] According to Indian teaching Kali is not only the goddess of death, but also the giver of life. […] Her various faces symbolize a view of the life-cycle which is free of illusions: man is born to die." This is how Horst Richter describes the mythological background. The contemporary reference is clear in the leaning, bent circus figure in a garment full of holes, "half Justice mourning in an unjust world, half suffering Job figure" (Evelyn Weiss), and also in the back view of the voluptuous naked woman (blind to fate) and the landsknecht's drum in front of a mirror and a telescope.

The stylistic devices of the mature Beckmann are easily read: expressive condensation and aggressive sharpening of form, powerful, sensuous colouring, outlines in the manner of the stained-glass window. Beckmann's affinity with the mediaeval method of simultaneous presentation, with the street-ballad, the circus and not least stage scenery, always for him the world-stage, is clearly to be seen: an affinity which has left its mark on precisely those areas of his work which are the most important.

Alongside this central piece almost all Beckmann's creative periods are represented. The series begins chronologically with the "Landscape with Balloon" (1917), painted in the same year as the self-portrait already mentioned, stamped with the terror of war. But this stylized landscape, almost without movement, portrayed in boldly tapered perspective and Jugendstil curves, seems on superficial consideration to be the work of a different artist. Not a trace remains of expressiveness unleashed. The figure lost in dreams at the side of the street, the balloon soaring above a scene devoid of human presence, the cool colours, all combine to give the picture a quality of glassy distance, a breath of unreality.

In the twenties Beckmann condensed form by simplification. The tonality becomes stronger, the drawing more artistic, contrasts between light and dark occur more frequently. The portrait of the collector Dr. F. G.

Max Beckmann, *The Organ-Grinder,* 1935

Max Beckmann, *Self-Portrait with Black Cap*, 1934

Max Beckmann, *Portrait of F. G. Reber*, 1929

Reber of 1929 is a perfect example of this, despite its "official," representative character.

What a contrast there is between the relaxed painting of this portrait and the well-known "Self-Portrait with Black Cap" of five years later! Beckmann was 50 years old when he created it. His painting handwriting now has the stimulating, spontaneous, powerful line characteristic of his mature work. The look in the excessively large eyes, the energetic, closed mouth in the concentrated, almost chiselled face, bear the stamp of the trials of his time. They point forward to the "Organ-Grinder" and the mythic depths of its relationship to the present. But Beckmann did not permit himself the luxury of sentimentality. He asks questions, he looks on the black side, but he doesn't moan. This will be so

throughout his life. The "Sea Beach" of 1935, a painter's elegy, lent an unassertive symbolism by the "swan necks" of the larger of the passing clouds, is an example of a related attitude demonstrated by one of Beckmann's favourite motifs.

Between 1937 and 1947 Beckmann lived as an emigrant in Amsterdam. This creative period between hope and despair, brought impressively to life in the painter's telegraphic diary, is particularly well represented in the Ludwig Museum. The polarity of sensation and subject is demonstrated in examples from the demi-monde: the "Tango" or "Rumba" of 1941 on the one hand, and the "Still Life with Three Glasses" of 1944 and "Three Women in Profile" of 1942 on the other, apparently filled with hope of an end to the suffering. The intimate picture of the "Lovers" (1940–43) links the two phases.

Beckmann has now developed his artistic technique to the full in terms of subject, form and colour: strong outlines, strong colouring, intensified to the point of harshness in the case of the three dancers painted in profile, grotesquely mask-like, lascivious faces, with a man lurking in the background. In "Two Women" (1940), an amply proportioned demi-mondaine stands in the street, dressed to kill, while the forlorn appear-

Max Beckmann, *Two Women,* 1940

Max Beckmann, *Still Life with Three Glasses,* 1944

ance of the two women contrasts with the caged look of the beautiful dream-face in the background of the picture; a narrow black shadow with a hint of a profile is watching the two women. The notion of being locked out, of isolation, of being shut in, is a constant theme of Beckmann's work, but it is never polemical, never seized upon for purposes of agitation. Beckmann makes the magic of reality visible in wonderful, richly graded colour and in powerfully aggressive, distinctive shapes. An everyday scene in the streets of Amsterdam becomes a painter's cipher of the forlornness of the human condition: in the foreground the banal hardness of a face without hope, behind bars the melancholy glimpse of a girl's face which has not yet been "marked," not yet been distorted. The scene is played out in front of an undefined pictorial space, with no definite location. By this Beckmann always means infinite space, which is beyond imagination, and which he feared; "Its foreground," he said therefore, "should always be filled with a bit of junk, so that we are not so aware of the awful depths behind." In the painter's undramatic vocabulary this "junk" is the supporting framework of the picture. Sometimes it can be the objects themselves: table, chair, bowl, bottle, glasses, bread

Max Beckmann, *Tango (Rumba),* 1941

and plant. This is the case in the beautiful harmony of contrasts in the "Still Life with Three Glasses", with its powerful, classically lucid structure and its rich colouring.

Beckmann's work owes its commanding position to the fact that expression and form are ideally balanced, that reality and myth interpenetrate. For all his sharp eye for the concrete problems of his times, the painter was never tempted to make them subjects of a superficial ideology in the foreground of his works, or to stand at the wailing wall. His attitude and his artistic power are in rare harmony.

Prelude to Classical Modern Art
The Masters of Cubism

Artists whose work inaugurates a new movement in twentieth century art are often also the most important in that movement. They set standards of quality sel-

Max Beckmann, *Three Women in Profile,* 1942

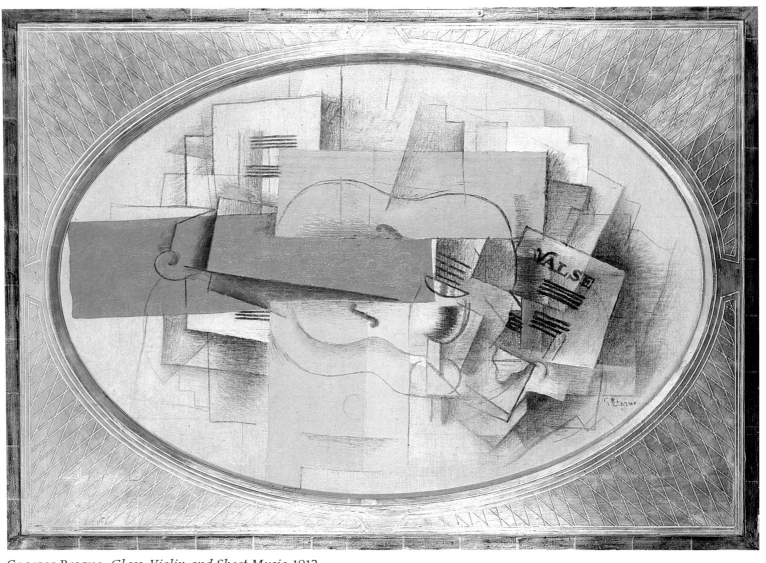

Georges Braque, *Glass, Violin and Sheet Music*, 1912

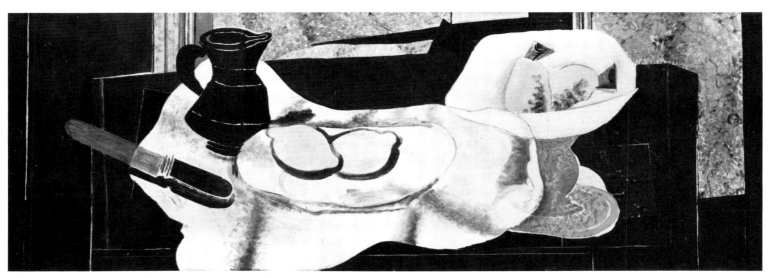

Georges Braque, *Carafe, Lemons, Fruit Bowl*, 1928

Juan Gris, *Syphon, Glass and Newspaper,* 1916

dom achieved by those who follow them. This is true of Matisse and the Fauves, of Kandinsky and abstract art, of Max Ernst and Surrealism, and also of Wols and the Informel, and of Pollock and Abstract Expressionism. It is also true of the most important movement of Modern Art as a whole. What is known as innovation, as fundamentally new in art, does not have to be, but often is, a sign of genius. Thomas Mann defined it in his speech on Lessing: "Genius […] is displayed when something unanticipated appears, when something of which one had no previous conception becomes real; genius manifests itself by making possible something which is new of its kind, something which could only be grasped, could only triumph, through the power and attraction of the creator personality. By this token genius in art would be something which is surprising and a source of astonishing delight, daring, and only recognizable as possible when it becomes reality."

In this sense Cubism, along with Fauvism, which started a few years earlier, is the great prelude to classical Modern Art. The outstanding personalities, Matisse and Picasso, have remained the leading figures and standard-setters until the present day; the boldness of the idea and the quality of their execution of it have not been surpassed throughout the decades.

There are several pictures which confirm this in the Ludwig Museum. The earliest is Picasso's "Woman with Mandoline" (1910), an exemplary "Analytic" Cubist picture. The faceted dissection of figure and instrument is taken to an extreme, and yet complete abstraction is just avoided. Pictorial symbols such as square and circular forms hint at the concrete subject of the picture and leave plenty of scope for the observer's imagination. The restriction of the palette, characteristic of Analytic Cubism, to the basic tones of grey and ochre is programmatically opposed to the colour fanfares of the Fauves; we are reminded of Manet's remark that shades of grey, correctly handled, are the hallmark of a master of painting.

Georges Braque's "Glass, Violin and Sheet Music" is in the same spirit, even if the range of tones between grey and ochre is somewhat more forceful and the dissection of form is not as radical as in the work of Picasso. The musicality of the composition and clearer indication of the objects in the picture make it easier to decipher this still life, presented in a distinctive oval. In contrast to Picasso, Braque, after his rejection of Fauvism, remained a Cubist, even if in later years he took up "Synthetic" Cubism and delineated objects more clearly. After 1917 Braque became the most spirited exponent of a new classicality ("Carafe, Lemons, Fruit Bowl", 1928) which had gone through the material and spiritual experience of Fauve and Cubist experiments and subordinated them to its own purposes: pictorial subject and pictorial space are placed in the same rela-

tionship to each other as colour and bulk. Braque's subject throughout his life was – apart from his later "excursions" into landscape – still life. He is the Chardin of the 20th century.

The third member of the league of leading Cubists, the sharp-minded Spaniard Juan Gris, was as close to Cézanne as he was to his friends Picasso and Braque. Although he was an analyst to a high degree, he was not involved in Analytic Cubism, but instead invented the "synthetic" version. One of the artist's precise aphorisms demonstrates what this means: "Cézanne made a cylinder out of a bottle, I make a bottle out of a cylinder." The German painter Werner Gilles later said: "The abstract in painting has to be conveyed in objects." This is precisely what Juan Gris did. In his work the individual elements of the picture retain their own, partial perspective, though this is subordinate to pictorial architecture with its own strict laws and compelling logic. "Syphon, Glass and Newspaper", dating from 1917, is the artistic and pictorial result of the application of these principles.

For Gino Severini, originally a Futurist, Cubism was only a stage on the route to the realistic classicism of "Valori plastici" ("plastic values"), a concept akin to those of the German Neue Sachlichkeit. His "Collage" (1912-15) is a good example of a "material picture" in the synthetic mode of Cubism. A harmonic, serenely classical pictorial composition is built up of banal, everyday materials, effectively enlivened by contrasts between light and dark. Instrument and figure are recognizable as such, but not precisely defined. This hovering between abstraction and objectivity gives the picture a particular charm.

The sculptor Henri Laurens, later a master of organic, three-dimensional figures with a mythological background, came into contact with the Cubists in 1911. His oval collage "Guitar, Glass and Pipe" of 1918 is an excel-

Henri Laurens, *Guitar, Glass and Pipe*, 1918

Fernand Léger, *The Pink Tug*, 1918

lent example of Synthetic Cubism in its late phase: the objects remain clearly recognizable, but are schematically simplified. Complex composition with changing viewpoints and graduated pictorial planes one behind the other, and rich nuances of restrained and noble colour, determine the high aesthetic quality of the work.

The principle of graduated pictorial layers is also used in the sculpture "The Guitar" (1914, see page 272), translated into three dimensions. The interlocking of structural sculptural elements, the alternation of concave and convex, the fusion of plastic form and the "framework" of drawing and colour, the balance of front and rear view are all achieved in a masterly fashion.

Fernand Léger brought a quite different idea to Cubism. Because of his love of tubular shapes, shown particularly impressively in the early "Contrastes de formes", he was known, with affectionate irony, as the "Tubist". A lavishly orchestrated late product in this magnificent series is "The Pink Tug" of 1918, an affirmation of technology, which Léger, in contrast to his friends, did not reject; indeed, he lent form to it, joyfully anticipating the future in the confident optimism

Fernand Léger, *The Twins*, 1929/30

of a glowing, occasionally harsh colour scheme based on red, blue and yellow. The person on the left-hand edge of the picture is robot-like, an indistinguishable component among the chimneys, chains, sirens, silos and warehouses in the docks where the tug has made fast. In contrast, technological and organic forms

Fernand Léger, *The Country Outing*, 1954

merge in the picture "The Twins" (1920-30). They float through the picture, a space with no concrete definition, some static and some moving.

The culmination of Léger's artistic development is the social utopia of a world free from oppression, equally happy whether working or at leisure (see also: "Social Utopia"). This world of the little man, with whom Léger the socialist remained in sympathy from the time he made his acquaintance during the war, is ideally represented in a place where work is play and play is work: in the world of the artistes, in the circus. The harmony achieved by Léger of person and object, man and thing,

Sunday and weekday, is unmatched in the art of the first half of the century.

"The Country Outing" (1954), painted a year before the artist's death, may be considered to exemplify Léger's late style. It is a Sunday picture, portraying the paradise of simple people. A group of five, a man with a blue jacket with a boater on his head, two naked women, a boy and a girl, are relaxing – sitting, lying, or standing by the water – on the bank of a river. Their attitude is partly casual and relaxed, partly a photographic pose: "group portrait with ladies." The figures are monumental, as in all the late work, without individual features. But they radiate happiness, untainted by problems. The formal devices are laconic simplification and stylization of figure and landscape, the colours cover broad areas and are without the nuances of aestheticizing peinture, the outlines are powerful and simple. The concealed classicality of this work can be traced back to Jacques Louis David, who was admired by Léger, but Piero della Francesca and Paolo Uccello are also seen to be kindred spirits.

Amadeo Modigliani came to Paris in 1906 and soon met the artists of the "Bateau-Lavoir" group. He was the Bohemian par excellence: a tall, handsome man much admired by women, but also a drinker and a drug addict, always in difficulties and incapable of handling money. In his painting Tuscan "disegno," harmony of line, lives again. He admired Toulouse-Lautrec's virtuoso drawing, and the Picasso of the pre-Cubist period and the "Demoiselles d'Avignon". He was also impressed by Cézanne as a painter of figures, and he came to sculpture through none other than the great Brancusi. In this field the influence of the Romanian cannot be overlooked, but alongside it is an unmistakable return to the art of the "Primitives", although the archaic style of the heads does have something of the elegance of the painted portraits and figures. The Italian found his models in the streets: girls and friends from the Bohemian society of Paris, people to whom he felt close. "The Algerian Girl" (1917) shows how Modigliani could take a simple girl and, by means of the calm beauty of his colours – intense black and terracotta brown – and the sovereign confidence of his drawing, give her psychological depth and a mysterious poetic distance from the world.

The French painter Robert Delaunay was a particular influence on German art before and after the First World War. The exhibition for the hundredth anniversary of his birth in Munich in 1985 showed the breadth and intensity of the impact of his work, furthered by personal contacts, in a way which was impressive, though controversial in some matters of detail. He affected the "Blaue Reiter" and the Rhineland Expressionists, and later also the Berlin "Sturm" circle around Herwarth Walden, and the Bauhaus.

Delaunay's early work – after he had assimilated ideas from Seurat and the Fauves – is a very personal, glowing variant of Cubism, which Guillaume Apollinaire, the poetic prophet of early classical Modernism, christened "Orphism". Delaunay had studied Chevreuil's colour theories and Cézanne's use of colour to create space, and had examined the Cubist pictures of Braque and Picasso closely, as well as African, Egyptian and Assyrian sculpture. He was a friend of Henri Rousseau, the greatest of the "naive" painters. In 1908 the Eiffel Tower appears in his work for the first time, a dominant theme in many later pictures in which he portrays the

Amadeo Modigliani, *The Algerian Girl,* 1917

inherent dynamics of the iron structure, using partially Cubist, partially Futurist techniques. In 1909 the series of pictures devoted to the church of Saint-Severin and its architecture appeared. The famous "Window Pictures", with their wonderful, glowing, transparent colours, followed in 1912.

Colour now becomes a subject in itself for Delaunay and his Ukrainian wife Sonia. The "harmony of colours," wrote the painter, "of colours dividing and joining to form a whole again in a single action," this "synchronous action should be seen as the actual and only subject for painting." In accordance with this the "disc," the "endless rhythms" of "circulating cosmic forms," becomes a central theme. The picture "Endless Rhythm" (1934) should be seen in this context. The colours of the spectrum are displayed in a circle, thus creating a rotating, dynamic, endless movement which is at the same time closed in on itself. The rigour of geometry has replaced Orphic vibrato and lucidity of colour. Unlike this, Sonia Delaunay's later work "Colour Rhythm" (1968), though related formally and

Robert Delaunay, *Endless Rhythm,* 1934

in its colouring, is built on the contrast of circular and rectangular forms in shining and decorative colour. Arthur Segal (1875–1944) was born in Romania; he is an unjustly neglected artist, closely associated with the Berlin "November Group" and the "Blaue Reiter", who left behind an œuvre which, although it showed the influence at first of Van Gogh and Matisse, later of Seurat and then the Cubists, nevertheless manifests a strong personal quality in his handling of the most varied influence. "The Port" (1921) is distinctive in that

Arthur Segal, *The Port,* 1921

the frame is incorporated into the composition of the picture, which is at the same time strict, yet made less formal by its narrative thrust. Design elements are reminiscent of Cubism in the style of Fernand Léger and also (in the circle segments) Delaunay's Orphism. The schematic figures seem to be influenced by Seurat, while the cool blue-grey-brown tonality shows Segal's independence as much as does the division of the surface of the picture into sixteen equal rectangles. This reflects the artist's conviction, held well ahead of its time, although based on mediaeval principles of simultaneous representation, that the composition should have no centre, because all the sections of the picture are equally important.

The Dynamics of Movement Documents of Futurism

A museum is not an encyclopaedia. Every so often we have to find the courage to say no. For a long time the Ludwig Museum thought that it was going to have to say no to Futurism. But then a new patron with a particular interest in twentieth century Italian art came on the scene, and since that time there have been good examples of this aggressive artistic movement in the museum.

Carlo Carrà, *The Woman and the Absinthe,* 1911

Carlo Carrà's picture "The Woman and the Absinthe" (1911) was painted before he moved on to "metaphysical painting" under the influence of Giorgio de Chirico. The work is a link between Cubism and Futurism. It dates from the time of Carrà's second journey to Paris. The influence of Analytic Cubism, with its faceted splintering of the surface of the picture, is clearly to be seen, the nuanced complementary tonality (turquoise and green against reddish brown and yellowy orange, with a subtly placed red accent) is certainly more dramatic than in the French and Spanish models, but nevertheless has a non-Futurist reticence. The figure of the woman and the back of the chair show movement, as does the pictorial space: for the Futurists, in whose 1912 exhibition Carrà was involved, this was the sign of living and life as opposed to the freezing of the moment in the static pictures of their predecessors.

Giacomo Ballà's representation of the "Speed of an Automobile" (1913/14) is almost a piece of Futurist "programme music." As soon as one sees it one thinks of the Futurists' view of speed as a new and independent quality, and of the famous remark that a racing-car is more beautiful than the Nike of Samothrace. Using reserved and tuneful colours, Ballà attempts to reflect the phases of a car journey – the continuous dislocation of perspective in movement, the spinning of the wheels – in dynamic shorthand. The intoxication of speed is to be conveyed to the spectator standing in front of the picture by means of moving shapes on a static, two-dimensional canvas: an indisputably bold intention, an attempt to square the pictorial circle. It led finally to "Kinetic" Art in the latter half of the century.

Gino Severini painted Futurist pictures before he turned to Cubism. His work is a mixture of the Pointillisme which he never abandoned and Futurist dynamism. The bright, cheerful colours are particularly reminiscent of Seurat. His "Ballerina" (1913) is one of a long series of pictures of dancers painted between 1911 and 1914. Their grace and body language show us movement of a very different kind from Ballà's motor-car dynamics. The play of light in space and on the costumes harmonizes with the airy colouring, in which the Pointilliste-Futurist whirl of figures and setting melts into unity.

Mario Sironi's "Yellow Aeroplane with Urban Landscape", which he painted as a war volunteer, is, despite the artist's martial inclinations, closer to Cubism, which finds an artistic response in the geometrical shape of the houses. Only the subject is really Futurist: the aeroplane (as an instrument of war) is even faster than the car and brings death and ruin. Only the spin-

Giacomo Balla, *Speed of an Automobile,* 1913/14

Mario Sironi, *Yellow Aeroplane with Urban Landscape,* 1915

ning reflection of the movement of the propellers shows Futurist intoxication with speed; the diagonal composition of the picture points more towards Expressionism, and the silence of the houses with their empty-windowed facades and the divided sky look forward to "pittura metafisica", a movement to which Sironi was later attached for a time.

Gino Severini, *Ballerina,* 1913

Radiant Energy – Suprematism – Ideology
The Russian Avant-garde

Before the Second World War there was lively artistic communication between Western Europe and Russia. The "Paris–Moscow" exhibition (1979/80) in the Centre Pompidou and in the Pushkin Museum in Moscow provided impressive documentation of this. Russian artists were great travellers. One has only to think of Kandinsky, Javlensky, Chagall, the Goncharova-Larionovs and not least the Parisian triumph of the Russian Ballet under Serge Diaghilev, which attracted an international group of musicians – Stravinsky, Milhaud, Falla, Hindemith – and also a similar group of fine artists. Apart from the Russians Leon Bakst, Benois, Larionov and Goncharova, Picasso, Braque, Gris, Matisse, Max Ernst, Miró and many others worked for the brilliant impresario. From 1905 onwards the collectors Jan Morosov and Serge Shohukin took pictures by leading members of the French avant-garde to Russia. Buyers of art on a grand scale, no longer rejected by the Soviet Union, before the outbreak of war in 1914 owned more than a hundred works by the great Western masters Matisse and Picasso. In 1917 the first Fauve exhibition went to Russia. In 1910 the Burliuk brothers, both painters, formed a Russian Futurist group. It is said that the art of the West was better-known and above all more sought after in Moscow at that time than in Paris, the Mecca of the avant-garde. After their early reliance on Western models the Russians began to reflect on their own tradition, and Eastern European avant-garde art became a force in its own right. Interest was reawakened in icon painting and folk art, and Western ideas were assimilated within this frame of reference. But above all it was the inspiration drawn from the concept of a socialist utopia, and enthusiasm for a future providing art for all in a classless society, that instilled new self-confidence and inspired independent formulations, which in their turn were broadcast to the West. Western art in subsequent years would have been different without the ping-pong effect of this uninhibited exchange of information. The artist couple Natalia Goncharova and Mikhail Larionov played an important pioneering role in overcoming the dominant influence of Western ideas. They had both taken part in the exhibition of Russian art organized by Diaghilev for the Paris Salon d'Automne of 1906, and were familiar with the Western artistic scene. At first they developed a personal variant of Fauvism-Expressionism with clear, programmatically intended backward looks at Russian models: icons, "primitive" peasant art, broadsheets, poster painting and even graffiti from the walls of the city; Larionov's "Still Life with Crab" (1907) is a typical example. His portrait of a man (presumed to be the painter Burliuk) of 1910 shows energetic formal condensation without illustrative detail and vital colour flooded with light, a clear pointer to the assimilation of Expressionist methods. Goncharova's "Still Life with Tiger-Skin", painted two years earlier, is a powerful demonstration of the mingling of the old Russian artistic tradition with a method of presentation which is still Expressionist in its glowing colour and light brushwork, with no dramatizing splintered distortion. Expressionist references figure more clearly in the "Nude on the Bank" (also 1908). The way the freely-handled figure is tied in with nature, with the flora and fauna, is close to German models in both form and subject matter.

A decisive step was taken in 1913 with the publication by Larionov of the "Rayonist Manifesto". The year before, the couple had left the "Jack of Diamonds" group, which was still dominated by Western influence. Rayonism marks the beginning of independent Russian art, the overcoming of Western models. Seen in this light, Larionov's "Rayonist Sausage and Mackerel", painted a year befor the publication of the manifesto, is a key picture. The painter emancipates himself from Cubist and Futurist influences. The idea of the picture is no longer the dissection of the subject outside perspective, nor is it the presentation of its movement within the pictorial space. Following the name of the movement (rayon = ray), the objects are dissolved into prismatic, much-broken rays; but it is not the thing itself, but its iridescent reflection, which is the subject. The dynamic pictorial event and its colourful echo take place outside concrete time and concrete space. The picture "radiates feelings," says Larionov, "which allow us to sense a fourth dimension." In her "Portrait of Larionov" (1913) Natalia Goncharova attempts to apply rayonist principles to the portrayal of her companion,

Mikail Larionov, *Still Life with Crab,* 1907

Mikail Larionov, *Rayonist Sausage and Mackerel*, 1912

to translate the "radiance" of his personality into colour and shape. Rayonist ideas and Futurist experience, Cubist refinement in the simultaneous portrayal "en face" and "en profil," as well as the naiveté of folk art, merge to form a highly individual artistic unity. Contradictory techniques in the application of pigment and formal design cancel each other out in a "harmony of contrasts."

There is a romantic attraction to the infinite in Rayonism, as well as references to contemporary trends and a desire to master them. This is also true of the movement which followed it, "Suprematism", in which Kasimir Malevich and his disciples established the second stage of the emancipation of Russian art. Malevich, too, had extensive experience of Fauvism-Expressionism, Cubism, Futurism, and Russian folklore. The "Landscape" of 1909, in its effective contrast of blooming colour tone and highly stylized, "structured" form, shows clear reminiscences of these movements, but also has a high degree of artistic independence. The plastic geometry of the mounds of earth balances the stylized cones of the treetops; the cylindrical trunks

are counterposed to the cubic buildings. The right-hand side of the picture is open to the observer in deep perspective, while the only human figure, in the centre of the picture, is presented "naively," with no regard for real proportion. Sovereign painting skill is combined with the consciously applied simplicity of "primitive" peasant art.

Four years later, after a series of Cubo-Futurist pictures, Malevich painted the icon of the world without objects, the "Black Square on a White Background" (1913), the elemental form of Suprematism, which according to Malevich signalled the supremacy of "pure feeling" over nature and the objective world in painting. The "Dynamic Suprematism" of 1916 shows Malevich the Suprematist at the height of his powers. One broad and two narrow trapeziums, red, black and yellow, climb towards the upper edge of the picture; they are set in front of an undefined, infinite background, and accompanied by geometric satellites made up of small sections. All the shapes float in front of the indeterminate pictorial background as a "construction of forces," while the colours are the "Roman-

Natalia Goncharova, *Portrait of Larionov,* 1913

Kasimir Malevich, *Dynamic Suprematism,* 1916

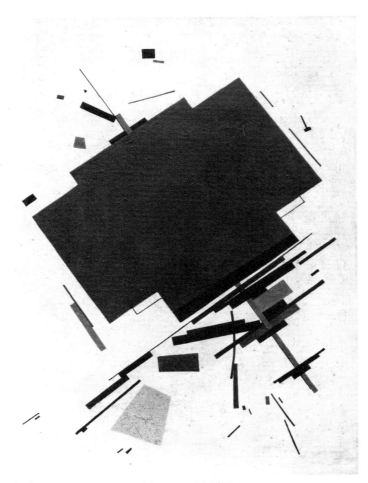

Nikolai Suetin, *Composition,* c. 1922/23

tic" bearers of energy. Disciplined structure renders the "supremacy of feeling" intellectually objective: intuition and reflection are held in soaring balance.

The "Red Square on Black" (c. 1922) is a late echo of the primaeval square of 1913; the "Suprematist Architekton" of 1926 is, like many other twenties works, proof of Malevich's conviction of the primacy of architecture in the planning of a new society. The clear concern of these models, which had a lasting effect on 20th century architecture, with reality, contrasts with the meditative lyricism of the pictures. A Romantic tendency towards the anarchic, the subversive and the infinite, and the will to bring about a concrete new order, lead to the enormous tension in the work of this artist (see also: "Art for the Collective").

The work of Malevich's twenty-year-younger colleague Nikolai Suetin is dominated more decisively by the constructive elements of an architect-draughtsman, as opposed to analysis of the science of colour, than was the case with the founder of Suprematism. "Composition" (1922/23) is clearly influenced by Malevich's floating geometry, but makes a more concrete impression, almost like an architectural blueprint for the world of tomorrow.

The painter Liubov Popova, who later gave up the "laboratory art" of the studio for applied art, or rather for the application of art to the creation of a new technical culture, was influenced at first by Malevich and

Tatlin to an equal extent. The two early pictures in the Ludwig Museum were painted at the height of her powers, while the "Artistic Architectonics" of 1920 shows signs of change to come, both in its subject and in the austerity of its reduced abstract forms.

"Female Nude Seated" (1913) and "Relief" (1915), on the other hand, are classic works of the Russian avant-garde. The nude shows the influence of Futurism and Cubism, but there are differences. Popova dissects shape, but makes no attempt to represent the progress of movement through time. In contrast to Analytic Cubism – she does not adopt the facet technique – the figure remains clearly recognizable and does not become a cipher. Her relatively "sturdy" method of presentation is powerful and dynamic when set against the austere intellectualism of Analytic Cubist formulations. Forms mingle, but do not dissolve. The prismatic play of shadows set "wrongly," the forward and backward movement of lines and surfaces, give the picture plasticity, without affecting its two-dimensional quality.

"Relief" already shows the elimination of the object. The inclusion of the third dimension should also be seen as part of the programme. The picture shows lively interplay between encapsulated shapes of equal value, which are not subordinated to any hierarchical principle of composition because of their intrinsic value. The strong colours clearly show the influence of Malevich and are in stark contrast with the Cubist purity which otherwise informs the picture.

Liubov Popova, *Female Nude Seated,* c. 1913

Liubov Popova, *Relief,* 1915

Ivan Puni, who later practised harmlessly illustrative Impressionism in exile in Paris as Jean Pougny, came to terms at an early stage with new trends in Western and Eastern art, without adopting a firm position. His "Sculpture" of 1915, a relief construction in the simplest of materials (wood, cardboard, tin) is obviously influenced by the contemporary work of Malevich's "Productivist" and diametrically opposed colleague Tatlin, who in his turn had been stimulated by Picasso in this field. Formal elements of pictorial composition are close to the formal world of Malevich in their lucidity and simplicity. This relationship is clearer in Ivan Kljun's "Suprematist Composition".

The works of Alexandra Exter are more clearly influenced by the West than those of her colleagues. This painter is one of the most prominent Russian exponents of Cubo-Futurism. This is clear if one considers her work in the Ludwig Museum, "Cubist Interior" and "Cubo-Futurist Composition" (both 1912). Western art was more influential in the groups of artists called "Sky-Blue Rose" and "Jack of Diamonds" with which Exter was connected than in the associations which bore the stamp of the nationalist avant-garde movement. Alexandra Exter's pictures have a delicacy of colour, an almost lyrical bloom, with overtones of

Impressionism, which is seldom found in the work of the early Russians. Dynamic Futurism is also tamed, Cubist analysis of form is not taken to extremes. The architectural fragments and the definition of space in "Cubist Interior" would have been inconceivable without the admired example of Robert Delaunay. It is not by chance that the painter, who had also worked for the great director Tairov, later concerned herself almost exclusively with designs for films, the theatre, fashion and interior decoration. Paris, to which she later emigrated, remained her real artistic home.

Aristarch Lentulov became known in the West as a result of the 1922 exhibition in the Van Diemen Gallery in Berlin, and fell into obscurity for a long time after that. He is one of the artists whose works combine Cubo-Futurist and Expressionist-Fauve influence with a vivid recollection of Russian folk art. The principal exponents of this style were the "Ace of Diamonds" group, to which Lentulov belonged. His own great model was Paul Cézanne, whose work also forms a link

Ivan Puni, *Sculpture – Variant No. 110,* 1915

Ivan Kljun, *Suprematist Composition,* 1916

Aristarch Lentulov, *Cypress Landscape,* 1913

with French Cubism. The austere compositional structure of "Cypress Landscape" (1913) is a reminder of this ancestry, and also of the early Cubist landscapes painted by Picasso and Braque in 1908 and 1909. The vigour of the picture on the other hand points to Futurism, and the refined sense of colour to the Fauves. Lentulov's painting assimilates stimuli from traditional sources and the present in a very personal and artistic way, combined with design of a very high quality.

Almost all the members of the Russian avant-garde were inclined not to restrict themselves to painting and sculpture, but to work on an interdisciplinary plane, as we would put it today. This is the case with Paul Mansuroff, whose title "The Wedding" is identical with that of a Stravinsky opera. The sensitive "Composition" of 1923 also combines picture and writing. The libretto is superimposed on the restrained Constructivist colour shapes in front of the ochre of the background.

There are echoes of the work of the early avant-garde in the pictures of Xenia Ender ("Spatial Composition", c. 1919). This whirl of expressive colour was created under the influence of scientific and analytical experiments by Malevich (later Matiushin), but despite its high degree of abstraction it has clearly recognizable links with "Brücke" Expressionism.

An example of Russian Post-Avant-garde away from the metropolises of Moscow and Leningrad is the work of Alexander Bogomasov, who lived in Kiev and experimented with the application of abstract principles to figurative representation ("Sleeping Woman", 1916). He finds a personal way of trying "to bring abstract painting into objects," The pictorial world of Kudriashov ("East", 1928), which is as far from the anti-art slogans of

Alexander Tyshler, *No. 4 of the Lyric Circle,* 1928

the Productivists as it is from the sentimental genre, is an example of an early "Post-Modern" with a Russian flavour.

The only consistently Constructivist-Productivist picture as Tatlin understood it is Vassily Ermilov's memorial tablet on the death of Lenin, "January 21, 1924". The day and time are sawn out of the upper wooden panel, the metal letters screwed on, the figures framed with nails. This bleak work draws its aesthetic quality solely from the gradation of the various levels of the picture, the typography, and the economical design. The picture "No. 4 of the Lyric Cycle" by Alexander Tyshler shows that Russian art in the twenties had connections with Surrealism; Tyshler did not accept the validity of "criteria of reality" in art.

Abstract and Concrete Painting
Variations on Constructivism

"Tableau I" by Piet Mondrian is a masterpiece of Western European Constructivism. It is the culmination of a long period in the artist's development which led him through traditional pictures in the tradition of old Dutch architectural painters via assimilation of the influence of Cézanne, Van Gogh and the Fauves first to

Vassily Ermilov, *Memorial-Tablet · 21. Januar 1924,* 1924

Piet Mondrian, *Tableau I,* 1921

his decisive confrontation with the Cubists and then to his association with Bart van der Leck and Theo van Doesburg. They gave the necessary impetus towards complete abstraction of form and colour with the goal of "universal harmony," as they formulated it in the "meditation tables" for a new spiritual human type. Monochrome colour fields are subordinated to strict, rectangular discipline by means of broad black border-lines. Finally, Mondrian restricts himself to the primary colours red, blue and yellow, and the "non-colours" black and white. To this extent "Tableau I" represents the opening phase of the mature work. The white is not yet "pure," there are still sensitively graded shades of grey, but the final step on the road to radical simplifica-tion, total abstraction and the expunging of the last traces of anything which reminds us of objects has been taken. Only Barnett Newman will go further by dissolving the rectangular frames of the geometrical colour fields and replacing them with a "zip" without a beginning or an end. It is scarcely credible that this wonderfully peaceful, meditative picture caused a scandal when Gert von der Osten acquired it in 1967 for less than a tenth of its present market value.

Mondrian himself saw his art, which he called "Neo-Plasticism", as the logical conclusion of all plastic or three-dimensional works realized in paint, because they were the only means of eliminating in complete harmony the individual, the random, the anxiety, and consequently the tragedy as well.

At first glance Mondrian's work is related to that of the late Bauhaus master Laszlo Moholy-Nagy. This is deceptive, however. The Hungarian is still strongly in-fluenced by Russian Constructivism, in particular the work of Malevich and El Lissitzky. Moholy-Nagy was not concerned with something "universal" and other-worldly, but with concrete social harmony here and now. For him technology seemed the most important instrument of art in a mass age. As a consequence of this he came to terms with kinetics, created the first moving objects, made light-machines and also includ-ed film, the new medium, in his work. He is famous for the first "Telephone Picture", completed according to instructions which were given over the telephone. His "Light-Painting" was later to influence the various Zero groups.

The pictures "Grey, Black, Blue" (1920) and "On a White Ground" (1923) are stages on the road to emancipation from traditional painting techniques. While the earlier work still shows the influence of Malevich (and per-haps of Mondrian as well), the later picture presents new solutions. There is an obvious contrast between transparently shimmering, almost floating colours and a more compact, denser and heavier tonality, which gives the work tension, heightened by emphatic grad-ing of the various layers of the picture. The spare geo-metry of segments and narrow bands of colour is coun-teracted by the dynamics of movement, again reminis-cent of Russian models.

A tendency towards "structured" pictorial composition is even more marked in Moholy-Nagy's fellow country-man Lajos Kassak, who returned to Hungary in 1926. In contrast to the Russians, however, Kassak was content with painted "pictorial architecture," and did not design architectural models, either as dreams or as intended buildings.

The Pole Stanislav Kubicki (shot by the Nazis in 1943) increasingly detached himself from Eastern Construc-tivism over the years and was stimulated by the West-ern version. His picture of the city of "Danzig" (1924) shows Cubist influence. The early work of Walter Dexel also bears the stamp of this movement, as is shown by the "Portrait of the Town of Jena" (1918). The later works of this artist, who was forgotton for a long time, were dominated by the Dutch "De Stijl" ("The Big H," 1924).

In the twenties Hanover was a centre of German Con-structivist and Abstract art; El Lissitzky designed his famous "Room of Abstracts" in the museum there, then under the direction of Alexander Dorner. Carl Buch-heister and Friedrich Vordemberge-Gildewart were the leading lights of "the abstract Hanovers," along with Kurt Schwitters. The former two artists were in contact with De Stijl, the Russians and the Bauhaus, and Vordemberge with the French association "abs-traction-création".

Central to Buchheister's work was a link with archi-tecture in the Russian manner as an important means of changing the world. His dynamic arrangements ("Composition Blue-Yellow Gradation", 1926, "Triangu-lar Composition", 1928) are alien to the peaceful and contemplative immersion of Mondrian. Buchheister was not concerned with the universal, but – like El Lis-sitzky – with concrete society. This is also true of the work of Erich Buchholz – abruptly broken off in 1933 – "Form Brings Along Its Own Formula"; he never recov-ered from the shock of being ostracized and died an embittered man in his adopted home town of Berlin.

Gunter Fruhtrunk studied architecture, and it is there-fore not surprising that he was impressed, after periods of study with Fernand Léger and Hans Arp, by Con-structivism, especially in Malevich's version. His prin-cipal theme, however, is the contrast of brightly glow-ing, even patches of colour arranged diagonally or horizontally, sensitively modulated at the edges with an intense black, which negates the light from which the colours come. Fruhtrunk, too, understands colour as form which should not be disturbed by any ele-ments of design.

Vordemberge-Gildewart's sensitive, highly-strung painting is much more meditative and inward, and

Laszlo Moholy-Nagy, *On a White Ground,* 1923

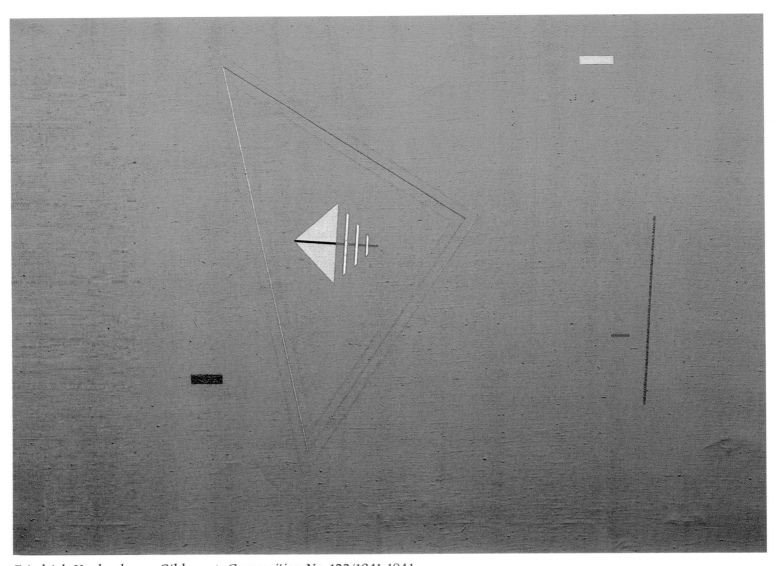

Friedrich Vordemberge-Gildewart, *Composition No. 122/1941,* 1941

Carl Buchheister, *Triangular Composition,* 1928

subject only to artistic, "art-inherent" disciplines without reference to the outside world, which it develops from within itself, as for example in "Composition 122" (1941), which places mainly yellow rectangles and triangles rhythmically against a green surface. A reticent, musically atmospheric lyricism distinguishes these paintings from the purist organizational schemes of the Mondrian he admired.

Constructivism underwent an independent Swiss variation in the work of the "Zurich concretes" Max Bill, Richard P. Lohse, Verena Loewensberg and Camille Graeser. They too aim for "purity, law and order" and the elimination of speculative and nebulous elements. The picture itself is the concrete object and the only subject; the Euclidian play of geometry and colour tones occurs within it, in accordance with the strict rules of logic, without any reference to the visible world outside. Graeser's late work "Yellow-Blue Volume 1 : 1, 1/18, Allegro" (1974) is an example which is as ingenious as it is stark. One-eighteenth of the area of the picture (hence the title) detaches itself from the symmetry of the yellow and blue area, makes room for the blue and thrusts into it. Remarkably, this bare

116

Josef Albers, *Homage to the Square: Green Scent,* 1963

Franz Wilhelm Seiwert, *Town and Country,* 1932

Camille Graeser, *Yellow-Blue Volume 1:1, 1/18, Allegro,* 1974 ▷

mathematical principle has a forceful effect and gives the picture a reticently dynamic quality.

There was a wonderful late flowering of these apparently puritanical trends in the work of the Bauhaus master Josef Albers; he was later to exert enormous influence in the USA through strict economy of means on the basis of crystal-clear artistic doctrine. There is no other painter of our times than this former primary-school teacher from Bottrop who has so clearly proved to us, by making them visible, that even the most elementary things are unfathomable. He always insisted on the diversity of his pictures as well as their originality. In his famous series "Homage to the Square" – the Ludwig Museum owns one of these pictures dating from 1963 with the felicitous subtitle "Green Scent" – area and space are perceived alternately. This is

Heinrich Hoerle, *Masks,* 1929

◁ Franz Wilhelm Seiwert, *Workers,* 1926

achieved by renouncing subjective "handwriting" and by a high degree of objectivization, and also colour sensitivity in the continual variety of the repeated essential shape of the square. "I paint as thinly as Brueghel," said Albers on the occasion of a visit to the "smallest workroom in the world" in New Haven, Connecticut, where he lived before he moved to Orange. "I want to realize myself, not to express myself; for I have learned to think and see: I did not learn art."

Changes of colour are brought about by a technique different from that of Mondrian, namely by juxtaposition, which makes it leap forwards and backwards. There is a fascinating "interaction of colour," of irritation and meditation of "physical state of affairs and psychic effect" (Albers). The painter set out to "create meditation pictures for the twentieth century." He not only set out to do this, he succeeded.

As we have seen, Eastern and Western Constructivism have a tendency to radical abstraction. The group of Cologne "Progressives" around Franz Wilhelm Seiwert and Heinrich Hoerle made a highly individual attempt to make Constructivism figurative on socialist principles, and therefore easier to understand.

119

Heinrich Hoerle, *Two Female Nudes,* 1930/31

"Masks" (1929) a Rhineland event, the carnival, becomes a metaphor of the world. Unlike Carl Hofer's work with the same title it is masked aggression and not forlornness and mourning that is hidden behind the stereotyped faces, or what is still visible of them. The "Two Female Nudes" of 1930/31 show certain characteristics of "Magic Realism" in the partial suspension of standardization in the figure turned towards the observer in the foreground, the background's resemblance to real landscape and a certain "atmosphere" tinged with melancholy.

The Kingdom In-Between
Paul Klee and the Bauhaus Masters

"Haste is not permitted when you want so much," Paul Klee noted in his diary. He was 34 years old when he was "called by colour" on a journey to Tunis with Macke and Moillet: "Colour has taken hold of me. I am a painter," runs the famous 1914 entry. Previously he had produced mainly drawings and illustrations. Kandinsky, who was a good friend, although Klee was not a member of the "Blaue Reiter", was very proud of having recognized Klee's genius at an early stage. Paul Klee is one of the great painters of the century, and brought

In his despair over the "inability of the Una Sancta Catholica to prevent mankind from destroying itself by mass murder," Seiwert abandoned Catholicism for Marxism and solidarity with the workers' movement. He came to Constructivism from Expressionism and Cubism, and restored its objectivity by working to strict formulae and standardization. The background landscape in the picture of "Workers" (1926) still has hints of realism, but the almost standardized workers (with one female worker) arranged in rows one behind the other are rigorously stripped of their individuality, are "representatives" of a concrete social group. Despite the limited number of figures there is an impression of the masses. "Town and Country" (1932) is reduced schematically to two men (with stylized hammer and sickle); at the same time they are unified by the handshake and a refined use of colour.

Seiwert's friend Heinrich Hoerle, who moved from "Dadamax" Ernst to the "Progressives", went to a similar source for his inspiration. His objective Constructivism is less spare, the grouping of the figures livelier, the presentation nearer to the concrete subject of the pictures. Aesthetic principles compel ideology to take a back seat, although the artist remained a militant socialist in his everyday life. In the picture entitled

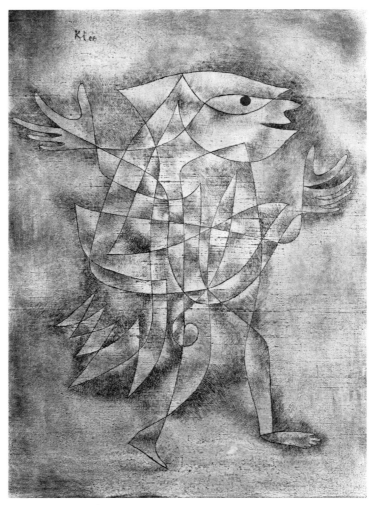

Paul Klee, *Fool in a Trance,* 1929

Paul Klee, *Highways and Byways,* 1929

Lyonel Feininger, *Bridge III*, 1917

Romanticism back into fashion; he has been called the "Romantic with a precise colour consciousness." In this respect Cézanne was the great teacher, while the theories of Robert Delaunay had paved the way for the liberation of colour.

"Highways and Byways" (1929), one of the most beautiful pictures in the Ludwig Museum, and certainly also one of the most important in the painter's entire œuvre, shows Klee at the height of his powers. It was painted in his "Bauhaus" period in response to a journey to Egypt, which proved just as important for him as the journey to Kairouan (Tunis) 15 years previously. Will Grohmann, Klee's biographer, said of the series of works produced as a result of that journey: "Even without the titles of the pictures anyone familiar with Klee's work would probably conclude from the structure of the pictorial framework, from the pyramids and cubes, that we were dealing with the Orient, and having seen the whole sequence would decide on Egypt without further prompting. Work had been done in advance on the pictorial scheme, but contact with country and his-

tory was needed to induce the birth of the Egyptian pictures."

Kairouan introduced the artist to colour and pictorial architecture, and Egypt allowed him to experience the timeless coexistence of permanence and transience. Thus "Highways and Byways", despite concrete location in place and history is, like so many other works, set in a kingdom in-between. The picture fulfils Klee's ideal not by reflecting the visible, but by making visible: light and sun, the structures of organic and constructed landscape are not depicted, but translated into coloured shapes and pictorial signs for pyramid and terrace, desert and fields, water and vegetation, man-made roads and pathways of life. This world of signs has many meanings: it is concrete, but points beyond itself; the horizontals at the top of the picture can mean sky or river. The hieratic structure of the picture is not schematic, but full of confusing irregularities: highways and byways can also lead us astray. "Genius is the mistake in the system," was Paul Klee's teaching. These confusions, "irritations in the system," fill this picture, awash with light, with vibrant life. As in all the work of this artist, "Highways and Byways" is a metaphor of creation, a design for a possible world outside our own.

The "Fool in a Trance", dating from the same year, represents another important group of works devoted to the world between appearance and reality, jest and earnest, gaiety and tragedy: the theatre, the circus, the world of variety. The figure of a fool with a drawn outline is performing a balancing act on an invisible rope; the figure is transparent, the background shows through. The picture bears the stamp of Klee's burlesque humour and draughtman's inclination to caricature. In contrast to the grotesquely comic formulations of his early years it has become an existential cipher between reality and dream.

Among Klee's colleagues at the Bauhaus were Lyonel Feininger and Oskar Schlemmer. Like Klee, Feininger was an outstanding musician. Like his friend, the American-German started out by drawing fantastic, "surreal" incidents, and as a caricaturist. For Feininger, too, the "Orphist" Delaunay was an important stimulus, but – apart from Seurat – he was most profoundly influenced by Cubism, although his strictly designed, as it were musical pictorial compositions are entirely individual. Cubism with its rules and crystal clarity meant, on his own admission, "a longing for the strict structuring of space – without a painting excess."

"Bridge III" dates from 1917, two years before the foundation of the Bauhaus in Weimar, in which Feininger was involved. The picture shows, in its prismatic, constructive order and reticent colouring, traces of his coming to terms with the constructive elements of Cubism. But it has depth, the pictorial space remains open, there is an unmistakable Romantic base to the mood, the austerity of the architecture is mitigated by the artistic atmosphere. His tendency to create "diaphanous" Gothic architecture and windows, transparent colour and form, shows much more clearly in the

Oskar Schlemmer, *Two Seated Figures,* 1935/36

picture of the "Towers Above the Town" of Halle (1931). The picture is glassily transparent and a certain tendency to dissolution of form cannot be overlooked. However, Feininger's will to impose shape makes for floating, elegant balance, not the least of the charming elements in this picture.

Oskar Schlemmer's work is also steeped in Romanticism, tinged with classicistic idealism. It was one of the blackest days in the history of German art when, of all the works of this very German artist, the Weimar Bauhaus mural was sacrificed to the barbarism of Nazi blockheads as early as 1930 (!).

Schlemmer's principal theme was the human figure in space. It is no coincidence that, as director of the Bauhaus theatre, he was also responsible for the creation of the "Triadic Ballet" and many other theatrical works. Schlemmer tried to connect the concept of an unindividualized, ideal human type, an "idol of the absolute," with the affirmation of technical, functionalistic control of the environment. This attitude is expressed with exceptional painting and organizational skill in the picture entitled "Group of Fourteen in Imaginary Architecture" (1930). Human beings dominate, as "organic human architecture has pushed constructed spatial architecture into the background," to use the formula-

Lyonel Feininger, *Towers Above the Town (Halle),* 1931

Oskar Schlemmer, *Group of Fourteen in Imaginary Architecture,* 1930

tion of Karin von Maur, Schlemmer's major biographer. The complicated rhythm of the group, its placing at various levels of the picture, shows the degree of communication within the group, but also its isolation in empty space, always related to structured, imaginary and idealistic architecture.

The smaller study "Two Seated Figures" (1935/36), however, painted when Schlemmer had gone into "inner emigration," is much more intimate. Here, too, the strict design of the chair backs responds to the standardization of the figures. Space is introduced into the picture by the diagonal position of the girl; the noiseless conversation is the highly symbolic representation of archetypal human behaviour by means of that brand of classicistic and cool Romanticism which is the hallmark of Schlemmer's highly-charged work.

Schlemmer's pupil was the Italian-German Werner Gilles, a likeable "poeta minor", also influenced for a time by Hans von Marées with his ideal figures in an ideal landscape. But in the last resort the influence of Expressionism, of Klee and above all – as the lyrical and

Werner Gilles, *Annunciation,* 1948

dramatic "Annunciation" (1948) demonstrates – that of Picasso, was stronger.

Werner Heldt was a close friend of Gilles. But his painting in the artistically crucial years after the war is of greater formal austerity and indeed unthinkable with-

Werner Heldt, *Still Life on the Balcony*, 1951

out the compositional doctrine of Synthetic Cubism. Despite the artist's mourning of the destruction of his home town of Berlin ("Berlin on Sea"), the intellectual attitude of his work is more distanced and less imbued with feeling than that of his friend. The "Still Life on the Balcony" (1951), set in front of the bare façades of the buildings and the empty windows, is a pictorial symbol of life submerged in a dead city.

Pocket Museum and Material Poetry
A Programme of Dadaist Contrast

The Ludwig Museum has a representative cross-section of the work of the grand master of the Dada movement, the refuser and driving force Marce Duchamp (see also: "The Great Refuser"), although in pocket size, 41 x 37.8 x 10. 5 cm: "La boîte en valise – The Portable Museum". There are 83 items from the most important phases of his work collected here: "Nude Descending a Staircase", the "Large Glass", the readymades, the Mona Lisa with a moustache, the chocolate mill, etc. The realization of Duchamp's idea of a transportable œuvre seemed more suitable than a book to its originator as a means of communicating his partially artistic, partially anti-artistic thinking, and its results. Certainly there are few cases which are so light, but which carry such a weight of ideas.

Franz Picabia's "Spanish Night" of 1922 sits fairly precisely on the borderline between Dada and Surrealism, and shows how much the latter movement owes to Dada and its exponents, a fact which André Breton was all too keen to suppress. One could almost say: the picture is in two halves, a white one and a black one, and one half is Dada, the other Surrealist. The black figure of a flamenco dancer in the white half of the picture presses against the figure of a woman seen from the front, standing like a passive female marksman's assistant in the black half; the aggressive eroticism of the

Marcel Duchamp, *The Portable Museum*, 1964

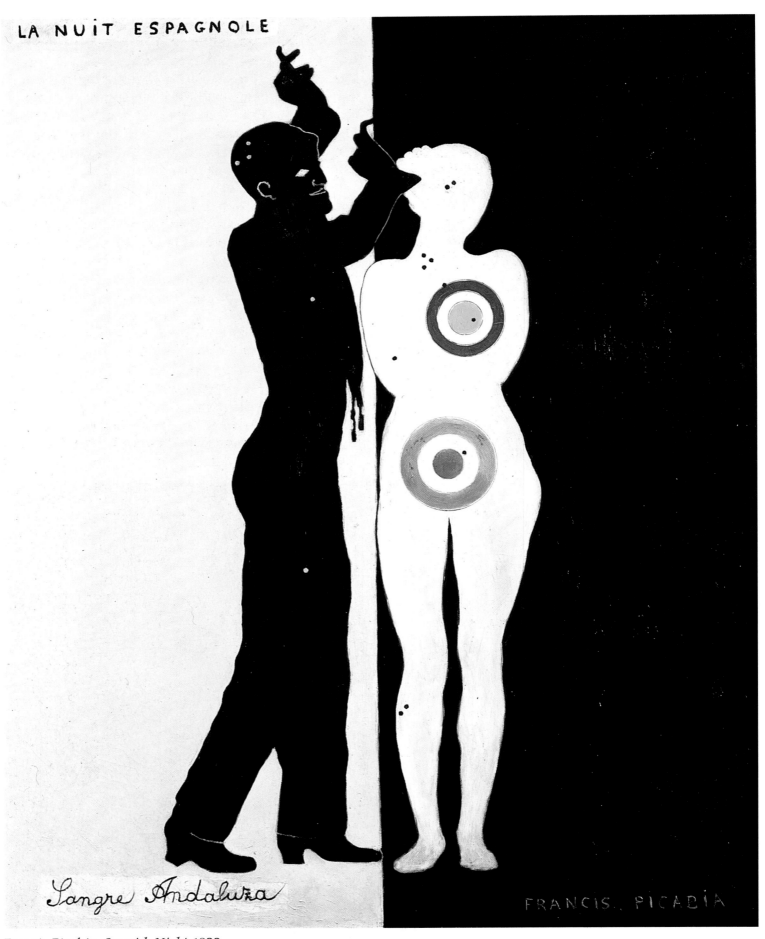

Francis Picabia, *Spanish Night,* 1922

Francis Picabia, *The Bride,* 1929

sculpted chessmen flank the spiral like anonymous watchers, stylized symbols of the increasing anonymity of man, but also of the power of reason. It has been pointed out that in ancient times and the Renaissance a left-hand spiral symbolized the destructive power of violence. Thus the picture, created on the eve of the Second World War, is without the irony of Dada, but still has two meanings, and represents opposing forces. As the title suggests, it is a final appeal to reason.

The Dada movement had a wonderful, valuable, poetic and Romantic flowering in Hanover. The most important German Dada artist, Kurt Schwitters, was "apolitical." He was not interested in either ideas or revolution; when he acted politically it was against something, not for a particular movement – above all against war. He made no bones about his pacifism. This led to years of argument with the left-wing Dada group around Richard Huelsenbeck, whom Schwitters scornfully called "Huelsendadas" – husk Dadas. Otherwise he saw his work as pure art, with no other ambition. "For Schwitters art was like the forest to a forester," Huelsenbeck later wrote in reconciliation.

In terms of form the North German was no innovator. In many fields, particularly the use of everyday mate-

subject-matter is heightened by the targets which mark the woman's primary and secondary "erogenous zones" with excessive clarity in harsh colours. Both figures are full of bullet-holes. The nature of the attack is documented by the title, originally "L'amour espagnol – Spanish Love", and the subtitle in the left-hand half of the picture "Sangre Andaluza – Andalusian Blood". Werner Spies also considers the female figure to be a blasphemous parody of Saint Sebastian in the black and white of Asian shadow-play.

"The Bride" (1929) is closer to Surrealism in the iconographic and historical references to Botticelli and the theme of the bridal Madonna, in the transformation of the sacred into the lascivious and erotic, in the alternating play of dream and reality, and the permeability of the various levels of the picture. The floral-architectural ornamentation – the snake lines, flower-stalks, petals and phallic temples – is also ironic on two levels and goes beyond Dada, which was usually more frugal, in its playful mixture of drawing and painting techniques.

Man Ray's oil painting "Return to Reason" of 1939 has the same title as his first film "Le Retour à la Raison" of 1923. It is a summary to remind us of the "prop-cupboard" of this all-round artist, who is also represented in the museum by photographs and a model of his famous "Lampshade" of 1919. The umbrella, unfurling in a spiral, is the central motif of the picture, created before Man Ray's second emigration to America. Two

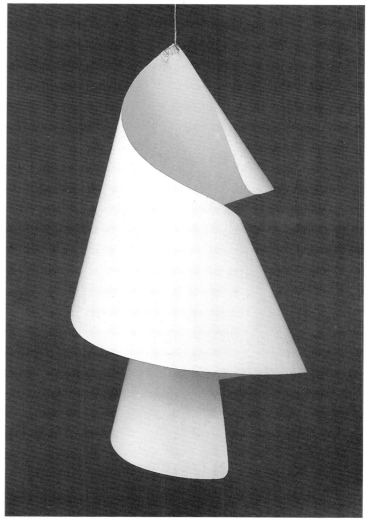

Man Ray, *Lampshade,* 1919 (1959)

127

Man Ray, *Return to Reason,* 1939

Kurt Schwitters, *Relief,* 1923

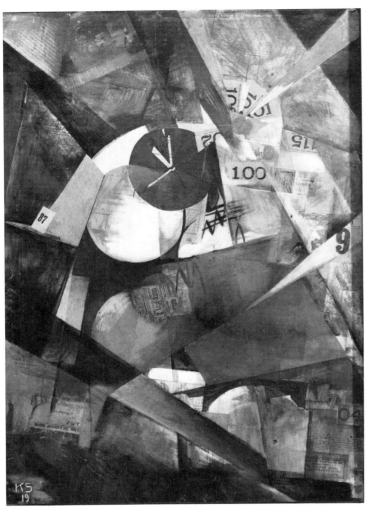

Kurt Schwitters, *Picture 9b (The Great I Picture)*, 1919

full element in the picture, but also the bearer of an immaterial poetic cipher.

Basic constructive elements are more and more in evidence in the work of the artist from 1922 onwards. The "Relief" (1923) shows Schwitters' response to stimuli from his friends in the Dutch "De Stijl" movement. The picture strives into the third dimension even more unambiguously than was the case in the Merz collages, an impression which is strengthened by the articulation of space through the placing of various levels of the picture one behind the other. Schwitters achieves additional compositional tension by the changing use of materials, above all by means of the contrast of larger, calm and smaller, more agitated fields. He avoids the temptation, however, of subordinating the contradictory poetry of individual elements to geometrical order in the rigorous manner of his Dutch friends.

The differences between Schwitters' work and Constructivism are completely clear if one compares their architectural concepts. Schwitters' striving for the "Gesamtkunstwerk" is set against the purism of the Dutchmen; he attempted to achieve this in his Merz buildings in Hanover, Norway and England. The fact that they all remained fragments is not due simply to the times, but also to the Romantic thinking which lies behind them, and which shows in the striving for the infinite as well as in the fact that the entire ambitious concept was not capable of realization.

rials, the Cubists and Futurists with their collages had done the same thing; in the matter of composition he owes much to Braque and Picasso, Boccioni and Ballà, indeed even to Feininger and Expressionists like Franz Marc, but above all – and this includes the organization of colour and space – to Robert Delaunay. "The new and special thing about his Merz pictures," wrote Werner Schmalenbach, "was the exclusive, unreserved and expressive use of old materials; not of paper, but of anything you can think of which was a waste product of everyday activity."

The Merz pictures of 1919–22 are among his artistically most outstanding, most poetical and most beautiful works. (The word "Merz" was found in just the same random way as "Dada", in a mutilated poster for the "Kommerz- und Privatbank".) "Merz Picture 9b", the "Great I Picture", (1919) is a classic example in its restrained, tuneful colouring and its radiantly rotating, Cubist-Futurist method of composition. It shows Schwitters' sovereign handling of the most banal of material on the one hand – consignment note, ticket, pieces of wood – and the way in which he "dyes" them in an artist's manner, lending to the trivial a dignity of its own. The material is informed with imagination and artistic intelligence, and by these means is not just a

Dreams – Madness – Reality
Early and Late Surrealism

In Max Ernst's famous picture "Rendevous of the Friends" (1922) Giorgio de Chirico, inventor and most important exponent of "pittura metafisica", is featured as a statue in a solemn pose among the group of past and present exponents of Surrealism. This shows the extent to which he was honoured by the Surrealists, and it is true that the metaphysical painting of the Italians is, along with Dada, the second most important artistic source of Surrealist art.

De Chirico is represented in the Ludwig Museum by pictures which date from later than the pioneering period of pittura metafisica. They cover two important creative phases in the career of the painter, who in 1919 had declared definitively that he was a "classical artist" ("pictor classicus sum"). Thus classical themes are a feature of his twenties work "The Roman Comedy" and "Metaphysical Interior" (both 1926). In both pictures the ancient world and the Renaissance are dominant thematically and formally, although there are clear echoes of anonymous lay figures ("manichini") on the model of antique-style architectural fragments in the toga of Comedy (on the left) and Tragedy (on the right).

Giorgio de Chirico, *Metaphysical Interior,* 1926

Giorgio de Chirico, *Furniture in a Valley,* 1927

◁ Giorgio de Chirico, *The Roman Comedy,* 1926

The ominousness of empty spaces, which gave a threatening pull to the early pictures, is much toned down in the portrayal of the background – which is still empty – with a hint of an oval amphitheatre. The same is true of the picture of "Furniture in a Valley", painted in 1927, which is also one of a series. The pieces of furniture are personified. They stand in isolation in a fragment of street, in front of an empty background landscape with scattered ancient remains, before which they seem to huddle together and enter into silent dialogue. In "Metaphysical Interior" the room is distorted by ancient elements as if by theatrical scenery, properties of the past, of which the blind heroic head in the foreground is a reminder. De Chirico's brother Andrea, who called himself Albert Savinio and was above all a musician and man of the theatre, painted properties from a colourful, theatre-like dream world ("Untitled", 1929).

Landscape and still life are the only subjects tackled by

Giorgio Morandi, *Still Life,* 1921

133

Max Ernst, *Laon,* 1916

the Bolognese Giorgio Morandi. The penetrating still-ness of his work gives pittura metafisica a very per-sonal, restrained and inward lyrical tone. Morandi's palette is muted, simple objects in their speechless existence become mementoes, timeless existential ciphers, although there are no human beings in these pictures. It is painting of extraordinary sensitivity and intensity, detached from the noisy bustle of the day. In the silent classical harmony of forms and the rich nuances of broken, darkly melancholic colours mov-ing from the muted ("Still Life", 1921) to the brightly-lit major key of lighter tones ("Still Life", 1938), Morandi's best pictures are comparable to those of an artist like Chardin.

In their spiritual attitude and withdrawn quality the emotional, archaic-looking works of Massimo Cam-pigli, who cannot be assigned to any particular move-ment, ("Violins" or "Concert", 1934) are related to Morandi's pictures, without reaching the spirituality of his still lifes with their anecdotal and busy style.

Max Ernst, the Cologne artist from the nearby town of Brühl, is of course the key figure in the Surrealist department of the Ludwig Museum. The sequence begins with two pictures from his Expressionist period, "Crucifixion" (1913) and the picture of the town of "Laon" (1916). Echoes of the work of Matthias Grüne-

wald, an artist much admired by the Expressionists, are unmistakably present in the dramatic representation of the dead Christ, torn from the centre of the picture, and of the mourning women. Ernst has adopted the historical custom of dressing the "dramatis personae" in contemporary clothes. The Expressionist-Gothic Jerusalem is Cologne, as is indicated by the bisected cathedral in the background.

The portrayal of the town of Laon, which Ernst painted during the war when he was staying nearby, is calmer, and also expressive, but owes much to Robert Delau-nay in its stricter structure and in its colouring.

The "Rendezvous of the Friends", as has already been indicated, announces both the farewell to Dada and the beginning of Surrealism. Four years after that (1926), Max Ernst painted the mocking "Virgin Smack-ing the Christ Child". This picture is a long way from the dramatic Ernst of the earlier "Crucifixion". In terms of cultural history the provocative scene is to be viewed in the context of the ancient theme of Cupid punished, and popular picture stories of the life of Christ. Of course, at the time it was painted it was above all a Sur-realist anti-clerical gesture, which in the case of Max Ernst is also connected with traumatic childhood memories of his strictly Catholic painter-father. The mannerist pose of the Virgin is influenced by Parmi-

Max Ernst, *Virgin Smacking the Christ Child,* 1926

Max Ernst, *Rendezvous of the Friends,* 1922

Max Ernst, *Shell Flowers,* 1929

giano ("Madonna with the Long Neck"), as is the exaggerated size of the Child. The stagey nature of the architecture is reminiscent of De Chirico's unnatural perspective of empty squares, while the blasé faces of the spectators (only Max Ernst's eyes are sparkling) and the Christ-Child's halo lying on the floor are typical pieces of Dada and Surrealist sarcasm. The picture was the subject of zealous protest from pious spirits at the Paris "Salon des Indépendants", just as it was in 1928 in Cologne, when the clerics wanted to close down a Max Ernst exhibition, and threatened excommunication; his artist father fervently agreed.

The small picture "Lark in the Wood" dates from the same time (1926/27) and is one of the Grätenwald series of pictures. Its apparently harmless lyricism is deceptive, as the spotted bird, Max Ernst's alter ego – known as Loplop, Hornebom or Max the Beak – is both hidden and caught up in the impenetrable forest. The "Shell Flowers" (1929) are specimens from a series of pictures of hybrids, half plant, half animal. The partly biological, partly geological shapes often contain coded references to the animal and the human kingdom. Max Ernst's love of indeterminate areas and associative transformations becomes deeply significant in shapes of this kind.

This inclination is expressed in a quite different way in

Max Ernst, *Spring in Paris,* 1950

Max Ernst, *Birth of Comedy,* 1947

Max Ernst, *Lark in the Wood,* 1926/27

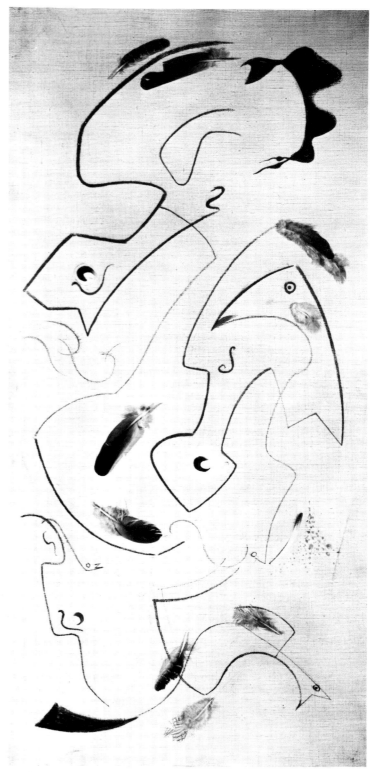

Andre Masson, *Bird-Eating Horses,* 1927

the "Grasshopper's Song to the Moon" (1953), which also contains memories of the Arizona home in exile. The swarm of grasshoppers grows into a ghostly landscape of craters and caves, watched over by a pale full moon in a pallid, empty sky. Its apparently harmless lyricism lures the onlooker into a trap and deceives him, until he sees that what is being portrayed is a world in ruins which has been gnawed away.

A more cheerful picture is "Spring in Paris" (1959), a pictorial representation of figurative metamorphoses in cool colours. The dream figure in the foreground, with a stone mask concealed inside it, "dances" with closed slit eyes, floating before an apparently theatrical setting, either a window hole with a broad frame or an open stage with proscenium area. On the stage a spindle shape is balanced on a pyramid, a mask hovers in front of the broad frame and is connected by taut threads to the magic shape, half plant, half stone, in the foreground.

The "Birth of Comedy" was inspired in title and content by the Nietzsche essay "The Birth of Tragedy from the Spirit of Music", in which the masks (persona = mask) of the performers play an important role in the chorus by indicating the anonymous origin of tragedy. Clear formal references to Oceanian sculptures and masks

can be recognized. The element of transformation once more has a role to play: a state of existence hovering between living and non-living figuration, represented – in a paradoxical reverse – by masks which are again almost personifications.

André Masson's pictures are a reminder of the Surrealist doctrine: "Beauty will be convulsive, or it will not be." Masson was openly in favour of the upheavals of the period. Conflict everywhere – animals fighting among themselves, human beings committing mur-

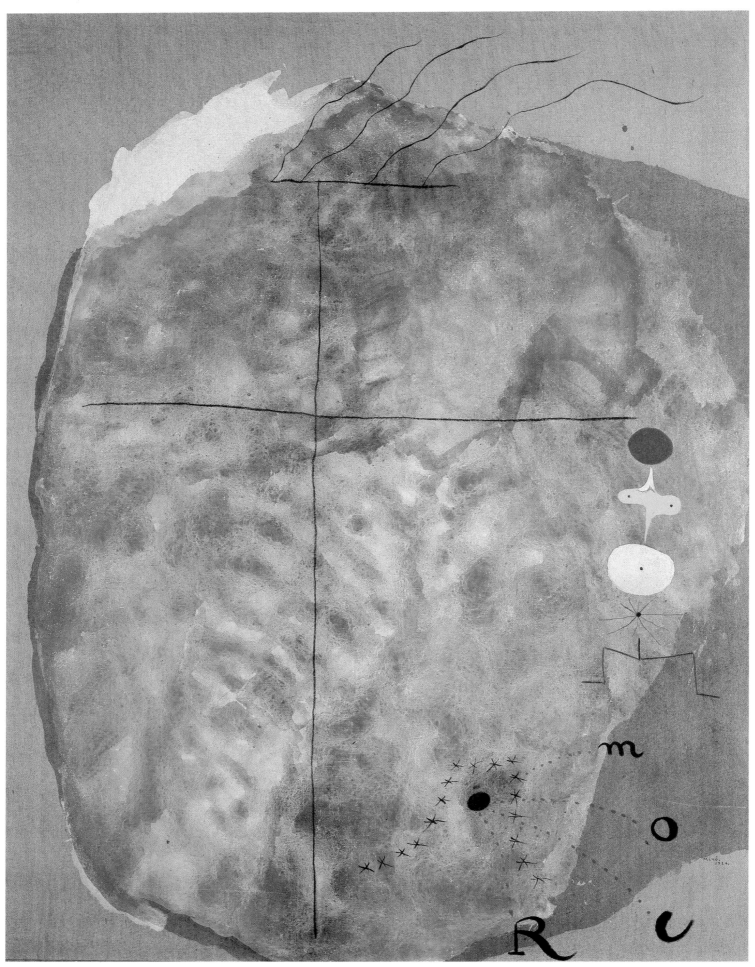

Joan Miro, *Amour,* 1926

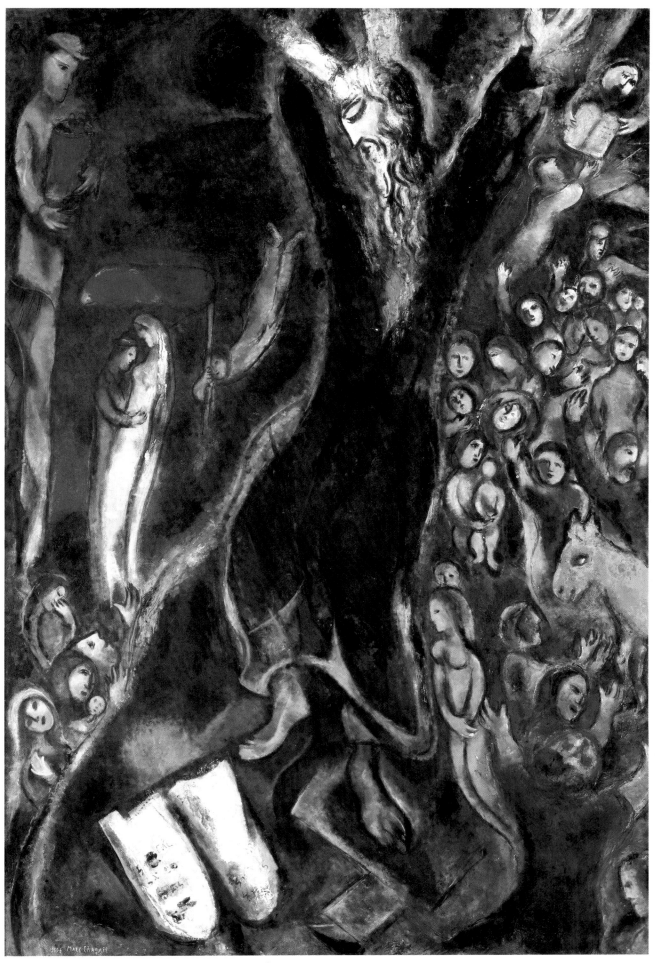

Marc Chagall, *Moses Breaking the Tablets of the Law*, 1955/56

Marc Chagall, *Sabbath,* 1910

der, racial struggles – is an idea from which he frees himself by the imposition of structure, in his own words "with energy, not [with] brutality;" there can be no great art without "délicatesse." In the picture "Bird-Eating Horses" (1927), the murderous subject-matter is handled with artistic "délicatesse" and highly individual technique. Birds' feathers are fastened onto a light background as elements in the picture, along with drawing and paint. Eyes, which were added later, observe the processes of eating and being eaten.

A year earlier Joan Miró, who Breton said was "perhaps the most Surrealist of us all," painted his picture "Amour", which belongs to the period of his "dream painting." Miró's work is also dominated by the theme of metamorphoses, fantastic transformations. The two-dimensional blue circular shape is programmatically contrasted with the Cubists' geometrical arrangements; the Catalan was influenced by them for a time. Through the shape runs a threadlike cross, which sprouts a few "hairs" in the upper part of the picture. Above the letters of the word "Amour" (reading clockwise), used as a constituent part ot the picture, appears the partly scribbled, partly naively painted figure of a dancing girl, who Miró himself said was the inspiration for the picture: "[…] The rising vertical line and the circles describe the movement." Miró was not an intellectual painter like Max Ernst, he did not need to shed layers of education to achieve the "second naiveté" of

Marc Chagall, *The Yellow House,* 1924

Salvador Dalí, *The Station at Perpignan*, 1965

the late-born artist. In him the relationship of form to colour was as spontaneous as the relationship to language of his fellow countryman, the poet Federico García Lorca.

Similar naiveté – in its Eastern, unaggressive version – is also always present in the work of Marc Chagall, one of the great artists who helped to pave the way for Surrealism. This is very clear in the dreamlike and detached early picture "Sabbath" (1910), painted by the artist in Paris in memory of his Russian home (Vitebsk). Its strong colours are a reminder of the early influence of the Fauves and above all of Van Gogh, with whom Chagall felt a fraternal bond. "The Yellow House" (1924) dates from after the second emigration from Russia, when the painter had come into conflict with the more wordly Constructivists, who were uncomprehendingly opposed to his fantastic world of stories of the Chassidim. It is again a memory picture in the blazing colours of summer, but still of this world, despite unmistakably dream-like moments.

The power of the late Chagall's surreal visions is given impressive artistic shape in the picture "Moses Breaking the Tablets of the Law" (1955/56), originally intend-

ed for the Calvary chapel in Vence. The boundaries of history and present, reality and dream are removed. The gigantic figure of the prophet dominates the various temporal and spatial planes of the work, which merge into pictorial unity as if in a mediaeval simultaneous representation. The angry, lamenting Moses blesses the couple under the Torah roll containing the law, while the emotional faithful watch the smashing of the tablets on the edge of the hill. On the other side of the picture the foolish people are still dancing around the Golden Calf, but above them the prophet receives the tablets for the second time.

One can hardly imagine a stronger mental contrast than that of Chagall's Chassidic piety and the provocative irrationalism of Salvador Dalí. "If one cannot get early Dalí any longer, at least one should buy the 'Station at Perpignan'," said a well-known artist of the middle generation whose own work starts in Surrealism. This huge picture dates from 1965, and now hangs in the Ludwig Museum. It is literally and figuratively a many-layered virtuoso work on various interdependent pictorial levels. The goods truck sets the scene in the French station on the way to Spain, with a hall with

Rene Magritte, *The Giantess,* 1929–31

the same measurements as Sigmund Freud's study – a fact which fascinated the painter with his psychoanalytic ambitions. The other stimulus decisive for the subject was François Millet's "Angelus Bell", to which Dalí constantly returned. The superficial humility of the woman corresponds to that of the female spider before the deadly mating. A X-ray of Millet's picture revealed a geometrical shape which Dalí took to be the coffin of his dead son. The floating crucified Christ in the Spaniard's late work indicates the place of the "sacrificed" son in the centre of the picture. On the left beside this is the bloody wound of the spear thrust. Dalí himself drops in various stages through the centre of the picture towards his wife Gala, who is waiting with a peasant's cart, above the countryside of their home in Port Lligat. The complex, contradictory content of the picture causes considerable confusion with its reversal of meaning, its mixture of dream and reality, sacred representation and blasphemous provocation, but also unleashes a chain of associative thoughts with neither a beginning nor an end.

Surrealist pictures tell stories. There is no other Sur-realist artist in whose work the literary element and the idea behind the picture are so much in the foreground as they are for René Magritte. The concept and the philosophical comment are more important for this admirer of Duchamp than the painting technique, which remains conventional. Magritte, like De Chirico, subscribes to the notion of "the dominance of poetry over painting." His subject is the puzzling nature of reality itself. "The Giantess" (1929–31) translates Baudelaire's poem from "Les Fleurs du Mal" into pictorial reality. It tells of a giantess who, scorning the gods, becomes the setting of the poet's life, and he strides through "her magnificent limbs" and "sometimes in summer" calmly falls asleep "in the shadow of her breasts." Magritte's pictorial interpretation puts a stop to the passage of time in the poem. The picture is a "snapshot," but one which reveals all the problems of Surrealist events.

In the work of Paul Delvaux, the most important Belgian Surrealist after Magritte, mythological scenes are set in civilized surroundings backed with archaic architecture. This is true of "The Dryads" (1966),

Paul Delvaux, *The Dryads,* 1966

Richard Oelze, *Growing Silence,* 1961

nymphs who have eternal youth. The statuesque figures in the foreground hover over the shallow water of a bathing pool with a bridge crossing it on the left. On the right is the framework of a springboard. The dryads wear fashionable hats dating from the turn of the century. The strict folds of the garments and ritualized gestures referring to nothing in particular stress their mental isolation. Only the figures in the background are moving, in a slow and measured fashion. A pallid, ghostly light underlines the unreality of the setting.

The pictures of the hermit-like lone wolf Richard Oelze show a forest which is not yet threatened, but threatening in itself. It becomes a mysterious, impenetrable thicket, somewhere between nature and architecture, in which demons with animal heads make their home and peer out from a thousand places, with pallid green eyes ("Growing Silence", 1961).

In the works of Roberto Matta the threat to man is more concrete and less timeless than in Oelze's pictures, which alienate nature: a fantastic quasi-technical fantasy world is given artistic shape ("Nude in a Group",

1965). Matta himself talks of "political Romanticism." His pictures gain tension from the contrast between "poisonous" misty colours and hard, sometimes dangerously spiky, drawn structures, fixed somewhere between paralysis and explosive movement. "It has become clear to us," says the painter, "that we are a reservoir for tension. This tension is our social reality, and even more our personal reality."

The pictorial world of Francis Bacon started in Surrealism, as the frightening crucifixion pictures of the early thirties clearly show; but even here the ever-increasing emancipation and independence of this great painter are beginning to make themselves felt. However stubbornly Bacon insists that his work is essentially aesthetic, and should be judged as pure painting by aesthetic criteria, it is equally clear that the theme of his masterly paintings is man as an endangered species. Damaged life and damaged reality are invoked by painting techniques. The horrified and the horrifying, the destroyed and that which can be destroyed, exploited man and gutted animals are not presented with evil joy, but are somehow inherent in the subject of the work. Recognition includes self-recognition; not only the world of the picture, but reality itself is fragmentary and distorted. Bacon, at home in the world above and in the world below, tells nothing but the truth, whether he uses Van Gogh, his friends or himself as an object – and the truth is something desperate. His fears are all our fears.

The "Painting" of 1971 – the first version is in the New York Museum of Modern Art – shows a fashionably-dressed figure in front of the "cross" of an animal which has been torn open; from time immemorial an artist's synonym for brutality and destruction. The figure, with distorted features and bleeding mouth, sits under the most banal of everyday properties, an umbrella. The railing, on which raw lumps of meat are impaled, isolates the human form like the Popes sitting in cages, which this artist also painted. In contrast to the earlier version, Bacon has formalized the shallow perspective of the "stage" and the background of the picture still further, while the movement of the figures is more intensely in evidence. This procedure creates artistic distance, which makes the intolerable tolerable, and the incomprehensible into a comprehensible pictorial metaphor.

Only Rudolf Hausner, the oldest of the Viennese "Fantastic Realists," pupils of the painter-writer Albert Paris Gütersloh, has remained a serious subject for artistic discussion. The virtuoso and allusive mannerism of the others – from Arik Brauer to Ernst Fuchs – is more on the level of high-class entertainment. Hausner's dominant theme is pictorial self-exploration. "Adam, Eve and Child" (1974/75) clearly shows a meditating and a sleeping adult and above them the smiling child,

146

Matta (Roberto Matta Echaurren), *Nude in a Group,* 1965

balancing a little playground with trees, ball and bobbin (Hausner's mother was a tailoress) on his forehead. The seated Adam wears a sailor suit as symbol of a dual longing: for childhood and for water, on which – as Hausner himself has put it – Odysseus floats towards his Penelope. The figure has his finger on a picture which indicates the mystery of existence in its mixture of earthly and heavenly material.

Truth instead of Reality
Realism after the First World War

Franz Marc said with reference to the explosive, Abstract Expressionist pictures of Kandinsky's "genius period" that they were the sort of pictures which should have been painted before the war, in order to set constructive order against the chaos to come. The realistic painters of the twenties had a quite different point of view. For them aesthetic formalism had run its course for the time being: it seemed like a withdrawal

into lack of commitment. They were concerned to unmask the times and their contemporaries by hard realism driven to the point of caricature, as practised in the early work of Otto Dix and by the young George Grosz. While Dix remained a remorseless analyst without illusions, Grosz was politically and ideologically engaged: as is well known, this engagement led to disillusionment and withdrawal.

There is an excellent example of a ruthlessly sincere portrait by the veristic Dix in the Ludwig Museum. The picture of his brother-in-law "Dr. Hans Koch" in his surgery is – stylistically and chronologically – of the first rank. The picture is painted with outstanding technique, modelled on the great portraitists of the Renaissance. The very precise representation of foreground, middle ground and background and the connection of the person with the tools of his trade are almost reminiscent of Hans Holbein, if the portrait were not so vicious, aggressive and ironic: the coolly psychological diagnosis of the painter presents the doctor almost as a caricature of himself; the instruments and their sur-

Francis Bacon, *Painting 1946* (Second Version), 1971

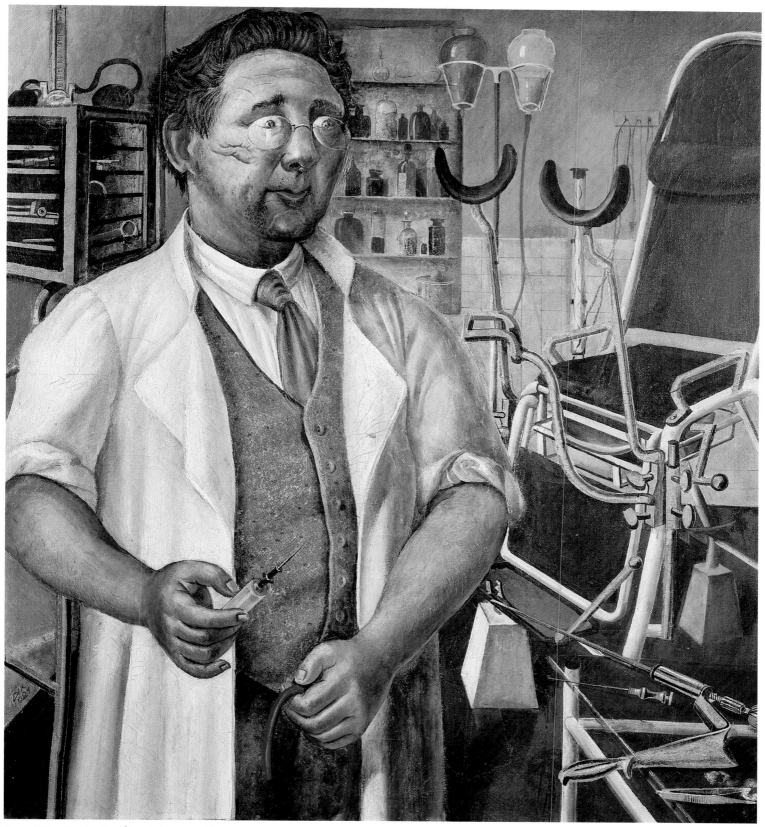

Otto Dix, *Portrait of Dr. Hans Koch,* 1921

Otto Dix, *Self-Portrait,* 1931

roundings are of a coldness which almost makes the grotesque an active threat.

The painter's self-portrait is as remorselessly sincere ("Self-Portrait", 1931). The analyst fixes the onlooker with deepset eyes under beetling brows. As in the picture of his brother-in-law, the props (easel, canvas, palette, paintbrush) give hints about the subject and his occupation, and at the same time make a framework for the picture and define the space. The painting technique is a little softer in this picture, painted ten years later; the sharpness and obsession with detail of the veristic early phase have faded. The crystal ball at the lower edge of the picture points to elements beyond the superficially visible.

George Grosz, *Dr. Eduard Plietzsch,* 1928

Otto Dix, *Portrait of Theodor Däubler,* 1927

Between these two works lies – again both chronologically and stylistically – the monumental "Portrait of Theodor Däubler". It shows the long-haired, bearded prophet's head and the voluminous forms of the poet's Expressionist visions, backed with the archaic architecture of the Academy on the Brühlsche Terrasse in Dresden. Däubler is sitting on a chair, which threatens to collapse under the weight of his body. The element of caricature, which one continually meets in the work of Dix, is less sharp here – sympathetic, and ironic in a friendly way. This is expressed in the soft, warm tonal-

150

ity of the picture. Anyone who is familiar with the huge, contradictory œuvre of the rhapsodic Däubler, swinging from expressive ecstasy to a Romanesque sense of form, will recognize that Dix has painted the writing as well as the writer in his picture.

There is not much of the aggression of the Dada critic of his times and bourgeois-baiter George Grosz in the portrait of the art historian "Dr. Eduard Plietzsch" (1928), just a certain almost amiable irony, like that in the Däubler portrait by Otto Dix, whom Grosz admired as a portraitist. The pointed precision of the veristic, pre-1925 pictures is replaced by softer and more fluent colour and form, with only a hint of caricature.

In the Rhineland, Carlo Mense, who came of age artisti-

Carlo Mense, *Portrait of H. M. Davringhausen,* 1922

cally among the Expressionists, turned temporarily to a cool version of "Magic Realism" which had, in contrast with veristic painting, a scarcely concealed classicistic component. This probably stems from the influence of Italian colleagues of the "valori plastici" group. It is these very "plastic values" which, combined with painting precision, lend distinction to the portrait of the somewhat distant but attentive artist and colleague Heinrich M. Davringhausen (1922), set in front of the empty, desolate background of suburbia.

Anton Raederscheidt's "Portrait of the Bishofs" (1923) is thematically close to the Davringhausen portrait, even though the painting is looser and less obsessed with detail. The sadness of the figures, who are walking arm in arm, but turning away from each other, is sharpened by the portrayal of the loneliness in each other's company of the autocratic man and melancholy woman, who, as it were, "steers him through the picture" (Raederscheidt). The motif of enmity between the sexes, which continually concerned the painter, runs like a basso continuo through his work.

Ludwig Ronig is a gentler, unaggressive exponent of "Neue Sachlichkeit", to which he lends quasi-Romantic traits. The "Lay Figure" (1930), falling to pieces as a symbol of transience, shows this in its reticent colouring, as does the still, inward-looking portrait of Liane Benner (1927).

Georg Schrimpf, the Munich artist, finally abandoned city life altogether and sought his subjects in the alleged innocence of nature. This return to the idyllic is characterized formally by coherently stylized Neo-Classicism. Schrimpf eschews individuality and details, and expresses himself by means of balanced compositions, in precise outline and three-dimensional form. Time seems to stand still in these pastoral scenes, which are of an artlessness out of tune with their times ("Swineherd" and "Girl at the Window", both 1923).

Georg Schrimpf, *Girl at the Window,* 1923

Renato Guttuso, *Caffè Greco,* 1976

Franz Radziwill's representations of the terror of the city are diametrically opposed to Schrimpf's idylls ("The Street", 1928). The empty street and the fortress-like, hostile architecture are somehow threatening. The sky is dark. Points of light and an aeroplane seem to prophesy impending doom, which was indeed soon to be visited upon towns and cities.

The line of realistic-veristic painting is continued most clearly to the present day by the work of Renato Guttuso. His artistic, political and socio-critical influence on the younger Realists is enormous, but even contemporary painters like Jörg Immendorff have been very much concerned with him. Immendorff's "Café-Deutschland" series would not have been possible without the inspiration of Guttuso's "Caffè Greco" (1976), however different the end products may be in

◁ Franz Radziwill, *The Street,* 1928

both style and content. The Café Greco is at the same time a real and an imaginary room, in which Guttuso meets real and imaginary people: Japanese tourists, Swedish girls, a lesbian couple, but also Giorgio de Chirico, André Gide, Buffalo Bill and Marcel Duchamp's hand holding a cigar. Reality and dream melt into a "collage" of realistic and fantasy painting.

Revolutionary and Traditionalist
The Works of Pablo Picasso

So far Pablo Picasso, the most important painter and sculptor of the century, has only been mentioned in the context of Cubism. There is a reason for this. The Spaniard's inner independence and ability to change make it impossible to attach a particular label to him. There is hardly a style, hardly a technique, on which he has not made a decided impact. Whatever he touches, whether it be the European masters of the past, Ingres, Delacroix, Velázquez or Cranach the Elder, Classicism or Surrealism, collage or sculpture in iron, which he invented – again always ahead of his fellow-countryman by a nose – with Julio González: he is always the first, and almost always the greatest as well. His imagination and staying power, which did not forsake him in old age, raise him well above his contemporaries. In

Pablo Picasso, *Woman with Mandoline,* 1910

Pablo Picasso, *Harlequin,* 1923

every guise he remains himself. However bold the experiment he does not lose his balance, stays on his fulcrum.

These qualities make him a classicist, however unclassical his dramatic gestures and the passionate expressiveness of large parts of his œuvre may be. Picasso is the painter and sculptor dramatist of this century. He is the creator of the most penetrating of artistic indictments of inhumanity: "Guernica" (1937), the expressive-realistic and at the same time emblematic-symbolic representation of the first air raid on the civilian population of a town.

The fragmentary, incomplete quality of many of his pictures allows a lot of freedom to make associations within the conscious openness. Just like the unbelievable productivity of the artist, his inventiveness, his continual testing of new forms and new means of expression, it shows that in the twentieth century there are no once-and-for-all solutions. In the last resort, what is incomparable in his work is the combination of innovation and tradition. This tireless experimenter is at the same time a great traditionalist. "I do not seek, I find," is his most famous saying. And so he

Pablo Picasso, *Mandoline, Fruitbowl, Marble Fist,* 1925

adopts what he finds – from negro sculpture to Dela-croix's "Woman of Algiers" – to subject it to his own formative will and transform it into something new, into something "unanticipated, of which one had no previous conception." The revolutionary Picasso was at the same time a late-born old master. There are excellent examples of many of the most important phases in the work of this artist in the Ludwig Museum. There are no pictures from the "blue" and "pink" periods, but the little bronze "Head of a Picador" (1903) already shows the mastery of the 22-year-old. The "Woman with Mandoline" (1910) represents Analytic Cubism, the "Harlequin" (1923) the relaxed calm of the Neo-Classical period, in which Picasso, under the influence of Cocteau, seemed to have broken with Cubism once and for all. The still life "Mandoline, Fruitbowl, Marble Fist" (1925) is a work of monumental reticence, and in its relief-like surface roughness and quiet, tuneful tonality it combines the harmonious balance of a composition on an emphatically two-dimensional plane, hinting at space only in the background, with a stronger reference back to the world of concrete

appearance. The "Vanitas" picture, inspired by histori-cal models, stands between the Neo-Classical and the quasi-Surrealist categories of Automatism and the unconscious, which he could not accept because of his lifelong inclination to the world of the senses, and to his unconquerable delight in conscious structuring. "Guernica" is not the only picture which shows that for him art was a part of life, and had to face up to reality, and that he was never tempted to withdraw into ivory towers beyond reality. The pictures painted during the war also show this clearly. One of the masterpieces of this difficult period is the "Woman with Artichoke" (1942), a symbol of deformed, oppressed, suffering man, who nevertheless retains his inviolable dignity. It is not by chance that Picasso's companion of the time, Dora Maar, was the model for this picture. The detached statuesqueness of Egyptian sculpture, pre-classical Greek art, and also the hieratic austerity of Byzantine Madonnas are the historical models Picasso makes into an exemplary picture for our time by means of a power of creative transformation that was uniquely his. In both the painting and formal fields he

Pablo Picasso, *Woman with Artichoke,* 1942

Pablo Picasso, *Île de la Cité – View of Notre-Dame de Paris,* 1945

applies the experience of his Cubist years in an unorthodox fashion. The alternation of viewpoint from full face to profile is an example of this. But the contemporary reference points beyond itself, the picture becomes a metaphor of permanent validity. The artichoke is at the same time sceptre and weapon: an indication of the range of meaning and profundity of perspective of the work. The clearly articulated colour and shapes are outlined with precision; they become weaker and dissolve towards the edge of the picture. The background is not completely painted, but sensitively shaded, allowing the canvas background to shimmer through: incompleteness is a determining element of the picture.

The only thing which the cityscape painted in the winter of 1945, "Île de la Cité – View of Notre-Dame de Paris," has in common with the "Woman with Artichoke" is the use of Cubist elements which have been developed further. In the Paris picture they become more strongly geometrical and prismatically united. The cool bluish-grey tonality of the picture and the compelling logic of its formal construction give it a harmonious classicality – an artistic point of repose in troubled times.

The beautiful "Head of a Woman Reading" was painted

eight years later. The meditative absorption of the woman gives the picture its open, uncramped atmosphere. The austere geometry is enlivened by the "Cubist" alternation of front and side view, undramatic on this occasion, by the free play of ornamental forms and by that light-hearted colouring which one so often comes across in the late work of the painter. The "Melon Eaters" (1967) and the "Musketeer and Cupid" (1969) show the artist, well over eighty years old, in full possession of his rich painting faculties. With sovereign virtuosity he runs the gamut of many decades of experience with colour and form. He is quite happy to quote himself as his own interpreter and commentator on occasions: glowing gaiety, cheerful irony and radiant colour in "Musketeer and Cupid", cryptic eroticism and a touch of the demonic in the muted tones of the "Melon Eaters". The Aachen art historian Adam C. Oellers writes: "Picasso's late painting is characterized by formal richness and intoxicating joie de vivre," and indeed these pictures are extraordinarily fresh, without a trace of tiredness or failing imaginative depth. What the older Picasso has overcome are superficial tendencies towards the avant-garde. But that was a course he never really embarked on. His invention came not from intention, but from plentiful

Pablo Picasso, *Head of a Woman Reading*, 1953

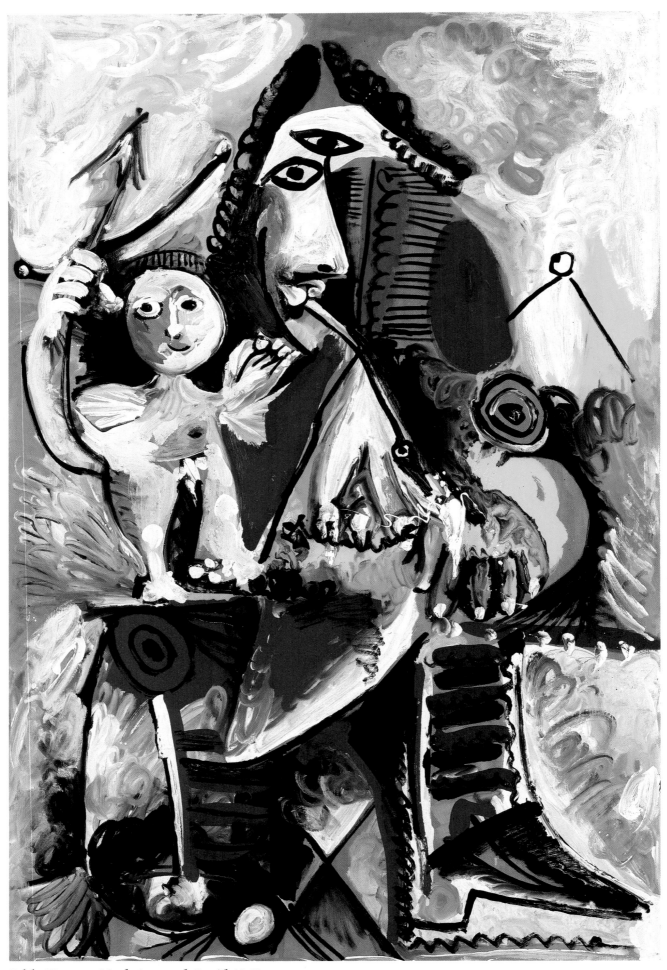

Pablo Picasso, *Musketeer and Cupid,* 1969

Pablo Picasso, *Melon Eaters,* 1967

reserves. In a quite different way from that of Matisse, Picasso's opulent late work, understandably uneven in quality, has its own significance, which has not yet been fully recognized.

The Unknown in Art
Abstract Painting after 1945

All dictators, whether of the right or of the left, have persecuted and repressed abstract art. After the Second World War it was rehabilitated in a triumphant fashion. If earlier pictures without subjects had been "flickers of freedom," they now became the Esperanto of fine art, a pictorial language which seemed to permit understanding across all borders and cultural barriers. "In our day," said a distinguished publication as late as 1962, "revolutions are not fought any more. The time of programmes and manifestos, the time of the artistic barricades is past. Art has [...] lost its ideological

character." The widespread desire for a return to reality by artists is seen to be an empty bubble. Shortly after that, Pop Art came to Europe – the foundations had been laid long since in America – and with it "reality" and the "picture object." It would be foolish to chaff the experts of the time about this. Art always jumps in a different direction to the one you anticipate.

The international abstract "Ecole de Paris" dominated the scene until well into the sixties, its place finally being taken by "Informel" in Europe and "action painting" in America. France celebrated the rebirth of "peinture" in the "tradition française." Bazaine, Manessier, Soulages, but also the German exile Hans Hartung, the Russians Sergei Poliakoff and Nicolas de Staël – the latter only semi-abstract – were the leading names among many others who have since been forgotten. In Germany Willi Baumeister and E. W. Nay restored contact with the international scene. Baumeister's writings on "The Unknown in Art" became the bible of abstract artists and their apologists. Today the products of those years have slimmed themselves back to health.

Jean Bazaine, *The Diver,* 1949

Pierre Soulages, *Painting,* 1964

The frippery has fled, and the substantial has stayed with us.

Jean Bazaine is perhaps the most cultivated of the painters in the "French tradition." There are always objective memories underlying his abstract pictures, whether they are of landscapes or figures. This is also true of the "Diver" (1949). Human being and nature merge indistinguishably, material dissolves in the light of colour. Bazaine's goal is to make visible "the pervasiveness, the great common structure, this great similarity between man and the world." The organization of his pictures is reminiscent of stained glass, which he had studied to his profit.

The painting of Pierre Soulages is quite different; his heavy black bands of paint are reminiscent of branches and trees, but also of the beams in Romanesque churches. Colour, still "Impressionistically" lightened in the work of Bazaine, is increasingly reduced by Soulages to silent black before light backgrounds. The gesture remains dynamic, but also shows great reticence ("Painting", 1964).

It was Alfred Manessier's ambition to set a personal abstract sign-world in the spirit of our times against the old religious symbols. His closeness to stained glass (he created the stained glass windows for St. Gereon in Cologne in 1964) shows clearly in the colour and structural organization of his picture "The Fire" (1957).

Sergei Poliakoff's pictures ("Composition", 1952) were for a time described as "abstract icons." They were influenced by Delaunay and the Cubists, but also by the coloured "building bricks" of the German Otto Freundlich ("Green-Red", 1939), who was living in Paris at the time. The filigree dream cities of the Portuguese Vieira de Silva on the other hand, with their floating high-level railway and metro stations and docks ("The Docks", 1953) are completely under the spell of a brand of hallucinatory Surrealism. Nicolas de Staël, the painter of the famous "Footballers" and the festive "Figure on the Beach", which has become a glowing red pictorial cipher, made a conscious return to objectivity at the end of his short life and struggled desperately to include the experience of his abstract paintings in his "New Realities". The bright colours of the apparently serenely floating "Shelf", dating from the last year of De Staël's life (1955), are, in treatment and the almost belligerent application of paint with brush and palette knife, living proof of the artist's fight to find the truth behind reality. Because he believed that he could never achieve it and would make no further progress as an artist, he committed suicide in desperation.

The work of two other artists, the German Hans Hartung and the Franco-Canadian Jean-Paul Riopelle, was of greater consequence for art after the "Ecole" than either De Staël's work, which remained a fragment, or his tragic life.

160

Otto Freundlich, *Green – Red,* 1939

Nicolas De Staël, *The Shelf,* 1955

Alfred Manessier, *The Fire,* 1957

Maria-Helena Vieira da Silva, *The Port,* 1953

The German, who grew up with Dresden Expressionism, soon found his way to abstract painting. But it was not until after the war, in which he lost a leg as a soldier in the foreign legion, that he became known in Germany. Technical brilliance and a sense of poetry, rationality and spontaneity form an unusual combination in his work. His tersely titled pictures ("T 55-3", 1955, "T 56-21", 1956) are psychograms, representations of emotional conditions, noted down in excited and expressive or meditative brush work. The theme of painting as writing is brought up to date by the independent inclusion of calligraphic elements in his work. Because of this Hartung, along with Wols, was one of the greatest initiators of the "Informel".

Riopelle came to abstract painting via Surrealism, not from Expressionism. His work, too, has its place between the "Ecole de Paris" and the "Informel", with references to the vitality of action painting. The paintings have no limitations, the colours and structure are not subject to any formal principle of composition, and thrust beyond the edge of the picture. Paint is applied powerfully, sometimes passionately, with a broad brush. Broad paths are drawn through the fields of colour with a palette knife ("Meeting", 1956), or thin threads of colour in small pieces are used to make small, dense, "Informel" net structures ("Star Dress", 1952). The universality of logical abstract painting is expressed in magnificent colour in pictures of this kind.

More important than his geometrical abstractions based on Constructivism are the serial works of Victor Vasarély, who was born in Hungary. They are the artistic result of the application of his own principle of replacing "craftsman technique" with "industrial technique," "personal language" with "universal language," and thus transforming "egocentric ethics" into "community ethics." This was an enormously powerful influence on "ars multiplicata", kinetic art and "Op Art" (with the Englishwoman Bridget Riley as its wittiest exponent). "Calota MC" (1965–67) is a typical work of the transition from the individual work to the series. Willi Baumeister found his own formal language by coming to terms with Cézanne, with Cubism (particularly in Fernand Léger's version), with the cave paintings of Altamira, with African rock pictures, and with Aztec and Babylonian art ("Epic of Gilgamesh"). He was important in German art as an artistic example, but also as a theoretician and above all as an outstanding teacher, especially after 1945. His pedagogic influence was just as great as that of his painting. Even in the early phases of the "Wall Pictures" for an intended building (c. 1920), he had developed the technique of roughening the surface of the picture with sand: only a step away from the "material picture." The archaistic "Standing Figure with Blue Plane" (1933) belongs in

Hans Hartung, *T 55-3,* 1955

this category; its artful primitivism is stamped with the Altamira experience. Baumeister's connection with architecture, with "built" shapes, which develop in the course of the painting process and are not "prefabricated," is also expressed in the series of "Form Plans", to which "Stonecutting" (1947) belongs.

In the final years of Baumeister's life he painted cycles of pictures ("Montaru", "Monturi", "Kessaua") which summarized his artistic and spiritual experience. "Montaru" and "Monturi" are under the spell of serious, dominant black formations. In "Monturi I A" (1953/54) the central discus shape is white, and the whole picture is exceptionally in a bright white major key. The disc is set against a rock-like pictorial element on the lower edge of the picture. The glowing colours, the dancing elation of the metaphorical accompanying figures, seem to have been influenced by Miró. "Kessaua on Yellow", dominated by a mysteriously anthropomorphic white figure in the left-hand half of the picture, exercises a strange, compelling magic. Insoluble floating pictorial ciphers move towards the schematic form. This sign-language leaves room for free association by the observer; Baumeister says: "Abstract shaping of the human mind is open to the transcendental."

Unlike Baumeister, Ernst Wilhelm Nay, a pupil of Hofer and then of Munch, bears the stamp of Expressionism. The stages of his development, right up to the free

Hans Hartung, *T 56-21,* 1956

Jean-Paul Riopelle, *Meeting*, 1956

Victor Vasarely, *Calota MC,* 1965–67

Willi Baumeister, *Standing Figure with Blue Plane,* 1933

Willi Baumeister, *Stonecutting,* 1947

Willi Baumeister, *Monturi, Diskus I A,* 1953/54

166

Willi Baumeister, *Kassaua on Yellow*, 1955

Ernst Wilhelm Nay, *Woman in the Taunus*, 1939

colour forms of his final years, can be followed almost without a single gap in the Ludwig Museum. The "Woman in the Taunus" (1939) is stylistically close to the Lofoten pictures of the lives of fishermen, painted while in exile in Norway. The recumbent nude is almost trifling as a motif, and the picture is structured austerely, with rhythmic ornamental movement. Natural forms, mountains and clouds, are no longer likenesses, but pictorial elements. Nay's palette unfolds even more lavishly in the magnificent colour-form orchestration of the "Hecate" period between 1945 and 1948, to which "Jacob's Ladder" (1946) belongs. Nay's understanding of colour as a form in its own right is clearly manifested in these pictures, despite the differentiated, allusive composition. The same is true of the "Girl's Head" of 1947 and its ornamental structure with internal shapes in small sections.

Once these associations had been established it was a relatively small step to the complete elimination of

Ernst Wilhelm Nay, *Blue Flood,* 1961

objective references. This step is taken in the picture "Rhythms Blue and Red"; the title also demonstrates the strong relationship of Nay's understanding of colour/form to music. The "rhythm" of both colour and form is clearly recognizable to the "reading" observer. In the subsequent "Disc Pictures", colour chromaticism finally comes of age in the logical emphasis on the two-dimensional quality of the picture ("Dark Sound", 1956, "Ecstatic Blue" and "Blue Flood", both 1961). The artist describes his procedure firmly as a "system of technique for setting colour." The floating, peaceful movement of the coloured discs is later opened up by expressive movement and dissolution of the closed circular form, by means of script cross-hatching, until in his final years the artist turns to emphatically two-dimensional pictorial symbols in economical, reticent, almost stark arrangements of laconic simplicity.

Fritz Winter studied at the Bauhaus under Kandinsky and Klee; the latter's influence can be seen in the famous series "Motive Powers of the Earth". With Nay, Hartung, Hubert Berke (who was also a pupil of Klee), Rupprecht Geiger, Emil Schumacher and others they founded the Munich group "Zen 49" in 1949, a group which was to be very important for German art after the Second World War. "Nocturnal Rain" (1952) is a characteristic example of Winter's always somewhat melancholy, thick-blooded painting, using calm forms with no direct relationship to the visible world, searching with a tinge of Romanticism for the non-visible behind all things. The work of Theodor Werner, ten

years older than Winter, and now almost forgotten, is characterized by the same artistic metaphysics ("Black, Green, Red", 1951).

Georg Meistermann, one of the few great stained-glass window artists of the period, was and still is a powerful advocate of post-war German art. He had hardly graduated when he also qualified as a "decadent artist." The objective becomes a pictorial emblem in a picture painted when he was in his thirties ("The Painter", which plumbs the depths of the period), a picture of mourning and of self-assertion. The whole of Meistermann is contained in this early picture. He is a painter who understands how to handle line as well as paint; he remains a drawing painter and a painting draughtsman, and, not to be overlooked, the builder and architect of his pictorial plans. "Fish Wanting to Become Bird" (1951) is a picture of the metamorphosis of abstraction and objective reality; it was also a key picture for young Germans after the war who were looking for some contact with what had been happening abroad. "Relief" (1910) shows the austere "pictorial plans" breaking up to become painterly. It also announces a central Meistermann theme for the first time, that of floating. In this case it is coloured rectangles that float in a cleverly disposed pictorial arrangement, stacking unoutlined coloured plans in layers one behind the other; the two-dimensional quality of the picture is thus rendered permeable to space, and it is transformed into a meditation tableau, moving and moved. The art of Joseph Fassbender is more in repose. He engages highly individual graphic and painting tech-

Ernst Wilhelm Nay, *Jacob's Ladder*, 1946

Georg Meistermann, *Fish Wanting to Become Bird,* 1951

Fritz Winter, *Nocturnal Rain,* 1952

Joseph Fassbender, *Untitled,* 1970 ▷

Hann Trier, *Scene of the Crime IV,* 1963

Hann Trier, *Puya I,* 1954

play of space and plane, thickly structured paint and the holding back of colour – structural painting of a high colouristic order, inspired by music and dance. It is no coincidence that action painting, using all physical and psychic reserves, came on the scene almost simultaneously in Europe and America. In the USA the major theme was the violent act of emancipation from European tutelage, under the leadership of Jackson Pollock. In Europe it was partly a revolt against geometry, partly a protest against regimented existence in a civilization which had become boring, and against the affluent society which was beginning to establish itself. The individual, the "human being in revolt," fought against being swallowed up by the collective. Existentialism supplied the necessary patterns of thought.

niques, structural and figurative formulations one within another, in withdrawn, earthy colours. In "Untitled" (1970) labyrinthine forms join to make compositions, the detail full of objective allusions; the constructive framework supplies overall pictorial control. "Dionysos" shows Fassbender's effortless mastery of the larger format.

Like Fassbender, Hann Trier, who is twelve years younger and was encouraged by the older artist, likes to paint ceiling and wall paintings. But, unlike his older friend, Trier is informed with the sense of colour of the great Italians, Veronese in particular, but also Tiepolo and – nearer to our own times – the French artist Pierre Bonnard. The rhythm of his pictures was influenced at an early stage by South American dancing ("Puya", 1954). The theme of movement and its spontaneous transfer to a picture ("Machine Writing", "Painting the Devil on the Wall") for a time appeared to bring Trier close to "Tachism" and the "Informel". But the theme of the labyrinth remained more important for him, the inter-

Wols (Wolfgang Alfred Otto Schulze-Battmann), *The Vowels,* 1950

The leading European figure was Wolfgang Schulze-Battmann, known as Wols. His "Blue Phantom" (1951) is a key picture. In this work the spiral turns again and the painter returns to his fantastic and surreal beginnings. The night face, floating in a ghostly position between becoming and passing away, emerges from a blue ground, and seems like a threatening personification of the artist's fears, which are also the fears of the entire age, without illusions and without hope. The central figure is beginning to decompose at the edges. The agi-

Wols (Wolfgang Alfred Otto Schulze-Battmann), *Blue Phantom,* 1951

Antoni Tàpies, *Grey Relief in Four Parts,* 1963

Antoni Tàpies, *Dream Garden,* 1949

Antoni Tàpies, *White with Pink Sign No. LXXVII,* 1958

Peter Brüning, *Picture No. 108,* 1962

tated scratches in the pigment, leading from the dark, many-eyed "face" to the edges, the long "neck," echoed by two smaller floating forms, all these conjure up the wretched smell of transience. In terms of the history of art this is a model demonstration of the close connection of nocturnal Surrealism with Tachism and Informel.

"Tapestry" (1949) and "The Vowels" (1950) were painted earlier, purged of all objective memories. The painter writes, tears, digs and scratches his feelings into the canvas, spontaneously and without interposing "aesthetic" control. He turns his inner feelings outwards, his ecstasies, his obsessions, his sufferings, his intoxication, his despair: the footprints of his existence. The colours stretch out, disintegrate, scatter in a tissue of illusory lights. His own wounds become a cipher for the "world wound." All this is a far cry from the controlled elegance of Hans Hartung's psychograms.

The painting of the Catalan Antoni Tàpies was origi-

nally also rooted in Surrealism. In the "Dream Garden" (1949), stimuli from oriental pictorial narratives are also assimilated. Later, it is only the use of certain materials (sand, wood, paper, glue) and techniques (perforation, imposition of surface relief) which indicates these origins.

The pictorial panels of his mature years are heavy, silent and earnest. Everyday experiences and memories are condensed into pictorial emblems, using simple, elemental form and withdrawn, melancholy colours inclining to the monochrome. Clues are buried in the wall pictures, which are almost partitioned off from the outside world: grooves, seams, beams, eyes and indecipherable "written" ciphers. They invoke ideas of a silent, archaic landscape, but also of injury, death, transience and oblivion. They will not yield up their mystery. In their still, undramatic silence they are as insoluble as the riddle of the world: "Grey Relief" in four parts (1963), "Great Black and Brown Craquelé",

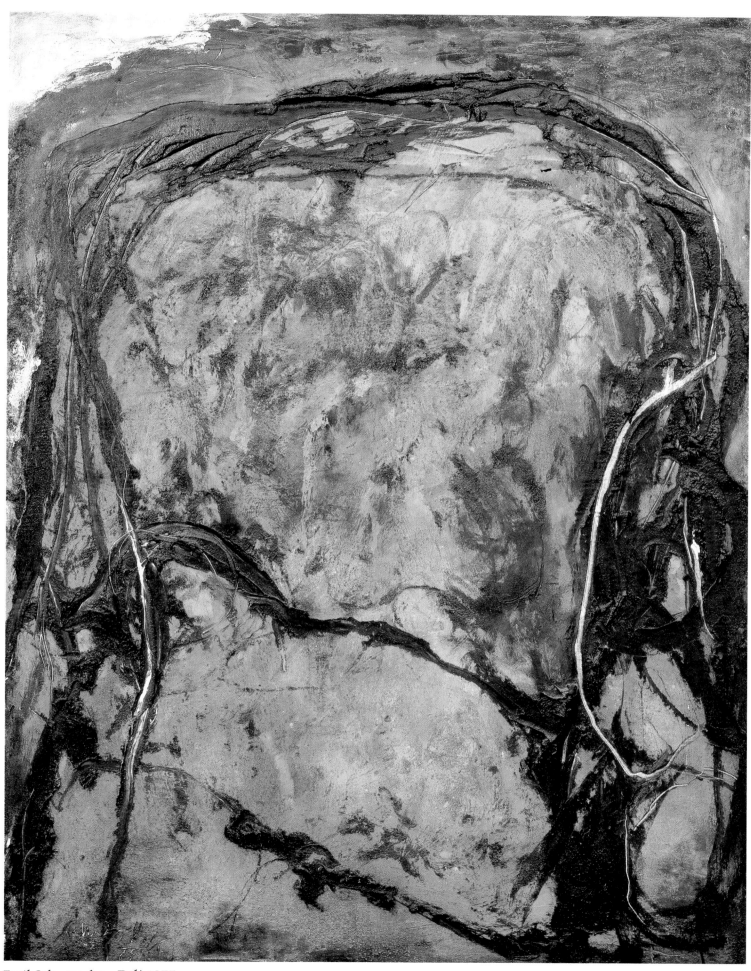

Emil Schumacher, *Deli,* 1975

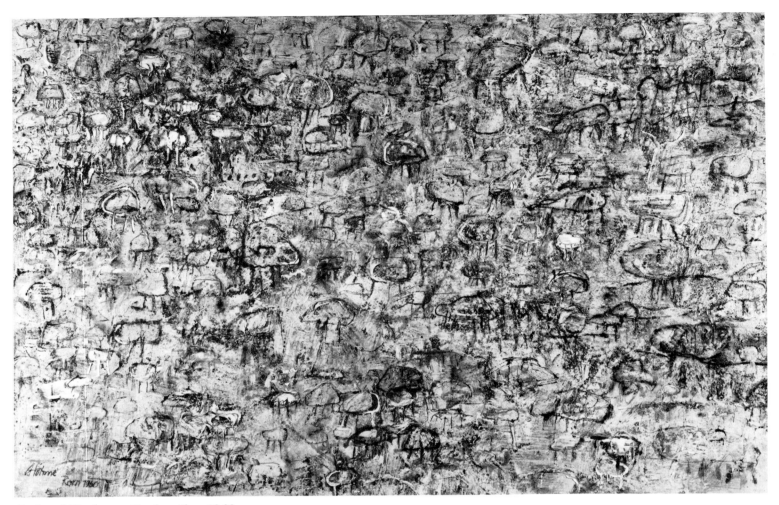

Gerhard Hoehme, *Conjuration,* 1960

Bernard Schultze, *Rubyrr,* 1957/58

"Signs of White Ovals" (both 1966). "White with Pink Sign" (1958) is a transitional work from the period in which Tàpies was starting to build up his personal language in a logical fashion. The action calligraphy of the witty showman Georges Mathieu ("Dana", 1958) is a long way from the existential, philosophically-based seriousness of Tàpies; Mathieu painted effectively and at great speed, and made spectacular public appearances in the fifties – almost a dress rehearsal for the happening.

Unusually, the Germans are far more to the forefront in this field than their French colleagues. Emil Schumacher, Bernard Schultze, Fred Thieler, K. H. Sonderborg, Gerhard Hoehme, K. O. Goetz are still working. Only Peter Brüning died young, but his serial pictures, created in parallel with the musical structures of the period, have lost none of their inspired and spontaneous freshness ("Picture No. 108", 1962). The expressive painting of today probably led to their rediscovery.

Emil Schumacher and Bernard Schultze show the most consistent development, Schumacher in deliberate, carefully thought out steps, Schultze in numerous variations which took his work beyond painting into a third dimension ("Headless Mannequin-Migof", 1967). Schumacher's pictures show a high level of involvement of a powerful personality, who engages mind and

Bernard Schultze, *Migof-Ursula-Family Tree,* 1963

body in a struggle with his material, leaving many clues as to the path taken. The thick material is given poetry and spirituality by the hands which seize hold of it. The dialectic of a ploughed-over painted surface, and graphic marks varying between the powerful and the light and delicate, give tension to these earthy pictures. They have been wrung from his own doubts and despair by a "happy painter" – Schumacher's own view of himself. The process of painting itself, the expression of his own being, becomes the unliterary theme of his artistic thinking. The "traditional compartmental division of body, soul and spirit," as Schumacher's biographer Schmalenbach put it, is removed in these serious pictures, close in their attitude to the work of Antoni Tàpies. This is true of the furrowed geology of the pigment in early pictures like "Yoop" (1963) and for "Deli", the piece of nature dating from twelve years later: "nearer to the Earth than to the stars" (Schumacher).

Bernard Schultze is a very German artist in his inclination to reflection and musing, and even when painting he can be seen to be an excellent draughtsman. His roots reach back to late Gothic via Surrealism, Romanticism and the Danube school. If one explores his pictorial landscapes ("Rubyrr", 1957/58), rich in figures and allusions, one comes across – sometimes in two, sometimes in three dimensions – "fleurs du mal" in poisonous, though sometimes pale, colours ("Migof-Ursula-Family Tree", 1963, "Migof-Parthenon", 1972). It is no coincidence that the Symbolists Baudelaire and Rimbaud, or eschatological poets like the Austrian Georg Trakl, are among the favourite creative artists of this inventor of an unfathomable fairy-tale world, who writes as well as paints. The old vanity motif appears in a new formulation drawn from the consciousness of a culture in its last days, and from the hallucinating mind of a late-born Alexandrian.

Karl Otto Götz, *Picture of 14. 09. 1954*, 1954

In Schultze's pictures the aesthetic of the ugly is extracted from the spirit of our times and set against the glittering world of visions of our threatened culture. "The earth might be uninhabited," says Krapp in Beckett's one-man play "Krapp's Last Tape". And Bernard Schultze states pertinently: "I am sure that nature will continue, it will grow and luxuriate as it does in my pictures, even if one day there are no more men."

Gerhard Hoehme's works "Conjuration" and "Ornamental Solemnity" have already abandoned unrestrained colour and the lack of concern for any formal elements. Structural arrangement once more underpins the picture. What have remained are a tendency to spill beyond the confines of the picture and the principle of accumulation. Pigment is also used as a means of creating relief, and transforms itself perceptibly into light. Hoehme met the American Cy Twombly in Rome, and like him drew inspiration from scribbled drawings on walls. The results are entirely different, however. Hoehme pulls together the thickly applied paint with graphic nets. Such pictures have to be "read." For, he says, "pictures are not on the canvas, they are inside people."

The dynamic works of K. O. Götz ("Picture of 14. 09. 1954") are produced in seconds. The basis of the process of realization is the Surrealist recipe: "Seize the miracle by the forelock by psychic automatism and paroxysm." Götz works in three phases. First, the pattern is sketched on a light background with dark, fluid paint. Then new tracks are made with a rubber applicator. Light and dark areas are mixed, splashes which occur by "controlled chance" are left as they are. A clean paintbrush is then drawn through the pigment while it is still wet, to establish structure. The high level of risk means a ratio of 15 or 20 to 1 between rejection and extinction on the one hand, and success and acceptance on the other.

The fantastic and ghostly early picture of the "Girlfriends" (1959), showing equal elements of Surrealism and Informel, occupies an exceptional place in the otherwise merely elegant and fashionable work of the highly erotic Paul Wunderlich. The technical virtuosity of the artist has not yet become an end in itself. "Violet Red, Vertical" (1961) is an urgent example of the early work of Arnulf Rainer, who is already possessed

178

Arnulf Rainer, *Violet Red, Vertical,* 1961

Jean Dubuffet, *The Dog on the Table,* 1953

by the themes of extinction, transience and death. This is true of his overpainted grimaces, his masks, and the expressive body language work, as well as the over-paintings, which bear the stamp of deep scepticism and eschatological melancholy of Austrian origin: "Painting comes into being to absorb, devalue and inter painting," as the artist himself said in 1962. But the dominating colours and traces of subjective handwriting remain visible, darkness leaves only a little corner available to light. To this extent "Violet Red, Vertical" is related to the Informel. In its attitude of contemplation, and the slow, reflective painting process of covering up and making invisible, it also comes close to other tendencies, from so-called monochrome painting to "Colour-Field Painting".

Superficially, H. E. Kalinowski's leather boxes and "ensachements" using old materials have nothing in common with the Informel, but in their taciturn, magically charged seriousness, their double meaning of protective casing and aggressive existence as objects, they are spiritually related to the early work of Tàpies ("Nocturnal Refuge", 1969).

The ever-changing work of Jean Dubuffet occupies an exceptional place in the art of the second half of the century. He did not turn to painting until he was forty, stimulated by the pictures of the naive school, but above all by the scribbled drawings of children and lunatics, and by coarse graffiti on suburban walls and in urinals. In protest against academicism he inaugurated "art brut" ("coarse art"), which introduced the epoch of Tachism and the Informel.

The "Street with Men" (1944) and also "The Dog on the Table" (1953) are good examples of this spontaneous, anti-aesthetic painting. Primitive drawn figurations and fragments of writing are written into the viscous paint with a vigorous delight in narrative, and with perspective which alters quite unconcernedly. In "Street with Men" the countryside is the subject, and in "The Dog on the Table" the questionable nature of affluent domesticity. Dubuffet's naiveté is of course put on; in fact, his cryptically ironic pictures question, sceptically but urgently, both reality and our understanding of it. Even in later phases of his work Dubuffet's sarcastic humour is expressed very originally, even though the

Jean Dubuffet, *The Street with Men,* 1944

Jean Dubuffet, *Portable Landscape,* 1968

uncompromisingly aggressive anti-aestheticism of the early works seems to have been toned down ("The Old Man in the Desert", 1955, "The Legend of the Steppe", 1961). Elements of draughtsmanship and graphics determine the structure of the picture, the "Informel" is brought into more pronounced rhythmic and compositional balance. Experience with lithographs and ink prints in the fifties is brought into the picture. The colour of the fairy-tale bright figurations, disintegrating like cells, in "The Legend of the Steppe" anticipate the cellular writing of the "Hourloupe" pictures, in which the real appearance of objects is subordinated to an invented, ornamental pattern.

It is only a step from here to the translation of this new formal language into the third dimension. The "Portable Landscape" (1968) sets limits to the limitless, subjective experience replaces objective reality, the real world is translated into a system of invented emblems in individual colouring. The secret demonism hidden behind the sarcasm of the early Dubuffet pictures dissolves into ironic gaiety.

An artist of great originality and imagination who does not fit into any historical pigeon-hole is Ursula (Schultze-Blum), the wife of the painter Bernard Schultze, but as a painter and maker of objects quite independent of him, the embodiment of the phrase "self-made woman." Her partly fairytale, partly deeply mythic world is by no means innocuous. Even the subjects ("The Great Cupboard of Pandora", 1966) point to the fact that beauty and death, sensuousness and transience are related. It is no coincidence that Jean Dubuffet, the high priest of "art brut", recognized the extraordinary talent of this self-taught artist, and the cryptic quality of her tension-filled and contradictory work at an early stage. Her chests and little boxes, lined in fur and filled with objets trouvés, are the secular continuation of the mediaeval tradition of pious reliquaries, richly decorated, full of beauty, but also full of hidden dangers. A similar duality, in decoration of feathers and fur, is the partly cheerful and bright, partly cryptic and demonic self-portrait "C'est moi" (1966), while the narrative vigour of the "Cologne Picture" (1972) transposes the city of Romans, churches and saints into an indeterminate kingdom of fantasy and magic.

Ursula (Schultze-Blum), *Cologne Picture,* 1972

Ursula (Schultze-Blum), *It's Me,* 1966

Action and Meditative Art
From "Cobra" to "Colour-Field Painting"

Between Informel and action painting is the Abstract Expressionism of North-Western Europe, as practised by the "Cobra" group (Copenhagen–Brussels–Amsterdam), founded at the end of the fifties in protest against abstract aesthetic academicism, and art that was politically and socially indifferent. The dominant figure as a personality and as an artist was the Dane Asger Jorn. His painting is also rooted in Surrealism, in the spontaneity of "automatic writing" and the combination of reality and dream. The thematic and artistic influence of the magic world of Nolde's pictures, also, cannot be overlooked. For Jorn, art had to be more than a social game, it had to have an effect on life, and take up a political attitude. In the later years of Jorn's life this view led to intensive contact with the politically active "International Situationists."

The vehemence of the act of painting, the obsessive "painting rage" of Asger Jorn, are unique among postwar European artists. The desire to destroy form, fully developed in the fifties after overcoming a difficult personal crisis, attacks both the detachment of exclusively aesthetic art and the snobbish society at which it is directed. However, Jorn's enormous power shapes

Asger Jorn, *The Blow,* 1962

the explosions of colour into a picture. "Grosskopfeter" is a blown-up, large-mouthed human-animal-being, realized in thickly applied paint and with an anatomy distorted in the manner of a caricature: large head, small body. Jorn's explosive, dynamic painting technique, with colour forms hovering between abstraction and objective reality, is expressed in an exemplary fashion in the mature work "The Blow". The magical and visionary pictorial forms, rising from an agitated sea of colour, are imagined dream figures (Jorn), set against the superficial "reality" of visible appearance. Planes of reality are displaced: the visible word becomes unreal, the unreal dream world becomes the true reality concealed "behind things."

The work of Karel Appel, who was influenced by Jorn, is of a similar kind; he also, in accordance with the tendencies of the period and the anti-aestheticism of the Cobra group, assimilated Dubuffet's "art brut". The "Figure" (1958) grows out of the picture towards the observer, without quite being identifiable. While for Jorn the grotesque has demonic features, in the work of the Dutchman the uncanny is often lightened with brightly ironic wit.

The pictures of Corneille (Cornelis van Beverloo) are calmer in their construction, and closer to the world of the visible and of experience. They show town structures and landscapes, often seen from above: "The White Town" (1955). The experience of flying had opened up new dimensions to artists in those years. The "Bird's Nesting-Place" (1960), painted in refined tones and divided into cells, invokes memories of this kind, suggesting that the painter might have painted the view from the nesting-place itself.

Pierre Alechinsky shows an even more marked departure from the expressive tendencies of the early Cobra years. "Dark Vessel" (1968) demonstrates the replacement of subjective handwriting by objective ornamentation, and the smoothing of the formerly rough surface of the picture, assisted by the use of acrylics, which flow more easily. The dual meaning of the half abstract, half objective figures remains.

American Abstract Expressionism is rooted in the work of the German Hans Hofmann, who emigrated to the USA in the early thirties. For almost 25 years his Hans Hofmann School of Fine Art was an influential centre of training and ideas: thus, a European, schooled by the pre-war Parisian avant-garde, was an important element in the emancipation of American art from European domination. It was not until the fifties that Hofmann detached himself from objective reality, and not until now that the inheritance of Expressionism has fully come through. Colour itself is the actual subject of the picture, form plays a subordinate and subservient role, and only reasserts itself in the later works.

Karel Appel, *Figure*, 1958

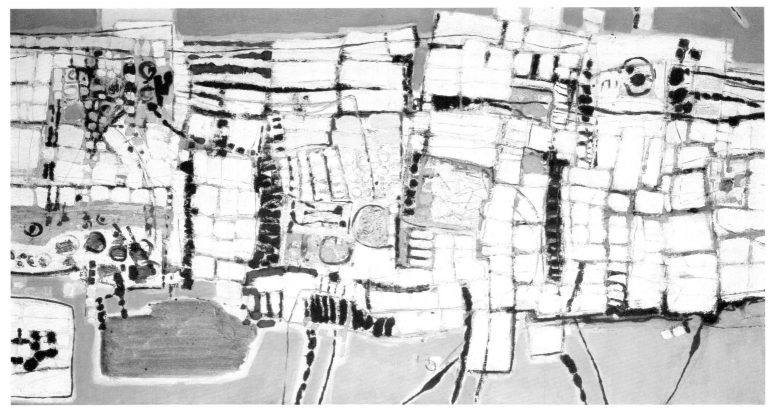

Corneille (Cornelis van Beverloo), *The White Town,* 1955

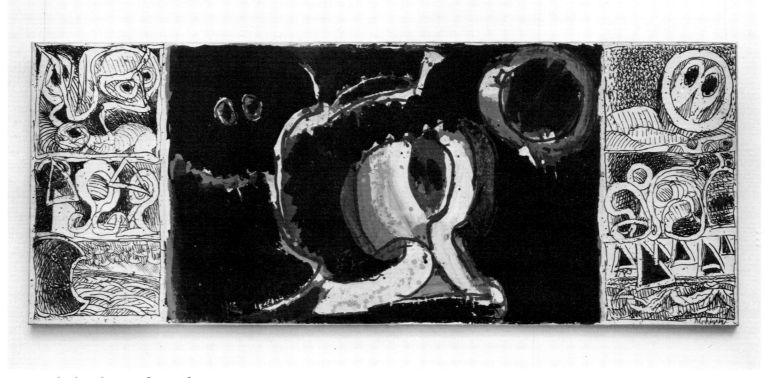

Pierre Alechinsky, *Dark Vessel,* 1968

Hans Hofmann, *Composition No. I*, 1952

Jackson Pollock, *Number 15,* 1951

"Composition No. 1" (1952), although relatively small, is a perfect example of Abstract Expressionism (action painting) as initiated by Hofmann himself. Suggestions of emblematic figurations disintegrate in violent swirls of colour, contrasts are bold and powerful, and the paint, applied on wood, is sometimes thick, sometimes transparent. The agitated "handwriting" expresses emotion quite directly, and without formal restraint. The essential idea is the understanding of colour as an emanation of light. "Colour is itself light," stated the painter. "In nature, colour is created by light. Colour is created by light in a picture." One could say there could have been no Tachist or Informel art without Hofmann, no action painting without Hofmann. This secures a dominant position in the art of the second half of the century for both the painter and his work, regardless of the aesthetic quality of the pictures. After studying under the great regionalist T. H. Ben-

ton and the Mexican revolutionary painter Siqueiros, Jackson Pollock came to Hofmann. Pollock's work represents not only the culmination of action painting, but also the great act of liberation of American artists. "Number 15" is the fifteenth of a total of 22 pictures which the painter showed in late 1951 in the Betty Parsons Gallery: monumental "drawings," painted in synthetic resin on unprimed canvas. Reminiscences of figurations from the early Surrealist period – also inspired by the ideas of Freud's adversary Jung, a lifelong influence of Pollock's thinking – wander through an abstract pictorial world of labyrinthine colour nets, applied with great physical effort and without a compositional centre, forcing their way beyond the edges of the picture. The painting process is executed with great concentration, with the possibility of instant correction, including final decisions about format. "Number 15" is a traditional picture. It is still allusively figurative, supported by abstract arrangement, and shows the obsessive character of Pollock's painting; he frees himself from his inner visions in the painting process itself.

Along with Jackson Pollock, Willem de Kooning, who was born in Rotterdam in 1904 and emigrated to America in 1926, is the most important exponent of the American school of Abstract Expressionism (action painting). His gestural, expressive brushwork is incomparably powerful. De Kooning was at first a figurative painter, but under the influence of Miró and Arshile Gorky, who was a friend of his, he soon turned to abstract work, without ever completely denying that he was stimulated by figure and landscape. In many of his early pictures the representation of unhistorical "landscapes" from his own inner mind, independent of external impressions, is reminiscent of Surreal-

Willem de Kooning, *Untitled VII,* 1984

ism. The more sovereign the painter becomes in handling his materials, the more the pictorial space is determined by spontaneous colour, applied however with great concentration and drama of gesture. De Kooning painted with unflagging imagination until a ripe old age; only the forms become looser and more economical ("Untitled VII", 1984).

The forceful dramatic gestures in the pictures of Franz Kline go back to the vigour of earlier brush-drawings. The painter restricted himself to capriciously shimmering black, and white tending to yellow, the "noncolours" according to Mondrian. It was not until his later years that his palette became more varied; for Kline colour is meaningless, peinture does not interest him. The stature of his pictures is determined by the contrast between movement and counter-movement, reminiscent in the vigour with which they are recorded not only of monumental calligraphy, but also of pro-

cesses in the world of machines. The pictures are "christened" by association. "Scranton" (1960) is the name of a place in Pennsylvania, which may have come into Kline's mind. The artist permits the observer to make his own associations: "I think: When long lines are used, what could they be? The only thing they could be is motorways or buildings or bridges." The

Franz Kline, *Scranton,* 1960

powerful, sometimes violent dynamic of an activist world filled with movement is given form in the gesture of these pictures.

Sam Francis, a pupil of Mark Rothko and Clyfford Still, met the group of Americans in Paris associated with Jean-Paul Riopelle during his stay in France in the early fifties, and was impressed above all by the delicate sense of colour of the late Matisse. His work was strongly influenced by the French approach to colour; in his early phase he preferred monochrome tones. Black and white clumps or clouds of colour, between which traces of running paint remain as a determining element in the picture, cover the canvas, usually large, in arrangements which are irregular but never fail to surprise the observer. Later, Francis increased the intensity of his colour to a powerful glow ("Composition bleu-verte").

Pollock's wife Lee Krasner's picture "Vernal Yellow",

Clyfford Still, *Untitled,* 1948/49

Mark Tobey, *Hurrying Patterns,* 1970

with its blazing colours and its contrast between spirited application of paint and disciplined pictorial organization, is particularly relevant in the context of the "violent" painting of today. In it Lee Krasner draws on the full range of her experience, from Matisse via Hofmann to the work of her husband.

Clyfford Still's work is the meditative variation on action painting. For him, too, painting means self-realization and commitment to a personal, independent world of the imagination. His "trademarks" are jagged forms which recur in a series of new variations, pushing through the surface of the picture like a wedge, or zig-zagging across like lightning. The picture "Untitled" (1948/49), at first glance almost monochrome, in fact consists of calm, graduated colour, effectively accentuated by precisely placed and contrasting red and blue. The controlled emotion of the powerful, layered pictorial presentation, effortlessly mastering the huge format, makes it one of Still's masterpieces.

Like Still, Mark Tobey also belonged to the so-called Pacific School, although he was later to say that he did not know what this was. It is true that all that happened was that a few contrasting artistic temperaments met on the West Coast (Rothko was also one of them), were a source of mutual inspiration and, as it were, prepared themselves for the contribution to American art which was innate in them. Tobey was an outsider; his painting was inspired by calligraphic, Eastern Asian art and thinking. Meditation, not action, is the motive force of his artistic production. The texture of his late work "Hurrying Patterns" (1970) is quite light in comparison with the dense tissue of some of his sensitively rhythmical pictures. The colour is also more intense than in other calligraphic pictures. There is usually a concrete experience behind them, and the meditative reflection of this is automatized in the calligraphic network of free forms.

The nervous, draughtsmanly art of Cy Twombly also stems from Abstract Expressionism, and it too has its thematic roots in Symbolism. In addition, connections with graffiti cannot be overlooked, but their elemental primitivism is reflected intellectually by the artist and transferred into the realm of art – his own art. The very title "Crimes of Passion" (1960) points to Twombly's leitmotiv, love and sexuality. The Marquis de Sade, also a cult figure for the Surrealists, was a spiritual ancestor of this picture. In others, the inspiration is mythology, whether ancient or modern. This artist's expressiveness of line, however, in accordance with his pronounced intellectualism, is by no means as elemental as Pollock's. It is closer to the wounded tension of an artist like Giacometti, although the principle of uncentred composition, spreading over the entire surface of the picture, stems from Pollock's "all over". The

Cy Twombly, *Crimes of Passion,* 1960

hermetic nature of Twombly's elitist work, full of literary and artistic allusions, is shown in the sequence of pictures "Treatise on the Veil" (1968). It is based on a photograph showing a woman in a bridal veil walking to the right, in various stages. Twombly seeks to represent the transience of duration in the emblematic representation of units of passing time in empty space. Edward Kienholz, the man from the West Coast, also started as a painter of almost barbaric vehemence, and this shows in many of his painted environments. Two other components are equally striking: alienation by quasi-surreal means, and the laconic impact of his condensed pictorial imagination, based on concrete, everyday settings and experiences. It makes no differences whether the subject is a bar and its clientele, as in the case of the famous "Beanery", or the memories of a dead woman ("Wait").

The notion of the everyday is important for Pop Art, at least as far as its theoretical basis is concerned. But Kienholz is not content with detached, frigid presentation of people and things. He is a critic, he interprets and comments: "I would first of all never insult this country (America)," he wrote in a reader's letter to a critic, with reference to the "Portable War-Memorial" (1968), "…as I love it perhaps even as well as you. I would, however, in my way presume to change it. My method, as is the method of most artists, is a system of focus and point of view." His work is precisely related to

Edward Kienholz, *The Portable War-Memorial,* 1968

a particular place and to concrete events, and tells stories without words. Kienholz has a striking ability to do
this without going outside art or resorting to literary
borrowings. Extremely complex events and situations
are translated into pictures which leave nothing out.
This range gives a depth and sympathy which are very
close to compassion. Occasionally he approaches the
fringes of Romanticism, and sometimes even sentimentality. Although Kienholz is not a political critic of
society, and also not a polemicist, his works speak so
directly that no-one can avoid their message. He does
not make the invisible visible, he makes the visible
conscious. The result is disconcerting.

The pictorial object "Night of Nights" (1961) makes a
laconic statement: it is the report of the death of a very
young girl in a deserted well, and the failure of all
attempts to rescue her, told in compressed artistic and
poetic pictorial emblems. A ballad-like effect, often a
feature of Kienholz's work, is reduced to a pregnant
formula of compelling urgency.

The famous "Portable War-Memorial" (1968) is based
on an equally famous war photograph of the flying of
the Stars and Stripes after the victory at Iwo Jima and

Edward Kienholz, *Night of Nights,* 1961

192

George Segal, *The Restaurant Window,* 1967

the copy of this in Arlington cemetery, which raises it to heroic levels. The personifications of patriotism, a bellicose Uncle Sam and the "front worker" Kathy Smith, placed in a barrel by Kienholz and stalwartly singing "God Bless America", and the warlike scene of soldiers hoisting the flag, are confronted with the banality of "business as usual" on the right-hand side of the picture – everyday life continues unaffected. Next to this is a black tombstone bearing the names of countries which have been wiped out in the meantime, with spaces for the names of those yet to be wiped out. Inside the heading "Portable War-Memorial" is a space in which to enter the date of the next "victory" day. The soldiers have no heads, and the flag is planted on a plain garden table instead of Mount Suribachi. The visitor buys his bottle of cola from a vending machine and can make himself comfortable (in theory – unfortunately, museum practice does not always allow this) but is jerked out of his relaxation when he suddenly notices that he is sitting by a second tombstone. At its lower end is old Tarzan, shrivelled and radioactive. In front of it sits a plaster dog, the bar has hot dogs for sale. The realism of this work (the artist always works with

realistic properties), which slides into the surreal and ghostly, is intended for use by the visitor. But although Kienholz calmly announces that as far as he is concerned he is happy for his works to be worn out and destroyed, so long as they are well documented, the gallery is obliged to maintain them.

Like Kienholz, Georges Segal also started as a painter. Among his teachers were the great masters of Abstract Expressionism Hans Hofmann and Jackson Pollock. While the artist from the West Coast was moving into three dimensions with his wooden reliefs, the New Yorker Segal was starting to experiment with hessian, wire and plaster. For him, the medium of painting was not real enough to reflect the reality of his own experience. Alan Kaprow, the master of the happening, acted as pacemaker to Segal's method of achieving a high degree of reality by the incorporation of everyday objects from the world of sculpture, specially selected by the artist. Thus, according to Kaprow, the happening became "a stage in the journey from picture to environment."

This new category of the expanding arts was further extended into the realm of sound by the Californian

Stephan von Huene, following the lead of the composer Edgar Varèse and linking up with ideas expressed by Schoenberg and Kandinsky.

Unlike Kienholz, Segal does not paint his figures. He also renounces detail. Thus, he does not create individuals, but a series of human types in everyday situations with which everyone is familiar: "Woman Washing Her Feet in a Sink" (1964/65), "The Restaurant Window" (1967). For these works the people around him, his wife and friends, sat for him in a familiar atmosphere. Everyday events like sitting, walking, washing, drinking coffee are made, without psychological overtones, into sculptural ciphers of human behaviour, of isolation and the loneliness of the individual in a mass society. The white of the plaster shows traces of the artist's shaping hand, but at once removes all superficial and naturalistic references and makes them into "symbols of our existence."

Like the great Austrian artist Alfred Kubin, who for half a century hardly ever left his home in Zwickledt, the American Joseph Cornell also lived in great seclusion. He never went abroad. And just as Kubin could say, "I have Brasil within me," so Cornell could have said that he had the absorbed world of Old Europe within him. But unlike Kubin he did not live on the "other side," where the magicians and demons have their home, but in the "good old days," which he invoked poetically with his relics of imagined memory. The Surrealist "objet trouvé" is given new and lovably fantastic form in his little boxes. All that Cornell had seen of the "Hôtel de l'Océan", an old-style Grand Hotel in Ostend, was the sticker on a globetrotter's case. That was enough to fire his poetic imagination and to conjure a microcosm of found objects into the little box (building bricks, clay pipe, stamps, tin sun and stellar orbits). His montages were as important for America, and Neo-Dada there, as the work of Kurt Schwitters was in Europe.

The Myth of Colour
From Mark Rothko to Yves Klein

It took a long time for Mark Rothko, an American painter of Eastern Jewish origin, to find his personal brand of artistic expression: "abstract icons" with their simple, floating rectangular forms dissolving at the edges and placed before a background of boundless space ("Earth and Green", 1955). Rothko had his confrontation with Surrealism, as did his friends the Abstract Expressionists. But his way did not lead to action, but to meditation. His monumental coloured figures require concentration and submersion in their silent, sacred dignity. After the interim phase of the Surrealist pictures, which invoke a fantastic submarine world, he abandons symbolism, allegories and historical reminiscences. There is no obstacle inserted between us and colour space, struggling to burst through the edges of the picture, and filled with floating internal forms: the picture admits the observer.

The controlled drama of Rothko's work is unthinkable without the Jewish world of his imagination and experience, and also his sense of the wide-open spaces of the American landscape. His works are variations on the theme of "infinity." But the ecstatic leap beyond the bound of space is subject to rational control. To the need for new myths Rothko gave the glow of his colour, consciously avoiding sharp contrasts, and the gentle force of his spare forms, hanging in the picture

Joseph Cornell, *Hôtel de l'Océan*, 1959/60

Mark Rothko, *Earth and Green*, 1955

194

Barnett Newman, *Midnight Blue,* 1970

like veils of the temple, shaped to satisfy the need for new myths. He proved that religious art, beyond the limits of denomination, is still possible today.

The same is true of Barnett Newman. His night piece "Midnight Blue" (1970) proves it. The beautiful even blue of the surface, bordered on the left by a strip of white, and divided on the right by a turquoise "zip" without a beginning or an end, gives pictorial presence to the "sublime," the "exalted" – for Newman the decisive category. The experience is not the same as it is with Rothko's painting, where the observer has the experience of penetrating the coloured space from a distance; here he has to stand close and allow himself to be enclosed by the colour, and leave the world of experience behind him as he meditates.

Brice Marden picks up this line of thought. Cutting across the tendency of his times, almost romantically, he compares the role of the artist with that of the priest, a mediator between man and myth. "Humilatio" (1978) is one of the series of pictures called "Annunciations"

and portrays Mary's behaviour while the angel is talking to her. Blue as the symbolic colour of the Mother of God is subjected to variations in an accumulation of two narrow and two double stripes, moving from blue-white via blue-black and ultramarine to blue-green.

Ad Reinhardt occupies a special position among the "Colour-Field" painters. He was a lone wolf, both traditionalist and utopian in his approach. For him there were no "new myths." His way inside himself led through a confrontation with Eastern culture. Despite this the German-American was not tempted to forget his Western origins. "Control and rationality are part of any morality," he said. He stood by this as a political human being and as an esoteric artist. Nevertheless, his pictures move with iron logic back to something elemental: to black, which hides its coloured or uncoloured depth on the even surface. This black brings us close to a zero point, to the verge of that which is no longer visible. To this extent Reinhardt's mature work is to be seen in the context of contemporary move-

Brice Marden, *Humilatio,* 1978

ments which led to the foundation of the various Zero groups, to the veneration of Albers' square, (he admired this artist), to Yves Klein's monochromes, to Rothko's and Barnett Newman's colour panels, while connections can be traced backwards to classical Cubism, which for Reinhardt was the great aesthetic event of the century. There are also links with Mondrian and Malevich.

Reinhardt's black is not a version of chiaroscuro. It is much more a form of light, total light, the source of light, while white is not the source of darkness. This light is inherent in the "black paintings." They have drawn it into themselves. It does not fall into the picture, as it does with Rothko, it has extinguished all form. The formations which show up from time to time (rectangle, cross or division into three), as in "Abstract Painting" (1954–59), have no formal or symbolic significance. Reinhardt's creativity, unlike Cézanne's, does not run "parallel to nature," but in opposition to it. "Art is always dead," he stated provocatively, "and 'living' art is a deception." His uncompromising attitude, which also led him into a legal confrontation with his equally belligerent erstwhile friend Newman, and his rejection of the "avant-garde business," meant that the path to success was closed to him. But success did come shortly before his death, when he was discovered by younger artists to be one of the few of their seniors who had paved their way to Minimal and Conceptual Art. Reinhardt's black paintings are the end of the road for easel painting. Just as Cézanne saw himself as a primitive at the beginning of something new, so Reinhardt saw himself as the last traditionalist. His work is that of a conservative utopian standing between today and tomorrow.

The title "Abstract Painting" (1954–59) describes a borderline situation between the early work in colour and the black paintings. The dominant black does allow some nuance to show: night blue, and a plum blue shading into violet. These tones indicate that Reinhardt's black includes all other colours: colour is an emanation of light. So light is also included, hermetically sealed in. The slender, tall format is unusual. It helps to establish the intermediate position of this, Reinhardt's last work before his final step into even deeper black and to the "objective" square, which no longer admits of any formal hierarchy. Structure and script only reveal themselves on concentrated consideration of the picture, without altering one's position or the quality and angle of the light, a way of looking at pictures which is asking a great deal in our hectic times.

Paint is used in a similarly meditative fashion, but without any metaphysical claims, in the work of Morris Louis (Bernstein), also the son of Russian immigrants. He lets the paint flow onto the canvas (or onto cotton

Ad Reinhardt, *Abstract Painting,* 1954–59

197

Morris Louis, *Alpha-Ro,* 1961

Morris Louis, *Daleth,* 1958/59

sailcloth) and penetrate into the priming coat. He uses acrylic paint, which "runs" easily. The series of "Veil" pictures, in which transparent widths of colour spread out like flowers ("Daleth", 1958/59) is followed by the "Unfoldings": in large diagonal formats freely-formulated colour spreads band-like in fourfold diagonal parallels, either through the middle of the picture ("Alpha-Ro", 1961) or diagonally to the right and left. The vegetable colour figures taper to the edge of the picture. The large worked-over plane which remains free gives an impression of breadth, the generously handled paint creates space. These pictures, whose colour was inspired by the beautiful light over Washington, invite the observer to relaxed, "worldly" meditation. The glowingly-coloured "stripes" are den-

ser in structure: "Pillar of Dawn" (1961), in which there are also traces reminiscent of American Indian painting. The column-like parallel stripes of colour are so close together that they give the impression of condensed three-dimensional form, in comparison with the openness of the "Unfoldings".

Like Louis, Kenneth Noland was stimulated to work with flowing colours by Helen Frankenthaler, the painter of abstract landscapes ("Flood I", 1974). As the years passed his work was dominated more and more by geometrical components. In "Provence" (1960), the disc made up of coloured rings dissolving at the edges is still floating at the outer edge; in the subsequent, more static pictures (V-forms, ellipses), the relationship between stricter colour form and the material in which the picture is painted is examined, while in the later strip pictures ("Shadow Line", 1967) paint and the background of the picture, which has now become insignificant, merge together, and the hard stripes of colour continue into unbounded space. Colour itself, liberated from concerns with composition and pictorial systems, is the only theme.

Colour is dominant in a quite different way in the work of Larry Poons ("Untitled", 1970); he paints over it in various layers and structures it by touching it with objects, then taking them away again. The impression is strengthened when the upper layers split as the paint dries, and the layers underneath become visible. In contrast with Poons, Jules Olitski ("4. Step", 1971) works with spray gun and compressor. The colour produced is not dense, it seems almost to have dematerialized and disintegrated into layers of coloured mist. Barbara

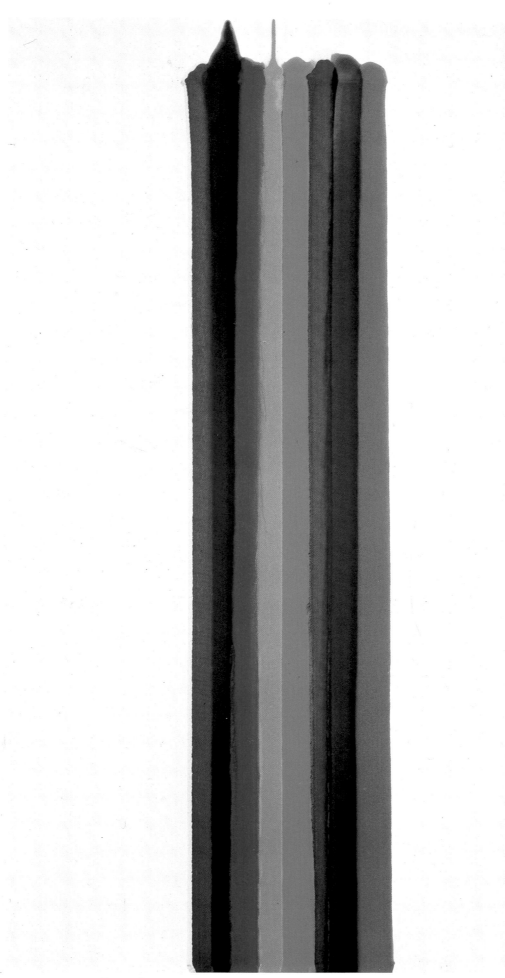

Morris Louis, *Pillars of Dawn,* 1961

Lucio Fontana, *Spatial Concept: Expectations,* 1960

Otto Piene, *Fire, Red and Black on White,* 1962

Rose also talks of "Abstract Impressionism", and it may well be that Monet's famous picture "Impression, Rising Sun" (1872) influenced the Russian-born artist as much as the misty landscapes of William Turner.

The revolt against the revolt of the European action painters, the Tachists and the monochrome utopia based itself on the idealization of light of the Zero Group, and began in 1957 with evening exhibitions in the Düsseldorf studio of Otto Piene. Like Geometrical Abstraction before it, Tachism was an academic movement, the sentimental spirit of existentialist Weltschmerz, expertly-handled gloom even in the realm of fine art, more at home with Françoise Sagan than Jean-Paul Sartre. The Zero movement met this with their vision – from the point of view of the present again a naive one – of a better world filled with light. The path led from the subjective "handwriting" of the Tachists to anonymous objectivity, from Wols to Yves Klein and Lucio Fontana – a beautiful communal work of the German Zero Group "Hommage à Fontana" was the crowning glory of "documenta III/1964".

Fontana's early work "White Manifesto" of 1946 was a kind of "Old Testament" for the Zero movement. Equally important were the two "Spatialist Manifestos" in which he described his methods of perforating ("buchi") or cutting through ("tagli") the canvas, and thus penetrating the space behind the picture.

Despite contempt for pictorial arrangement, which he saw as "variations for the public," Fontana's rectangular or elliptical perforations and incisions, which have also been compared with the Primitives' notches, are composed with precision. The sequence of five incisions of irregular breadth and length in "Spatial Concept: Expectations" of 1961 is comparatively speaking "dramatic" and full of movement, while the three cuts of varying length in the 1960/61 picture of the same name are calmer and more contemplative. In the perforations and pigment, applied in relief with a palette knife, of "Spatial Concept: Marriage in Venice" (1960/61) he reflects impressions of reality and translates them into a subjective pictorial arrangement. "Spatial Concept: Private Theatre" (1966) has a protruding wooden proscenium area. The picture is a concise symbolic interpretation of the "Small World Theatre" (1966), set before invisible space, which enters the picture through the perforations. Fontana was also concerned, like the later "t" group in Italy and "Groupe de la Recherche d'Art Visuel" in Paris, with removing the distinctions between painting and sculpture. In the flat "Spatial Sculpture" of 1957 he applies his principles in reverse: he extends two-dimensional pictures into the third dimension by cutting and perforating, but the plastic form remains flat.

Yves Klein, "Yves le Monochrome", was even more important to the Zero movement than Fontana; Klein died at the early age of 34, in the midst of his hectic pursuits, which contrasted so paradoxically with his meditative monochrome painting, influenced by Zen Buddhism and the teachings of the Rosicrucians. His "IKB" (International Klein Blue), a very deep ultramarine, was discovered in 1955 after many experiments with the assistance of a Parisian chemist: the pigments are formulated on a petroleum base, rather than the usual one.

Yves Klein used different means from those employed by Barnett Newman to enable the spectator to sink in meditation into the pure sheet of colour, unbroken by any additional pictorial elements, not even a "zip." The pulsation of the colour is echoed in the retina, and is supposed to penetrate into one's innermost being in

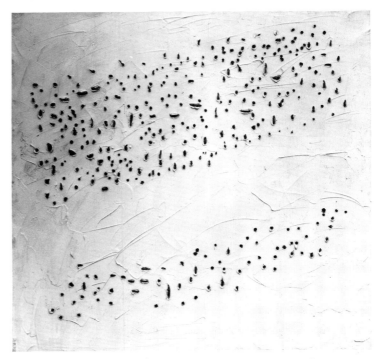

Lucio Fontana, *Spatial Concepts: Marriage in Venice,* 1961

this way. Klein, too, speaks of plunging into a space "which is greater than infinity." On a new plane of consciousness it is the blue of the Romantics, the blue of the sky, which is the means used to invoke infinity ("Monochrome Blue IKB 73", 1961). The blue plane is occasionally interrupted with sponges ("Blue Sponge Relief: RE 19", 1958). This combination came about while he was working on the new theatre in Gelsenkirchen (architect: Werner Ruhnau).

When Klein joined the "New Realists", founded by the critic Pierre Restany, a group who used real materials to create their works of art, he extended his subject range to include prints of the human body on paper and canvas ("Anthropométrie: Ant 130", 1960). Very occasionally he used the colour red, and sometimes the symbolic weight of gold ("Monogold: MG 18", 1959–61); but he was extremely displeased if monochrome

Yves Klein, *Blue Sponge Relief: RE 19,* 1958

Yves Klein, *Anthropométrie: ANT 130,* 1960

pictures in different colours were placed together to make decorative arrangements. This contradicted his quasi-metaphysical intentions, and his strict sense of artistic sensibility and of the presence of the immaterial in the material of colour.

Otto Piene, sometime chief ideologist of the Zero Group, was in sympathy with this thinking. He worked with new techniques and methods of presentation which were a continuation of the work of Fontana, and also of Moholy-Nagy: light-ballets, theatre of light, museum pieces for light, air and fire are all proof of this. After his early monochrome half-tone pictures his "Smoke Pictures" are important ("Fire, Red and Black on White", 1962). The idea came to him when he saw smoke from a candle pouring through screen foil. The red-edged "black sun" of the fire pictures was created by burning pigment on paper or canvas. The outer red ring is retained, while the disc becomes black, and traces of the smoke spread out over the circular form. Heinz Mack, who dabbled in Tachism while still a kind of infant prodigy at the Düsseldorf Academy, invented "vibration" as his stylistic method, and used it in many of his beautiful early pictures. But then he discovered the magic of reflected light by accidentally

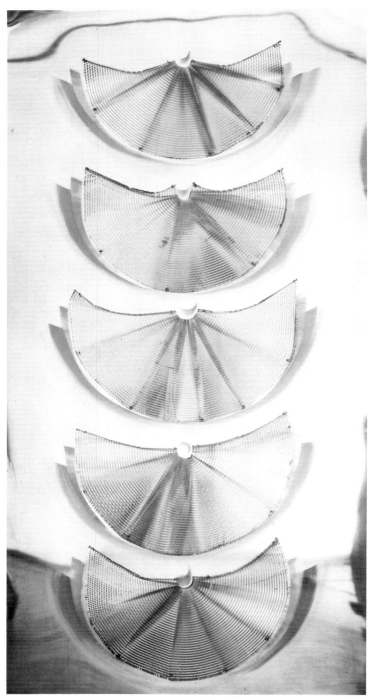

Heinz Mack, *Five Wings of an Angel,* 1965

treading on a metal plate on a sisal carpet. This set the style for his art of the future, which increasingly involved the three-dimensional. "Five Wings of an Angel" (1965) and "Silver Sun" (1967) are logical developments on the basis of this first discovery. For the wings he used high-grade aeroplane and rocket aluminium. The material was cut into blocks and pulled apart by hand. The way the light strikes it transforms it, and gives it a hint of the immaterial. Thus the technical is combined with the metaphysical, and rationality with romanticism. Mack quotes Leonardo da Vinci in support: "He was an engineer and he painted angels." The rotating "Silver Sun" shows the important step to kinetics. The famous Sahara project ("10 Columns of Light in the Desert Sand", 1968) was one of the high

Gotthard Graubner, *Colour–Space–Body – Diptych,* 1977

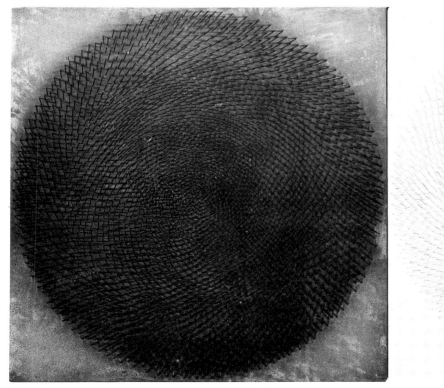

Günther Uecker, *Great Spiral I (Black), II (White),* 1968

spots of this development, leading far beyond the confines of painting.

The same is true of Gunter Uecker's moving and static nail pictures and objects. The nail as a medium creates space by the alternation of dense and open structures, of light and shade. Both moving and static objects change under the changing light and as a result of the movement of the observer as he passes, approaches or backs away. This is equally true of both the nail relief "White-White" (1961), dating from the early Zero years, and the later "Great Spiral I (Black), II (White)" (1968), with its impressive contrasts of light and dark, gaiety and melancholy. Carefree optimism, belief in a "white world," streaming with light in an equally bright future, is here already tinged with scepticism, day and night thoughts are poised in uneasy balance.

In the early stages there were loose links between Zero and Gotthard Graubner. His "Colour-Space-Bodies" are also artistic manifestations of the infinite which the observer looks at before they enfold him ("Colour-Space-Body – Diptych," 1977). Colour is an emanation of light, and the confines of light are immeasurable. Graubner encloses it in his corporeal picture-organisms and lets it shine back. Thus the spiritual becomes open to experience by the senses, the immaterial materializes: light is wave and corpuscle.

Graubner's work also has links with Romanticism, above all with C. D. Friedrich, but equally with Turner and beyond that with most of the great European colourists. His subject-matter, however, is entirely different from that of the Zero artists: it is colour itself, as it breathes within the organism of the picture. In "Twin Picture" (1977) the meditative and muted colour of the two panels is based on an anthracite grey which shimmers first towards green and then towards a reddish plum blue. In the centre these two shades approach one another in a discreet, cautious manner. Intensity of observation is the deciding factor in how deeply one can penetrate into these breathing coloured spaces.

Raimund Girke's sensitively nuanced white studies ("12 Horizontally Graded Progressions", 1971) are more reserved. The horizontal bands of white modulate the surface of the picture with gentle vibration. These quiet pictures with their reticent structure deliberately set the purity of their varied white against the coarse attractions of an environment flooded with banal images.

Even more radical is "Achrome" ("Colourless", 1960) by Piero Manzoni, a restless spirit whose short life took his work from the Informel via the happening and Fluxus to the most rigid monochromism: "For me, infinity is monochrome or, better still, devoid of colour. [...] For me the question is to produce a completely white (or better a completely colourless, neutral) area, beyond

Piero Manzoni, *Colourless,* 1960

any painted phenomenon [...]: a white that is not a polar landscape, not an associative object, not a thing of beauty, not a sensation, not a symbol or anything else: an area of white which is an area of white [...]."

Art for All – Art for Artists
Pop Art in New York

The incorporation of everyday objects in pictures is also one of the stylistic devices of Pop Art, not least in the work of Jasper Johns and Robert Rauschenberg, who paved the way for later artists. Otherwise, Pop Art is a description which – unlike the musical equivalent – no longer fits. We have discovered in the meantime that Pop Art, for all its frivolous apparatus of comic strips and Coca-cola bottles, can be very demanding. Of course this kind of art, typical of a democratic mass society, is not just aimed at an elite, but at a wider audience; but in contrast to the familiar, popular subject-matter, the artistic devices employed are by no means always lightweight, in fact in many cases they are of considerable complexity. This art for consumers is also art for artists and connoisseurs, and a far cry from the sort of artistic dilettantism which is sometimes thought to be a mark of genius. To this extent it has much in common with the work of an artist like Fernand Léger, to whom the movement owes a great deal. A look at the work of Jasper Johns, one of the artists who influenced the movement, shows how outstanding the artistic quality of Pop Art can be. "Deeper mean-

Jasper Johns, *Map,* 1967–71

ing" is renounced, but great thought is applied to finding a basis of reality, and this thinking is not restricted to external appearances. In the two-dimensional world of the picture the painter places "exalted" and banal objects, as they are, or as they seem to be; it might be the national emblem, the Stars and Stripes ("Flag on Orange Field", 1958), a target, or the writing on a board, in the theatre ("15′ Entr'acte", 1958) announcing the interruption of an artistic activity. The new reality which is created inside the picture is contrasted with reality outside the picture. Planes of reality are displaced, there is no definite answer to the question whether Johns' Stars and Stripes is a picture or a flag. The thing itself changes when it becomes the subject of a picture. Thus the works of this artist, apparently so simple, ask urgent questions of reality: "What is real?" It would be just as legitimate to ask, as Pilate did: "What is truth?" The answer – as in the famous Japanese film "Rashomon" (1951) – will always be different, according to the point of view and experiences of the observer. A thing, as the artist says, "is always different from what it was," and it will always be "different from what it is." But this profound and pragmatic thinking does not get right to the bottom of the American's art. "Entr'acte" shows outstanding technical skill in the dynamic handling of paint, in virtuoso gradation of areas of light and shade and dense and transparent areas of colour, a

technique developed by Johns through intensive study of mummy portraits. He uses liquid wax as well as oil as a bonding agent for the application of hot pigments and for working with a heated palette knife ("encaustics"). He employed this technique for the displaced rows of numbers in the picture "Large White Numbers" (1958), which is one of the masterpieces of our time in its artistic sensibility and the differentiated richness of its nuances. The numbers do not have a meaning, they do not point beyond themselves, they stand for themselves. The picture becomes a Kantian "thing in itself." The question again arises of the reality of the picture and the thing depicted, and again various answers are possible.

The same underlying problems are found in the monumental and richly painted "Map" (1967–71), which the artist created with reference to architect Buckminster Fuller's map of the world cut into triangles to show the two-dimensional quality of the surface of the earth without distortion. The changing relationship between external reality and the reality of the picture is formulated in a very complicated fashion in "Passage" (1962). On the one hand Johns follows Robert Rauschenberg's example by assembling real materials as part of the picture (ruler and nail on a grey quarter-circle), and on the other hand he provides merely the imprint of an iron, with the heading "Iron A real fork,

Jasper Johns, *Flag on Orange Field,* 1957

Jasper Johns, *Passage,* 1962

Jasper Johns, *Untitled,* 1972

held by chain and wire, is answered by the painted shadow of a wire. Ideas originated by Magritte and developed by Marcel Duchamp are for Johns no longer an end in themselves, but motivate brilliant painting, transcending the theme in a way which is diametrically opposed to Duchamp's approach; there is an abundance of "passsages," and elements of external reality are combined with painted pictorial reality, a procedure which Johns' friend Rauschenberg continually uses in his "combines." Johns uses the same process in the stronger, almost "poppy" colours and stricter formalization of "Edingsville" (1965): the leg in the left-hand half of the picture is painted, the hand on the right is set between banal objects which can be folded out.

Various phases of the work of this great artist are combined in the picture "Untitled" of 1972. On the right is a relatively coarse montage of fragmentary casts of bodies and clumsy "rulers," in the centre is a stylized group of city murals, and on the left is the braid-like structure of a motif which Johns discovered on a passing car and which crops up in numerous variations in his subsequent work. The apparent abstractness is also a reflection of reality. The fragmentation of the world, the destruction of orders which unite and engender commitment, the blurring of the borderlines between the exalted and the banal, the picture and what is depicted, are all given shape in the work of this artist. The boundless complexity of the real world is confronted with the serial structure of a world of art working with fragments of reality.

The use of everyday materials is also an important feature of the work of Robert Rauschenberg, who quotes the brilliant "rag-collector" Kurt Schwitters in justification; Schwitters' ideas were just as important, if not more important, for him than the theories of Marcel Duchamp. Rauschenberg's approach to the bridging of the gulf between the real world and the world of art,

between artist and observer, is more concrete than that of his friend Johns, and his attitude is more optimistic. In the fifties and sixties, which were an influential period for him, he believed in the possibility of overcoming the antinomy of art and reality, and of wresting the recipient non-artist out of his passivity and making him a creative participant.

"Odalisque" is an exemplary demonstration of the removal of the boundary between picture and subject, high culture and trivial culture. The title refers to the lasciviously erotic picture of the same name by Jean Auguste Dominique Ingres – the cushion is reminiscent of this – and of the "Bathers at Valpencon" by the same painter. The support on which the illuminated collage stands has pushed in the surface of the cushion in just the same way as the body of Ingres' naked lady has pushed in the downy bed of that sinful linen.

The collages on the illuminated case relate to the same theme: they are reproductions of famous pictures by old masters, and of their classical subjects: women in erotic poses, aggressive and sporting men, landscapes, animals, death and transience. Above the whole thing is a crowing cock as a symbol of male vanity. Anything exalted is reduced to absurdity. Many Pop Art themes are sounded for the first time in this picture: the triumph of the trivial over the exalted, which is only seen through the prism of irony, the use of cheap everyday materials and the crossing of genre boundaries.

Similar tendencies can also be detected in the three-part "Allegory", a "combine" made up of pigment, umbrella fabric, turned metal columns, sackcloth and other materials. But in this case the characteristics of a picture are more strongly in evidence; the composition is interesting and deliberate, and the rhythm of the picture is powerful and varied, moving from the dramatic, small-scale structure of the right-hand section via the concentrated dynamic of the narrower central section

Robert Rauschenberg, *Odalisque,* 1955–58

Robert Rauschenberg, *Soundings,* 1968

Robert Rauschenberg, *Wall Street,* 1961

to the calmer, almost classical organization of the larger third section, which makes up more than half of the "triptych." The artist's origins in action painting are clear in the format, composition and artistic handwriting of this picture, which could be called, to use Peter Ludwig's phrase, a "historical picture for our times."

"Combines" like "Black Market" and "Wall Street" (both 1961) bear the stamp of Rauschenberg's desire to merge the real world and the world of the picture, life and art. "Black Market" consists of objets trouvés: street sign, car numberplate, photograph, note-books with metal covers, and on the floor a case filled with everyday objects and rubber stamps with stamp pads. The visitor is politely invited to help himself to the objets trouvés and leave something else in exchange, and to record the swap in writing, thus taking an active part in changing the work of art, and being redeemed from his passive role of spectator. This intention is in tune with the idealistic views of Kennedy-era democracy, but is unlikely to be realized in the context of everyday museum practice, as the "new man," who would be the ideal, creative museum visitor, does not yet exist.

The "Soundings" (1968) are much more in tune with actual museum practice. They came into being in the context of euphoric experiment by artists, engineers and technicians (these experiments are usually euphoric) called "Art and Technology", and intended to bring the two disciplines closer together. Using the technique of screen printing, two chairs are projected onto perspex panels. When the visitor enters the (darkened) gallery, all he sees at first is himself, reflected on silvered panels. When he talks loudly to others, dances around or claps his hands, the sound activates

Robert Rauschenberg, *Allegory,* 1959/60

Robert Rauschenberg, *Axle,* 1964

Robert Rauschenberg, *Radiant White 952,* 1971

lights, and the chairs become visible in various arrangements and disappear into the darkness again.

Rauschenberg was encouraged to use offset, screen print and other techniques by Andy Warhol, but he mixes them in an unmistakably personal and always artistic fashion in "combines" like "Axle" and "Frog" (both 1964). In these cases, too, it is legitimate to speak of simultaneous historical pictures created in the spirit and using the devices of our times: fetishes, symbols and leading figures meet, sometimes even twice over, as with John F. Kennedy in "Axle". They are separate and yet connected by overlapping arrangements: eagle and Statue of Liberty, nature and technology, rural cabin and emblems of the city, parachutist and the Rubens Venus.

The monumental cardboard pieces in the style of "Radiant White" (1971) are more unyielding than these pictures, which have already become classics. Here again the artist used the simplest possible materials (cardboard cartons, labels, laths of wood) in order to achieve a lucid pictorial arrangement and once more to prove his theory – based on Schwitters – that one could just as easily make a picture with a pair of socks as with wood, nails, turpentine, oil and canvas.

There are also Dadaist paradoxes in the work of the third founding father of Pop Art, Claes Oldenburg. He made hard things soft, soft things hard, small things large and large things small, the insignificant significant and the significant insignificant. The cryptic qualities of this Swede in New York, his profoundly roguish humour and the accuracy of his wit are unequalled in the art of our times. European and American sharpness are combined in a unique fashion in his work. He too is a child of action painting, as can be seen in his early pictures. He is also, along with Alan Kaprow, one of the pioneers of the happening. The figure of the "Street Chick" and the caricature "Pear" as "Passer-by's Head" (both 1960) date from these pioneering days. They are at the same time "leading actors" and properties. The "Green Legs with Shoes", the "Brown Jacket" and the "White Shirt and Blue Tie" (all 1961), made of material and plaster held together with wire and painted with enamel, are products of the search for an equally untraditional but more durable material than card-

board and newspaper, which he had used in the "Street Scene" period. His wife Coosje van Bruggen wrote that the thick layer of plaster and the green paint of a kitchen in his neighbourhood inspired him, as did the bulges and mysterious irregularities in the plastered walls of his staircases, which showed up particularly clearly through the gleaming paintwork.

"Soft Washstand" (1965) and "Giant Soft Swedish Light Switch" (1966) are excellent examples of the monumentalization of objects in everyday use. Their transformation from hard to soft, from mini to maxi format, are signs of Oldenburg's strange sense of humour and of paradox, and also of his humane and forgiving nature. The (hard) "Bathtub" in wood and cardboard of 1966 shows the wealth of associations which a simple object can evoke when treated by Oldenburg. The thinly-painted bath has been turned through 90 degrees and stood on its end, and is reminiscent of a sentry-box and an Egyptian sarcophagus. There are various examples in the Ludwig Museum of his drawings suggesting anti-heroic monuments to objects in everyday use (umbrella, clothes-peg, toothpaste tube, builder's trowel or garden spade). They include the "Proposed Colossal Monument for Coronation Park, Toronto" (1967), in the form of a drainpipe.

Claes Oldenburg, *Men's Jacket with Shirt and Tie (Brown Jacket),* 1961

Claes Oldenburg, *Green Legs with Shoes,* 1961

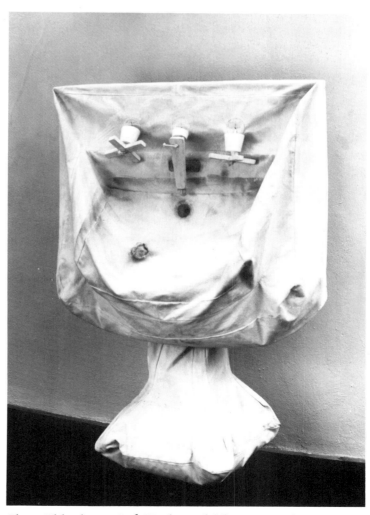

Claes Oldenburg, *Soft Washstand (ghost version),* 1965

Claes Oldenburg, *The Mouse Museum*, 1965–77

The "Mouse Museum" (1965–77) is externally a stylized Mickey Mouse, and contains a summary of all these ideas. The home-made objects, relics of the working process, the altered and the found objects (Oldenburg finds them wherever he goes) relate closely to the entire œuvre, to the artist and his world, but also to the observer, who comes across similar things (toothpaste tube and dishcloth, garter and lipstick, toaster and hamburger) every day.

The "Ray Gun Wing" (1969–77), like the "Mouse Museum" a "musée infini", is a demonstration of endless variations (which can be added to and are interchangeable) on a prototype, the ray gun which makes its owner invincible, and which occupies a central role in Oldenburg's work. The serial arrangement and the pictorial organization betray a childlike and naive delight in playing with this property from comics and science fiction, and also Oldenburg's reflective ennoblement of the trivial – finally taken seriously – and his unerring instinct for exciting aesthetic arrangements. Both these environments are key works to the understanding of Oldenburg's aesthetic world. Jim Dine was also originally an action painter, as is shown by a work like the "Pleasure Palette" of 1969. He too was one of the pioneers of the legendary New York happening period. When he says that his Polish maternal grandfather, who ran a shop which sold paint, tools and plumbers' utensils, was the greatest influence on his work, this casual remark cannot be dismissed either as a gag or a superficial indication of his preference for robust tools. An inclination towards the sturdy and the concrete is in tune with the undramatic self-knowledge of the generation of American artists to

which Jim Dine belongs. Behind the apparent simplicity of all this is a noble, humane spirituality, full of allusions, ironic layers of meaning and paradoxes. Dine never wanted to be an innovator. "I do not understand," he said, "why everything has to be new. That is just a destructive attitude. Everything is new [...], but without the old standards of beauty one cannot make a success of a picture."

Dine's pictorial thinking also deals with the juxtaposition of real and artistic objects. "Six Big Saws" (1962), a real saw and several painted ones, is a striking example of this. On seeing the "Pleasure Palette" one asks oneself: Are these paints the artist's materials or a portrait of them? The view of a blue sky adds to the confusion: Is the palette just a tool of the painter's trade, or the object on which the picture is painted? The heart – Dine's favourite item of vocabulary as a painter – also stresses the confusing change from reality to non-reality. A similar case in the "Roman Color Chart" (1968), a gigantic coloured landscape in serial arrangement.

It is quite clear that Dine is not concerned simply with mere representation when one considers his tripartite, mysteriously Surrealistic monument "Angel for Lorca" (1966): a profound memento in which the hats used as properties cannot be explained exactly, despite their apparent realism. Dine is anyway not prepared to accept a direct link between life and art: "There's art and there's life. ... If the object is used, the people say that the object is used to bridge the gap – it's crazy. The object is used to make art, just like paint is used to make art."

James Rosenquist, too, is not prepared to bridge the gap between art and life. In fact he draws a firm line be-

216

Jim Dine, *Roman Color Chart,* 1968

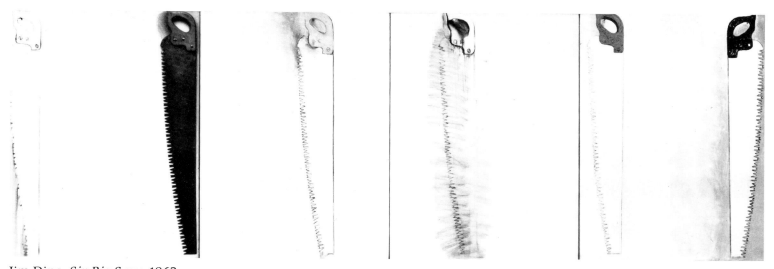

Jim Dine, *Six Big Saws,* 1962

tween them, he does not wish to depict experiences, but to bring about new experiences through the medium of his pictures. Rosenquist, who in his younger days used to paint gigantic billboards for the cinema, shows us fragments of reality, enlarged, larger than life, clearly definable but not isolated, as in many pictures by his Pop Art colleagues, but always in the context of other fragments. The same fragment of reality can be central in one section of a picture and at the same time the context of another. Everything relates to something else, meshes with everything else, is part of an overall monumental conception. Formerly one would probably have said "composition." The simultaneous awareness of abbreviated pictures forces the eye to keep on the move, to "see" in an abstract manner.

Rosenquist's experience as a billboard painter contributes to this. Advertisement hoardings cannot be grasped as a whole if you stand directly in front of them. And the painter may make his own decision to bring things closer to the observer, life-size or even larger than life-size, because things change and become alien when you look at them from close up. The artist's monumental major work in the Ludwig Museum, the environment "Horse Blinders" (1968/69), resulted from following such principles through. The sequence of pictures has no centre, there is no direction in which one is compelled to "read" it. It doesn't matter where you start or stop. This random element is introduced from the outset by the differing heights of the individual panels. Everyday things are enlarged to

James Rosenquist, *Horse Blinders,* 1968/69

gigantic proportions in a typically poppy "blow-up": paintbrush, key, whisk, telephone cable, a piece of melting butter, a thumb with paint under the nail, the grain of a piece of wood. No part is complete, everything remains fragmentary, there are no hierarchies of form or theme. The sequence of pictures runs like a film sequence, but makes absolutely no attempt to tell a story. At the corners the objects depicted are reflected again in polished aluminium plates. In this way the observer sees pictures within a picture. It is a new way of experiencing the world, given artistic form in this work: the city-dweller's way of seeing – rapidly, simultaneously, and in excerpts.

It has sometimes been a source of amusement to Rosenquist that many people seem to believe that Pop Artists identify with the mass idols whom they portray: "They really love Marilyn Monroe." When he depicts another star, Joan Crawford ("Joan Crawford Says…", 1964), the subject is not really the actress, but the commercialized cult of the star, here at the service of a tobacco company. It is not Joan Crawford whose "portrait" is painted, but a placard: the picture interprets the commercially effective, large-grained way in which it is put together. Rosenquist's pertinent experience as

a painter of advertisements is employed consciously, but not affirmatively and without comment, rather with critical distance.

Various materials are introduced in the collage "Rainbow" (1961). Chance also plays a part, quite deliberately. The artist left remains of a pane of glass broken in transit as part of the picture.

Roy Lichtenstein's work combines powerful simplicity with elegant refinement and intellectual precision, as Diane Waldmann of the New York Guggenheim Museum has pointed out. "Exactitudes", the title of a book by the Comtesse de Noailles, could stand motto for this Pop Artist par excellence. Perhaps it is this inborn inclination to accuracy combined with an ability to distance himself coolly which has protected Lichtenstein from the danger of quoting himself and making the attempt, doomed to failure, of continuing ad infinitum the pioneering days of Pop Art, with its monumentalizing transformation of the everyday object into a fetish, its trivial superman and its comic-strip sentimentality. Nevertheless, Lichtenstein was stimulated by the comic-strips. He concentrated their forms, generalized their content and alluded to past styles, e.g. the art nouveau of "Takka Takka" (1962).

James Rosenquist, *Untitled (Joan Crawford says…)*, 1964

Roy Lichtenstein, *Takka Takka*, 1962

Roy Lichtenstein, *Stillife with Net, Shell, Rope and Pulley*, 1972

Roy Lichtenstein, *Modular Painting with Four Panels No. 1*, 1969

Even before the work of the mature years, rich in quotation and allusion, Diane Waldmann noted that just as Ingres was in a position to present the ideal woman, Lichtenstein is able to communicate a new vision to us, based not on the comic-strip […] but on his understanding of Modern Art. It is not by chance that the name of the great classicist Ingres is used here, and also no coincidence that Mondrian and Van Doesburg played as important a part in Lichtenstein's artistic development as the dabbing colours of the Impressionists ("Rouen Cathedral", after Monet, 1969). He was influenced above all, however, by the Cubists in general and Picasso and Léger in particular (study for "Preparedness", 1968). Of course, the reflective stance also points back to Cézanne, and it is certainly not by chance that the Egyptian pyramid and Greek temple are subjected to the same formal schemes as a peasant's hut ("Red Barn II", 1969) or a hot dog.

In the eighties, Expressionist ideas feature increasingly as subjects for his pictures, from the expressive dramatist Picasso to the Germans Marc and Heckel, Kirchner and Schmidt-Rottluff ("Landscape with Figures and Rainbow", 1980). However, unruly expressive elements are always included in Lichtenstein's formalized schemes, which are only superficially simple, actually highly refined and derived from the reproductive techniques of our times, in a manner which gives them irony, a cryptically allusive quality, and the power to pay hidden tributes, all of which reflects the high level

Roy Lichtenstein, *M-Maybe (A Girl's Picture)*, 1965

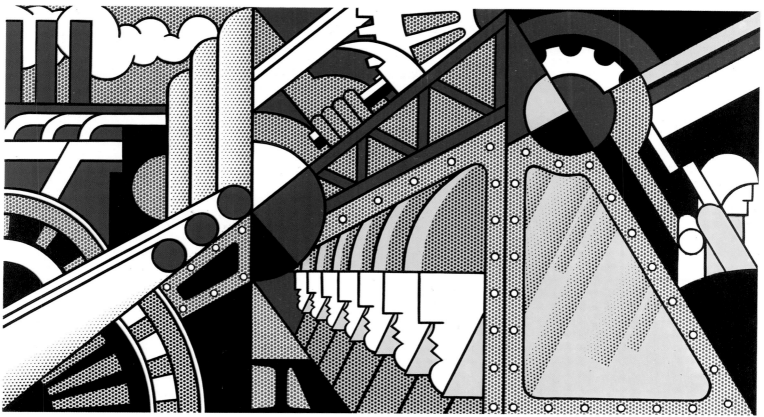

Roy Lichtenstein, *Study for "Preparedness"*, 1968

Roy Lichtenstein, *Landscape with Figures and Rainbow*, 1980

Roy Lichtenstein, *Rouen Cathedral (Seen at three different times of the day), Set No. 2,* 1969

of consciousness of a late culture. Lichtenstein today is creating "art about art," against the trends of the times he is establishing a timeless classicism, closer to Ingres than to Delacroix, closer to Cézanne than to Van Gogh, closer to Mondrian than to the expressive artists, whose longing to flaunt themselves he submits to the rigorous laws of his intelligent pictorial composition ("Modular Painting with Four Panels No. 1", 1969). This classical quality is also inherent in the early work of this artist. His blow-up monumentalizations of comics are close to the formulations of the late Léger and his "proletarian Olympus" – in artistic quality as well ("M-Maybe" – "P-Possibly", 1965).

The same is true of the still lifes. They strike a sensitive balance between objectivity and abstraction. The subject of the picture remains clearly recognizable, but is also part of an abstract and decorative pictorial arrangement ("Stillife", 1972). This fits in with the artist's statement that what he does is to impose form, what he would like to do is to impose unity. On the one hand the exalted is trivialized (whether it is Monet's "Cathedral" or a 17th-century Dutch still life), on the other hand the trivial is not only enlarged, but in Lichtenstein's pictures is invested with new dignity, placed side by side with the "exalted." This technique of making an alloy of disparate elements, and the "discrepancy between the hollowness of the content and the high rhetorical level of execution" which can often be detected, as Bernhard

Kerber, the Berlin interpreter of American art has put it, make Lichtenstein one of the most consistent of Pop Artists.

But the most radical among them – before he finally joined the jet-set at the price of his substance as an artist – was Andy Warhol, the son of Czech emigrants, almost as successful in his twenties as an advertising man as he is today although not quite as famous. Contemporary society saw itself reflected in his even-handed cynicism, whether genuine or expertly assumed, and it still does today. Thus, Andy Warhol became the drawing-room darling of the smart set.

He also did "do-it-yourself" painting kits ("Do-it-yourself Landscape"), the top of a Pepsi-Cola bottle and also all sympathy, from his art. He is the super-cooled reporter of the times, and simultaneously their symbol. In 1962 he "painted a portrait" of something of which he had always been very fond: bank notes ("80 Two-Dollar Bills").

He also did "do-it-yourself" painting kits ("Do-it-yourself Landscape"), the top of a Pepsi-Cola bottle ("Close Cover Before Sitting") and, with the same chilly detachment, the front page of a newspaper reporting a terrible aeroplane crash ("129 Die in Jet", all 1962), a filmed report of a revolt ("Red Race Riot", 1963), a wanted man ("Salvatore V", 1963) and the rock-star Elvis Presley ("Two Elvis", 1963). The "poppy" monumentalized "Flowers" (1964) appeared a year later as ironic

Andy Warhol, *Do-it-yourself – Landscape,* 1962

223

Andy Warhol, *Flowers*, 1964

Andy Warhol, *129 Die in Jet-Plane Crash*, 1962

Andy Warhol, *Red Race Riot*, 1963

Tom Wesselmann, *Bathtub No. 3*, 1964

symbols of "flower power" and the "flower children" of those hippy years.

In the world of Warhol's pictures (and his technique), everything is standardized, everything is of equal value. Scholars squabble over whether this is radically democratic or totalitarian, and some also do not trust the star painter's cold detachment, considering him to be a rigorous moralist and critic of his times. The complexity of Warhol's work is shown by the extent to which people are prepared to quarrel over it. There will never be an unequivocal answer to all these questions, and it is hard to deny the allegation that Warhol neither can nor wants to supply it from the depths of his intelligent and contradictory nature. The only thing which can be proved is that his work – if one sets aside the hastily-produced output of recent years – is not as simple as it appears at first glance. Despite the technological devices there is a wealth of sensitive gradation of colour and variation of form, even in the series

("Texan, Portrait of R. Rauschenberg", 1963). The anonymous perfection which Warhol himself sees as his highest goal ("I should like to be a machine") he has hardly ever achieved. He too is subject to "accidents" during production, which he does not eliminate, but incorporates in the picture; Klee's remark that genius is "the mistake in the system" is also true of Warhol.

Tom Wesselman's predominant theme is the world of consumerism, in which even sex is packaged as a clinically clean consumer article. The environment "Bathtub 3" (1964) makes man-made materials its target: the faceless advertisement ideal of the slim woman behind a plastic curtain in a plastic bath with plastic tiles behind it, and next to them a genuine wooden door and a yellow towel. They are all, including the female body as a sexual object, derivatives: symbols and properties of a chilly pseudo-sexuality without an erotic element. This is even clearer in the tripartite "Great American Nude No. 98" (1967). Even the numbering

Tom Wesselmann, *Great American Nude No. 98*, 1967

Tom Wesselmann, *Landscape No. 2*, 1964

reinforces the clichéd repetition of symbols of sexuality and civilization: "sinful" lips, budding breasts, fresh orange, ashtray and burning tipped cigarette – "enjoyment without regret."

Rather more complex is the combination of an almost life-size Volkswagen by a plastic tree in a landscape, with a family idyll in the background ("Landscape No. 2", 1964). The denaturization of nature and the way it is beaten back by "progress" in a technological environment are combined into a succinct pictorial formula.

John Chamberlain's "White Shadow" (1964) presents us with the detritus of civilization. Parts of wrecked cars become an abstract symbol of vanity as they thrust, aggressive, sharp and threatening, into the space. Quite independent of this interpretation is the admirable sculptural form which Chamberlain imposes on these bits of wreckage.

Robert Indiana's letter and figure pictures based on his own experiences are much more optimistic and by no means directed against the emblems of civilization. They stylize the visual charms of the advertizing world and, by means of strict formalization, make them – always with agreement and affirmation – into pictorial statements with some autobiographical references. "USA 666" (1966/67) takes the motif of the warning cross at level crossings; the first 6 refers to the month of his father's birth, the 66 and the contrasting red and green are a reminder of the "Philips 66" petrol company for which his father worked, and of Federal Highway 66, which led to the Golden West. Finally 666 is the name of a cold cure. "The American Gas Works" (1961/62) poeticizes symbols of the world of technology: yellow is a sign for combustible gases, the combination of black and yellow is the symbolic colour for warning beacons, the parallel stripes are an allusion to the national flag, the dials remind one of gas meters, and the stencilled lettering is a symbol of the world of standards. The sculpture "Zig" (1960), on the other hand, also includes historical material: reminders of Red Indian totems and Greek steles, combined with comparatively reticent indications of our own times given by the functionless wheels and schematic letters and signs.

Allan d'Arcangelo is also on the trail of new realms of experience in modern civilization, without subjecting

John Chamberlain, *White Shadow*, 1964

226

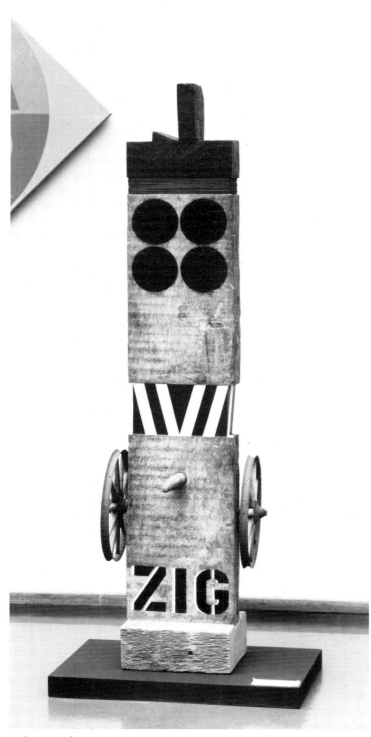

Robert Indiana, *Zig*, 1960

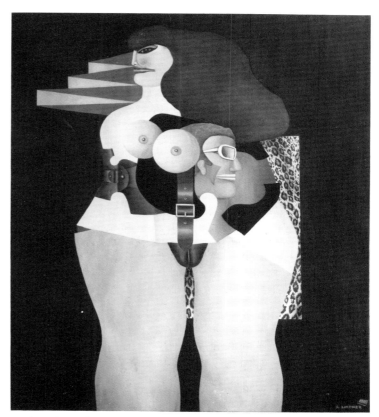

Richard Lindner, *Leopard-Lilly*, 1966

Richard Lindner, *Disneyland*, 1965

them to critical questioning. This shows in "Street Scene No. 12" (1965), in which a schematized road leads towards an area of gleaming green under a glowing blue sky, while the direction of the drive is indicated by bright red parallelograms set in the green.

Wayne Thiebaud also affirms the charm of the transient world of consumerism. He is interested in the impermanent "architecture" of a "Cake Counter" (1963) and also that of a "Hamburger", which he unconcernedly places beside a Frank Lloyd Wright.

The painting of Richard Lindner, a German emigrant originally from Nuremberg, occupies a special place on

Robert Indiana, *The American Gas Works,* 1961/62

Richard Lindner, *Target No. 1*, 1960–62

the American scene. His work is rooted in European Magic Realism. Lindner adapts elements of advertising and caricature, and approaches Pop Art independently via life in the fascinating city of New York, without losing his independently European and critical attitude.

Woman appears in Lindner's precisely painted pictures as both the agent and the object of seduction, as earth-mother and whore, demon and sacrifice ("Disneyland", 1965, "Leopard-Lilly", 1966). But she is always stronger than man, even if he is clearly, as in "Cushion" (1966), a member of the demi-monde or the underworld. The artistic device is that of the painted collage, with symbolically oversized breasts and legs, stylized faces, unlinked juxtapositions of brightly-coloured areas, the use of laconic and above all sexual symbols (target, riding kit, leather belt, whip, lolly, parrot's head, sunglasses, sun top) and the language of neon signs and advertising. He is always concerned with the relationship between man and woman ("Target No. 1", 1960/61) and the dangers of cosmopolitan life in the New Babylon of New York, which Lindner adored body and soul. The outsider Larry Rivers was an admirer of his. He too went his own way, although it was a very different one, on the fringes of Pop Art. "Moon Man – Moon Lady" (1973) demonstrates that Rivers was inspired by commercialized pictures which had been reproduced a thousand times, and developed his own pictorial ideas from clichés. Science fiction, trips to the moon, and the way in which they were fashionably marketed were just as much the begetters of "Moon Man – Moon Lady" as the tendency of many Pop Artists to place motifs next to each other in pairs.

Between Fascination and Criticism
Pop Art in London

British Pop Art always looked quite different from its American counterpart. This can already be seen in its rejection of "blow-up" techniques, and the choice of relatively small formats. This is not just a superficial decision about form, it is much more a question of attitude and inner adjustment. Naturally, the world of consumerism, from Mickey Mouse to the refrigerator, is a theme in England as well. At first it is presented with admiration for the achievements of the "brave new world," and then increasingly critically. Marcel Duchamp's intelligent scepticism was a much stronger influence on Pop Art in England than it was in America, particularly in the work of Richard Hamilton, and also Paolozzi.

The guiding spirit of the movement was Richard Hamilton, who founded the "Independent Group" in

the fifties along with some of his friends, and made the incorporation of trivial culture into their work (film, adverts, fashion, comics, consumer goods) part of the programme. The collage "Towards a Definitive Statement on the Coming Trends in Men's Wear and Accessories" (1963) is in both title and content influenced by "Playboy" and its virility cult, including a fashionable shirt, as well as astronaut John Glenn. Hamilton adopts a critical attitude to this kind of material, however, and examines it for questionable elements. What interests him in the series of press photographs of Marilyn Monroe ("My Marilyn", 1964) some accepted, some not (crossed out), is the simultaneous existence of the star's man-crunching vitality and the vulnerable quality which lies beneath it, as expressed in the way she "crosses herself out" in some of the photographs. At the same time we are made aware of a basic trait of the consumer world: the elimination of anything original, or non-conformist. The anodyne selection of things considered good is intended for instant consumption by an audience which is treated as stupid. Anything imperfect, which might disturb the balance with its awkward corners and edges, is eliminated.

Richard Hamilton, *Towards a Definitive Statement on the Coming Trends in Men's Wear and Accessories,* 1963

Richard Hamilton, *My Marilyn (Paste Up)*, 1964

Advertising's consecration of the everyday and the trivial by means of transfiguring interpretation and ennobling design is unmasked in "Still Life" of 1965. It shows two elegantly-shaped glasses in front of a diffuse background, and an advertisement photograph of a toaster placed with the measured dignity of an altarpiece. The ironically titled "Swingeing London" of 1968 shows Mick Jagger and gallery proprietor Robert Frazer after their arrest for the possession of dangerous drugs. By his adaptation of a press photograph, which caused a furore at the time, Hamilton unmasks the excessive nature of the police action by the handcuffs with which the two leading figures of the "swinging" London of those days are fastened together. He attacks the disturbance of private life by the brutal curiosity of the media and, through that, the vulnerability of all people. In the painted photograph "Trafalgar Square" (1965–67) and the collage "Bathers I", also based on a photograph, Hamilton brilliantly presents his vision of mass society and the loneliness of the individual, and also individual modes of behaviour which bear the stamp of this society.

The outstanding painter Ronald Kitaj is also a collector, traveller, literary figure, film and information expert and art historian. This gives his work a richly allusive intellectual framework. "Austro-Hungarian Foot-Soldier" is a relatively uncomplicated picture based on memories of student days in Vienna, where Kitaj was taught by the poet-painter Albert Paris Gütersloh. The portrayal of the Kaiser's soldier is a combination of concrete experience and historical knowledge, both real and dream-like, brought to our awareness by the realistic painting of the upper part of the picture and the dematerialized and openly fragmentary style of the lower section. More complicated and less easy to decipher is "Casting of the Parts" (1967), an only super-

231

Richard Hamilton, *Swingeing London 67 II*, 1968

ficially simple typology in picture and words of a girl in
a Californian brothel. Her example shows the clichéd
nature of role distribution in a thoroughly rationalized
society which firmly restricts the individual's opportu-
nities to expand his personality.

Peter Blake's "Bo-Diddley" portrait (1963) is easier to
understand; it is an artistic refinement of an effective
pop-music poster from the early days of the Beatles
and "swinging London".

Allan Jones, who painted formally extraordinarily interesting and colourful abstracts well into the sixties
("Figure Falling", 1964), as a second generation pop
artist created the prototype of the "sexy girl" in a Las-
Vegas erotic style which was as lucid as it was cool. "Perfect Match" (1966/67) is a pictorial representation of
woman as the plaything of the consumer world.

David Hockney expressed the feel of life in those days
in a quite different way; he spent them in temporary
voluntary exile in sunny California. Simplified, realistic presentation without psychological comment, and

spirited handling of stylized forms in changing per-
spectives and bright tonality characterize the homo-
erotic picture of the "Sunbather" (1966), which contrasts strongly with the obstinate scribble of this
artist's earlier pictorial narratives ("Untitled", 1963).

A reticently parodistic version of Pop Art came from
the French former Neo-Realist Martial Raysse, who
tried to unmask the world of clichés raised to the level
of idols by the use of stereotyped reproduction and
artistic "alienation." "Elle" (1962) is a completely unnatural representation of an idealized woman's head with
total lack of expression; "Simple and Quiet Painting"
(1965) shows fake nature in a plastic world, and at the
same time reveals the boredom to which men are
exposed within it.

In crass contrast to this innocuous irony is the committed critical attitude of the German Wolf Vostell, who
is also the father of the European happening. Vostell is
out to provoke. His sense of the social and political
responsibility of the artist sets him apart from the

Ronald B. Kitaj, *Austro-Hungarian Foot Soldier,* 1961

Allan Jones, *Perfect Match,* 1966/67

majority of the Pop Art scene. Something of German idealism has survived in his moralism, however unclassical his pictures, environments and actions may be. What he is criticizing is the partly open, partly concealed inhumanity of the industrial and post-industrial world, on the one hand thoroughly rational, and on the other full of irrational fears and aggression. His devices for confronting it are the happening, the "Décollages" (tear-off pictures) as abbreviated and condensed interpretations of a "torn" world ("Coca-Cola", 1961) and, more directly, his pictorial spaces and panel pictures, for which he uses all kinds of materials and techniques. This tendency is seen to the full in "Homage to Henry Ford and Jacqueline Kennedy" (1963–67), his response to the assassination of the American president. The target of his accusation is the everyday terror which bursts from below the surface in spectacular crimes like the Kennedy murder, but is always potentially present. Harder and colder still is the juxtaposition of the notorious murder of a shackled Vietcong

Peter Blake, *Bo-Diddley,* 1963

David Hockney, *Sunbather,* 1966

Martial Raysse, *Simple and Quiet Painting,* 1965

media's daily news show, which mixes the terrifying with the banal in a way which blunts response. It is just this which makes the famous photograph of the barbaric shooting a memento beyond its day.

The Poetry of the Real From Pop Art to Nouveau Réalisme

In the work of the French artist Arman (Fernandez) everyday objects are not just incorporated in the picture – as they are in the work of Schwitters, Rauschenberg or Vostell – but are much more its actual subject. This marks the most radical position within the group of "Nouveau Réalistes", At the beginning of the development Arman was still under the influence of "Informel", even though he uses ready-made materials (rubber stamps) in his picture "Free Copy" ("Nominatif", 1952–58). He goes a step further in the portrait of the photographer Charles Wilp (1961) by "accumulating," apparently randomly, everyday objects from the life

with the false glamour of a beauty queen dancing blindfold over the horrors of the world ("Miss America", 1968). For this "combine" of photograph, glaze and screen-print – rather like Rauschenberg and Warhol, but with a polemical intention – Vostell uses the

Wolf Vostell, *Miss America,* 1968

Arman (Armand Fernandez), *Torso with Gloves,* 1967

236

Arman (Armand Fernandez), *Accumulation of Jugs,* 1961

César (César Baldaccini), *Compression,* 1981 ▷

and surroundings of the "subject," thus producing a picture of the person without his making an appearance at all. The final development of this technique is the "Accumulation of Jugs" (1961) in a glass case. Here we are made aware of the concealed beauty of the apparently ugly without any adaptation by the artist. The picture and what is depicted are identical, the jugs no longer simply serve as models, they are the picture itself. A variation is "Torso with Gloves" (1967) which, together with a number of other similar works, was cast in a polyester form.

César's "Compression" of 1981 is a – compressed – "memorial" to a racing car. Unlike Chamberlain, César, who liked fast cars himself, does not see the motor car as scrap for the slag-heap of civilization. For him the "Compression" is a stele, a fetish, the act of compression a "metamorphosis" of the object, omitting all anecdotal material and, by condensation, making reality into its own monument.

It is no coincidence that Daniel Spoerri, the Romanian-born Swiss, compiled "Anecdotes towards a Topography of Chance One of the co-authors was, together with Spoerri, the originator of "Robert's Table": the French artist Robert Filliou. The two worked and

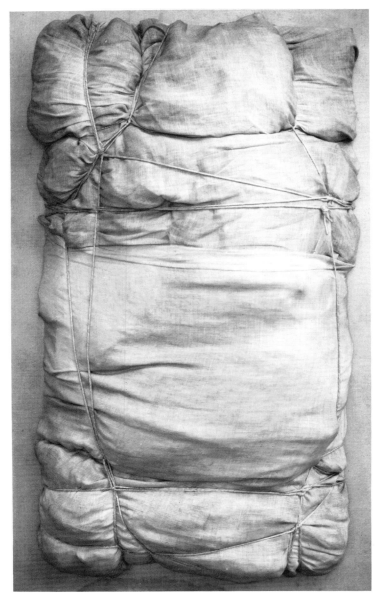

Christo, *Wrapped Object,* 1963

Daniel Spoerri, *Robert's Table,* 1961

ate together in the flat which Filliou then had in Copenhagen. Spoerri recorded the remains of a "working meal" for the two friends in his "Trap Picture". A second between birth and death is lent permanence, the table in its plain ordinariness and ugliness becomes a reliquary of the everyday.

Christo's package work ("Wrapped Object", 1963) has no other aim than to give everyday things their own dignity and poetry. Packing them up removes everyday items from view in a way which alienates them, and gives them an aura of the mysterious and hidden. Christo's reliquaries of the everyday are different from Arman's accumulations in that they have two layers: the unmanipulated one, which cannot be seen, and the outer skin, which is the work of the artist, who in a way both cryptic and ironic questions the status and significance of the packing and its contents. Thus the concrete object is transferred to a different aesthetic plane. Christo is not always able to leave this design stage because his art is public art and therefore of short

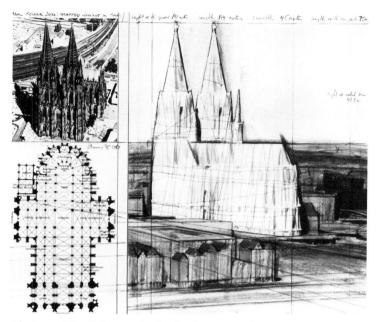

Christo, *My Cologne Cathedral Wrapped – Project for Cologne,* 1980

duration if carried out at all. "My Cologne Cathedral Wrapped" (1980) gives an idea of what it might look like in reality (see also: "Breaking Out of the Museum").
Raymond Hains' "Tattered Placard" (1961) should be mentioned in the context of comparable work by Vostell, but the use of monochrome paper reveals the work's closeness to Tachism, the Informel and Impressionist structures. Hains' principle is one of destroying the beautified surface of the world of the placard in order to make visible the unseen reality beneath it. In the décollage of 1961, polemical considerations yield pride of place to aesthetic ones.
One of the most consistent exponents of "Nouveau Réalisme" is Jean Tinguely, whose partly cheerful, partly cryptic and ironic machine objects, always capable of motion, are also made of "pieces of reality," but reduce this reality to the absurd in a light-hearted fashion, and above all question technological perfection. In Tinguely's work homo ludens, man at play, is cheerfully resurrected. Like all this artist's devices "Balouba No. 3" (1959) is a mechanical toy which is quite pointless, circling within itself to remind us, both by its title and its bright colours, of the dancing of an African tribe, mocking the lack of imagination of civilized society in the nonsense of its movement. The "Great Water Machine" (1966) is similarly conceived, but here cheerful racket and colour have been replaced by lively water games. "Vehicle No. 8" (1968), with its permanent forward and backward movement, satirizes the eternal to-ing and fro-ing of a mobile society. The constant repetition of the same movements combines the static and the dynamic in a paradoxical fashion in these works of art, which still deal in a philosophical way with the theme of time and transience, despite their playful attitude. Sometimes Tingue-

Raymond Hains, *Tattered Placard,* 1961

Jean Tinguely, *Vehicle No. 8,* 1968

Jean Tinguely, *Balouba No. 3,* 1959

Frank Stella, *Ctesiphon III,* 1968

ly's irony slips into black humour when one of his machines destroys itself: the final result of senseless, busy automatism which has become an end in itself.

Ascetic Utopias
Minimal Art Variants

Minimal Art could not have existed without Eastern and Western European Constructivism. This is not an indication of dependence, but of related artistic thought and spiritual attitude. Minimal Art came into being under different historical, geographical and social conditions. But aspects of the work of the Russians Tatlin, Rodchenko, Malevich, Lissitzky, Gabo and Pevsner, the Dutchmen around Mondrian, Van Doesburg and Vantongerloo and finally the teachings of the Weimar Bauhaus were picked up, thought through and continued independently.

Frank Stella, *Color Maze,* 1966

The drama of Abstract Expressionism, the enthronement of the trivial by Pop Art, the decorative arrangements of Op Art, were followed by the extreme "objectivity" of Minimal Art, which took the concept to its limits and beyond. It is art of an unyielding kind, working with the simplest elements. It operates with the plainest of forms, though the thought behind them

241

Frank Stella, *Bonin Night Heron No. 1,* 1976/77

can be very complicated. Minimal Art should not be understood in aesthetic terms alone. Minimal Art, particularly in its American version, is out to change the world. It questions all tradition, it proclaims the end of the individual genius with his individualistic "handwriting." In the background – as with the Constructivists – is a concrete utopia, the utopia of new art for all. Finally we should remember the American art which preceded Minimal Art, or which introduced it and formulated many of its ideas: the painting of artists like Mark Rothko, Barnett Newman, and above all Ad Reinhardt, and lastly the influence of younger artists like Kenneth Noland and, in particular, Frank Stella.

Frank Stella's black pictures structured with a narrow geometrical pattern of stripes are forerunners of the movement. The "Color Maze" (1966) in its glowing, sixfold colouring is a long way from such barrenness, but close to it in the "minimalist" simplicity of the juxtaposed "right-angled spirals" in three triangular shapes. This use of colour also characterizes "Ctesiphon III" (1968), which is formally influenced by Delaunay's

coloured discs, in affirmation of the decorative pattern of Matisse. The picture is purged of any kind of "meaning." It does not mean anything other than itself, it is its own "pictorial object." In his late work Stella increasingly detached himself from these purist colour shapes, thrust forward into the third dimension, first used loose, "Informel" colour structures ("Bonin Night Heron", 1976/77), and finally acknowledged Red Indian ornamentation in his use of increasingly dense structure and colour.

Ellsworth Kelly also makes the picture an object ("Three Panels: Blue Yellow Red," 1966). The picture and its base are at one. "Three Panels" consists of three rectangular sections, completely covered with glowing colours. Their extent is determined (as in late Noland) solely by the material on which the picture is painted, and the euphony of their proportion determines the beauty of the picture, colours mingling and merging with their base.

Lewis Stein extends asceticism even further by moving radically reduced shapes – in the picture "Untitled" of

Ellsworth Kelly, *Three Panels: Blue Yellow Red,* 1966

Richard Tuttle, *Mountain,* 1965

Imi Knöbel, *Untitled,* 1967–75

1969 two small white in two red squares – to the lower edge of a picture on a large canvas: a painting of "next to nothing," an extreme challenge to the observer's ability to react.

Minimal art content as a programme features uncompromisingly in the work of Joe Baer. The picture "Untitled" (1969–71) is the visual realization of intensive reflection about art. In this six-part group the picture becomes the subject. Coloured strips edged in black are painted over the stretcher edges of the empty white panels; the stripes establish contact with the wall. In this way there is interaction between picture and wall, which is then recognized as the actual "material on which the picture is painted." Baer's theme is the relationship of colour and the pictorial surface to space. It is a question of making an idea visible, "art about art": the boundaries between it and Conceptual Art are fluid.

The pictures and objects of the Venezuelan Jesús Rafael Soto ("White Curved Lines on White", 1966) also belong to Minimal Art in its widest sense, although their moving elements make them less unyielding and more graceful; he wished to set Mondrian's works in motion by the use of kinetics.

The much younger artist Richard Tuttle tries to minimalize his pictorial devices in a radical fashion, but without the use of geometrical shapes, which makes his usually small works seem more relaxed and playful

("Mountain", 1965). He sees his fabric objects ("Untitled", 1969) as "drawings of three-dimensional structures in space," as the Munich art historian Hermann Kern put it, while "Wheel" (1965) is assembled from "alien" materials, and is reminiscent of mechanisms which no longer work.

It is remarkable that some of the most important younger German artists working as Minimalists come from the school of Joseph Beuys. It is less surprising, given their origins, that there is a stronger meditative component in their work than in that of the more pragmatic Americans. This is true of the eight-part picture "Untitled" (1967–75) by Imi Knoebel, and of the four aluminium panels which make up "Points of the Compass" (1976) by "Blinky" Palermo (Peter Heisterkamp), who died young. Knoebel's picture combines the monumental quality of work on a large scale with the sensitivity of gentle, precisely-calculated displacement of proportion. The contrast between the static repose of the four lower panels and the soaring lightness of the four upper ones, getting smaller by stages so that visually they seem to be set back, is intelligently calculated. The purist reticence of the organization of the white panels corresponds to the unobtrusive – almost musical – distortion of tempo (agogics) in the rhythmic quality of the picture, which stimulates greater intensity of contemplation.

For his "Points of the Compass", Palermo painted on aluminium plates instead of canvas, in order to avoid the alteration of pigment texture by the weave of the material. The distance between the pictures must correspond precisely to their format when they are hung. The rectangular forms outlined with narrow strips of paint on the upper and lower edges of the picture are determined by reference to geometrical laws which the painter considers to be in tune with the geometry of the cosmos. Pigment is applied in many layers on a white ground, and finally given resonance; it symbolizes the unpredictable mutability of human experience.

The conceptual works of Heijo Hangen ("Double Picture from Extension Series No. 5", 1969) and Attila Kovacs ("Co-ordination P 3–14–1974", 1974) are on the borderline between Constructivism, Minimal Art and

Blinky Palermo (Peter Heisterkamp), *Points of the Compass,* 1976

Rune Mields, *Untitled, (B 31/1971),* 1971

Conceptual Art, and also point to the joyous fact that art cannot be labelled. Hangen's double picture develops a module by dividing the square; the module then establishes the basic formal structure, which can be put together in numerous ways. Choice of colour and arrangement of the individual pictures remain variable.

Kovacs' theme is the relationship between a black area and a grid system. Alteration of the grid leads to alteration of the shape. This is made visible in sequences of pictures. Kovacs: "My 'Co-ordinations' are relativized articulations of works which are created operatively [...] If I take graphics as a starting point, I can relativize them in such a way as to make them seem quite different from what they actually are." The making visible of processes of perception on a scientific and philosophical basis is the actual theme of this difficult and intellectual art.

Paolo Uccello is the great historical model for Rune Mields, because he combines artistic calculation with the vividness of reality. The uniting of reason and imagination, the translation of recognition processes into artistic and draughtsmanly forms is the ground base in the work of this artist. It can not be definitely classified as Minimal Art, Conceptual Art, or "New Myths". In Mields' early pictures the tube appears "to stand for power, technology, aggression and rationality," as the ideal medium for the definition of relationally under-

stood space ("Untitled"), which transcends visible reality. She later disturbed expressivity of form by her artistic search for the mathematical harmony of a world in which the distinction between science and imagination is removed.

The Idea as a Work of Art
Thought and Design in Conceptual Art

The name and definition of Conceptual Art came from an artist whose work still falls within the category of Minimal Art, but which in many ways points forward to the new movement. It was Sol LeWitt, who published his "Paragraphs about Conceptual Art" in "artforum" in 1967. This was followed two years later by his "Basic Principles" on the same subject. In this he pointed to the lines of contact which have already been described, leading directly to Minimal Art, and further back to the classical and in some ways, the first "conceptual" movement of Modern Art, Cubism. The key sentences read: "Ideas alone can be works of art." And: "All ideas need not be made physical." Georg Japp, the publicist now living in Hamburg, logically spoke of the "liberation of the hypostatized work of art by a creative act." Ideally, the open, process-like nature of the formulation of design should give the observer a new role, the role which Lessing saw as ideal for the spectator in the theatre, that of finishing the play for himself. Behind this of course lay also a desire to escape from commercialism and the embrace of beneficence. The basic idea that in art it is the idea and not its execution which is the decisive factor was not entirely new. What was new was the radical way in which it was pursued from the late sixties onwards. In retrospect the range of these attempts is broader than one would like to believe, or have others believe. It includes Walter de Maria's mythic hole in the ground, and the polemical diagnoses of Hans Haacke.

The diagram pictures of the Japanese artist Shusaku Arakawa are a preliminary stage of Conceptual Art; he does not in fact renounce the making visible of his ideas, but he does break off presentation in drawing or paint at the moment when imagination begins to formulate things ("Untitled", 1964/65). Arakawa is concerned with the "mechanism of meaning," that is to say, the relationship between things and the means by which they run their course, which appears as open coloured or drawn, static or dynamic forms on monochrome planes. To the extent that they are open to rational resolution they make heavy demands on the intellectual co-operation of the observer, or alternatively require readiness of sympathy and meditative absorption.

Douglas Huebler's "Variable Piece No. 48" (1971) con-

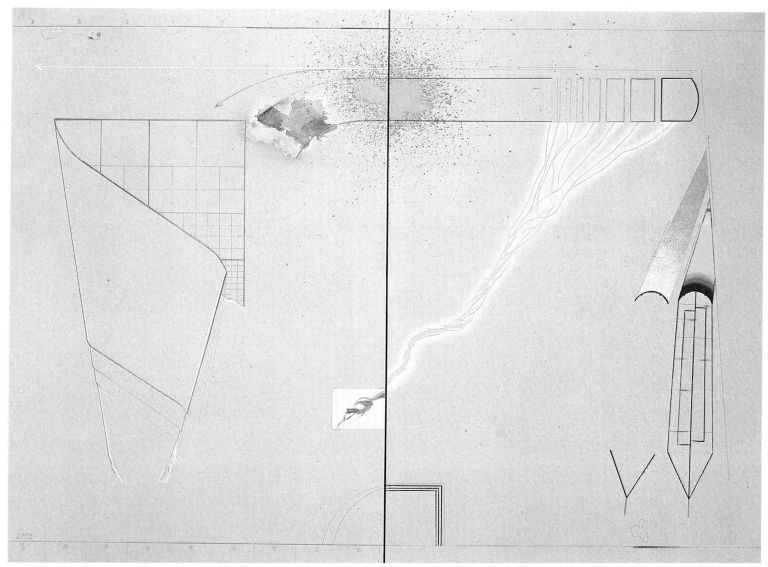

Shusaku Arakawa, *Untitled,* 1964/65

Joseph Kosuth, *Frame – One and Three,* 1965

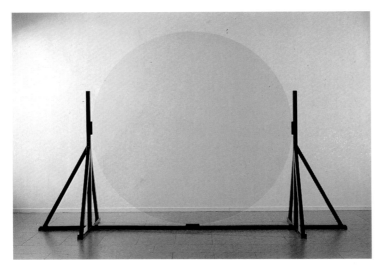

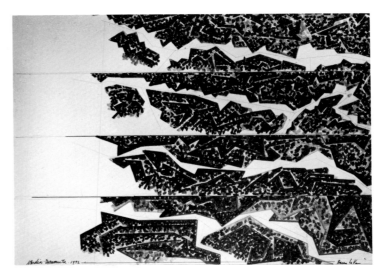

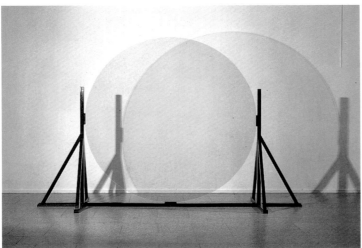

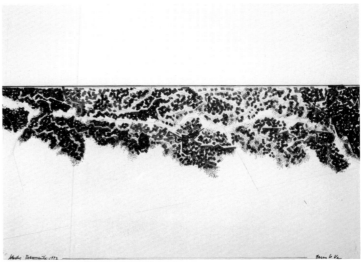

James Lee Byars, *The Golden Speaking Hole,* 1982

Barry Le Va, *Three Studies for documenta 1972,* 1972

tains a statement by the artist and is one in itself: a selection of 650 photographs which Huebler took on a journey from Bradford to New York, and which he had put together by others in any way the temporary owner or the observer wished. He is not concerned with making a "picture," but with representing visual phenomena and processes of perception.

Joseph Kosuth is the most important American member of the group "Art & Language", and replaces appearance with concept within Conceptual Art. "Frame – One and Three" (1967) places equal weight on the dictionary definition of the word frame, alongside a real frame and a life-size photograph of it. "Art as Idea – Definition 'Abstract'" is linked with the theories of Ad Reinhardt and provides only an enlargement of the dictionary definition of the word "abstract." This is one of the last outposts of Conceptual Art, challenging the observer to think his way into the theory underlying the statement.

James Lee Byars belongs neither to Action Art nor to Conceptual Art. He operates on the fringes. Sometimes he writes letters, sometimes he appears, blindfold or in shadow, in deep black, concentrates, purses his lips and leaves the room: "The Perfect Kiss" has been breathed

into the air. In Berlin he wanted to proclaim the Golden Age from the tower of the Gedächtniskirche, but was prevented by German narrow-mindedness. If anyone provides a legible text to accompany Byars' "appearance" he makes it illegible by reducing it in size or removing the punctuation: the idea does not admit of description. But sometimes a limited number of objects is left behind. For example a perfect form, like the glass circle with a much smaller circle in the middle, the "Golden Speaking Hole" (1982), which is available to anyone who is prepared to entrust his ideas to the opening in the transparent disc. Minimal Art? Conceptual Art? Or an emotional and living property as the bearer of ideas? The question remains open. At "documenta V/1972" Barry Le Va "marked" a dangerous path in broken glass on the floor of a corridor, for the visitor to "explore" ("Three Studies for documenta 1972"). "Forest Path, to Be Objectivized" (1971) is a statement for intellectual and visual completion by the observer, with the footprints of the walker seen from above and in cross-section on the left, and a photograph of the edge of the forest and a thicket on the right.

Hanne Darboven's theme is superficially the aesthetic attraction of formulae and numbers, but principally the representation of the passage of time, either speeded up or slowed down, using a system of numbers on the basis of the sum of the digits. "24 Songs" (1974) is one of her more all-embracing works. "The subject of the songs," writes Evelyn Weiss, a curator at the Ludwig Museum, "is 24 letters of the alphabet. One song is devoted to each letter, and is divided into three stanzes, again each with three lines. The artist has written two indices for each song and noted down three stanzes with them. The scheme or key […] is the division of the lines. Each line is divided into 10 horizontal and vertical sections, and the artist also provides a basic count of 10 to 100."

Ger Dekker's "Orchard near Emmeloord" (1974) is a sequence of photographs on the subject of the peaceful contemplation of a tract of cultivated countryside from various points of view, a landscape in which the balance between nature and its utilization has not yet been upset by man.

"Film-Painting: Black Vase Horizontal" (1972) by Jan Dibbets makes visible a passage of time which cannot be perceived in reality, and the alteration of an object (in this case a vase) which takes place during it. The artist pans a film camera past a vase at a constant distance. The position in the picture of the "wandering" vase shows Dibbets' different viewpoints as he moved past.

The theme of the London-based Yugoslav Braco Dimitrijević is doubt in history, its traditions, its assessments and its cult of personality. His motto is: "There are no mistakes in history. History is a mistake." Dimitrijević takes photographs of "Casual Passers-by", sets up monumental enlargements in public places, and so gives the people portrayed the significance they might have had if history had been different. He built an obelisk in the grounds of Schloss Charlottenburg in Berlin with the inscription "This could be a place of historical importance." There is a tablet bearing the same message in the West wall of Cologne cathedral.

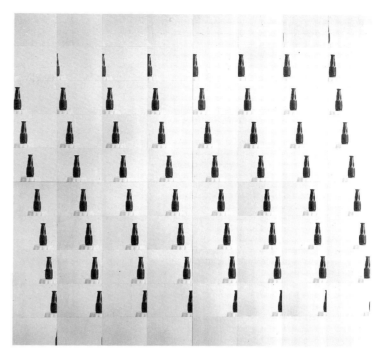

Jan Dibbets, *Film Painting: Black Vase Horizontal,* 1972

Braco Dimitrijević, *Triptychon Post Historicus,* 1984

Dimitrijević's radical doubts naturally include the history of art. Thus he says in his "Story about Two Artists" (1969): "Once upon a time there lived, far away from cities and towns, two painters. One day the King, who was out hunting nearby, lost his dog. He found him in the garden of one of the two men. He saw the work of this man, and took him back to the palace. The name of this painter was Leonardo da Vinci. The name of the other has been lost for ever to the memory of man." In the picture "Two Steps Ahead" (1972–79) a leopard is wandering through a picture by Jackson Pollock. The regular natural pattern of its coat is contrasted with the studied, free structure of the dripped paint, which

249

Franz Gertsch, *Marina Making Up Luciano,* 1975

obeys no laws at all. In the "Triptychon Post Historicus" the borders between art, nature and the everyday are finally broken down: it combines a picture by De Chirico ("Furniture in the Valley") with "Table, Ladder and Ancient Bust, Transported by Herr König" and a pear (1984). The name of the museum worker is just as important as that of the artist, only nature, in the form of the ironically placed pear, remains anonymous. The revaluation is clear: De Chirico's picture becomes an object, ladder and table are just as much part of the "Gesamtkunstwerk", courtesy of Dimitrijević, as the transient fruit. Complex problems are not only made comprehensible, but also laid open to visual experience in a remarkable way. The Yugoslav has found a startling solution to the crucial question for Conceptual Art, "How do I go about making abstract ideas visible?" without compromising the idea and without impinging unduly on the work of art.

Questioning Reality
Ways of Playing the Neo-Realism Game

The early eighties were dominated by the triumph of the "violent" expressive artistic gesture. Thus the various forms of seventies Neo-Realism were pushed into the background, like the opposite pole, artistic purism, which appeared in its most extreme form in the ascetic intellectualism of Conceptual Art. A glance at some of the work of its protagonists in Europe and America, varied both in form and subject-matter, shows how wrong it is to dismiss all Neo-Realist art as superficial naturalism. The Swiss "Photorealist" Franz Gertsch says of his work: "A picture must always remain a picture and not a substitute for reality." For him, preparatory sequences of photographs serve as a sketch-book. The formal process begins with the selection of the final copy of the picture. An important stylistic device is the change to a large format, which alienates reality to a high degree and makes the familiar seem unfamiliar.

It is no coincidence that Gertsch prefers to turn to non-conformist, "eccentric" people, whose personality has not yet been annihilated by the consumer world, whose faces are not yet in tatters ("Marina Making Up Luciano", 1975). Gertsch does not act as an "insider," but as someone standing outside, who is friendly and sympathetic. He has so far employed an almost Pointilliste style of painting, using a pointed brush, which results in melodious colour, flooded with light and structurally very dense. There are no hierarchies of subject-matter: foreground and background, figure and cos-

250

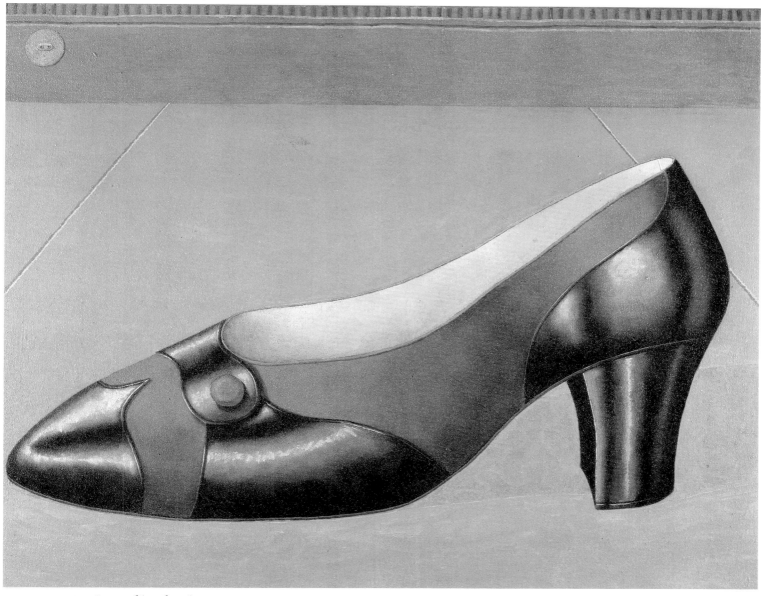

Domenico Gnoli, *Profile of a Shoe,* 1966

tume, room and decor are all treated with the same painstaking care. Large and small formats are not just copies, but autonomous coloured spaces, which have their own order and formal significance, independently of the motif. The Lausanne art historian Erika Billeter was right to point out that every centimetre of Gertsch's work has "the purity of a monochrome picture by Yves Klein." This man from Berne is a very European painter. His "friendship pictures," an extension of a traditional theme, are not neutral documentation, but rich artistic interpretation. They are a far cry from unresonant naturalism.

Domenico Gnoli is not a naturalist either. People have either disappeared from his pictures, or been made entirely anonymous ("Man with Two Fronts", 1964). On the other hand, everyday objects are invested with threatening presence, and become fetishes ("Profile of a Shoe", 1966). Gnoli: "For me, the everyday object itself, enlarged by the attention it has been paid, is more beautiful and terrible than any invention or ima-

gination could have made it. It tells me more about myself than anything else, and fills me with fear, disgust and delight." Gnoli has succeeded in incorporating his own fears, shared by many of his contemporaries, into his painted magic objects in an almost Surrealist way.

Michelangelo Pistoletto, who in the meantime has turned to other artistic forms, stands at one of the farthest outposts. His mirror pictures ("Party Conference No. 2", 1965) include the observer and his surroundings in the picture by the use of mirrors, without eye contact with the collage of people in the picture. The artist's aim is to use pictures like this "to carry art to the edge of life."

The work of the American Richard Estes ("Foodshop", 1967) shows in an impressive fashion that photograph and picture are not identical in serious Photorealism. In his work also, foreground and background are represented down to the last detail with almost surreal sharpness of focus, of the kind one does not find in real-

Michelangelo Pistoletto, *Party Conference No. 2,* 1965

Richard Estes, *Foodshop,* 1967

Howard Kanovitz, *Journal,* 1972/73

ity. The settings are devoid of human presence, the neon signs have congealed, there is no movement. The subject of the picture becomes a memorial to itself. The silent calm of this picture is reminiscent of the empty squares of "pittura metafisica".

In contrast, Malcolm Morley brings pictorial "handwriting" back onto the scene in his representations of the banal and everyday ("St. John's Yellow Pages", 1971). This gives a certain plasticity to the surface of the picture. It is used by Morley as a distancing stylistic device to reveal the illusory character of reality.

Howard Kanovitz is a product of action painting, but this particular pupil of Franz Kline was subsequently more strongly impressed by Pop Art, an influence which can also be seen in the work of other Photorealist artists. Kanovitz developed a special variation ("Journal", 1972/73), giving the original, here the title

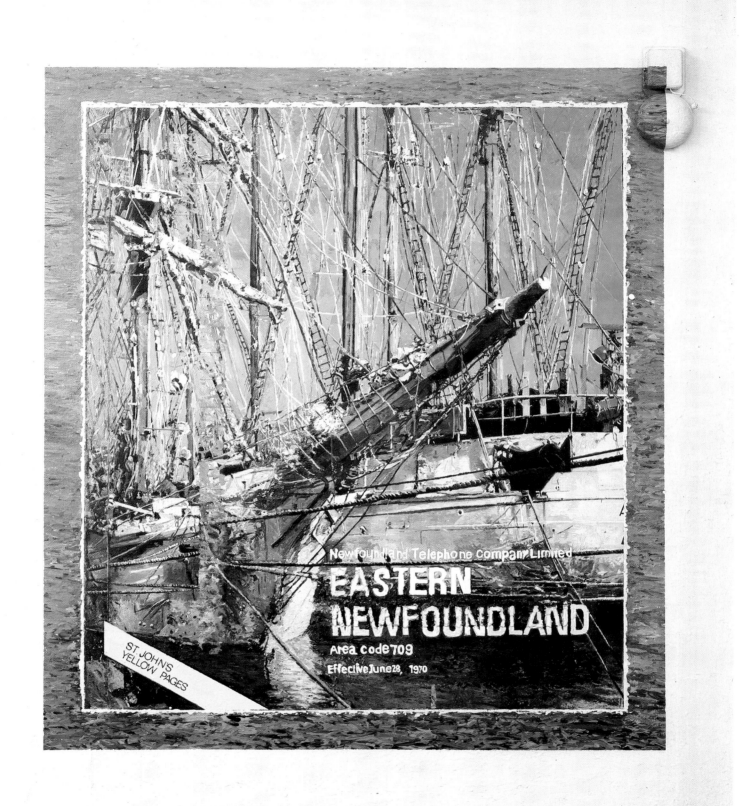

Malcolm Morley, *St. John's Yellow Pages,* 1971

Öyvind Fahlström, *Roulette, Variable Painting,* 1966

page of the magazine "Ladies' Home Journal", new meaning by the use of apparently small, alienating additions. The title page of the gossip magazine floats in front of an undefinable background, gigantic in format as the result of a poppy "blow-up." The diva's eyes reflect a reality outside the picture, the slightly misty acrylic paint gives the whole picture an unreal quality. The overlapping of reality and illusion, the "illusion of illusion," is the matter of primary interest to the artist. The painting technique of the Canadian Alex Colville is many-layered and very precisely calculated. He does not work with photographs. He develops a geometrical model structure from a series of preliminary drawings. "The final stage is the preparation of drawings from live models, which he proportions in accordance with the

module selected. He paints on compressed wooden boards prepared with acrylic and smoothed with plaster; the module of the painting is now transferred to the wooden board. It is then painted over, first with thin colours; then, over a period of perhaps three months, the forms are worked over in greater detail to make an even opaque surface." Thus his biographer David Burnett. Colville's theme is everyday mythology, which the fine artist, in his opinion, should not leave solely to poets of the calibre of James Joyce. His silent pictures are static, but almost all of them tell a story of laconic brevity. Simple human situations are the theme, as simple as they are complex: loneliness, isolation, love, strangeness, farewell and work.

The everyday becomes pictorial legend in the symme-

Alex Colville, *Truck Stop*, 1966

Alexander Petrov, *House by the Railway*, 1981

Boris Birger, *Married Couple*, 1981

trical structure of "Truck Stop" (1966): the petrol-pump attendant stares into the distance under a Caspar David Friedrich sky, the lorry is a monument with a snuffling dog in front of it, the scene is filled with silence. The precise form is exactly in tune with the un-dramatic, melancholy sparseness of the content. Colville strikes a balance between imagination and artistic detail, with almost incomparable skill. The surreal lurks behind the real and ordinary. Time becomes transparent, an artistic report on daily life in our times becomes the "legend of mankind."

In Öyvind Fahlström's kaleidoscope-like "Roulette, Variable Painting" (1966), realistic figuration is com-bined with Surrealist and Dadaist techniques of mon-tage. The sections of the picture are scenes – some overpainted – from newsreels, war and light entertain-ment films (including Johnny Weissmueller as Tarzan), the movable central figures, manipulable like mario-nettes, indicate the role of man as a mere object in a consumer-oriented society, and as the victim of war and violence.

The Soviet Union also has a school of realism free from transfiguring drama. Alexander Petrov's "House by the Railway" (1981) is from a distance reminiscent of the mirror effects in the pictures of Richard Estes. But the woman by the window is the actual theme. The re-flection of the surroundings in the window panes is also a reflection of the contemplative attitude of the old person. Petrov is not depicting to objectify, but using subjective feelings.

Jan Kryshevski's "Harbour Pier in Winter" (1981) is a pictorial composition combining Romantic and Con-structivist inspiration. The figure looking at the sea is reminiscent of the work of Caspar David Friedrich.

The painting of Boris Birger, inward, removed from any reality, and streaming with subdued light cannot be assigned precisely to any historic or contemporary movement; his entire interest is devoted to intellectual

Gerhard Richter, *Abstract No. 484*, 1981

Gerhard Richter, *Ema – Nude on a Staircase*, 1966

and spiritual relationships beyond everyday problems (see "Married Couple", 1981). This painter was a particular favourite of Heinrich Böll.

The most varied and versatile contemporary German artist, the brilliant painter Gerhard Richter, also worked with photographs. One only has to compare his work in this vein with that of Estes or Franz Gertsch to see how complex and contradictory painting which has been forcibly dubbed "Photorealism" can be.

As soon as Richter escaped from "Social Realism" in the then still very doctrinaire GDR and came to the "Golden West" to practise what he ironically called "Capitalist Realism" he could, in the opinion of Berlin critic Heinz Ohff, "paint like an old master." Photography plays an important role in many areas of his work. He uses photographs from brochures, magazines and books, which are transferred to canvas in faded, partly grey and partly coloured tones, and partially overpainted. His subjects are the world of advertising and popular magazines, everyday objects and private family pictures. His witty and ironic variation on Duchamp's "Nude Descending a Staircase" falls into this category. Richter's then wife was coming downstairs to sit for him, he took her photograph and overpainted the "faded" image with thin paint, translating the chiaroscuro of the photograph into painterly terms with great sensitivity ("Ema – Nude on a Staircase", 1966). The precise representation of phases of move-

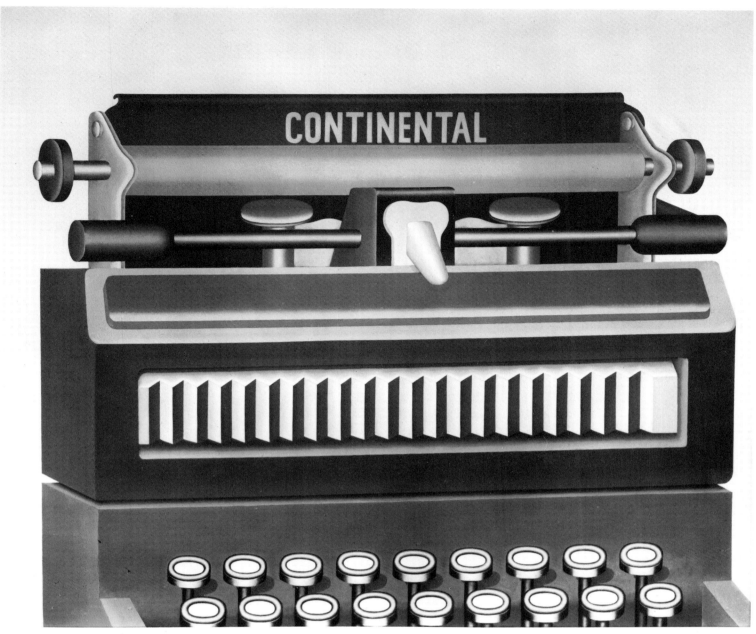

Konrad Klapheck, *The Superman,* 1962

ment in the picture of "Five Doors" (1967) contrasts with the conscious "lack of focus," disconcerting the observer in his perception of reality, in the picture of the nude. The rhythm of the presentation, the delicate grey-white of the colouring, the contrasting hard contours and areas of the picture creating a painterly, soft "atmosphere" remove the work from any superficially naturalistic category.

Between this work and the third picture in the Ludwig Museum ("Abstract No. 484", 1981) the city pictures were painted, expressive in gesture and reticent in their reduction of colour to black, white and grey, then the ironically alienated landscapes imitating Romantic motifs, followed by the monochrome grey structures, the conceptual colour panels, the series of figures from contemporary history and latterly, as a preliminary to what for the time being is the final phase, the highly-coloured loop and streak pictures. Richter circles con-

stantly around the theme of reality and the problem of capturing it in a picture. It was the years of rejection of a personal style of "handwriting" – the return of art to the idea of the picture and the painting process – which smoothed the way to his highly-coloured expressive pictures. Technique is made comprehensible by coarsening and opening up the procedures of painting and layers of pigment. Broad areas of colour show the layers underneath them through breaks in the pigment. Planned and spontaneous gestures alternate. Violent tonality emphasizes the agitation of line and design in the picture. Richter sees his abstract work as entirely relevant to his attempts to approach reality from constantly changing positions: "Abstract pictures are fictive models, because they illustrate a reality which we can neither see nor describe, but which we can conclude to exist."

Magic and Expression
Aspects of Contemporary German Painting

Where art of the seventies and above all the eighties is concerned, the Ludwig Museum is a "musée infini", open to the art of the present and future, and the pathway to expansion of the collection has been marked out. It also includes works by artists who defy labelling. In the realm of German painting the work of the lone wolf Konrad Klapheck, a member of the middle generation, should be mentioned in this context; he has always run counter to the trends of the moment. His work under consideration here introduces a magic reality, unmasked by touches of irony, to human behaviour and society. It began when the Tachist storm was still blowing at full strength. As early as 1955 Klapheck painted, with painstaking accuracy, an old-fashioned typewriter as the only object in a still life. The pictures in the Ludwig Museum also represent humanized machines with "souls": "The Ancestors" (1960) are symbolized by a reduced and statuesque mixture of calculating machine and typewriter. The monotonous rows of keys stand for the equivalent arrangement of family trees which, in the period of the Third Reich, were used to prove Aryan descent, and which could legitimize or, if no proof was forthcoming, have fatal consequences. "The Superman" (1962) is again a typewriter with an entirely uncryptic phallic symbol in the centre. The highly formalized instrument undergoes a "sex change" in the work of Klapheck. The machine (feminine in German) "on which," as the artist says, "the most important decisions of our life are made," stands in his eyes "for the father, the politician and the artist." The "Soldier Brides" (1967), on the other hand, are (feminine) shoemakers' sewing machines, who march threateningly past in a bellicose column greedy for booty. "The Dictator" (1967–70) is a stiff, windowless anthropomorphic monument, monotonous and threatening like the architecture of the administrative fortresses of our times. A cash-register handle towers steeply and dangerously into the picture as a sceptre-like instrument of power.

Klapheck's machines are archetypes of technical existence, but also indirect "portraits," representing human feelings and behaviour: lust and fear, hope and despair, brutality and, sometimes, a hidden tenderness.

The elimination of individual handwriting, the objectifying anonymity of the figures of a cold myth is a cryptic and ironic prism, the protective shield behind which Klapheck hides his feelings. "Only if armed with the cold might of precision," he says, "do we have access to the fires of the soul, and only under the mantle of the joke can we express what we have seen."

His formal austerity is based on Jan Vermeer, whom he admires. The combination of precision and imagina-

Konrad Klapheck, *Soldier Brides,* 1967

Bruno Goller, *Various Pictures,* 1955

tion comes from Surrealism, from models like Tanguy via Oelze to Dalí, and also from Richard Lindner's cosmopolitan mythology, and Magic Realism. His closeness to the trivial world of Pop Art, of which Klapheck knew nothing when he painted his first machines, is probably partly due to his teacher Bruno Goller. Goller was admired by Pop Artists like Richard Hamilton and Claes Oldenburg, and because of his shy, withdrawn nature he is one of the least known of the important painters of the century. He had already discovered the magic of simple things and of numbers in the twenties, but the detached, coolly protesting impartiality with which the Pop Artists make us conscious of the phenomena of the advertising and consumer world was something which remained alien to this sensitive and typically European artist. Goller's pictorial figures, whether they are people, animals or things, have the austerity of idols despite their refined decorum and their fantastic nature, which transcends reality. But love cannot be overlooked in this little world ("Various Pictures", 1955). Discretion and alienation exlude sentimentality. Goller's pictures are not confessional, but objective, the composition is disciplined and playful at the same time, the colour tuneful and reticent. The painting technique is masterly, and denies itself loud tones and virtuoso snatching at effect. The painter is conscious of isolation, unfamiliarity and alienation in a way which is distanced, but at the same time gentle and sympathetic; this shows in his use of separating framing for the subjects of his pictures – human, animal, thing, number, ornament.

Michael Buthe develops his own mythology from a confrontation with unconsumed myths from alien cultures, and juxtaposes them with the senseless, pre-programmed labels of an unimaginative world of culture and billboards ("Mask", 1973). He reacts spontaneously to the strange, colourful world of Africa, above all Morocco, without wanting to submit it to intellectual

Bernhard Heisig, *Last Portrait of My Mother,* 1978

Michael Buthe, *Mask,* Nigeria–Marrakesh–Madrid, 1973

assimilation. His pictures, collages and environments in various materials reflect the artist's fascination and emotional involvement with strong colours and inventive forms.

Horst Antes is famous for the figure of the cephalopod, emphasized and pushed forward almost in the manner of a relief by the expressive tonality of the background and the creature's own bodily existence. "Third Landscape Picture" (1968) shows a serene version of the double form, male and female version, which can seem both eerie and threatening, although the artist himself insists that he is not necessarily dealing with "demonic beings or monstrous products of Hell." The beginning of the sporting and erotic competition before a hilly landscape over which a flying chair is sailing away strikes a delicate balance between cryptic irony and latent danger.

As well as painting, objective pictorial drawing plays an important part in the work of C. O. Paeffgen. In the wall object "Black on White" (1968–72), insignia of might and emblems of love meet in a witty, allusive arrange-

Wolfgang Mattheuer, *What Now?,* 1980

ment, which takes aim with double irony but without bitterness at banal symbols like the lovers' moon, a three-fold heart standing on its head, and also sacred objects like sceptre and cross.

Douglas Swan paints pictures about pictures. His allusive, commenting art is the product of a late culture and requires intellectual confrontation if it is to be decoded. His triptych "The Laundress" (1979) is a series of variations on the famous picture with the same name by Degas, although Swan is only interested in a fragment of it, which he interprets in a contrary fashion. The painter jams a painted plastic hood over the painted canvas. Thus the picture unfolds on two planes, which are not equal in meaning. The air space between them, indicated by the word AIR, is the only "real thing" to thrust between the layers of the picture and thus to transform "the hard object-structure into airy painting" (Swan).

Traditionalist painting in the GDR is represented by examples of the work of the ebullient Bernhard Heisig,

influenced by Kokoschka and above all Beckmann ("Freedom Bridge Budapest", 1972, "Last Portrait of My Mother",1978), and by pictures by Wolfgang Mattheuer, who introduces the notion of "unhoped-for-invention" in the Surrealist sense. Despite this he is not a Surrealist, as he is concerned not with dream and madness, but with the "meaning and effective conclusion" of a picture ("What Now?", 1980).

An introduction to the dominant tendency of art in the Federal Republic, neo-expressive "violent" painting, is provided by nine important works by pacemakers Georg Baselitz and A. R. Penck. The importance of these two artists for the return to expressive, gestural painting is comparable with that of Johns and Rauschenberg for the rise and establishment of Pop Art.

Georg Baselitz hit the headlines with his early pictures in the sixties. The painting of those wild years, vital in gesture but morbid in subject-matter, by means of which he protested not only against the sterile academic quality of late abstract art, but also against the

Georg Baselitz, *Whip Woman,* 1965

Georg Baselitz, *The Wood Upside Down,* 1969

code of conduct of bourgeois decency and deceitful sexual morality, drove those he was attacking onto the barricades. Over two decades later the scandals have been forgotten, but these pictures have still lost none of their artistic energy. "The Great Night in the Bucket" (1962/63), a macabre representation of a boy, out of proportion and with a head and penis which are both far too large, has become a key picture in the revolt against convention. In the "Whip Woman" (1965) dancing over grave mounds, the world is already starting to turn: a preliminary stage to the works, standing on their heads and more clarified, of the later period. The text of "Pandämonium" 1 and 2 provides a literary commentary on these works, of which the wickedest is probably the bitter mockery of long-commercialized Christmas customs. The author of the "Theatre of Cruelty", Antonin Artaud, on whom the Surrealists and Tachists had already based their cases, Lautréamont, guiding figure of the Surrealists, and also Van Gogh, were the ancestors of these truly "wild" writings.

Baselitz, who, incidentally, studied under Hann Trier, learned in good time that you can't be an enfant terrible all your life. This perception was probably one of the reasons for his radical rejection of his early work. The goal of the mature Baselitz, an admirer of Corinth and the "degenerate" Expressionists, is to make the quality of painting effective, independently of subject and form. In order to achieve this, and in order to illustrate the insignificance of any given subject visually, rather than intellectually, he stands his pictures upside down ("The Wood Upside Down", 1967–69, "Bedroom", 1975). Objectivity is now only a check. It should be used to avoid abstract arbitrariness and to fix the structure of the picture. "Pure" painting as a sensuous experience for artist and observer is the only theme, demonstrated in the changing cold and warm tones, density and openness, calm and agitation.

There is a series of five pictures by A. R. Penck. Two date from the mid-sixties and two from the mid-seventies. The friendship picture "Untitled" (1964) is still under the spell of symbolically-charged Expressionism in glowing colours, but in the abbreviated sign language of the accompanying figures it points forward to the system pictures which are to follow: matchstick man in the hand of filmmaker Böttcher, birds over the head of Wolf Biermann, slide-rule in the hand of Penck-Picasso, sickle staff for the "ghost of the night" Georg Baselitz. In these works archaistic, signal-like sign language is combined with abstract cybernetic symbols. "A Possible System" (1965) shows complex procedures in abbreviated, condensing formulae: brutal fighting with an axe on the right, in the middle an assembled group, fenced in and divided into two – one half participating excitedly, the other static – a man dancing for joy beside the group on the left, and at both extremities

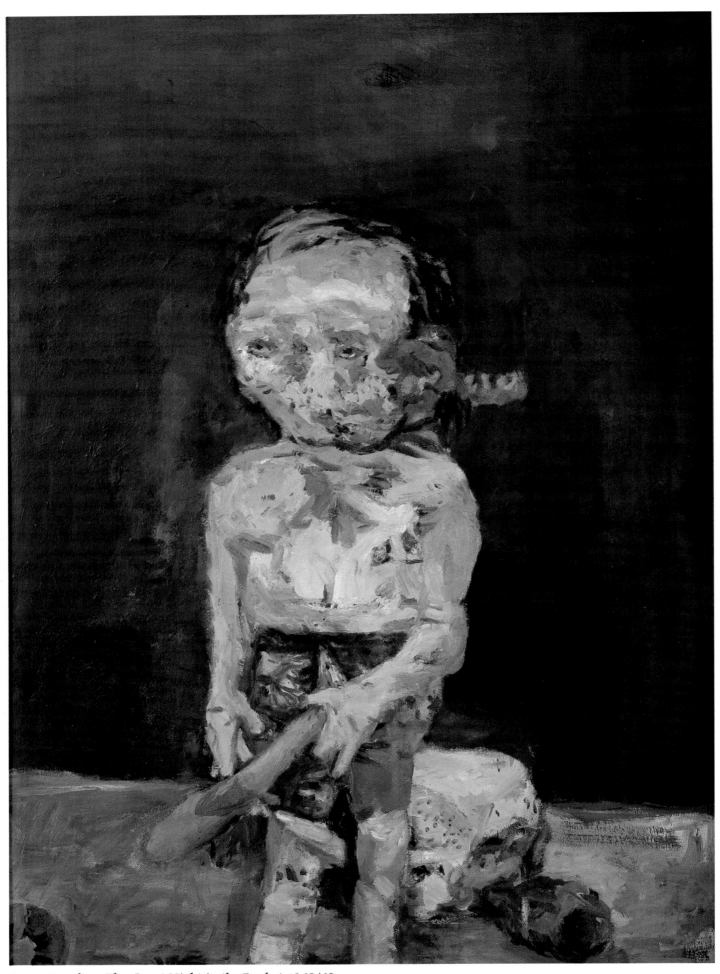

Georg Baselitz, *The Great Night in the Bucket,* 1962/63

A. R. Penck, *Untitled,* 1964

A. R. Penck, *A Possible System,* 1965

Jörg Immendorff, *Café Deutschland I,* 1978

figures holding up placards. The one on the right is pointing to the people fighting and showing a card with the ambiguous formula "A = I and I = B", the one on the left holds in one hand a picture of the silent, uninvolved group in the pen, and in the other the formula "A = A". Action, news and commentary, archaic behaviour which is still significant today, are summarized in artistic formulae in this "physics of human society."

The "Structure Picture" (1974) shows an area filled with abstract and figurative grammalogues. Figurations of age-old irrationalism break in on the rational sign language of a highly technical world. The picture of a girl, "Untitled", dates from the same year. The expressively melancholy face is surrounded by a system of dots and grids. Man has completely transformed the external world, but his aggressions and fears remain the same. Jörg Immendorff's meeting with Penck was of crucial

importance; Immendorff was one of the highly political group around the great Joseph Beuys. The meeting took place in 1976, a few years before Penck moved to the West. "We want to be a good collective. A collective which includes opposites," announced Immendorff in an article written in the same year. The simultaneity of closeness through friendship and separation by different political systems to which neither of the painters, either over here or over there, felt he belonged, became an important pictorial motif in Immendorff's central work "Café Deutschland", the sequence of pictures which made him the leading figure among the few painters in the Federal Republic attempting to use their art to further political ends.

The second important stimulus came from Renato Guttuso, not in person, but from his key picture "Caffè Greco", and Immendorff's resistance to the thesis of the Italian painter and active socialist: "I do not believe

Karl Marx, *Paolozzi III,* 1978

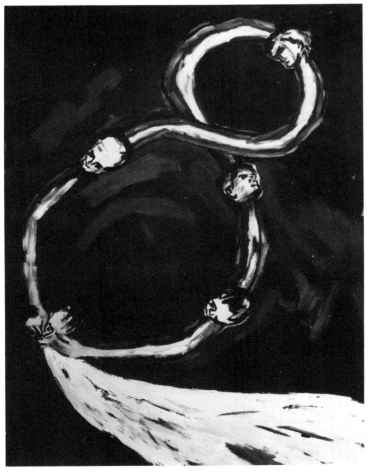

Volker Tannert, *Untitled,* 1982

that the artist confronts reality with the intention of changing it […] A painter paints things, not ideas." In the stage-like setting, seen from above, of "Café Deutschland I" (1977/78) the painter's hand is shown breaking through the (Berlin) wall, while the head of his friend Penck is seen as a reflection on a pillar, with the Brandenburg Gate behind him. Left of this Immendorff appears again, dancing, and pointing – like a character in one of Brecht's didactic plays – to a swastika held in the talons of an eagle. The playwright Brecht himself looks down from the upper right of the picture, a bringer of light, carrying a candle to illuminate the lively scene. Immendorff obviously sees him exclusively positively, even in the political field, a judgement which is not shared by other politically committed artists and writers.

What prevents Immendorff's picture sequence, which is at the same time a narrative and a commentary, from falling into the trap of mere illustration and pure agitation politics is his ability to give historical depth to a concrete political situation as well as his personal one, to present the figures involved in all their unstylized realism, not just as individuals but also as "representatives" of a political system and an intellectual attitude. The distillation of the objects, painted almost three-dimensionally (eagle, watch-tower, candle, ice, barbed wire, wall), to striking pictorial symbols is also in tune with this concept.

A painter whose work has been caught up by contemporary movements is the Cologne university lecturer Karl Marx. Sexuality and death, lust and fear, orgy and annihilation, loneliness and alienation, are the basic themes of his passionate art, sometimes aggressive, and owing much to German Expressionism. The painter's vehement handwriting is as clearly present in the portrait of the sculptor Eduardo Paolozzi (1978) as it is in his obsessive and erotic works. Head and hand not only fill the picture, they force their way out of it, which gives the picture striking presence, despite the shadowy and withdrawn quality of the face.

Before Volker Tannert, a pupil of Gerhard Richter, recently turned to Romantic-Symbolist landscape painting, he created impressive pictorial ciphers of existential human situations between fear and hope, executed with great artistic vigour in comparatively spare tonality, restricted to a few, carefully accentuated contrasts ("Untitled", 1982).

Horst Münch is an outstanding figure among the group of younger German artists who have produced excellent painting in a manner which is independent but does not deny tradition. His work combines spirituality with spontaneity of attack and a reflective quality with command of form, even in the realm of richly nuanced tonality. Münch's figures occupy a half-way position between abstraction and objectivity, between

265

Horst Münch, *Victory,* 1983

Charly Banana, *The Stag Under Cross-Examination,* 1983

a conscious critical recourse to tradition and free invention, between expression and construction, and thus create pictorial images of unusual imaginativeness and originality ("Victory", 1983).

Charly Banana (alias Ralf Johannes) is an outsider who moves from one extreme to another, partly in the world above (Johannes), partly in the world beneath (Banana). One can only assume that artist Banana and citizen Johannes are driven by a vehement longing for life, a longing whose reverse is awareness of transience. Paradox, alienation of the familiar, the distorting mirror and monumentalized triviality are the devices used by this Jekyll and Hyde character to penetrate the surface, to destroy illusion and to show what lies behind it: emptiness, substitute worlds, isolation, speechlessness. Investigations on the light and the dark side of reality, by day and in dreams, are part of the artistic process. Banana-Johannes exposes himself to reality before commenting on it or standing it on its head, when for example a man throws his wealth to poor gangsters, while he himself is threatened by a deer which has gone wild, or when – in a later picture – a stag is cross-examined by shrieking shades ("The Stag under Cross-Examination", 1983).

"Woe betide the man who sees symbols!" This is the last sentence of the addenda to Samuel Beckett's novel "Watt", and Horst Münch liked to use it. It could also stand as motto to the collage work of Tina Juretzek, in which spontaneity of painting (and draughtsmanly)

technique and glowing colour are combined with controlling reflectiveness and formal precision, abstract ciphers with living objectivity ("June Women", 1983). The openness of the pictorial space is in tune with this sensitive balance and leaves the observer with plenty of room for his own associations.

Sigmar Polke, who combines cryptic wit and an inexhaustible wealth of ideas with sovereign mastery in the application of extremely varied techniques of painting and drawing, is represented by his large early work "Head" (1966). It is one of a series of grid pictures painted by Polke when he was still in his twenties, between 1963 and 1969. At first glance it looks like a rendezvous between Pointillisme and Pop Art. A second glance reveals the major differences and the independence of Polke's procedure: while reality is eliminated by the Neo-Impressionist dots, they are also used by Polke in several layers as elements in building autonomous pictorial reality. They differ from Lichtenstein's grid methods in the carefully thought out and highly unusual "craft" with which they are applied to the monumental area of the picture. This leads to a tense counterpoint between pictorial construction and free interplay of the elements of the picture. "The dots are my brothers," says the painter, "I too am a dot. We used to play together, now we each go our own way. We only meet now at family parties and ask each other: How are you?"

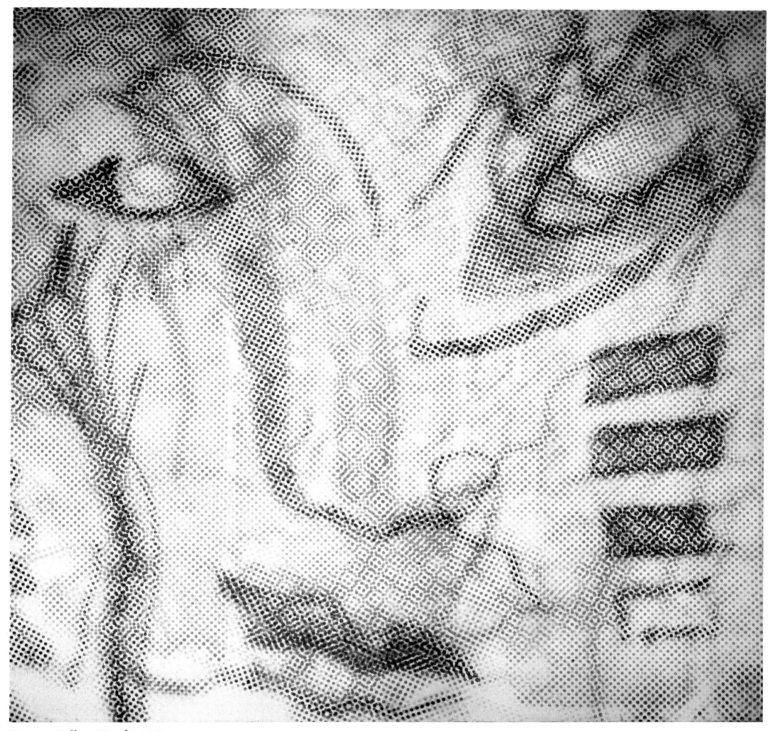

Sigmar Polke, *Head,* 1966

Nancy Stevenson Graves, *Shaman,* 1970

Utopian Archaeology
The Designs of "Spurensicherung"

The aim of "Spurensicherung" is to draw connecting lines between lost cultures and the present, to lead man back to the roots of his historic, prehistoric and biological existence, to reconcile art and nature and to restore depth and perspective to our shallow, hectic lives.

Years ago, when Nancy Graves exhibited astonishingly lifelike camels in art galleries, it was possible to believe at first glance that this was a trendy gag or a specific manifestation of Hyperrealism. But that was the wrong conclusion: it was already "Spurensicherung" (looking for lost traces in the dust, the sand, the ashes). "Ceridwen, Out of Fossils" (1966–77) is evidence of this. Ceridwen is the Welsh name of the goddess who watches over both death and immortality. The subject of the sculpture is again a camel, but a prehistoric rather than a modern one, and we are presented with its fossilized remains, not its living appearance. Nancy Graves' work is a contemporary "memento mori" challenging us to meditate on space and time, being and

passing, and the inexorable evolutionary change and shifting of the earth.

The ten-part environment "Shaman" is based on the lost culture of a tribe of North-West American Indians who died out in the 19th century. The items consist of feathers, bones, insects and skin-like strings. They are 4.2 m high, and cannot be taken in at a glance. They have to be walked around and studied from close up and from further away. The subject is the ritual of a medicine man and the people involved in it. As in "Ceridwen" we are concerned with the "Spurensicherung" of myths of the past and their cultic meaning, which embraces origin, life, death and survival.

Charles Simonds is also fascinated by the life and myths of the American Indians, not least by the "Anasazi", who disappeared from the American Mid-West for unknown reasons in the (European) Middle Ages. Their wonderfully humane architecture, the "dwellings" of their little towns cut into the rock, are for him historically based primaeval pictures of accommodation which is worthy of human beings. In his hands the utopia of a worthy human life in contact with nature, which should return once more to the unimaginative

Nancy Stevenson Graves, *Ceridwen, Out of Fossils,* 1969–77

Charles Simonds, *Park Model/Fantasy I,* 1974–76

Anne and Patrick Poirier, *Ausée*, 1975

stone deserts of the cities, grows from the creative invocation and memory of these lost worlds ("Park Model I, II, III" 1974–76). Simonds wants to "break up the present with the past," in order to create the possibility of "seeing" the present "in a different light." The past of his imaginary "little people" becomes the model for a society in which even a constantly changing world is able to retain its identity, and which understands how to live in a rational, more humane, less murderous, less profit-orientated way than contemporary man with his suicidal pragmatism. This is the point of Simonds' utopian archaeology.

The word "Spurensicherung" is derived ironically from criminology. It means both "covering one's tracks" and "looking for traces," as many examples of utopian archaeology demonstrate. The scientific basis is fictive, the documentation is often invented. In the work of Anne and Patrick Poirier both the concrete past and the legendary European past have a role to play. In their case artistic vision includes future as well as past decay, including the decay and destruction of their own work. The Romantics anticipated these ideas.

Many representatives of Spurensicherung are just as much stimulated by their thoughts and dreams as they are by Lévy-Strauss's societies beyond historical experience, by Duchamp's objectivity of things or by the objet trouvé of Surrealism and the "nouveau roman". "Ausée" (1975) does not refer to a real place, but to a reconstruction recalled in a vision – or better, the poetic construction – of the ruins of a legendary town containing the seat of an oracle. The work is a monument to force us to be aware of the danger of sinking into a state in which we have no history, a danger which was particularly real in the seventies, when "Ausée" came into being. "Ausée" with its theatres, towers, gates, squares and cult sites cuts through the ages, belongs to no particular historical period. Its ruins are, in the words of critic Günter Metken, "a metaphor for the patchy historical memory of mankind." In this sense "Ausée" is an image and an appeal to our imagination which has been given form, a plea to remember, because without memory there can be no mastering of the present, and no design for the future.

2. Sculpture in the Ludwig Museum

From Classical Harmony to Cubism

The first major focal point in the Ludwig Museum's collection of sculpture is German Expressionism, as in the painting section, but chronologically it goes back a little further. The starting point is Medardo Rosso ("Carne Altrui", 1883, "Ecce Puer", 1906), whose work establishes a link between the 19th and the 20th centuries, between Genre, Impressionism and Symbolism, with hints of social criticism. The beautiful "pre-existent" boy's head, with a face still freeing itself from the material to be endowed with life and soul, is a mature work in the spirit of Rodin. The Italian was the first artist after Rodin to transfer Impressionism to sculpture, as is later also shown in the mobility and artistic treatment of the surface of the work of Renée Sintenis ("Daphne", 1930). The work of Aristide Maillol demonstrates the turn away from Rodin and back to sculpture of classical harmony, based on the teaching of Adolf Hildebrand. His sculpture differs from that of the Neo-Classicists with their latent intellectual colourlessness in its sense of reality, derived not from abstract idols, but from live models, and combined with a marked sense of proportion and form. "Leda" (c. 1902), with its discreetly restrained mobility, is still reminiscent of classical models, but the allegory of the "Ile de France" (1925) embodies a new, self-assured type of woman and reveals Maillol's understanding of sculpture as pictorial architecture. Charles Despiau, 13 years younger, was influenced by him, but in his work the tendency to standardize is mellowed by realistic detail ("Assia", 1938). The French were a strong influence on German sculpture up to the period before the Second World War.

Cubist sculpture is represented in great beauty and purity by Henri Laurens' "Guitar" (1914), which has already been mentioned; in subsequent years he turned to the heavy, mythologizing sculpture of self-contained volume which made him famous ("The Parting", 1941). This work took the artist back to idols from the early days of mankind, and also to his older contemporaries Maillol and, above all, Brancusi. "Seated Woman" (1914) by Raymond Duchamp-Villon – in stark contrast to his legendary "Big Horse" – is, despite its early date, closer to de-individualized archa-

Renée Sintenis, *Daphne,* 1930

ism than the futuristic Cubism which has filtered in, as is hinted at by some formal elements.

The work of Alexander Archipenko, a sculptor who came to Paris from Russia, is more consistent: "Flat Torso" (1914) uses the formal devices of Cubism to integrate hollow space in his sculptures by means of alternating positive and negative forms (convex and concave); Jacques Lipschitz ("Woman Reading", 1919)

271

Aristide Maillol, *Leda,* 1902

transferred elements of Analytical and Synthetic Cubism to sculpture before he turned back to organic forms with mobile surfaces in the twenties ("Géricault", 1932); Ossip Zadkine ("Intimacy/Narcissus", 1950) retained the vocabulary of Cubism to the end.

The sculpture "Ascension" (1929) by the German emigrant Otto Freundlich occupies a position between Cubist and abstract sculpture. One might be reminded of Hans Arp's organic shapes derived from nature were it not for the fact that Freundlich's almost violent forms thrust upward and entwine with considerably greater drama.

Revolutionary Constructivism is represented by the brothers Antoine Pevsner ("The Last Upswing", (1961/62) and Naum Gabo ("Construction in Space – Crystal", 1937). In 1920 both demanded in their "Realistic Manifesto": "1. If it is to respond to real life, art must be based on two fundamental elements: space and time. – 2. Volume is not the only expression of space. – 3. Kinetic and dynamic elements permit the expression of real time; static rhythms are not adequate for this. – 4. Art must cease to be imitative, in order to discover new forms."

The two kept to these guidelines throughout their lives. This is quite clear when we realize that "The Last Upswing" is also Pevsner's last work. (The title was sug-

Aristide Maillol, *Île de France,* 1925

272

Henri Laurens, *The Parting,* 1941

Henri Laurens, *The Guitar,* 1914

Raymond Duchamp-Villon, *Seated Woman*, 1914

Alexander Archipenko, *Flat Torso*, 1914

gested by his widow.) This important work is an all-round sculpture with no particular viewpoint. Statics and dynamics, repose and movement, are set in tense confrontation. Here, too, empty space surrounded by laconic forms and radial surface is as important as volume.

This consistent principle is taken further in Gabo's "Construction in Space" by the use of light, transparent perspex in the arrangement of the complicated, contradictory figure with its overlapping and encapsulations. As the light changes, dynamic processes are revealed –

strengthened by formal movement and counter-movement connected with the graphic structures. Sculpture becomes a pictorial cipher of cosmic events. In their mature years, both brothers believed in the possibility of changing and perfecting the world on the basis of Constructivist design. The three-dimensional material object "Construction" (1919) by Konstantin Vialov is a useful part of the collection as an example of early revolutionary avant-garde art in Russia; it was created in the spirit of Vladimir Tatlin and under his instruction.

Jacques Lipchitz, *Woman Reading,* 1919

Antoine Pevsner, *The Last Upswing,* 1961/62   ▷

Otto Freundlich, *Ascension,* 1929

Naum, Gabo, *Construction in Space – Crystal,* 1937

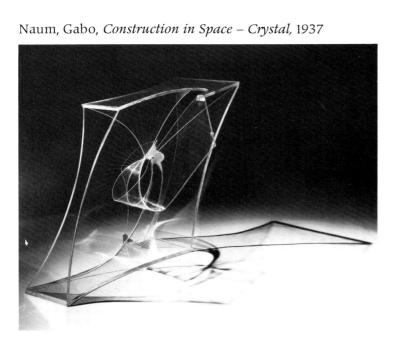

Ernst Barlach, *The Avenger*, 1914

Between East and West – the Expressionists

At the opposite pole to the cool passion of these designs for a concrete better world is the work of a man who did not come from the East, but who felt himself drawn thither, and that man is Ernst Barlach, the Expressionist poet-sculptor. His introspective sculptures combine precise observation with contemplative immersion, precision of simplified form with emotional heightening of expression. He always resisted the elevation of his art to a mystery. Myth and oracular pronouncements are more readily to be found in the somewhat strained, whispering symbolism of his plays. The poet Hans Carossa has described the humane element and even the ambiguity of the ecstatic Barlach figures, brilliantly taking the example of the "Berserk," which forms a group with the "Avenger" (1914) and the "Sword-Drawer": "If I ask myself [...] what touched me in this work of art, it was certainly not just that great gesture of anger, but much more the way it contradicted the face of the raging man, which

was gentle, even timid by nature, an impression which is confirmed by the full monk's habit. And so in fact it was something invisible that seized one: the inhuman and hostile power which was capable of driving this quiet being to such madness." This thoughtful note can also apply to the "Avenger" without forcing the issue, even if the violent, bursting dynamic of the second figure is more under control.

Even more sovereign in the laconic simplification of form, and more casual, even though in an attitude of complete concentration, is the "Singing Man" (1928). Tension and relaxation are kept in balance, and not without concealed humour. The late work "Old Woman Crouching" (1933), dating from five years before Barlach's relatively early death, shows the artist's return to closed, block form without expansive gesture. Barlach's expressively heightened lyricism now shows only in the overlarge hands and feet and in the urgent arrangement of the old woman's features, drawn from life.

After Barlach, Wilhelm Lehmbruck is the second Ger-

Ernst Barlach, *Singing Man,* 1928

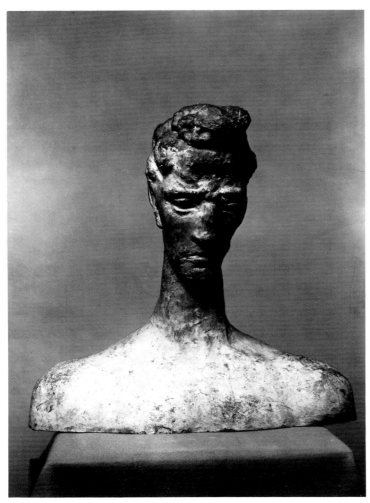

Wilhelm Lehmbruck, *Youth's Head*, 1913

Wilhelm Lehmbruck, *Female Torso*, 1910

man Expressionist sculptor of European calibre. For the visionary and ecstatic North German the East was his artistic destiny from an early age, but for the quieter Lehmbruck confrontation with France – the France of the cathedrals as well as the France of Rodin and Maillol – was the decisive experience. In coming to terms with great contemporary and historical models, including Michelangelo, this son of a Duisburg miner found a form of his own, which was to be influential until the middle of the century and beyond. Both Henry Moore and Joseph Beuys are admirers of Lehmbruck. A few days before his death Beuys started his last speech with the words: "I thank my teacher Wilhelm Lehmbruck."

The "Female Torso" of 1910 still shows the influence of Maillol, but its austere classicality is alleviated by a restrained lyricism, expressed in the inclination of the head and the light, open turn of the body. The melancholy charm of many of Lehmbruck's figures, the lyrical line, the reticent, soft bloom of the handling of the surface are all innately present in this work, as in the stone cast "Bust of Frau L.", dating from the same year. The most famous example of the development of the mature, personal Lehmbruck style is the introspective figure of the "Kneeling Woman" of 1911, which now enjoys world-wide popularity, but which in the twen-

Käthe Kollwitz, *Lament*, 1938

Georg Kolbe, *Dancer,* 1922

Rudolf Belling, *Alfred Flechtheim,* 1927

ties was knocked over by boorish fanatics in the name of morality and decency. The "Gothic" elongation of the slender limbs is used on Expressionist principles to heighten expression and spiritualize forms. Lehmbruck took the application of these principles to a logical conclusion two years later with the "Youth Rising" (1913). Anything sensuous and earthbound, the emphasis of volume – as in the work of Maillol, is reduced in importance, and so is Rodin's dramatic treatment of surface, with his bumps and hollows. The empty space between the parts of the body becomes part of the sculpture. The ascetic austerity of the elongated heads and bodies points far ahead, to Giacometti's elimination of volume. The "Bowed Woman's Head" (1911) is an accompanying independent study for the "Kneeling Woman", the "Youth's Head" (1913) belongs formally and thematically to the group around the "Youth Rising".

The impressive woman's head "Lament" (1938), almost a self-portrait, created by Käthe Kollwitz in mourning at the death of Ernst Barlach, also has expressive features, always present below the surface in the Dramatic Realism of this committed pacifist and compassionate critic of society. The figures of "Father and Mother" (1931/32), copied by pupils of Ewald Mataré in 1954 and

placed among the ruins of the Cologne church of St. Alban as a memorial for the dead of two world wars, are more austere in their block-like unity and more restrained in the expression of their inward mourning. Rudolf Belling's work in the twenties was a mixture of Expressionist and Cubist tendencies. The portraits from this period are important, and of them the rudimentary "Portrait of the Art Dealer Flechtheim" is one of the best-known and most successful. Although Belling restricts himself to an expressively fanciful presentation of eye, nose, mouth and forehead with hairline, the essential characteristics of the strong, unusual face are expressed most originally and strikingly.

In the passion of its movement and the trance-like detachment of the facial expression, Georg Kolbe's floating "Dancer" (1922) belongs to the sculpture of Expressionism. It has a formal boldness which distinguishes it from Kolbe's later work, which is a pale shadow of its models, and from the partly realistic, partly archaistic work of Richard Scheibe, the Post-Expressionist Edwin Scharff and his pupil Hermann Blumenthal, or Kurt Lehmann.

Poetry and Demonism

The mature work of the Alsatian sculptor Hans (Jean) Arp is lavishly represented by works drawn from 30 years of his creative life. In his younger years the sculptor-poet was one of the most intellectually vigorous of the Dadaists and Surrealists, but also the gentlest and the most conciliatory. He was an unequivocal critic of the lack of imagination and belligerent rationalism of the period, but his contribution was not so much aggressive protest as the presentation of a poetic counter-design for a humane pictorial world. He juxtaposes round, organic primaeval forms and three-dimensional architectural shapes as metaphors of natural growth on the one hand, and harmoniously geometrical constructions as examples of human creativity on the other, all with equal status. All these shapes, products of a teeming, self-disciplined, free formal imagination – whether they are sculpture or relief (such as the surreal "Nadir", 1959), metamorphosis of human, animal or plant – aim for the reconciliation of man and nature, and are full of gentle, unassertive humour. "Cobra-Centaur" (1952), "Clawalu" (1942), "Snake Movement" (1955) are clear proof of this, as is "The Little Theatre" (1959); its obliquely placed and supported peepshow becomes the scene of an ironically abbreviated "Little World Theatre" with abstract figures.

Arp's sculpture does not copy nature and architecture; it is a creative response to the world of appearance, which he confronts with his autonomous artistic

Hans Arp, *Cobra-Centaur,* 1952

Hans Arp, *Architectonic Construction,* 1965

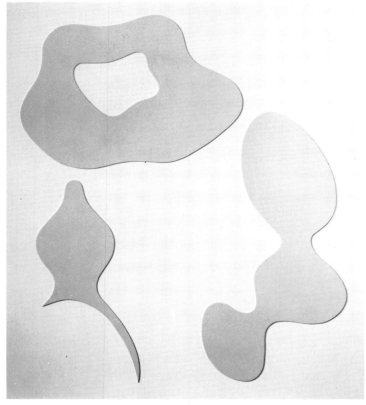

Hans Arp, *Relief Nadir,* 1959

Alberto Giacometti, *Place,* 1950

figures, with their own laws of form and growth ("Architectonic Construction", 1965). Human beings, too, become part of nature in their physicality ("Female Torso", 1930–53) and in their reflective spirituality ("Attentive – Thoughtful", 1960).

The elongated "Surrealist" figures of Alberto Giacometti are diametrically opposed to Hans Arp's blossoming, swelling organic forms: Giacometti's figures become more elongated as the years pass – emblems in space, which often seem to dissolve in the artist's nervous hands. He is the most unfathomable and probably the most significant sculptor of the century, and at the same time one of the most sensitive and profound painters of the period, and he "found" the most urgent pictorial ciphers for "the existential situation of man, his isolation, his lack of contact and his hopelessness" (Eduard Trier).

As in the work of Beckett, an element of grim caricature and Chaplinesque humour against a background of massive, silent seriousness cannot be overlooked in the work of Giacometti. This shows in the pointed "Nose" (1947), aggressively thrusting into space; the nose belongs to an imprisoned ghostly head with a shouting mouth, hanging in a cage; both the nose and the sack-like, sagging neck seem to have been skinned. But the nose thrusts at the visitor, pointed and threatening, and provocatively challenges him to think.

The "Place" (1950) shows a group of rudimentary, thin figures of various lengths, not communicating at all, a good distance from each other and from any real contact, on a relatively broad base-plate on four feet. The narrow, silent, isolated figures define the space which surrounds them by their differing sizes. The way in which man is "thrown" into a senseless existence, as described by Sartre, is given urgent visual force by Giacometti's figures.

Germaine Richier's "Claw Being" (1952), at the same time demonic and grotesque, is related in spirit; it seals

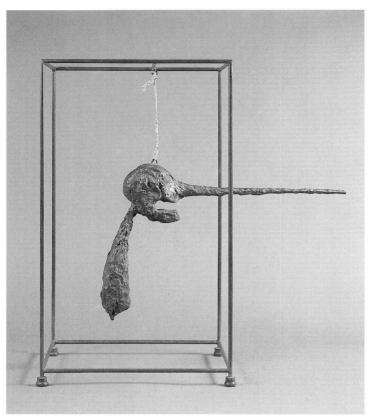

Alberto Giacometti, *The Nose,* 1947

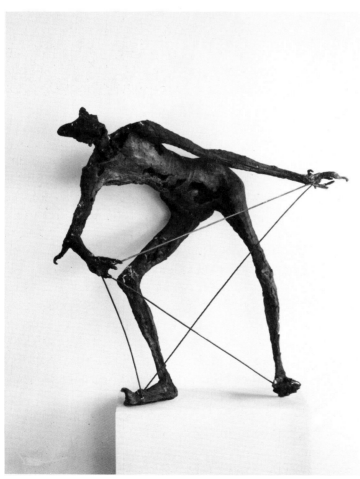

Germaine Richier, *Claw Being,* 1952

itself off from the observer. In Richier's work the whole form is always shown, although it is full of holes, eaten to pieces, and seems to be disintegrating. Formally and intellectually the abstract framework means something different from Giacometti's cages. It defines not just space, but also the evolution of movement, and, confronted with decaying nature, has an emblematic and occult significance.

Julio González, who together with Picasso invented iron sculpture, and who was an outstanding draughtsman, saw sculpture programmatically as an emblem in space, before he returned in his later years to work which was closer to nature. "Dancer with Daisy" (1956) is a copy of a late iron sculpture dating from 1937/38. The ritualized, expressive gesture, the reduction of the figure to its outline, the wayward grace of the movement, all give the work a macabre and grotesque demonic quality, lacking in hardness because of the change of material – bronze instead of iron.

Henry Moore and After

If Giacometti is the most difficult and extreme of the sculptors of this century, Henry Moore, the Yorkshire miner's son, is the most influental and famous. Until he came on the scene there had been no significant English sculpture since the Middle Ages. There were no portents of liberation from a lack of ideas and a pale imitation of traditional models when Moore appeared: no "new hope," no "promising talent," but just straight away the dominant figure among the sculptors of the first half of the century.

The idea of becoming a sculptor came to him at Sunday-school, when a teacher was giving an edifying talk about Michelangelo. From then on he assimilated a wealth of impressions: African sculpture, the Etruscans, the art of pre-Columbian Mexico, the European Middle Ages, the "disegno" of the Italian quattrocento, Brancusi, the Neo-Classical works of Picasso. These powerful impressions did not paralyze his creative powers, but liberated them, particularly as he never lost contact with nature in its monumental and minimal forms. Thus he logically saw sculpture as art for open spaces in the open air, changed by the play of light and shade.

In this spirit the "Hellenistically" clad "Reclining Draped Figure" (1952/53) is an "archetypal figure in the art-historical sense, as well as in the sense of the psychology of C. G. Jung, […] descendant of all earthly goddesses, of Venus and the river nymphs […]. pure woman, […] object of love and source of life," as the British art historian Norbert Lynton put it. The "Reclining Figures" of 1938 derive their formal tension from the interplay of bulk and hollow space, whereas in the

Henry Moore, *Draped Reclining Figure,* 1952/53

larger work the unified form of the partly earthbound, partly detached figure is dominant; the empty spaces are subordinate parts of the whole.

The stunted figure "Warrior with Shield" (1952/53), an echo of Moore's experience as a war artist, shows the artist's astonishing ability to give an inner monumental quality to smaller works.

In the fifties and sixties it seemed that Henry Moore was to find equally talented successors in his own country in the triumvirate of Kenneth Armitage ("Seated Woman", 1961), Reg Butler ("Girl", 1953) and Lynn Chadwick ("Moon of Alabama", 1957), but the artistic impetus of those years, which showed in original and highly individual thematic and formal innovations, could not be sustained, neither by Armitage, the creator of disc figures, nor by Butler, whose excessively thin, Mannerist figures of girls made a great impression at the time, nor by Chadwick with his aggressive, archaistic watchman figures in steel, stone and bronze. It is a personal tragedy for Butler that his most important concept, the design of a "Memorial to the Unknown Political Prisoner", with which he won a Berlin competition in 1953, against prominent sculptors from

all over the world, was never executed in the Federal Republic, which was too busy celebrating its economic miracle and suppressing its past. The essayist Hans Egon Holthusen wrote in 1956 in a personal opinion aimed at the realization of the work: "Are we Germans not well on the way, like many people in other countries, in an atmosphere of a spiritual trip down the old, well-worn track, of a mental habit of living from hand to mouth and of powerless forgetfulness about the catastrophic circumstances of the epoch; are we not about to degenerate into provincial and witless strivers towards a restoration of the old Biedermeier period?" And it was so. And unfortunately little had changed thirty years later, as is shown by the removal of a sculpture by Serra in New York.

Further development – or rather, new formulations – in British sculpture finally came about in opposition to the over-powerful father-figure. One of the most important opponents – in the meantime reconciled with the grand old man – was Eduardo Paolozzi, one of the co-founders of Pop Art, with his ever-changing work. The bronze idols of a wicked world were followed by architectural and constructive towers, closed

Eduardo Paolozzi, *The Last of the Idols,* 1963

Anthony Caro, *Prospect II*, 1964

Along with Norbert Kricke, who is twenty younger, Hans Uhlmann is the most important German sculptor of the post-war period, leaving aside Joseph Beuys, who defies classification. Before the Second World War he was making highly original figures and heads in wire, a continuation and development of Cubism. His most important work, assimilating the experience of the thirties, came after 1945. Following the lead of Vladimir Tatlin and Julio González, he found his own form, in which the architectural austerity and clarity of the early Russian are combined with free play of clustered and intertwining curves and circles ("Steel Sculpture", 1956). In the course of time the last traces of the figurative disappeared, and forms were further reduced and concentrated ("Great Triangle", 1964). Alongside these consistently abstract innovators, the post-war scene has been dominated by the two father-figures Gerhard Marcks and Ewald Mataré. Gerhard Marcks is the more conservative, the custodian of the classical tradition, who left the Bauhaus at an early stage when over-technical tendencies towards a mass culture were dominant. His confrontation with Expressionism and the abstract movement remained an epi-

tubular form was followed by open tubular form, and that in its turn by chromium-plated, reflecting steel. "The Last of the Idols" (1963), made of prefabricated components, "a totem-pole of the machine age," is simultaneously tower, anthropomorphic art figure and machine memorial. The pop-style painting is an indication of the idea Paolozzi then had of painted sculpture, which was to lead to the complete abolition in the future of the distinction between sculpture and painting: an idea which, in its many variations, was to have far-reaching consequences. "Molik I" (1967) shows a quite different side of this tirelessly searching artist, never to be pinned down to a single style. The wavy, abstract figuration reflects the form and colour of its surroundings and makes them part of the sculpture. The observer catches sight of himself, his surroundings and the way they change as if in a duplicated distorting mirror. The boundaries between sculpture and its effect are blurred.

Anthony Caro's sculptures without plinths look at first like continuations of Constructivist designs, but the prefabricated industrial shapes are alienated from their purpose. They have no function ("Prospect II", 1964). The form, heightened by painting and assembled without purpose, is set against the thoroughly rational, purposeful world of technology. The heavy and light sections are sensitively balanced on their diagonal.

Hans Uhlmann, *Steel Sculpture*, 1956

Gerhard Marcks, *Prometheus Bound II,* 1948

places, one of which is the Stefan Locher fountain (1955/56) in the courtyard of the old Wallraf-Richartz Museum, and above all for his cathedral and church doorways of Cologne, Salzburg and Hiroshima. Compared with these, his autonomous three-dimensional work, schooled by Expressionism and Cubism, has taken a back seat in terms of public interest. And this is wrong. Mataré's relatively small works in bronze and above all in wood show a highly successful combination of natural and abstract form. In his hands, natural form becomes pictorial emblem, concentrating completely on the essential, whether it is in "Sleeping Cat" (1929), "Cow" (1929) or "Female Torso" (1932). All anecdotal embellishment is avoided. The careful polish on the surface, consciously including the grain of the wood, strengthens the impression of the concentration of a natural phenomenon into artistic form, without the aliveness of the sculpture suffering in any way. These works appeal to our sense of touch. They are pleasant to pick up. "Dürer is quite right," the artist noted in his diary, "when he says that the artist can wrest art from nature; it is just hidden, and it takes a little trouble…"

"Wresting out" form is not an end in itself. It serves much more as a means of making complex reality vis-

sode. A stay in Greece confirmed his view of himself as guardian and continuing exponent of the classical European-Occidental inheritance. Despite this he was persecuted and suppressed by the Nazis as a "degenerate artist."

Marcks' artistic devices are generous simplification of form and introspective expression. In the figure "Eos" (1934) all physical qualites have given way to a column-like unity of form. The goddess of the dawn, given the features of a pupil of Marcks, seems to rise weightlessly from the plinth, to soar. Closer to the earth, but with comparable sensitivity of expression, is the figure of a woman mourning on the "Cologne Memorial to the Dead" in the cloister of the church of St. Maria in the Capitol (1946/49). The act of mourning is internalized both literally and figuratively; it is immanent in the face in repose, in the slight inclination of the head, and in the arms under the protecting cloak. More strongly accentuated is the seated, bowed-down figure of "Prometheus Bound" (1948), a personification of the suffering caused by the period and by man. The space enclosed by the body is an active part of the composition, unlike the closed form of the female figures. Ewald Mataré, a pupil of Corinth and later teacher of Joseph Beuys, Erwin Heerich and Gunter Haese, was much more open with regard to the movements of his period. He became famous for his works in public

Ewald Mataré, *Female Torso,* 1932

286

Alfred Lörcher, *Conversation While Bathing,* 1955

ible in pictorial form. This is not primarily a question of
aesthetics. A piece of sculpture should be a "necessary
object." "I no longer want an aesthetic work of art,"
wrote Mataré in 1947 to Albert Schulze-Vellinghausen,
the most influental German critic of the first two
decades after the war, "I'm making myself a fetish." It is a
straight road from this position to the magic of the
object in the work of Mataré's pupil Joseph Beuys.

The miniature sculptures of the Swabian artist Alfred
Lörcher are original and lively; he has made the sculptural group portrait his subject. His lovable works
("Conversation While Bathing", 1955), which represent
everyday scenes, are at the opposite pole to the unfathomable depths of Giacometti's existentialism:
although they are less demanding, they are full of
movement and a delight in communication.

The next generation of German sculptors is represented by Karl Hartung and Bernhard Heiliger. Hartung,
taking his example from Brancusi, Lehmbruck and
Arp, develops his abstract emblems from primaeval
natural forms, as in "Monument" (1954), reminiscent of
a flayed torso, and further developed as a memorial to
the victims of tyranny. Heiliger's forms are nearer to
those of the classical canon in their elegant reduction,
and their combination of organic and technical form.
He took his direction first of all from Brancusi and Arp
("Figure with Raised Arms", 1949). His portraits are
unconventional and highly expressive, formally
reduced and concentrating entirely on the essential
elements of a character ("Karl Hofer", 1951).

The early work of Otto Herbert Hajek and Emil Cimi-
otti represents German sculptural Informel in the late
fifties, which remained a mere episode in this field. In
Hajek's "Space Knot" (1958), the broken planes, spatial

Bernhard Heiliger, *Karl Hofer,* 1951

Günter Haese, *Oasis,* 1964

287

constructions and layers show a particular understanding of architecture in their combination of scaffold-line structures and vegetable forms, an understanding which is the hallmark of the artist's more recent work.

The works of Wilhelm Loth, which at the same time stress and objectify female sexuality ("Outspread Torso", 1972), are outside current trends. This is also true of the sculpture of G. F. Ris ("Round Relief", 1967/68), which combines the organic with the constructive, often with reference to architecture, and of Gunter Haese's graceful, serenely ironic wire sculptures, which had early success in the United States. They are poems written in the air, full of charm, witty and precise ("Oasis", 1964).

"Thinking is Sculpture"

The most complex figure of all is, of course, Joseph Beuys – and not just for Germany. He was a sculptor, object maker, painter, draughtsman, an artist of the environment, the happening and the Fluxus. He founded the "Free University for Creativity" with Heinrich Böll in 1974, he was a political thinker and, without denominational allegiance, a homo religiosus. Because of his faith in the creative force within all men, and his view of sculpture as the sum of all mankind's social and intellectual activities – even "thinking is sculpture" – he broke through all genre boundaries and broadened the concept of art as no-one had done before him. His cultural understanding embraces politics, myth, magic and, in the last resort, religion. Art is not just a part of life, life itself should become a work of art. The concept of "social sculpture" which Beuys invented anticipates the realization of this utopian vision, which goes far beyond any historical idea of the "Gesamtkunstwerk". The Frankfurt critic Peter Iden rightly pointed out in his obituary for the great magician, who died early in 1986, that Beuys "never ceased to insist on the notion of a society in which art could be abolished and would be abolished, society as the sculpture of humane possibility." This idea is realized in various materials. Fat, honey, copper and sulphur are conductive, warm materials, felt isolates, cold metal is repellent: coldness leads to alienation, love manifests itself in an unceasing stream of spreading warmth. This is the key to his rich life's work, however impenetrable it may seem to many. The sensitivity and vulnerability of Beuys, both as an artist and as a human being, speak directly from his drawings, but also from many of his collages ("King's Daughter Sees Iceland", "Bisected Felt Cross with Dust Picture Martha", both 1960). A cross is engraved under the profile of the king's daughter – a sign which crops up throughout his work. A magic hand next to it seems

Joseph Beuys, *Bisected Felt Cross with Dust Picture Martha*, 1960

to combine heathen with Christian symbolism. Sledges suggest cold, the sun-ring warmth. The symbolic language of the "Dust Picture Martha" needs little decoding: a human being declining into dust together with a letter in the simple reliquary of a crude frame. The bisected cross is an emblem of the separation of Rome and Byzantium, of Europe and Asia ("Eurasia"), but also of the division of the world in our time. A Greek cross on a piece of paper is fastened to the bisected felt: with the simplest of means Beuys has created a vivid pictorial metaphor which penetrates deeply into the depths of history and human consciousness.

The sculpture "Sibylla-Justitia" (1957), with the dumb-bell spheres on the ends of the "scale of justice," the suspended eyes and the engraved organic forms, is also full of profound allusions. The sheltering bowl of "Val" (1959/69) conjures up the idea of valley, grave and human being, the "Double Aggregate" (1958/69) with its sucking hollow spaces seems to be a monumental formulation of threatening forces. The dialectical confrontation of a sulphur block and a sulphur mash in a bowl with three air-pumps ("Destroyed Battery S → Sul-

Joseph Beuys, *King's Daughter Sees Iceland,* 1960

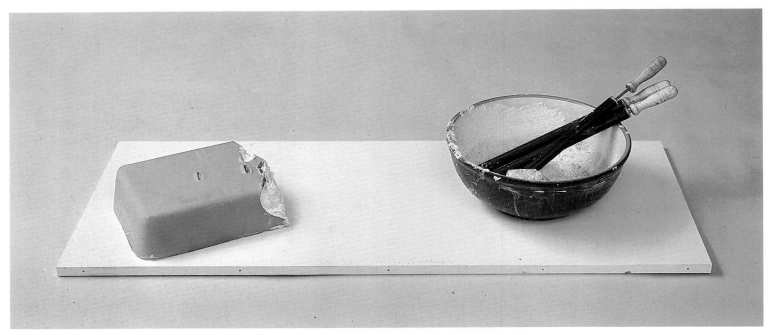

Joseph Beuys, *Destroyed Battery S → Sulphur,* 1969

Joseph Beuys, *Double Aggregate,* 1958 (1969)

phur", 1969) seems to draw a parallel between ourselves and that early period in which the undivided material still had a higher, "unstirred" significance. This puzzling piece cannot be completely deciphered, and it is probably not intended to be. The irrational is an important factor for Beuys. In a radio interview (1969) he said of the origins of sculpture: "The point of origin is completely undifferentiated, is a streaming chaos of the undifferentiated." This "streaming chaos" is also omnipresent in his works. They are not perfect in the Classical, but open in the Romantic sense. The magic object, Mataré's "fetish," is not open to rational explanation, even though much is revealed to anyone who allows himself to become involved with the work. And there is no great art without a little mystery remaining.

The specific quality of the material also plays an important part in the work of Beuys' pupil Reiner Ruthenbeck. His "Glass Plate in Material Bag II" (1971) not only has no plinth, it hangs on the wall. Its subject is the contrast between hard and soft, ductile and rigid, transparent and opaque, stability and instability, open and closed form. The glass forces the lower part of the pocket into a tight rectangle, the upper part – slightly gathered – surges like a tent roof above the limits of the glass. Confusion of the senses of sight and touch leads the observer to critical examination of the processes of perception.

The sculptures of Erwin Heerich, with their incorruptible discipline and comprehensive clarity of form, are at the opposite pole to the incantatory magic of an artist like Joseph Beuys. Their apparent closeness to

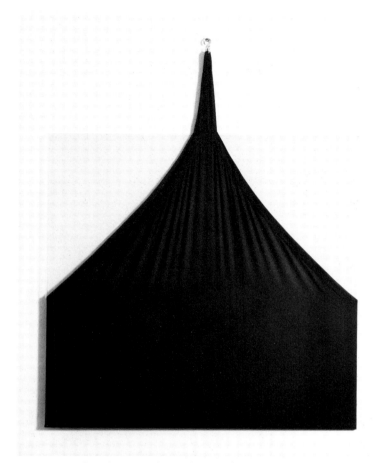

Reiner Ruthenbeck, *Glass Plate in Cloth Bag II,* 1971

Erwin Heerich, *Cardboard Object,* 1969

Ulrich Rückriem, *Triangle,* 1979

the work of the American Minimalists is deceptive. For Heerich, who has French Huguenot blood as well as German, is concerned with composition in accordance with the strict laws of sphere, cube and cylinder, cuboid and pyramid. The bodies are arranged with compulsive logic and his extraordinary "gift for emphatic formulation;" his designs are based on preliminary drawings. "His preferred techniques, the drawing of a line, the cutting of a seam, the bending of an edge," wrote one of his discoverers, Hans van der Grinten, "are handled with a high degree of culture, but they are also primitive in their being, and cannot be reduced to even simpler planes." His sculptures in simple cardboard ("Cardboard Object", 1969) show that he is concerned with form and not with material. These exemplary works always exist on the basis of possible transfer to other materials and to other sizes ("Untitled", 1969). Such transformations are possible without loss of substance, because all the works – in their striving for extreme objectivity – are based on exact plans which determine their execution. The idea is the highest category for Heerich, not what is produced as a result of it.

Things are quite different in the work of Ulrich Rückriem. For him the material is an essential component of his work, whether it is wood, iron or stone. Its specific character remains unaltered, it is the point of origin of the artistic conception: "The material, its form, its qualities and its dimensions, influences and limits my artistic activity," said the artist. Stones are taken apart and reassembled or rearranged to relate to each other, without any encroachment on their material condition. The range of forms is limited to rectangle, square, cross, triangle, trapezium and other basic geometrical shapes. The stone is split or – as in the "Triangle" of 1979 – cut. The smooth sharpness of the cuts gives a higher degree of abstraction than splitting with a hammer and chisel. By taking apart and reassembling in a precisely calculated way – in the case of the "Triangle" by placing the two pieces one on top of the other, with a slight displacement – a piece of nature becomes a work of art in a different context. Nature is not just "exhibited," although the original condition is always visible, without alienation. For, as Rückriem says: "The way in which I adapt the material determines the object itself and the way in which it relates to its site." Because of the way in which it enables one to perceive the dialectic of nature and art, Rückriem's work has to be set in a man-made environment. It has nothing to do with archaism and mysticism. And thus it is entirely comprehensible that the artist once said almost in passing: "Actually I am a Constructivist."

The works of the Soviet sculptress Nina Shilinskaya (b. 1926) are of astonishing strength and independence in their assimilation of historical stimuli. She herself names Gothic sculpture and architecture and Old Russian icon painting as her sources of inspiration. What cannot be overlooked however is a powerfully expressive sense of design, controlled by formal discipline of a Cubist stamp, as found also in the works of Liubov Popova ("The Crossbearer", 1979).

The sculpture of the post-war European heroes who caused such a furore around 1950 at "documenta" I and II has, like the painting of the Ecole de Paris, grown older, and been subjected to bitter criticism. In the Ludwig Museum it is represented mainly by Italians. There is a "Lamenting Horse" (1950) by Marino Marini, paralyzed with terror, a sculptural expression of the "apocalypse now" feeling of the years after the Second World War. Pietro Consagra's "Encounter" (1956) translates an old subject into an abstract vocabulary, rich in form and operating on many levels. Finally, Arnaldo Pomodoro uses the technical vocabulary of the period to represent natural, human and cosmic systems of order in his "Mathematician's Tablet", constructed on a cellular basis.

Mondrian's Constructivism and Moholy-Nagy's experiments with light and movement are the source of inspiration for the Hungarian Nicolas Schöffer, who lives in Paris, and his idea of a quasi-technical Gesamtkunstwerk consisting of mobile (light) painting, sculpture and architecture. In his work structured time

Nina Ivanova Shilinskaya, *The Crossbearer*, 1979

Marino Marini, *Lamenting Horse*, 1950

Niki de Saint-Phalle, *Black Nana,* 1968/69

Nicolas Schoeffer, *Chronos 5,* 1960

plays an important part, unfolding rhythmically, sometimes controlled by the environment and sometimes not, including the aleatory element, guided chance (noise and silence, cold and warmth, light and movement). At the end of all this is the utopia of the "cybernetic town," the world as a work of art for all. Essentially, the sculptures are just pointers to this goal. "Chronos 5" (1960) consists, like many of Schöffer's other sculptures, of polished, moving metal parts and revolving coloured foils. Schöffer, as the title indicates, sees the partly programmed, partly random permanent change of colour and three-dimensional appearance in space as time made visible.

The original "Nana" image by the French artist Niki de Saint-Phalle is the unforgettable monumental figure "Hon" ("She"), who spread her legs in the Moderna Museet Stockholm in 1966, inviting visitors to enter the entertaining interior of the figure, which offered

diversions such as games, a bar and aquaria. Subsequent "Nana Figures", including the one in the Ludwig Museum (1968/69), are cheerful variations on the centuries-old theme of the primaeval mother, good-humouredly but uncompromisingly juxtaposed with the commercialized refrigerator eroticism of the relevant voyeur magazines.

Focus on America

The stock of sculptures by post-1945 American artists, of whom Alexander Calder and David Smith have long since achieved classical status, is rather more significant. Calder is represented by a relatively early "mobile" and a later "stabile". Mobiles, a creative continuation of the first wire sculptures and the legendary miniature circus, are manifestations of the artist at play, and have become extraordinarily popular. "Thirteen Spines", hanging on a thread, apparently floating freely in a delicately staggered arrangement, are kept in unstable balance by a large heart-shaped plate and three smaller steel plates. A breath of air is enough to

Alexander Calder, *The Boot,* 1959

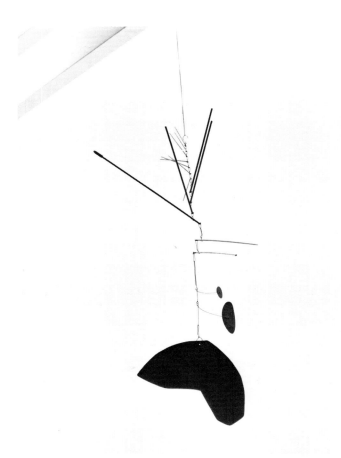

set them in motion. This cheerful game of chance is so carefully calculated by the artist that despite the wide range of possibilities, it cannot possibly go completely wrong.

Calder sees a serious and more intellectual meaning behind this cheerful game. Like Moholy-Nagy before him he saw his kinetic structures as metaphors of the movement of the universe. This system, or part of this system, became the deeper meaning behind all forms in his work. The plinthless, earthbound, immobile, sometimes even threatening stabiles are consciously set against such programmatic content.

It was David Smith – along with Calder, who was more strongly bound up with Europe – who gave American sculpture decisive impetus and new standards. Nevertheless, he always saw himself as a link in a historical chain, and never denied the stimulus he had been given by the work of Picasso and González: "The best artists are presumably both innovators and children of their parents. My parents were all artists who came

Alexander Calder, *Thirteen Spines,* 1940

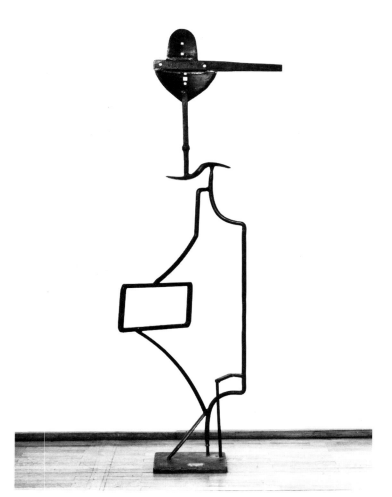

David Smith, *Untitled,* 1953

David Smith, *Voltron XV,* 1963

295

Mark di Suvero, *Martian Ears,* 1975

before me, whose work I knew." Unlike Picasso, he did not see himself as someone who finds without seeking, but as someone who makes selections from an available supply. Sculpture did not interest him as an aesthetic system, but as an emblem of life.

"Untitled" (1953) is one of a group of works inspired by writing, signs in space which Smith believed everyone could understand. It is no coincidence that the sculptor was also an outstanding draughtsman. And so "Untitled" is a draughtsman's "writing" transferred into the third dimension. "Voltron XV", so called in honour of a steel firm and its workers in the Voltri in Italy, is one of the "totem" works, the totem being, like writing another highly significant concept for Smith. The anthropomorphic sculpture is made of industrial materials and assembled with fitting-tools. The almost monstrous, threatening figure is expressive in its mass, and indicates the potential for aggression within each and every human being.

Mark di Suvero is, as the steel sculpture with the provocative title "Martian Ears" (1975) shows, a legitimate heir of David Smith. The "ears," cut from a heavy steel slab and folded upwards and downwards, rock on the narrow tip of the support, statically secured by broad forms at ground level. Ornament and movement para-

doxically contradict the heaviness of the material and the industrial manufacturing process: Smith's aggressive seriousness is tinged with irony.

Minimal Art finally removed sculpture from its pedestal. Formats run counter to the name of the movement by often being gigantic. When looking at these purist works it is often possible to notice that drama, programmatically dismissed for ever, occasionally manages to creep in again by the back door, even if this is on a quite different basis and with quite other aims than those of the heyday of the individual "handwriting" of the self-confident artist "personality," which developed so intoxicatingly at the time of action painting.

When Minimal Art began to make itself felt, the historical programme of anonymous art for all, the ideal of Constructivism, was almost forgotten. Minimal Art is once more classless art without hierarchies, which, in the view of the pioneers of the movement, reflects traditional European social structures. In the early stages Robert Morris sought confirmation of this in the example of Tatlin, Rodchenko, early Gabo and Vantongerloo. Minimal Art, and sculpture in particular, does not exist unconnected in empty space. It always refers to its environment and is usually conceived specifically for it: for a landscape, for a particular architectural context or, as in the case of Carl André and Dan Flavin, directly for the museum.

André's "Timber Object" (1964/70) is related to its environment, and also stems from the world of his own experience as a railwayman. The artist encapsulates prepared wooden beams within each other as "monuments" to human activity, and makes them into a massive, defensive tower. His "Lock Series" (1976) takes a decisive step further forward. The "sculpture" is made up of square steel plates and can be walked on; it is no

Carl André, *Lock Series,* 1976

296

longer three-dimensional, but flat and horizontal: "The idea of sculpture is that of a 'street.' The parts are interchangeable, even the form can be altered by different ways of putting it together, according to the shape and requirements of the surrounding space into which the series is to be integrated, or which it is supposed to define." The part played by theory in these conceptual works, radically questioning the whole traditional concept of "sculpture," cannot be overlooked. Dan Flavin is to an extent right not to allow some of his work to be called "sculpture." "This project" – the installation of fluorescent lamps – "was wrongly designated sculpture, and by people who should have known better," said the artist himself. The title of his work in the Ludwig Museum shows that his artistic thinking is also based on Constructivism: "Monument 7 for V. Tatlin" (1964/65). The work of art is executed in standard fluorescent tubes, and is totally anonymous. Even so, it is possible to make associations: organ pipes, cathedral façade, flying machine. But what it is really about is the emission of light, and the effect which this has of changing the things on which it shines. Flavin wishes his work to be considered soberly. His stimulus is the lights of the city, and not the lights of the universe. He is suspicious of spiritualistic or sociological speculation.

Don Judd is no longer prepared to accept the distinction between content and form, world and order. He certainly does not want any of his work to be all-embracing or universal in the usual sense, as he once said. A form, a mass, a surface is already something in itself and thus should not be hidden as part of an entirely different whole. Forms and materials should be seen without a context. The result of this thinking is the regular lining up of the same objects without hierarchy. "Untitled: 8 Modular Units, V-Channel Piece" (1966/68) is a typical example. Its effect is enhanced by the space in which the modules are placed, into which they extend, and which becomes a part of them.

Minimal Art is only a phase, although it is an important phase, in the work of Robert Morris. His wire-netting "bed" ("Untitled", 1968) is also a series made up of identical parts. The transparent surface of the object includes space, and the way in which it is changed by the play of light and shade. The neutral tone of the material is intended to maintain this impression, which should not be disturbed by the distractions of colour. At the same time Morris stresses the demands of unformed material without limiting geometrical structure: "Unformed masses can be thought just as capable of development as cubes, rags just as acceptable as steel poles." These considerations – and his coming-to-terms with Beuys – led to his amorphous felt pieces. Sol LeWitt did not want to instruct the observer, he wanted to inform him, wrote Lucy R. Lippard, who

Dan Flavin, *Monument 7 for V. Tatlin,* 1964/65

Robert Morris, *Untitled,* 1968

Donald Judd, *Untitled (eight modular units, V-channel piece),* 1966–68

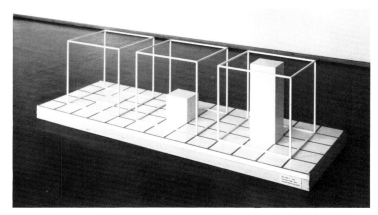

Sol LeWitt, *3 Part Set 789 (B),* 1968

coined the term "Primary Structures" for Minimal Art. The "Three-Part Set" (1968) is a good example of this. A square becomes a cube, and with the assistance of a modular number, three other bodies are created. The process is made visible by the light, open framing. Sculptures of this kind are designed in the studio and executed elsewhere; this is made possible by the renunciation of individual shaping, handwriting and expression. LeWitt's wall drawings are also realized by assistants. The supposition, mooted in the sixties, that one day the object would be superfluous, became a reality in Conceptual Art.

Monument and Thought Games

Minimal Art reaches its most serious, valid, and therefore probably most provocative formulation in the work of Richard Serra, which has already been assigned to the "Post-Minimal" generation – that's how quickly things move today! For Serra, art is too important to be left to the aesthetes. His works are a concentrated expression of concrete experience. For this reason the label "Concrete Art", as understood by the De Stijl artist Van Doesburg, is probably the most accurate. Serra was once a steel worker. Thus his experience in dealing with the material of his choice, the qualities of which are precisely known to him, is existential in the literal sense of the word. The effect of the heavy steel plates held in precarious balance is best described, using the example of the Bochum "Terminal", by a man

Richard Serra, *Moe,* 1971

who has worked at a blast furnace himself: "I spent a long time at the blast furnace," he wrote, "melting rusty plates and also working with huge machines on large rusty brown plates like the ones the Terminal is made of. Now when I pass the Terminal I am reminded of the difficulties, the work, and also the satisfaction I had when a piece of work came out well. I can't help thinking then that I might have made it."

This kind of unprejudiced directness beyond any aesthetic high-mindedness is unlikely to be encountered in the very people who ought to find Serra's concrete art of emblematic compression of concrete experience most accessible. The misapprehension that art is non-compulsory leisure entertainment, a reflection of an intact world outside reality, is the reason for this. Even mass-manufactured industrial steel is rejected as too "raw" a material for a work of art set in an industrial landscape, even though it is used for buildings without a second thought. Art is supposed to be smooth, highly polished and "clean." High-grade steel would be preferable (see also: "Counterpositions").

So for the time being the safest place for Serra's powerful, silent and serious works is the museum. "Moe" (1971) was created to this end. The sculpture weighs several tons, and like all Serra's work from the lead "Card House" of 1969 onwards, its tension is derived from the contrast between the apparent precariousness of the erection and the enormous weight of the three steel plates held in place by a long metal tube. It gives an impression of threat and danger. The sculpture has no front, all sections of it – in accordance with the principles of Minimal Art – are of equal value. The artist wishes the visitor to walk around "Moe", in order to see the work in all its aspects and constantly changing visual conformations. The laconic simplicity of the juxtaposed plates is deceptive in terms of the complex thought processes on which Richard Serra's formal concept and its realization are based. Stubborn prejudice maintains that you need to have studied the history of art to be able to understand these processes, but this is not so. They are all incorporated in the visible work, and therefore visually available to anyone who has his eyes open.

Michael Heizer is famous for his "Land Art" (he calls it "Earth Works") in the Nevada desert and elsewhere. He applied the experience he acquired from this in the shaping of his precisely formulated sculptures, strewn over the floor in alternately positive and negative forms. The wooden sculpture "Circle I" (1976) is one such work. The subject of this beautiful work in many parts is the relationship of segments of a circle to the ideal circle.

Walter de Maria's floor sculpture "Pentagon" comes from the "5 to 9" series (1973), which consists, as the title suggests, of five immaculate polygons of equal size, from a pentagon to a nonagon. The theme is growth, progression. In the open shape of the individual pieces there is a sphere, which can be rolled: a laconic, striking visual formulation of the contrast between repose and movement. It is clear from the background of his contemplative work that this important Land Artist was also concerned with mystical and religious matters, with artistic metaphors of classification systems, with the connection of early man with his modern counterpart (see also: "Breaking out of the Museum").

David Rabinowitch, *Elliptical Plane in 3 Masses and Scales,* 1973

Walter de Maria, *Pentagon (Series 5 to 9),* 1973

Royden Rabinowitch, *Barrel Construction,* 1964

Alain Kirili, *Commandment I,* 1979

Eva Hesse, *Accession II,* 1968

Floor sculpture is the most logical version of sculpture without a plinth. David Rabinowitch's "Elliptical Plane in 3 Masses and 2 Scales" (1973) is a radical example of the minimalization of form. The observer is supposed to walk around the work, and as he does so (as Manfred Schneckenburger, twice director of "documenta", put it) "to make the concrete experience of space while walking part of the three-dimensional effect." That is to say: the non-visible, the observer's associations, become part of the sculpture. An additional bonus is that as one walks around the work the asymmetric division of the whole area continually changes visually in the relationship of the parts to each other and to the whole. The works of David Rabinowitch's brother Royden also require "witnesses" with physical and mental flexibility. The starting point for his work is horizontal sculptures made of parts of oak barrels, which he arranges in a new and contradictory order. The subject is the contrast between bulge and hollow (convex and concave), between the rounded form of lid or base and the fixed rectangular form of the whole in relationship to the observer ("Barrel Construction", 1964).
The works of younger sculptors like Alain Kirili signal a resistance to the purism of Minimal Art by the use of the new media among other things (video, performance, photography, etc.) "Commandment I" (1979) is

a floor sculpture consisting of 26 wrought iron parts in variable arrangements and slightly differing heights. Floor, wall and room are seen as active components of the sculpture. The pieces seem like letters of a forgotten language set in the third dimension, and in fact Kirili was stimulated to create this work by Jewish cult objects. He says: "This sculpture [...] is a translation of emblems, it is a field of emblems."
Eva Hesse died early; she was a pupil of Josef Albers. Her open fibre-glass cube "Accession" (1968) is a striking, sensitive demonstration of the contrasting pairs hard and soft, smooth and rough, solid and hollow, achieved by the simple device of introducing slender plastic tubes through the wall into the interior of the box.

Imagination and Reality

The cheerfully ironic figure world of Marisol is just as far removed from the rigour and formal puritanism of the Minimal Artists as from the elitist thought games of the Conceptualists. Her assemblages in various materials are close to Pop Art, particularly as she is keen that her work should take account of the danger that art might become something for a circle of initiates only, if it is too intellectual. She differs from most Pop Artists in being no stranger to social criticism, although she does not see herself as a political artist. She often features in her own work, as in her montage "The Visit" (1964) as "second on the right." The heavy irony of this representation of a questionable family idyll is easily recognized in the stiff attitude of the three ladies and their impersonal, inhibited facial expressions, the child which has been pushed aside and forced into a cask, and the total lack of communication.
Although they are put together from relics of the everyday world, the wooden shrines of Louise Nevelson have an aura of magic and cult. "Royal Tide IV" (1959/60) is set up like an altar. Everyday objects are not denounced here, but raised to the status of a work of art in a Baroque-Romantic fashion. The gold colour emphasizes the dignity with which everyday things are imbued in the sight of this artist. In her very personal, slightly dramatic and highly imaginative way Louise Nevelson seeks to make life visible in its totality by means of the properties she collects and combines. The work of Paul Thek bears the stamp of cult and ritual from primaeval times down to hippy culture. Death as the nocturnal, reverse side of life plays a central role in his work – to the extent of the identification of the artist with a dead hippy. The splinted arm decorated with feathers ("Untitled", 1967) is at the same time both relic and fetish, as Thek's symbol language demands, in which heathen and Christian elements

Marisol, *The Visit,* 1964

Louise Nevelson, *Royal Tide IV,* 1959/60

Paul Thek, *Sedan Chair,* 1968

Robert Graham, *Untitled,* 1965

John de Andrea, *Untitled,* 1977

combine as the alienating components of an "individual mythology." The "Sedan Chair" (1968) is more brutal, and without a trace of transfiguring Romanticism. Platform, scaffold and chair are apparently the scene of the ritual murder of a blood-stained child, hanging in chains. The piece of raw meat on the seat makes the shock greater.

The sarcastic cheerfulness of Robert Graham's veristic miniature "Untitled" (1965) contrasts strongly with such extreme forms of neo-sacral "new myths." The target of his mockery is the substitute pleasure of "better people" in advanced years: the imitation of Californian glamour à la Hollywood and the eroticism of a bourgeois world which has declined into unimaginative sexism.

John de Andrea is one of the artists who have taken hyperrealism in sculpture to extreme lengths, but his work is far from being flat and superficially naturalistic. This is clear from the reticent painting in neutral colours, avoiding any noisy demonstrations of virtuosity. The same is true of the choice of the unspectacular, calm situations in which he places his figures. They are usually private and intimate ("Untitled", 1977). Also, he always chooses the models for his plaster casts from his own surroundings, from people he knows well. He is concerned with the precise representation of unrepeatable, unique individuality, as expressed in physical appearance. Flat, photographic reproduction is not enough for him. He wants the whole person, and so he produces three-dimensional snapshots in which time stands still.

Duane Hanson goes far beyond De Andrea's private sphere. His theme is a Balzacian "Comédie Humaine". What he asks of art is that it should be a "document" giving reliable information about the times and contemporary society. Hyancinthe Rigaud's official portrait of the sun king Louis XIV is a key work for Hanson, but the painter he admires the most – more even than Goya and Ingres – is Hans Holbein the Younger. His highly focused presentation seems exemplary to Hanson, because it can reveal traits of character which the untrained eye would otherwise miss; reality is enhanced, condensed and concentrated by extreme precision. It is also important to Hanson that properties are not a random ingredient, but belong to the sitter and deliver a commentary on him. The American has been trying to get closer to this precision since 1967, the year in which he opted for lifelike sculptural realism. The way led from the accusing scenarios of his early years ("War", "Bowery Alcoholic") to the undramatic representation of what is strange and everyday, using simple people "in a complex, confused and cross-

Duane Hanson, *Woman with a Purse,* 1974

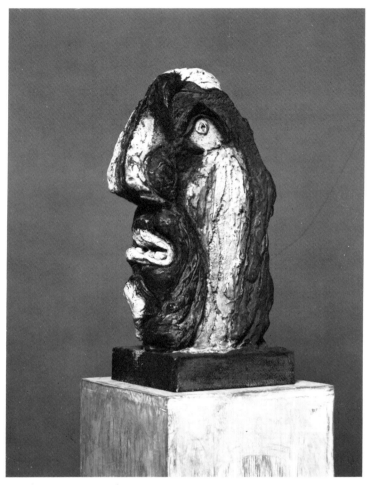

wise world," as he once said. Hanson presents them in poses which are typical of themselves. The individual becomes the representative of a social group within a real situation, which in the hectic rush of everyday life one does not usually notice. Such a figure is the "Woman with a Purse" (1974), whose face mirrors the entire forlornness and melancholy of an average life. Neo-Expressionist sculpture is for the time being only represented by a few vehement sculptures ("Il Principe", 1983) by Markus Lüpertz, who now teaches in Düsseldorf.

New Media

The Ludwig Museum has been able to build up a remarkable photographic department based on the L. Fritz Gruber collection, but only a modest beginning has been made in the field of the new media (video, art film, performance). In terms of quality, however, the standard is excellent. The impressive photographic sequence "Formalization of Boredom" (1979/80) by Jürgen Klauke has been acquired. Klauke is an outstanding draughtsman and painter as well as a "performer," and the work in question is the "short score" of a performance transferred into another medium. It

Markus Lüpertz, *Il Principe,* 1983

Franz Erhard Walther, *Towards an Understanding of Brutality,* 1967

Jürgen Klauke, *Formalization of Boredom,* 1979/80

shows the artist in a struggle, as desperate as it is absurd, with a chair, which has become an active participant: an urgent sequence on loneliness, mistaken identity of person and prop, and hopeless entanglement.

Franz Erhard Walther is an artist who has taken the demand for an active recipient seriously, not just in theory, but also in artistic practice. The objects which make up "Towards an Understanding of Brutality" are not autonomous works of art. They are intended to be used to activate trains of thought and action. Without the involvement of the observer the object remains dead; not until it is actively "used" does it become an instrument for making experience conscious. Walther has been able to prove that this involvement works in many places, using volunteers from various walks of life and different age-groups. His work has opened up new possibilities for relating to art. The process which he set in motion is by no means at an end.

Rebecca Horn's preoccupation is with the extension of sensual and spiritual experience. Her artistic media were at first objects and performance, later video and film. The object can be personalized in her case as well. In the film "The Gigolo" a table dances a tango as a "complete gentleman" and doppelgänger of a blind dancer. Isolation, alienation of self, speechlessness, the garrulous automatic mechanism of disturbed interpersonal relationships, circling in the dark, the "interchangeability of things and human beings, reality and illusion" (Germano Celant), are the themes of Rebecca Horn's first feature film "La Ferdinanda". In it objects are as important as the people whose activities they reflect. Peacocks play an important role in this. The "Peacock Machine" (1981) in the cellar of the Villa Ferdinanda accompanies and comments upon what is happening in the upper rooms, and spreads out in all its splendour, or collapses tremulously. Its feather-lightness and remote control give the peacock wheel the unconscious grace of a marionette. Action and sculpture: these are the poles between which Horn's work moves. The object exhibited and the textual setting combine emotion and reflection in a poetic metaphor.

Rebecca Horn, *The Peacock Machine,* 1981

Literature

Art of the Twentieth Century, General Texts

Arnason, H. H.: A History of Modern Art. New York 1976/London 1977.
Ashton, Dore: A Reading of Modern Art. Cleveland/London 1969.
Battcock, Gregory (ed.): The New Art: A Critical Anthology. New York 1973.
Canaday, John: Mainstreams of Modern Art. New York 1980.
Frascina, Francis and *Harrison, Charles:* Modern Art and Modernism. London 1982.
Gottlieb, Carla: Beyond Modern Art. New York 1976.
Haftmann, Werner: Painting in the Twentieth Century. London 1968.
Herbert, R. L. (ed.): Modern Artists on Art. New York 1965.
Hofmann, Werner: Turning Points in Twentieth-Century Art. London 1969.
Hughes, Robert: Shock of the New. London 1980.
Lucie-Smith, Edward: Art Now. London 1977.
Oliva, A. B.: Europe/America, The Different Avantgardes. New York 1976.
Read, Herbert: Concise History of Modern Painting. London 1975.
Richardson, Tony and *Stangos, Nicos (eds.):* Concepts of Modern Art. Harmondsworth/New York 1974.
Rubin, William (ed.): "Primitivism" in 20th Century Art. New York 1984.
Russell, John: The Meanings of Modern Art. London 1981.
Schapiro, Meyer: Modern Art: Nineteenth and Twentieth Centuries. New York 1982.
Shone, Richard: The Century of Change. Oxford 1977.
Solomon, Frederick: Critique of Modern Art. Sevenoaks, Kent 1970.
Walker, John A.: Art since Pop. London 1975.

General History of Art

Chipp, Herschel B.: Theories of Modern Art. Berkeley/Los Angeles 1968.
Dvorak, Max: The History of Art as a History of Ideas. London 1984.
Gombrich, E. H.: The Story of Art. London 1983.
Janson, H. W.: History of Art. New York 1974.
Meier-Graefe, Julius: Modern Art. Being a Contribution to a New System of Aesthetics. Salem NH 1968.
Osborne, Harold (ed.): Aesthetics. Oxford 1972.
Read, Herbert: The Philosophy of Modern Art. London 1964.
Spies, Werner: Focus on Art. New York 1982.

Sculpture

Bowness, Alan: Modern Sculpture. London 1965.
Burnham, Jack: Beyond Modern Sculpture. New York 1968.
Elsen, Albert E.: The Origins of Modern Sculpture. New York 1974/London 1978.
Elsen, Albert E.: Modern European Sculpture. New York 1979.
Hammacher, A. M.: The Evolution of Modern Sculpture. London 1969.
Krauss, Rosalind E.: Passages in Modern Sculpture. London/New York 1977.
Read, Herbert: Concise History of Modern Sculpture. London 1964.

Trier, Eduard: Form and Space. London/New York 1968.
Tucher, William: The Language of Sculpture. London 1974.

Individual Countries

Austria:
Frampton, Kenneth: Austrian New Wave. London 1980.
Sotriffer, Kristian (ed.): Modern Austrian Art. New York 1965.
Vergo, Peter: Art in Vienna 1898–1918. Oxford 1975.

France:
Hunter, Sam: Modern French Painting 1855–1956. New York 1956.
Kelder, D.: Great Book of French Impressionism. New York 1984.
Marchiori, G.: Modern French Sculpture. New York 1963.
Paris and the American Avant-Garde 1900–1925. Michigan 1980.
Van Dyke, John C.: Modern French Masters. Gloucester 1984.

Germany:
Barr, Alfred H.: Modern German Painting and Sculpture. Salem NH 1972.
German Art in the Twentieth Century – Painting and Sculpture 1905–1985. Royal Academy of Arts, London 1985.
Haftmann, Werner: German Art of the Twentieth Century. Salem NH 1972.
Händler, G.: German Painting in Our Time. Berlin 1956.
Neue Sachlichkeit and German Realism of the Twenties. London 1978.
Ritchie, Andrew C. (ed.): German Art of the Twentieth Century. New York 1957.
Roethel, Hans K.: Modern German Painting. New York 1957.
Roh, Franz: German Art in the 20th Century. Greenwich CT 1968.
Roters, Eberhard: Berlin 1910–1933. New York 1982.
Selz, Peter: German Expressionist Painting. Berkeley 1957.

Great Britain:
Bertram, Anthony: A Century of British Painting 1851–1951. London 1951.
Bowness, Alan: Contemporary British Painting. London 1968.
Farr, Denis: English Art 1870–1940. Oxford 1978.
Harrison, Charles: English Art and Modernism 1900–1939. Bloomington IN 1981.
Ray, Paul C.: The Surrealist Movement in England. Ithaka/London 1971.
Read, Herbert: Contemporary British Art. London 1964.

Italy:
Carrieri, Raffaele: Avant-Garde Painting and Sculpture (1890–1955) in Italy. Milan 1955.
Soby, James T. and *Barr, Alfred H.:* Twentieth-Century Italian Art. New York 1949.

Russia:
Avantgarde in Russia (cat.). Los Angeles 1980.
Barooshian, Vahan D.: Russian Cubo-Futurismus 1910–1930. Amsterdam/Berlin/New York 1974.
Cook, Catherine: Russian Avant-Garde Art and Architecture. London/Paris 1983.

Dodge, Norton (ed.): New Art from the Soviet Union. Washington 1977.
Gray, Camilla: The Great Experiment: Russian Art 1863–1922. London 1962.
Russian and Soviet Painting (cat.). New York 1977.

United States:

Ashton, Dore: American Art since 1945. Oxford 1982.
Brown, Milton W.: American Art. New York 1979.
Cahill, Holger: American Painting and Sculpture. New York 1970.
Geldzahler, Henry: New York Painting and Sculpture 1940–1970. New York 1970.
Goodrich, Lloyd: Pioneers of Modern Art in America. New York 1963.
Heller, Nancy and Williams, Julia: Painters of the American Scene. New York 1982.
Hunter, Sam and Jacobus, John: American Art of the Twentieth Century. New York 1974.
Johnson, Ellen H. (ed.): American Artists on Art from 1940–1980. London/New York 1982.
Lane, John R. and Larsen, Susan C.: Abstract Painting and Sculpture in America. Pittsburgh 1983.
Rose, Barbara: American Art since 1900. New York 1967.
Rose, Barbara: Readings in American Art since 1900. New York 1968.
Sandler, Irving: The Triumph of American Painting. New York 1975.

Expressionism and Fauvism

Dube, Wolf Dieter: The Expressionists. New York 1972.
Elderfield, John: Fauvism and Its Affinities. New York 1976.
Giry, Marcel: Fauvism. New York 1983.
Lankheit, Klaus (ed.): The Blaue Reiter Almanac. London 1969.
Meyers, Bernhard S.: Expressionism: A Generation in Revolt. London 1963.
Muller, J. E.: Fauvism. London 1967.
Schneider, Pierre: Matisse. London 1984.
Vogt, Paul: The Blue Rider. Woodbury NY 1980.
Whitford, Frank: Expressionism. London 1970.

Cubism and Futurism

Appolonio, Umbro: Futurist Manifestos. London 1973.
Cooper, Douglas: The Cubist Epoch. London 1970.
Daix, Pierre: Cubists and Cubism. New York 1983.
D'Harnoncourt, Anne and Celant, Germano: Futurism and the International Avant-Garde. Philadelphia 1980.
Fry, Edward F.: Cubism. London 1965.
Golding, John: Cubism, a History and Analysis. London 1971.
Kozloff, Max: Cubism – Futurism. New York 1973.
Martin, Marianne W: Futurist Art and Theory. Oxford 1969.
Nash, J. M.: Cubism, Futurism, Constructivism. London 1974.
Rosenblum, Robert: Cubism and Twentieth Century Art. New York 1976.
Rye, Jane: Futurism. London 1972.
Schwartz, Paul Waldo: The Cubists. London 1971.
Tisdall, Caroline and Bozzola, Angelo: Futurism. London 1977.
Wadley, Nicholas: Cubism. London 1970.
Wilson, Simon: What Is Cubism? London 1983.

Bauhaus, Constructivism and De Stijl

Barr, Alfred H.: De Stijl 1917–1928. New York 1961.
Douglas, Charlotte E.: Swans of Other Worlds: Kazimir Malevich and the Origins of Abstraction in Russia. Ann Arbor MI 1980.
Gray, C.: The Russian Experiment in Art, 1863–1922. London 1974.
Jaffé, H. L. C.: De Stijl 1917–1931. London 1956.

Rickey, George: Constructivism: Origins and Evolution. New York 1967.
Roters, Eberhard: Painters of the Bauhaus. London 1965.
Rotzler, Willy: Constructive Concepts.
Whitford, Frank: Bauhaus. London 1984.
Wingler, Hans M.: The Bauhaus. Cambridge MA 1969.

Dada and Surrealism

Ades, Dawn: Dada and Surrealism Reviewed. London 1978.
Breton, André: What Is Surrealism? New York 1973.
Cardinal, Roger and Short, Robert S.: Surrealism, Permanent Revelation. London 1970.
Erickson, John: Dada: Performance, Poetry and Art. Boston 1984.
Gershmann, Herbert S.: The Surrealist Revolution in France. Ann Arbor MI 1969.
Lippard, Lucy (ed.): Surrealists on Art. Englewood NJ 1974.
Motherwell, Robert (ed.): The Dada Poets and Painters. New York 1951.
Nadeau, Maurice: The History of Surrealism. London 1965.
Picon, Gaetan: Surrealism 1919–1939. London 1977.
Richter, Hans: Dada. London 1965.
Rosemont, Franklin: André Breton and the First Principles of Surrealism. London 1978.
Rubin, William S.: Dada and Surrealist Art. New York 1969.
Schneede, Uwe: Surrealism. New York 1974.
Verkauf, Willy (ed.): Dada. London 1975.
Waldberg, Patrick: Surrealism. London 1966.
Wilson, Simon: Surrealist Painting. Oxford 1975.

Post-1945 Movements (Main Tendencies)

Barrett, Cyril: Op Art. London 1970.
Battcock, Gregory (ed.): Idea Art. New York 1973.
Battcock, Gregory: Super Realism. New York 1975.
Carrà, Massimo (ed.): Metaphysical Art. London 1971.
Celant, Germano: Arte Povera. Milan 1985.
Compton, Michael: Pop Art. London 1970.
Finch, Christopher: Pop Art. London 1968.
Guilbaut, Serge: How New York Stole the Idea of Modern Art: Abstract Expression 1940–1948. Chicago 1983.
Hobbs, Robert C. and Levin, Gail: Abstract Expressionism. Ithaka/London 1978.
Joachimedes, Christos and Rosenthal, Norman (eds.): Zeitgeist (cat.). New York 1984.
Kaprow, Allan: Assemblage, Environments and Happenings. New York 1965.
Lippard, Lucy: Pop Art. New York 1968.
Lippard, Lucy: Changing. New York 1971.
Lippard, Lucy: Six Years: The Dematerialization of the Art Object. London 1973.
Lucie-Smith, Edward: Movements in Art since 1945. London 1969.
Lucie-Smith, Edward: Art in the Seventies. London 1980.
McShine, Kynaston L. (ed.): Information. New York 1970.
Meyer, Ursula: Conceptual Art. New York 1972.
Popper, Frank: Origins and Development of Kinetic Art. Greenwich CT 1968.
Russell, John and Gablik, Suzi: Pop Art Redefined. London/New York 1969.
Schmalenbach, Fritz: Picasso to Lichtenstein. London 1974.
Shapiro, David (ed.): Social Realism: Art as a Weapon. New York 1973.
Wilson, Simon: Pop Art. London 1974.
Wolfe, T.: The Painted Word. New York 1978.

Ludwig Museum

Handbook to the Ludwig Museum, Art of the 20th Century. Contributors: Alfred M. Fischer, Gerhard Kolberg, Ursula Peters, Dieter Ronte, Karl Ruhrberg, Evelyn Weiss. Vol 1 & 2, Cologne 1983.

List of Illustrations
A. Twentieth Century Art/Of Collectors and Collections

Jankel Adler, *Katzen (Cats)*, 1927
Oil on canvas, 100.7 x 120.5 cm
Donation Haubrich, 1946

Josef Albers, *Homage to the Square: Green Scent*, 1963
Oil on fibre board, 120 x 120 cm
Donation Ludwig, 1976

Pierre Alechinsky, *Coupe Sombre (Dark Vessel)*, 1968
Acrylic on parchment on canvas, 100 x 244 cm
Anniversary donation, 150 years WRM, 1974

Carl André, *Lock Series*, 1976
36 steel plates, each 100 x 100 cm
Donation Ludwig, 1976

John de Andrea, *Untitled*, 1977
Glass fibre, PVC, plaster, cloth, paint, male figure, h. 185 cm
(standing), female figure, h. 115 cm (seated)
City of Cologne, 1978

Karel Appel, *Personnage (Figure)*, 1958
Oil on canvas, 116 x 89 cm
Donation Haubrich, 1959

Shusaku Arakawa, *Untitled*, 1964/65
Mixed media on canvas, 2 parts, each 245 x 160 cm
Donation Ludwig, 1976

Alexander Archipenko, *Flat Torso*, 1914
Bronze, h. 38.2 cm
City of Cologne, 1964

Arman (Armand Fernandez), *Accumulation de brocs
(Accumulation of Jugs)*, 1961
Enamel Jugs, Plexiglass, 83 x 140 x 40 cm
Donation Ludwig, 1976

Arman (Armand Fernandez), *Torse aux Gants
(Torso with Gloves)*, 1967
Plastic hands in polyester, 170 x 55 cm
Donation Ludwig, 1976

Hans Arp, *Kobra-Kentaur (Cobra-Centaur)*, 1952
Plaster, 78 x 43 x 30 cm
Gift of Mrs. M. Arp-Hagenbach

Hans Arp, *Relief Nadir*, 1959
Pavatex on wood, 152.5 x 130.5 cm
Gift of Mrs. M. Arp-Hagenbach, 1971

Hans Arp, *Construction Architectonique
(Architectonic Construction)*, 1965
Plaster, 84 x 60 x 25 cm
Gift of Mrs. M. Arp-Hagenbach, 1972

Francis Bacon, *Painting 1946* (second version), 1971
Oil on canvas, 198 x 147 cm
Donation Ludwig, 1976

Giacomo Balla, *Velocità d'automobile
(Speed of an Automobile)*, 1913/14
Oil on canvas, 49.5 x 67 cm
On loan, private collection, 1981

Charly Banana, *Der Hirsch im Kreuzverhör
(The Stag Under Cross-Examination)*, 1983
Dispersion paint on nettle cloth and material collage,
190 x 170 cm

Ernst Barlach, *Der Rächer (The Avenger)*, 1914
Bronze, h. 44 cm
City of Cologne, 1944

Ernst Barlach, *Singender Mann (Singing Man)*, 1928
Bronze, h. 49 cm
Gift of Farbenfabriken Bayer Leverkusen, 1950

Georg Baselitz, *Der Wald auf dem Kopf
(The Wood Upside Down)*, 1969
Oil on canvas, 250 x 190 cm
Donation Ludwig, 1976

Georg Baselitz, *Die große Nacht im Eimer
(The Great Night in the Bucket)*, 1962/63
Oil on canvas, 250 x 180 cm
Donation Ludwig, 1976

Georg Baselitz, *Die Peitschenfrau (Whip Woman)*, 1965
Oil on canvas, 162 x 130 cm
Donation Ludwig, 1976

Willi Baumeister, *Steinschliff (Stonecutting)*, 1947
Oil on canvas, 46.5 x 65 cm
Collection Haubrich, 1948

Willi Baumeister, *Stehende Figur mit blauer Fläche
(Standing Figure with Blue Plane)*, 1933
Oil and sand on canvas, 82 x 65.5 cm
Collection Haubrich, 1949

Willi Baumeister, *Kessaua auf Gelb
(Kessaua on Yellow)*, 1955
Oil on cardboard, 65 x 81 cm
Donation Peill, 1976

Willi Baumeister, *Monturi, Diskus IA*, 1953/54
Oil and sand on fibre board, 185 x 135 cm
City of Cologne, 1979

Jean Bazaine, *Le Plongeur (The Diver)*, 1949
Oil on canvas, 147 x 115 cm
City and Land NW, 1963

Max Beckmann, *Landschaft mit Luftballon
(Landscape with Balloon)*, 1917
Oil on canvas, 75.5 x 100.5 cm
City of Cologne, 1954

Max Beckmann, *Bildnis Reber (Portrait of F. G. Reber)*, 1929
Oil on canvas, 140.5 x 72 cm
Gift of Farbenfabriken Bayer Leverkusen, 1955

Max Beckmann, *Selbstbildnis mit schwarzer Kappe
(Self-Portrait with Black Cap)*, 1934
Oil on canvas, 100 x 70 cm
City of Cologne, 1957 (Legacy Georg and Lilly von
Schnitzler, 1979)

Max Beckmann, *Der Leiermann (The Organ-Grinder)*, 1935
Oil on canvas, 175 x 120.5 cm
City of Cologne, (Legacy Georg and Lilly von
Schnitzler, 1979)

Max Beckmann, *Zwei Frauen (Two Women)*, 1940
Oil on canvas, 80 x 61 cm
City of Cologne, 1949

Max Beckmann, *Tango (Rumba)*, 1941
Oil on canvas, 95.5 x 55.5 cm
City of Cologne, (Legacy Georg and Lilly von
Schnitzler, 1979)

Max Beckmann, *Drei Frauen im Profil
(Three Women in Profile)*, 1942
Oil on canvas, 85 x 55 cm
Donation Haubrich, 1946

Max Beckmann, *Stilleben mit drei Gläsern
(Still Life with Three Glasses)*, 1944
Oil on canvas, 95 x 56 cm
Collection Peill, 1976

Rudolf Belling, *Alfred Flechtheim*, 1927
Bronze, h. 19 cm
Collection Haubrich, 1958

Joseph Beuys, *Zerstörte Batterie S → Schwefel
(Destroyed Battery S → Sulphur)*, 1969
Mixed media, 28 x 112 x 44 cm
Donation Ludwig, 1976

Joseph Beuys, *Halbiertes Filzkreuz mit Staubbild Martha
(Bisected Felt Cross with Dust Picture Martha)*, 1960
Gouache and mixed media, 108 x 68 cm
Donation Ludwig, 1976

Joseph Beuys, *Doppelaggregat (Double Aggregate)*,
1958 (1969)
Bronze, 108 x 214 x 78.5 cm
Donation Ludwig, 1976

Joseph Beuys, *Königstochter sieht Island
(King's Daughter Sees Iceland)*, 1960
Gouache and mixed media, 114 x 99 cm
Donation Ludwig, 1976

Boris Birger, *Married Couple*, 1981
Oil on canvas, 120.5 x 110 cm
On loan, private collection, 1982

Peter Blake, *Bo-Diddley*, 1963
Acrylic, Scotch Tape on fibre board, 122.4 x 78.3 cm
Donation Ludwig, 1976

Georges Braque, *Pichet, Citrons, Compotier
(Carafe, Lemons, Fruit Bowl)*, 1928
Oil on canvas, 40.5 x 120.5 cm
City of Cologne, 1958

Georges Braque, *Verre, violon et papier á musique
(Glass, Violin and Sheet Music)*, 1912
Oil and charcoal on canvas, 64.5 x 91.5 cm
Donation Kuratorium und Förderges. Landesregierung
NW, 1962

Peter Brüning, *Bild Nr. 108 (Picture No. 108)*, 1962
Oil on canvas, 120 x 145 cm
City of Cologne, 1962

Carl Buchheister, *Dreieckskomposition
(Triangular Composition)*, 1928
Oil on plywood, 152 x 152 x 135 cm
Gift of Mrs. E. Buchheister, Hanover, 1968

Michael Buthe, *Maske (Mask)*, Nigeria–Marrakesh–Madrid,
1973
Papercollage, opaque paint, gold bronze, 137 x 80 cm
City of Cologne, 1978

James Lee Byars, *The Golden Speaking Hole*, 1982
Glass and gold, circ. 280 cm
City of Cologne, 1982

Alexander Calder, *Thirteen Spines*, 1940
Steel, 220 x 220 cm
City of Cologne, 1969

Alexander Calder, *The Boot*, 1959
Sheet iron, h. 195 cm
City of Cologne, 1962

Heinrich Campendonk, *Frau mit Fischen
(Woman with Fish)*, 1929
Verre églomisé, 67 x 48 cm
Donation Haubrich, 1952

Anthony Caro, *Prospect II*, 1964
Painted steel, 260 x 215 cm
Donation Ludwig, 1976

Carlo Carrà, *La donna e l'assenzio* or *Donna al caffè
(The Woman and the Absinthe)*, 1911
Oil on canvas, 67.5 x 52.5 cm
On loan, private collection, 1980

César (César Baldaccini), *Compression*, 1981
Compressed car body, 162 x 56 x 53 cm
Loan of Ford-Werke, Cologne, 1982

Marc Chagall, *Moses zerbricht die Gesetzestafeln
(Moses Breaking the Tablets of the Law)*, 1955/56
Oil on paper on canvas, 228 x 154 cm
Loan of Wallraf-Richartz-Kuratorium, 1960

Marc Chagall, *Sabbath*, 1910
Oil on canvas, 90.5 x 94.5 cm
Donation Haubrich, 1946

Marc Chagall, *Gelbes Haus (The Yellow House)*, 1924
Oil on canvas, 54.7 x 37.8 cm
Donation Haubrich, 1946

John Chamberlain, *White Shadow*, 1964
Welded (car) scrap, h. 172 cm
Collection Ludwig, 1969

Giorgio de Chirico, *Meubles dans une valleé
(Furniture in a Valley)*, 1927
Oil on canvas, 100 x 135 cm
On loan, private collection, 1983

Giorgio de Chirico, *Intérieur metaphysique*
(Metaphysical Interior), 1926
Oil on canvas, 100 x 73 cm
On loan, private collection, 1982

Giorgio de Chirico, *La Comédie romaine*
(The Roman Comedy), 1926
Oil on canvas, 147 x 117 cm
On loan, private collection, 1982

Christo, *Wrapped Object*, 1963
Canvas, string, 81 x 45 cm
Gallery R. Ricke, Cologne, 1969

Christo, *My Cologne Cathedral Wrapped – Project for
Cologne*, 1980
Enamel Paint, pastel, charcoal, photograph, photocopy
and technical data, collage in two parts:
71 x 28 cm and 71 x 56 cm
On loan, private collection, 1980

Alex Colville, *Truck Stop*, 1966
Acrylic on fibre board, 91.6 x 91.6 cm
Donation Ludwig, 1976

Corneille (Cornelis van Beverloo), *La Cité blanche
(The White Town)*, 1955
Oil on canvas, 79 x 146 cm
Collection Haubrich, 1959

Joseph Cornell, *Hôtel de l'Océan*, 1959/60
Mixed media, 21.5 x 36 x 10.2 cm
City of Cologne, 1970

Salvador Dalí, *Der Bahnhof von Perpignan
(The Station at Perpignan)*, 1965
Oil on canvas, 295 x 406 cm
Collection Ludwig, 1978

Robert Delaunay, *Rhythme sans fin (Endless Rhythm)*,
1934
Oil on canvas, 208 x 51.9 cm
City of Cologne, 1973

Paul Delvaux, *Les Dryades (The Dryads)*, 1966
Oil on canvas, 149.5 x 237.5 cm
Collection Ludwig, 1977

André Derain, *Vue de St. Paul-de-Vence
(View of Saint-Paul-de-Vence)*, 1910
Oil on canvas, 60.5 x 80.5 cm
City of Cologne, 1947

Jan Dibbets, *Film Painting: Black Vase Horizontal*, 1972
80 Photos mounted on aluminium plates, 24 x 19 cm each,
total 190.0 x 192 cm
Donation Ludwig, 1976

Braco Dimitrijević, *Triptychon Post Historicus*, 1984
Photo made after an installation for an exhibition at the
Ludwig Museum with Giorgio de Chirico's "Furniture in a
Valley." (1927)
On loan, private collection

Jim Dine, *Six Big Saws*, 1962
Oil, saw, nails on canvas, 4 parts, 122.5 x 368 cm
Donation Ludwig, 1976

Jim Dine, *Roman Color Chart*, 1968
Canvas, screws, tapes, two parts, 213 x 416 cm
Donation Ludwig, 1976

Otto Dix, *Bildnis Dr. Hans Koch
(Portrait of Dr. Hans Koch)*, 1921
Oil on canvas, 100.5 x 90 cm
Donation Haubrich, 1946

Otto Dix, *Selbstbildnis (Self-Portrait)*, 1931
Oil and tempera on wood, 100 x 80 cm
Donation Haubrich, 1946

Otto Dix, *Bildnis des Dichters Theodor Däubler
(Portrait of Theodor Däubler)*, 1927
Tempera on plywood, 150 x 100 cm
Donation Haubrich, 1946

Kees van Dongen, *Bildnis Ana (Portrait of Ana)*, c. 1905/06
Oil on canvas, 55 x 46.4 cm
City of Cologne, 1911

Jean Dubuffet, *La Route aux hommes
(The Street with Men)*, 1944
Oil on canvas, 129 x 96 cm
Donation Ludwig, 1976

Jean Dubuffet, *Le Chien sur la table
(The Dog on the Table)*, 1953
Oil on canvas, 89.7 x 116.5 cm
City of Cologne, 1966

Jean Dubuffet, *Paysage portatif (Portable Landscape)*, 1968
Polyurethene, 100 x 140 x 100 cm
Donation Ludwig, 1976

Marcel Duchamp, *La Boîte en valise
(The Portable Museum)*, 1964
Wood, paper, glass, plastic, photos, 83 parts in a red
leather case, 41 x 37.8 x 10.5 cm
City of Cologne, 1971

Raymond Duchamp-Villon, *Seated Woman*, 1914
Bronze, gilded, h. 73 cm
Collection Ludwig, 1976

Vassily Ermilov, *Memorial Tablet "21. Januar 1924"*, 1924
Metal and enamel, 79 x 79.5 cm
Collection Ludwig, 1979

Max Ernst, *Laon*, 1916
Oil on canvas, 65.6 x 100.5 cm
Donation Haubrich, 1946

Max Ernst, *Au Rendez-vous des amis
(Rendezvous of the Friends)*, 1922
Oil on canvas, 129.5 x 193 cm
City of Cologne, 1971

Max Ernst, *Die Jungfrau Maria verhaut den Menschensohn
(Virgin Smacking the Christ Child)*, 1926
Oil on canvas, 100 x 81 cm

Max Ernst, *Lerche im Wald (Lark in the Wood)*, 1926/27
Opaque paint on cardboard, 37 x 25 cm
Collection Haubrich, 1948

Max Ernst, *Fleurs-Coquillages (Shell Flowers)*, 1929
Oil on canvas, 100 x 80 cm
City and Land NW, 1963

Max Ernst, *Birth of Comedy*, 1947
Oil on canvas, 53 x 40 cm
Donation Peill, 1976

Max Ernst, *Printemps à Paris (Spring in Paris)*, 1950
Oil on canvas, 115 x 89 cm
Loan of the Land NW, 1966

Richard Estes, *Foodshop*, 1967
Oil on canvas, 166 x 123.5 cm
Donation Ludwig, 1976

Öyvind Fahlström, *Roulette, Variable Painting*, 1966
Oil on photo, vinyl, paperboard and magnets,
152.5 x 166 cm
Donation Ludwig, 1976

Joseph Fassbender, *Ohne Titel (Untitled)*, 1970
Oil on canvas, 150 x 104.5 cm
Anniversary Donation, 150 years WRM, 1974

Lyonel Feininger, *Brücke III (Bridge III)*, 1917
Oil on canvas, 80.5 x 100 cm
Collection Haubrich, 1951

Lyonel Feininger, *Türme über der Stadt (Halle)*
(Towers Above the Town), 1931
Oil on canvas, 88.3 x 124 cm
Collection Haubrich, 1952

Dan Flavin, *Monument 7 for V. Tatlin*, 1964/65
Fluorescent tubes, 300 x 100 cm
Donation Ludwig, 1969

Lucio Fontana, *Concetto Spaziale: Attese*
(Spatial Concept: Expectations), 1960
Water colour on canvas, 80 x 100 cm
Gift of the Kölnischer Kunstverein, 1963

Lucio Fontana, *Concetto Spaziale: Sposalizio a Venezia*
(Spatial Concept: Marriage in Venice), 1961
Oil on canvas, 152 x 154 cm
Donation Ludwig, 1976

Otto Freundlich, *Ascension*, 1929
Bronze, 200 x 104 x 104 cm
City of Cologne, 1978

Otto Freundlich, *Grün – Rot (Green – Red)*, 1939
Oil on canvas, 65 x 54.4 cm
City of Cologne and Land NW, 1963

Naum Gabo, *Construction in Space – Crystal*, 1937
Plexiglass, 57.2 x 57.2 x 46 cm
City of Cologne, 1969

Franz Gertsch, *Marina schminkt Luciano*
(Marina Making Up Luciano), 1975
Acrylic on untreated cotton, 234 x 346.5 cm
Collection Ludwig, 1976

Alberto Giacometti, *Le Nez (The Nose)*, 1947
Bronze, 38 x 7.5 x 66 cm
Collection Ludwig, 1979

Alberto Giacometti, *Place*, 1950
Bronze, painted, 56.2 x 56 x 42.5 cm
Collection Ludwig, 1979

Werner Gilles, *Verkündigung (Annunciation)*, 1948
Oil on canvas, 45 x 65 cm
Collection Haubrich, 1948

Domenico Gnoli, *Scarpa di Profilo (Profile of a Shoe)*,
1966
Oil on canvas, 110 x 139.5 cm
Donation Ludwig, 1976

Karl Otto Götz, *Bild vom 14. 9. 1954*
(Picture of 14. 09. 1954), 1954
Mixed media on canvas, 90 x 120 cm
Collection Ludwig, Köln

Bruno Goller, *Verschiedene Bilder (Various Pictures)*, 1955
Oil on canvas, 170 x 140 cm
Donation Ludwig, 1976

Natalia Goncharova, *Portrait of Larionov*, 1913
Oil on canvas, 105 x 78 cm
Collection Ludwig, 1980

Camille Graeser, *Gelb-Blau-Volumen 1:1, 1/18, bewegt*
(Yellow-Blue Volume 1:1, 1/18, Allegro), 1974
Acrylic on canvas, 120 x 120 cm
City of Cologne, 1976

Robert Graham, *Untitled*, 1965
Painted clay, plexiglass, 43 x 25 x 36 cm
Donation Ludwig, 1976

Gotthard Graubner, *Farbraumkörper – Diptychon*
(Colour-Space-Body – Diptych), 1977
Oil on canvas on synthetic cotton, 248 x 248 x 15 cm each
City of Cologne, 1978

Nancy Stevenson Graves, *Shaman*, 1970
Steel, latex, gauze, oil paint, marble dust, acrylic,
426 x 426 x 365 cm
Donation Ludwig, 1976

Nancy Stevenson Graves, *Ceridwen, Out of Fossils*, 1969
Bronze, c. 5 x 5 m
Collection Ludwig, 1978

Juan Gris, *Syphon, verre et journal (Syphon, Glass and*
Newspaper), 1916
Oil on canvas, 155 x 46.5 cm
Donation WRM-Kuratorium und Fördergesellschaft, 1964

George Grosz, *Dr. Eduard Plietzsch*, 1928
Oil on canvas, 110 x 79.5 cm
Collection Haubrich, 1949

Renato Guttuso, *Caffè Greco*, 1976
Oil on canvas, 282 x 333 cm
Collection Ludwig, 1977

Günter Haese, *Oase (Oasis)*, 1964
Brass wire, 29.5 x 27 x 30 cm
Donation Ludwig, 1976

Raymond Hains, *Affiche déchirée (Tattered Placard)*, 1961
Coloured paper on zinc, 200 x 100 cm
City of Cologne, 1971

Richard Hamilton, *Towards a Definitive Statement on the*
Coming Trends in Men's Wear and Accessories, 1963
Oil, collage, plastic foil on wood, 122.3 x 81.2 cm
Donation Ludwig, 1976

Richard Hamilton, *My Marilyn (Paste Up)*, 1964
Photos, oil, paper, 50.4 x 51 cm
Donation Ludwig, 1976

Richard Hamilton, *Swingeing London 67 II*, 1968
Silk screen, oil on canvas, 67 x 85 cm
Donation Ludwig, 1976

Duane Hanson, *Woman with a Purse,* 1974
Polyester, resin, talcum, reinforced with fibreglass,
oil paint, articles of clothing, wig, 163 cm (real size)
Donation Ludwig, 1976

Hans Hartung, *T 55-3,* 1955
Oil on canvas, 100 x 72 cm
Collection Peill, 1976

Hans Hartung, *T 56-21,* 1956
Oil on canvas, 180 x 114 cm
City of Cologne and Land NW, 1963

Erich Heckel, *Fasanenschlößchen bei Moritzburg*
(Pheasant Lodge near Moritzburg), 1910
Oil on canvas, 97 x 120.5 cm
City of Cologne, 1949

Erich Heckel, *Kanal in Berlin (Canal in Berlin),* 1912
Oil on canvas, 83 x 100 cm
Donation Haubrich, 1946

Erwin Heerich, *Kartonobjekt (Cardboard Object),* 1969
Cardboard, 60 x 60 x 60 cm
Donation Ludwig, 1976

Bernhard Heiliger, *Karl Hofer,* 1951
Bronze, h. 46 cm
City of Cologne, 1956

Bernhard Heisig, *Letztes Bildnis meiner Mutter*
(Last Portrait of My Mother), 1978
Oil on pressed pasteboard, 118.5 x 83 cm
On loan, private collection, 1982

Werner Heldt, *Stilleben auf dem Balkon*
(Still Life on the Balcony), 1951
Oil on canvas, 57 x 71 cm
Collection Haubrich, 1959

Eva Hesse, *Accession II,* 1968
Fibreglass, 80 x 80 x 80 cm
Donation Ludwig, 1976

David Hockney, *Sunbather,* 1966
Acrylic on canvas, 183 x 183 cm
Donation Ludwig, 1976

Gerhard Hoehme, *Beschwörung (Conjuration),* 1960
Mixed media on canvas, 128 x 200 cm
Donation Kölnischer Kustverein, 1961

Heinrich Hoerle, *Masken (Masks),* 1929
Oil on canvas, 68.5 x 95.5 cm
Donation Haubrich, 1946

Heinrich Hoerle, *Zwei Frauenakte (Two Female Nudes),*
1930/31
Oil on plywood, 108 x 73 cm
Donation Haubrich, 1946

Carl Hofer, *Maskerade (Masquerade),* 1922
Oil on canvas, 129 x 103 cm
Donation Haubrich, 1946

Hans Hofmann, *Composition No. I,* 1952
Oil on plywood, 76.2 x 60.9 cm
Collection Ludwig, 1980

Rebecca Horn, *Die Pfauenmaschine (The Peacock Machine),*
1981
Metal, peacock feathers, electro motor, installation with
three glass tubes, 4 m height each, with text, 2 glass boxes
with caput mortum filled with ash
City of Cologne, 1982

Jörg Immendorff, *Café Deutschland I,* 1978
Acrylic on canvas, 278 x 326 cm
Collection Ludwig

Robert Indiana, *Zig,* 1960
Wood, wire, iron, oil paint, 165 x 45 x 41 cm
Donation Ludwig, 1976

Robert Indiana, *The American Gas Works,* 1961/62
Acrylic on canvas, 152.5 x 122 cm
Donation Ludwig, 1976

Alexei von Javlensky, *Stilleben mit Vase und Krug*
(Still Life with Vase and Pitcher), 1909
Oil on paperboard, 49.5 x 43.5 cm
Collection Haubrich, 1947

Alexei von Javlensky, *Märchenprinzessin mit Fächer*
(Fairytale Princess with Fan), 1912
Oil on paperboard, 65.5 x 54 cm
Donation Peill, 1976

Alexei von Javlensky, *Variation,* c. 1916
Oil on cloth, cardboard, 37.8 x 26.2 cm
Donation Haubrich, after 1946

Jasper Johns, *Flag on Orange Field,* 1957
Encaustic on canvas, 167 x 124 cm
Donation Ludwig, 1976

Jasper Johns, *Passage,* 1962
Encaustic, part of a ruler, metal chain, fork, paper,
collage on canvas (3 parts), 178 x 102 cm
Donation Ludwig, 1976

Jasper Johns, *Map,* 1967–71
Encaustic, pastel and collage on canvas, 22 parts,
500 x 1000 cm
Donation Ludwig, 1976

Jasper Johns, *Untitled,* 1972
Acrylic and wax on canvas, boards, waxcasts and mixed
media, 4 parts, 183 x 490 cm
Donation Ludwig, 1976

Allan Jones, *Perfect Match,* 1966/67
Oil on canvas, 280 x 93 cm
Donation Ludwig, 1976

Asger Jorn, *The Blow,* 1962
Oil on canvas, 125 x 199 cm
City of Cologne, 1980

Donald Judd, *Untitled (eight modular units, V-channel*
piece), 1966–68
Stainless steel, 120 x 313 x 318 cm
Donation Ludwig, 1976

Vassily Kandinsky, *Moscow, Zubovskiy Square III,*
c. 1916
Oil on canvas, 180 x 200 cm
Collection Ludwig

Vassily Kandinsky, *White Stroke,* 1920
Oil on hessian, 98 x 80 cm
City of Cologne, 1977

Vassily Kandinsky, *Shrill Peaceful Pink,* 1924
Oil on paperboard, 63.6 x 48.2 cm
Collection Haubrich, 1952

Howard Kanovitz, *Journal,* 1972/73
Acrylic on canvas, 273 x 243 cm
Donation Ludwig, 1976

Ellsworth Kelly, *Three Panels: Blue Yellow Red,* 1966
Oil on canvas, 210 x 153.5 cm
Donation Ludwig, 1976

Edward Kienholz, *Night of Nights,* 1961
Zinc, steel wool, plaster head, 77 x 74 x 20 cm
Donation Ludwig, 1976

Edward Kienholz, *The Portable War-Memorial,* 1968
Mixed media, 285 x 960 x 240 cm
Donation Ludwig, 1976

Ernst Ludwig Kirchner, *Weiblicher Halbakt mit Hut
(Half-Nude Woman with Hat),* 1911
Oil on canvas, 76 x 70 cm
Donation Haubrich, 1946

Ernst Ludwig Kirchner, *Die Russin (The Russian Woman),*
1912
Oil on canvas, 150.5 x 76 cm
Collection Haubrich, 1947

Ernst Ludwig Kirchner, *Fünf Frauen auf der Straße
(Five Women in the Street),* 1913
Oil on canvas, 120 x 90 cm
Collection Haubrich, 1947

Ernst Ludwig Kirchner, *Die Eisenbahnüberführung
(The Bridge Over the Railway),* 1914
Oil on canvas, 79 x 100 cm
Gift of W. Franz, Cologne, 1960

Ernst Ludwig Kirchner, *Eine Künstlergemeinschaft
(A Fellowship of Artists),* 1925
Oil on canvas, 168 x 126 cm
Collection Haubrich, 1953

Alain Kirili, *Commandment I,* 1979
Forged iron, 26 different pieces of various sizes, between
22.5 and 37 cm in height, 10 and 28 cm breadth, and
5.5 and 18 cm depth
Collection Ludwig, 1980

Ronald B. Kitaj, *Austro-Hungarian Foot-Soldier,* 1961
Oil, collage, canvas, 152.5 x 91 cm
Donation Ludwig, 1976

Konrad Klapheck, *Der Supermann (The Superman),* 1962
Oil on canvas, 140 x 170 cm
Donation Ludwig, 1976

Konrad Klapheck, *Soldatenbräute (Soldier Brides),* 1967
Oil on canvas, 120 x 170 cm
Donation Ludwig, 1976

Jürgen Klauke, *Formalisierung der Langeweile
(Formalization of Boredom),* 1979/80
5 part photography, each 110 x 180 cm
City of Cologne, 1982

Paul Klee, *Kleiner Narr in Trance
(Fool in a Trance),* 1929
Oil on canvas, 50.5 x 35.5 cm
Collection Strecker, 1958

Paul Klee, *Hauptweg und Nebenwege
(Highways and Byways),* 1929
Oil on canvas, adjustable frame, 83 x 67 cm
City of Cologne, 1974

Yves Klein, *Relief éponge bleu: RE 19
(Blue Sponge Relief: RE 19),* 1958
Wood, sponges, pigment, synthetic resin, 200 x 165 cm
Donation Ludwig, 1976

Yves Klein, *Anthropométrie: ANT 130,* 1960
Pigment and synthetic resin on paper and canvas,
194 x 127 cm
Donation Ludwig, 1976

Franz Kline, *Scranton,* 1960
Oil on canvas, 177 x 124.5 cm
Collection Ludwig

Ivan Kljun, *Suprematist Composition,* c. 1916
Oil on canvas, 70 x 45.5 cm
Collection Ludwig

Imi Knoebel, *Ohne Titel (Untitled),* 1967–75
Oil on nettle cloth, 8 pieces: 260 x 160 cm (4 x),
160 x 130, 160 x 140, 160 x 150, 160 x 160 cm
Collection Ludwig, 1975

Oskar Kokoschka, *Bildnis Tilla Durieux
(Portrait of Tilla Durieux),* 1910
Oil on canvas, 56 x 65 cm
Donation Haubrich, 1946

Oskar Kokoschka, *Die Heiden (The Heathens),* 1918
Oil on canvas, 75.5 x 126 cm
Donation Haubrich, 1950

Oskar Kokoschka, *Dresden, Neustadt III,* 1921
Oil on canvas, 70 x 99 cm
Donation Haubrich, 1949

Oskar Kokoschka, *Ansicht der Stadt Köln vom Messeturm
aus (View of the City of Cologne from the Exhibition Tower),*
1956
Oil on canvas, 85 x 130 cm
Gift of Kulturkreis im BDI, 1956

Georg Kolbe, *Tänzerin (Dancer),* 1922
Bronze, h. 66 cm
City of Cologne, 1948

Käthe Kollwitz, *Klage (Lament),* 1938
Tinted plaster, 28 x 25 cm
City of Cologne, 1947

Willem de Kooning, *Untitled VII,* 1984
Oil on canvas, 195 x 223.5 cm
Collection Ludwig

Joseph Kosuth, *Frame – One and Three,* 1965
Wooden frame, 60 x 60 cm, 2 formica boards,
100 x 100 cm each, collage on cardboard, 12.5 x 7.5 cm
Donation Ludwig, 1976

František Kupka, *Boîte à musique (Musical Box),* 1946
Oil on plywood, 51.4 x 50 cm
City of Cologne, 1961

Mikhail Larionov, *Nature morte à l'écrevisse
(Still Life with Crab),* 1907
Oil on canvas, 80 x 95 cm
On loan, private collection, 1982

Mikhail Larionov, *Saucisson et maquereaux rayonistes (Rayonist Sausage and Mackerel)*, 1912
Oil on canvas, 46 x 61 cm
Collection Ludwig, 1979

Henri Laurens, *La Guitare (The Guitar)*, 1914
Sheet iron, painted, h. 44 cm
Collection Ludwig, 1979

Henri Laurens, *Guitare, verre et pipe (Guitar, Glass and Pipe)*, 1918
Collage, 49 x 62 cm
City of Cologne, 1967

Henri Laurens, *L'Adieu (The Parting)*, 1941
Bronze, 70 x 85 x 82 cm
City of Cologne, 1967

Fernand Léger, *Le Remorqueur rose (The Pink Tug)*, 1918
Oil on canvas, 65.5 x 92 cm
City of Cologne, 1961

Fernand Léger, *Les Gémeaux (The Twins)*, 1929/30
Oil on canvas, 73 x 92 cm
City of Cologne, 1970

Fernand Léger, *La Partie de campagne (The Country Outing)*, 1954
Oil on canvas, 194.5 x 194.5 cm
WRM Kuratorium und Förderergesellschaft, 1978

Wilhelm Lehmbruck, *Frauentorso (Female Torso)*, 1910
Bronze, h. 115 cm
City of Cologne, 1925

Wilhelm Lehmbruck, *Jünglingskopf (Youth's Head)*, 1913
Stone cast, h. 46 cm
City of Cologne, 1946

Aristarch Lentulov, *Cypress Landscape*, 1913
Oil on canvas, 64.5 x 61 cm
Collection Ludwig

Barry Le Va, *Three Studies for documenta 1972*, 1972
Felt pen, coloured crayon, ballpoint pen on paper, 73.2 x 102.2 cm each
Donation Ludwig, 1976

Rudolf Levy, *Bildnis des Malers Purrmann (Portrait of the Painter Purrmann)*, 1931
Oil on canvas, 93.3 x 73.2 cm
City of Cologne, 1956

Sol LeWitt, *3 Part Set 789 (B)*, 1968
Coloured steel, scotch tape, 80 x 208 x 50 cm
Donation Ludwig, 1976

Roy Lichtenstein, *Takka Takka*, 1962
Magna on canvas, 173 x 143 cm
Donation Ludwig, 1976

Roy Lichtenstein, *M-Maybe (A Girl's Picture)*, 1965
Magna on canvas, 152 x 152 cm
Donation Ludwig, 1976

Roy Lichtenstein, *Study for "Preparedness"*, 1968
Magna on canvas, 142.5 x 255 cm
Donation Ludwig, 1976

Roy Lichtenstein, *Rouen Cathedral (Seen at three different times of the day), Set No. 2*, 1969
Magna on canvas, 3 parts, 160 x 106.8 cm each
Donation Ludwig, 1976

Roy Lichtenstein, *Modular Painting with Four Panels No. 1*, 1969
Magna on canvas, 4 parts, 137.3 x 137.3 cm each
Donation Ludwig, 1976

Roy Lichtenstein, *Stillife with Net, Shell, Rope and Pulley*, 1972
Magna and oil on canvas, 152 x 234.5 cm
Donation Ludwig, 1976

Roy Lichtenstein, *Landscape with Figures and Rainbow*, 1980
Oil and magna on canvas, 213.4 x 304.8 cm
Collection Ludwig, 1980

Richard Lindner, *Target No. 1*, 1960–62
Oil on canvas, 152.4 x 101.5 cm
Donation Ludwig, 1976

Richard Lindner, *Disneyland*, 1965
Oil on canvas, 203 x 127 cm
Donation Ludwig, 1976

Richard Lindner, *Leopard-Lilly*, 1966
Oil on canvas, 177.8 x 152.4 cm
Donation Ludwig, 1976

Jacques Lipchitz, *Woman Reading*, 1919
Bronze, h. 77 cm
City of Cologne, 1961

Alfred Lörcher, *Gespräch beim Baden (Conversation While Bathing)*, 1955
Bronze, 14.3 x 8.8 x 12 cm
City of Cologne, 1962

Morris Louis, *Daleth*, 1958/59
Acrylic on cotton oil cloth, 250 x 350 cm
Donation Ludwig, 1976

Morris Louis, *Alpha-Ro*, 1961
Acrylic on canvas, 267 x 546.5 cm
Donation Ludwig, 1976

Morris Louis, *Pillars of Dawn*, 1961
Acrylic on canvas, 220 x 122 cm
Donation Ludwig, 1976

Markus Lüpertz, *Il Principe*, 1983
Bronze, gilded, 40 x 19.5 x 24 cm
On loan, private collection

Heinz Mack, *Fünf Flügel eines Engels (Five Wings of an Angel)*, 1965
Aluminium on wood, 200 x 103 cm
Donation Ludwig, 1976

August Macke, *Dame in grüner Jacke (Lady in a Green Jacket)*, 1913
Oil on canvas, 44 x 43.5 cm
Collection Haubrich, 1947

August Macke, *Lesender Mann im Park (Man Reading in the Park)*, 1914
Oil on canvas, 86.5 x 100.3 cm
Collection Haubrich, 1948

René Magritte, *La Géante (The Giantess)*, c. 1929–31
Oil on canvas, paperboard, paper, tempera, 54 x 73 cm
City of Cologne, 1974

Aristide Maillol, *Leda,* about 1902
Bronze, h. 28.5 cm
Donation Haubrich, 1946

Aristide Maillol, *Ile de France,* 1925
Bronze, h. 166.5 cm
City of Cologne, 1954

Kasimir Malevich, *Suprématisme dynamique
(Dynamic Suprematism),* 1916
Oil on canvas, 102.4 x 66.9 cm
Collection Ludwig, 1978

Alfred Manessier, *Le Feu (The Fire),* 1957
Oil on canvas, 80.5 x 100 cm
City of Cologne, 1958

Man Ray, *Lampshade,* 1919 (1959)
Sheet iron, painted white, h. c. 87 cm
City of Cologne, 1967

Man Ray, *Retour à la Raison (Return to Reason),* 1939
Oil on canvas, 200 x 124.5 cm
City of Cologne, Kuratorium und Förderergesellschaft
WRM/ML, 1980

Piero Manzoni, *Achrome (Colourless),* 1960
Fabric, sewed and treated, 80 x 60 cm
Donation Ludwig, 1976

Franz Marc, *Wildschweine (Wild Boars),* 1913
Oil on canvas on paperboard, 73.5 x 57.5 cm
Gift of Autohaus Fleischhauer, 1954

Gerhard Marcks, *Gefesselter Prometheus II
(Prometheus Bound),* 1948
Bronze, h. 78 cm
City of Cologne, 1951

Brice Marden, *Humilatio,* 1978
Oil and wax on canvas, 213 x 244 cm
Collection Ludwig, 1979

Walter de Maria, *Pentagon (Series 5 to 9),* 1973
5 Aluminium sculptures, each 120 cm diameter
City of Cologne, 1975

Marino Marini, *Klagendes Pferd (Lamenting Horse),* 1950
Bronze, h. 51.5 cm
Collection Haubrich, 1954

Marisol, *La Visita (The Visit),* 1964
Multi media, 152.5 x 226 cm
Donation Ludwig, 1976

Albert Marquet, *Bon Regret, Rabat (Fond Memory,
Rabat)* 1935
Oil on canvas, 50 x 61 cm
City of Cologne, 1960

Karl Marx, *Paolozzi III,* 1978
Oil on fibre board, 100 x 90 cm
Gift of the artist, 1982

Andre Masson, *Chevaux dévorant des oiseaux
(Bird-Eating Horses),* 1927
Oil and feathers on canvas, 110 x 50.5 cm
City of Cologne, 1967

Ewald Mataré, *Weiblicher Torso (Female Torso),* 1932
Teak wood, h. 20 cm
Collection Haubrich, 1955

Henri Matisse, *Jeune fille assise (Girl Seated),* c. 1909
Oil on canvas, 41.5 x 33.5 cm
Collection Strecker, 1958

Henri Matisse, *Femmes et singes (Women and Monkeys),*
1952
Collage, 71.7 x 286.2 cm
Collection Ludwig, 1978

Matta (Roberto Matta Echaurren), *Nu d'ensemble
(Nude in a Group),* 1965
Oil on canvas, 156 x 200 cm
Land NW und Wallraf-Richartz-Kuratorium, 150 years
Museum, 1974

Wolfgang Mattheuer, *Was nun? (What Now?),* 1980
Oil on fibre board, 100 x 125 cm
On loan, private collection, 1982

Georg Meistermann, *Fisch will Vogel werden
(Fish Wanting to Become Bird),* 1951
Oil on canvas, 101 x 151 cm
Collection Haubrich, 1952

Carlo Mense, *Bildnis H. M. Davringhausen
(Portrait of H. M. Davringhausen),* 1922
Oil on canvas, 86.5 x 59.5 cm
Donation Haubrich, 1946

Rune Mields, *Ohne Titel (B 31/1971) (Untitled – B 31/1971),*
1971
Oil on canvas, 250 x 150 cm
City of Cologne, 1972

Joan Miró, *Amour,* 1926
Oil on canvas, 146 x 114 cm
City of Cologne, 1965

Paula Modersohn-Becker, *Stilleben mit Kürbis
(Still Life with Pumpkin),* 1905
Oil on paperboard, 69.5 x 89.5 cm
Collection Haubrich, 1947

Paula Modersohn-Becker, *Selbstbildnis (Self-Portrait),* 1906
Oil on paperboard, 45.7 x 29.7 cm
Collection Haubrich, 1948

Amadeo Modigliani, *L'Algérienne (The Algerian Girl),* 1917
Oil on canvas, 55 x 30 cm
Collection Strecker, 1958

Laszlo Moholy-Nagy, *Auf weißem Grund (On a White
Ground),* 1923
Oil on canvas, 101 x 80.5 cm
Gift of W. Franz, 1962

Piet Mondrian, *Tableau I,* 1921
Oil on canvas, 96.5 x 60.5 cm
City of Cologne and WDR, 1967

Henry Moore, *Reclining Draped Figure,* 1952/53
Bronze, h. 102 cm
City of Cologne, 1954

Giorgio Morandi, *Still Life,* 1921
Oil on canvas, 44.7 x 52.8 cm
On loan, private collection, 1981

Malcolm Morley, *St. John's Yellow Pages*, 1971
Oil on canvas, 159 x 137 cm
Donation Ludwig, 1976

Robert Morris, *Untitled*, 1968
Aluminium wire, 92.5 x 360 x 360 cm
Donation Ludwig, 1976

Otto Mueller, *Zwei Mädchenakte (Two Nudes)*, c. 1919
Distemper on hessian, 87.4 x 70.6 cm
Donation Haubrich, 1946

Otto Mueller, *Zwei Zigeunerinnen mit Katze
(Two Gypsies and Cat)*, c. 1926/27
Oil on canvas, 144.5 x 109.5 cm
Collection Haubrich, 1952

Horst Münch, *Victory*, 1983
Mixed media on nettle cloth, 200 x 240 cm

Heinrich Nauen, *Der barmherzige Samariter
(The Good Samaritan)*, 1914
Gouache on paper on canvas, 170 x 120 cm
Collection Haubrich, 1952

Ernst Wilhelm Nay, *Frau im Taunus (Woman in Taunus)*,
1939
Oil on canvas, 95.5 x 115.5 cm
Collection Haubrich, 1955

Ernst Wilhelm Nay, *Die Jakobsleiter (Jacob's Ladder)*, 1946
Oil on canvas, 96 x 81 cm
Donation Peill, 1976

Ernst Wilhelm Nay, *Blauflut (Blue Flood)*, 1961
Oil on canvas, 190 x 340 cm
Donation Peill, 1976

Louise Nevelson, *Royal Tide IV*, 1959/60
Wood, gold paint, 35 parts, 335 x 426 cm
Donation Ludwig, 1976

Barnett Newman, *Midnight Blue*, 1970
Oil and acrylic on canvas, 193 x 239 cm
City of Cologne, 1976

Emil Nolde, *Rote und gelbe Rosen (Red and Yellow Roses)*,
1907
Oil on canvas, 64.5 x 83 cm
Donation Haubrich, 1946

Emil Nolde, *Familie (Bonnichsen) (The Bonnichsen Family)*,
1915
Oil on canvas, 73.3 x 89 cm
Collection Haubrich, 1948

Emil Nolde, *Schwärmer (The Enthusiasts)*, 1916
Oil on canvas, 100.7 x 86.4 cm
Donation Haubrich, 1946

Emil Nolde, *Junge Frau und Männer
(Young Woman and Men)*, 1919
Oil on plywood, 101 x 73 cm
Donation Haubrich, 1946

Richard Oelze, *Wachsende Stille (Growing Silence)*, 1961
Oil on canvas, 98 x 125 cm
Gift of BDI 150 years WRM, 1974

Claes Oldenburg, *Men's Jacket with Shirt and Tie
(Brown Jacket)*, 1961
Wire, fabric, plaster, enamel varnish, 115 x 80 cm
Donation Ludwig, 1976

Claes Oldenburg, *Green Legs with Shoes*, 1961
Plaster, wire, fabric, enamel varnish, 149 x 100 x 20 cm
Donation Ludwig, 1976

Claes Oldenburg, *Soft Washstand (ghost version)*, 1965
Canvas, kapok, paint, wood, h. 135 cm
Donation Ludwig, 1976

Claes Oldenburg, *The Mouse Museum*, 1965–77
Inventory: 389 objects, room size: 263 x 950 x 1020 cm
Collection Ludwig, 1978

Blinky Palermo (Peter Heisterkamp), *Himmelsrichtungen I
(Points of the Compass)*, 1976
Acrylic on aluminium, 4 parts, 26.7 x 21 cm each
Collection Ludwig, 1976

Eduardo Paolozzi, *The Last of the Idols*, 1963
Aluminium, oil paint, 244 x 71 x 64 cm
Donation Ludwig, 1976

Max Pechstein, *Das grüne Sofa (The Green Sofa)*, 1910
Oil on canvas, 96.5 x 96.5 cm
Collection Haubrich, 1953

A. R. Penck, *Ohne Titel (Freundesgruppe) (Untitled)*, 1964
Oil on fibre board, 170 x 275 cm
Collection Ludwig, 1976

A. R. Penck, *Ein mögliches System (A Possible System)*, 1965
Oil on canvas, 95 x 200 cm
Donation Ludwig, 1976

Alexander Petrov, *House by the Railway*, 1981
Oil on canvas, 150 x 120 cm
On loan, private collection, 1982

Antoine Pevsner, *Dernier Elan (The Last Upswing)*,
1961/62
Bronze, gilded, h. 66.8 cm
City of Cologne, 1965

Francis Picabia, *La Nuit espagnole (Spanish Night)*, 1922
Ripolin (enamel paint) on canvas, 200 x 161 cm
Collection Ludwig, 1979

Francis Picabia, *La Mariée (The Bride)*, c. 1929
Gouache on wood, 121.5 x 96.5 cm
Collection Haubrich, 1960

Pablo Picasso, *Femme à la mandoline
(Woman with Mandoline)*, 1910
Oil on canvas, 91.5 x 59 cm
Collection Ludwig, 1976

Pablo Picasso, *Harlequin*, 1923
Oil on canvas, 129 x 96 cm

Pablo Picasso, *Mandoline, compotier, bras de marbre
(Mandoline, Fruitbowl, Marble Fist)*, 1925
Oil on canvas, 97.5 x 131 cm
Collection Strecker, 1958

Pablo Picasso, *La Femme à l'artichaut
(Woman with Artichoke)*, 1942
Oil on canvas, 195 x 132 cm
Collection Ludwig, 1978

Pablo Picasso, *Île de la Cité – Vue de Notre-Dame de Paris
(26. Février 1945) (Île de la Cité – View of Notre Dame de
Paris)*, 1945
Oil on canvas, 80 x 120 cm
Collection Ludwig, 1973

Pablo Picasso, *Tête de femme lisant (Head of a Woman Reading)*, 1953
Oil on plywood, 45.8 x 38 cm
City of Cologne, 1953

Pablo Picasso, *Mangeurs de pastèque (Melon Eaters)*, 1967
Oil on canvas, 114 x 146 cm
Donation Ludwig, 1976

Pablo Picasso, *Mousquetaire et Amour (Musketeer and Cupid)*, 1969
Oil on canvas, 194.5 x 130 cm
Donation Ludwig, 1976

Otto Piene, *Feuer, Rot und Schwarz auf Weiß (Fire, Red and Black on White)*, 1962
Oil, pigment on canvas, 110 x 110 cm
City of Cologne, 1971

Michelangelo Pistoletto, *Comizio Nr. 2 (Party Conference No. 2)*, 1965
Polished steel, collage, 215 x 120 cm
Donation Ludwig, 1976

Anne and Patrick Poirier, *Ausée*, 1975
Corkboards, charcoal, c. 10 x 5 m
Collection Ludwig, 1980

Sigmar Polke, *Kopf (Head)*, 1966
Oil on canvas, 297.5 x 305 cm
Anniversary donation, 150 years WRM, 1974

Jackson Pollock, *Number 15*, 1951
Duco on canvas, 142.2 x 167.7 cm
City of Cologne, 1972

Liubov Popova, *Female Nude Seated*, c. 1913
Oil on canvas, 106 x 87 cm
Collection Ludwig, 1978

Liubov Popova, *Relief*, 1915
Oil on paper and paperboard on wood, 66.3 x 48.5 cm
Collection Ludwig, 1977

Ivan Puni, *Sculpture – Variant No. 110*, 1915
Wood, tin plate, cardboard, painted, 70.5 x 40.5 x 12 cm
Collection Ludwig, 1979

Hans Purrmann, *Blumen und Früchte (Flowers and Fruits)*, 1949
Oil on canvas, 81.5 x 100 cm
Collection Haubrich, 1958

David Rabinowitch, *Elliptical Plane in 3 Masses and Scales*, 1973
Solid steel, 7.7 x 305 x 274 cm
City of Cologne, 1979

Royden Rabinowitch, *Barrel Construction*, 1964
Oak
David Bellman

Franz Radziwill, *Die Straße (The Street)*, 1928
Oil on canvas, 80.5 x 87 cm
Collection Haubrich, 1955

Arnulf Rainer, *Violettrot, vertikal (Violet Red, Vertical)*, 1961
Oil on canvas, 200 x 130 cm
Collection Ludwig, 1976

Robert Rauschenberg, *Odalisque*, 1955–58
Multi media, 205 x 44 x 44 cm
Donation Ludwig, 1976

Robert Rauschenberg, *Allegory*, 1959/60
Multi media, 183 x 305 cm
Donation Ludwig, 1976

Robert Rauschenberg, *Wall Street*, 1961
Multi media, 182 x 226 cm
Donation Ludwig, 1976

Robert Rauschenberg, *Axle*, 1964
Oil and silk screen on canvas, 274 x 610 cm
Donation Ludwig, 1976

Robert Rauschenberg, *Soundings*, 1968
Plexiglass, silk screen, electronic installations, 244 x 1100 cm
Donation Ludwig, 1976

Robert Rauschenberg, *Radiant White 952*, 1971
Cardboard, plywood, 230 x 991 x 36 cm
Donation Ludwig, 1976

Ray, see Man Ray

Martial Raysse, *Simple and Quiet Painting*, 1965
Photograph on cardboard, oil on canvas, plastic fabric, plastic flowers, 130 x 195 cm
Donation Ludwig, 1976

Ad Reinhardt, *Abstract Painting*, 1954–59
Oil on canvas, 276 x 102 cm
City of Cologne, 1978

Germaine Richier, *Le Griffu (Claw Being)*, 1952
Bronze, h. 91 cm
City of Cologne and WDR, 1966

Gerhard Richter, *Ema – Akt auf einer Treppe (Ema – Nude on a Staircase)*, 1966
Oil on canvas, 200 x 130 cm
Donation Ludwig, 1976

Gerhard Richter, *Abstrakt Nr. 484 (Abstract No. 484)*, 1981
Oil paint on canvas, 200 x 320 cm
Donation Ludwig, 1982

Jean-Paul Riopelle, *Rencontre (Meeting)*, 1956
Oil on canvas, 100 x 81 cm
Collection Haubrich, 1957

James Rosenquist, *Untitled (Joan Crawford says…)*, 1964
Oil on canvas, 242 x 196 cm
Donation Ludwig, 1976

James Rosenquist, *Horse Blinders*, 1968/69
Oil and luminous paint on canvas, aluminium, 23 parts, 275 x 2530 cm
Donation Ludwig, 1976

Mark Rothko, *Earth and Green*, 1955
Oil on canvas, 231.5 x 187 cm
City of Cologne and Kuratorium, 1971

Ulrich Rückriem, *Dreieck (Triangle)*, 1979
Natural stone, h. 110 cm, 100 cm length on each side
City of Cologne

Reiner Ruthenbeck, *Glasplatte in Stofftasche II (Glass Plate in Cloth Bag II)*, 1971
Glass, fabric, 100 x 100 cm
City of Cologne, 1979

Niki de Saint-Phalle, *Schwarze Nana (Black Nana)*, 1968/69
Painted polyester, 293 x 200 x 120 cm
Donation Ludwig, 1976

Oskar Schlemmer, *Zwei Sitzende auf geschwungenen Stühlen (Zwei Mädchen) (Two Seated Figures)*, 1935/36
Oil on paper, 61.5 x 43 cm
Collection Haubrich, 1946

Oskar Schlemmer, *Vierzehner Gruppe in imaginärer Architektur (Group of Fourteen in Imaginary Architecture)*, 1930
Oil, tempera on canvas, 91.5 x 120.5 cm
City of Cologne and NW, 1956

Karl Schmidt-Rottluff, *Stilleben mit Äpfeln und gelben Blumen (Still Life with Apples and Yellow Flowers)*, 1908
Oil on canvas, 66 x 48 cm
Collection Haubrich, 1958

Karl Schmidt-Rottluff, *Stilleben mit Negerplastik (Still Life with Negro Sculpture)*, 1913
Oil on canvas, 73 x 68.5 cm
Donation Haubrich, 1946

Karl Schmidt-Rottluff, *Gruß an Nolde (Greeting to Nolde)*, 1936
Oil on canvas, 89.5 x 76.5 cm
City of Cologne, 1946

Nicolas Schöffer, *Chronos 5*, 1960
Duralumin, plexiglass, electro motors, h. 200 cm
Donation Ludwig, 1976

Georg Schrimpf, *Mädchen am Fenster (Girl at the Window)*, 1923
Oil on canvas, 52.5 x 37.5 cm
Donation Haubrich, 1946

Bernard Schultze, *Rubyrr*, 1957/58
Wire, textiles, plastic mass and oil on canvas, 120 x 120 cm
Gift, 150 years WRM, 1974

Bernard Schultze, *Migof-Ursula-Ahnentafel (Migof-Ursula-Family Tree)*, 1963
Mixed media, wire, textiles, plastic mass on canvas, 125 x 150 x 32 cm
City of Cologne, 1968

Emil Schumacher, *Deli*, 1975
Oil on canvas, 170 x 130 cm
City of Cologne, 1982

Kurt Schwitters, *Merzbild 9 B (Das große Ichbild) (Merz Picture 9 B [The Great I Picture])*, 1919
Collage, 96.8 x 70 cm

Kurt Schwitters, *Relief*, 1923
Material collage, 35.5 x 30 cm
City of Cologne, 1974

Paul-Adolf Seehaus, *Bergstadt (Town in the Mountains)*, 1915
Oil on canvas, 100 x 77 cm
Donation Haubrich, 1946

Arthur Segal, *Der Hafen (The Port)*, 1921
Oil on canvas, 147 x 187.5 cm with frame
Collection Ludwig, 1980

George Segal, *The Restaurant Window*, 1967
Plaster, restaurant windows, wood, metal, plexiglass, neon tubes, chair, table, 243 x 335 cm
Donation Ludwig, 1976

Franz Wilhelm Seiwert, *Arbeiter (Workers)*, 1926
Oil on canvas, 81 x 60 cm
City of Cologne, 1957

Franz Wilhelm Seiwert, *Stadt and Land (Town and Country)*, 1932
Oil on plywood, 70.6 x 80.7 cm
Gift of Dr. H. Schmitt-Rost, Cologne, 1957

Richard Serra, *Moe*, 1971
Steel plates, 244 x 610 x 366 cm

Gino Severini, *Ballerina*, 1913
Oil on canvas, 61 x 50 cm
On loan, private collection, 1981

Nina Ivanovna Shilinskaya, *Crossbearer*, 1979
Wood, painted
On loan, private collection, 1982

Charles Simonds, *Park Model/Fantasy I*, 1974–76
Clay, photographs, 3 parts, 81 x 51 x 18 cm each
Collection Ludwig, 1978

Renée Sintenis, *Daphne*, 1930
Bronze, h. 145 cm
City of Cologne, 1949

Mario Sironi, *Aeroplano giallo con paessagio urbano (Yellow Aeroplane with Urban Landscape)*, 1915
Gouache, collage, 71 x 53 cm
Collection Ludwig, 1980

David Smith, *Untitled*, 1953
Steel, h. 215 cm
Collection Ludwig, 1979

David Smith, *Voltron XV*, 1963
Steel, h. 190 cm
City of Cologne, 1979

Pierre Soulages, *Peinture (Painting)*, 1964
Oil on canvas, 202 x 143 cm
Donation Ludwig, 1976

Daniel Spoerri, *La Table de Robert (Robert's Table)*, 1961
Wooden plate with assembled objects, 200 x 50 cm
Donation Ludwig, 1976

Nicolas De Staël, *L'Etagère (The Shelf)*, 1955
Oil on canvas, 88,5 x 116 cm
Land NW/Kuratorium/City of Cologne and anniversary donation, 150 years WRM, 1974

Frank Stella, *Color Maze*, 1966
Acrylic on canvas, 160 x 160 cm
Donation Ludwig, 1976

Frank Stella, *Ctesiphon III*, 1968
Fluorescent acrylic on canvas, 300 x 600 cm
Donation Ludwig, 1976

Frank Stella, *Bonin Night Heron No. 1*, 1976/77
Aluminium, acrylic, 1975 x 325 cm
Collection Ludwig, 1977

Clyfford Still, *Untitled,* 1948/49
Oil on canvas, 206 x 172.7 cm
Collection Ludwig, 1977

Nikolai Suetin, *Composition,* c. 1922/23
Oil on canvas, 65 x 48 cm
On loan, private collection, 1982

Mark di Suvero, *Martian Ears,* 1975
Steel, 200 x 170 x 180 cm
Collection Ludwig, 1979

Antoni Tàpies, *Traumgarten (Dream Garden),* 1949
Oil on canvas, 96 x 128.8 cm
City of Cologne, 1964

Antoni Tàpies, *Blanc avec signe rose No. LXXVII
(White with Pink Sign No. LXXVII),* 1958
Wood, sand, canvas, paint on canvas, 130 x 162 cm
Donation Ludwig, 1976

Antoni Tàpies, *Graues Relief in vier Teilen
(Grey Relief in Four Parts),* 1963
Mixed media (sand) on canvas, 150 x 217 cm
City of Cologne, 1965

Volker Tannert, *Ohne Titel (Untitled),* 1982
Dispersion paint on canvas, 300 x 200 cm
City of Cologne, 1982

Paul Thek, *Sedan Chair,* 1968
Wood, plastic, paint, metal, 200 x 100 x 100 cm
Collection Ludwig, 1969

Jean Tinguely, *Balouba No. 3,* 1959
Wood, metal, bulb, electro motor, h. 144 cm
Collection Ludwig, 1969

Jean Tinguely, *Char No. 8 (Vehicle No. 8),* 1968
Metal, wood, electro motor, 70 x 267 x 100 cm
Collection Ludwig, 1969

Mark Tobey, *Hurrying Patterns,* 1970
Tempera on paperboard, 98.5 x 69.5 cm
Anniversary donation, 150 years WRM, 1974

Hann Trier, *Puya I,* 1954
Tempera on canvas, 65.5 x 80 cm
Collection Haubrich, 1959

Hann Trier, *Tatort IV (Scene of the Crime IV),* 1963
Tempera and oil on canvas, 97 x 130.5 cm
City of Cologne, 1963

Richard Tuttle, *Mountain,* 1965
Acrylic on canvas and wood, 116 x 119 cm
Donation Ludwig, 1976

Cy Twombly, *Crimes of Passion,* 1960
Oil, crayon, pencil on canvas, 190 x 200 cm
Donation Ludwig, 1976

Alexander Tyshler, *No. 4 of the Lyric Circle,* 1928
Oil on canvas, 73.4 x 55.6 cm
Collection Ludwig, 1982

Günther Uecker, *Große Spirale I (Schwarz), II (Weiß)
(Great Spiral I [Black], II [White]),* 1968
Nails on canvas and wood, 150 x 150 cm each
Collection Ludwig, 1969

Hans Uhlmann, *Stahlplastik (Steel Sculpture),* 1956
Galvanized steel, h. 125 cm
Gift of BDI, 1961

Ursula (Schultze-Blum), *C'est moi (It's Me),* 1966
Velvet bust, feathers and fur, 52 x 25 x 23 cm
Donation Ludwig, 1976

Ursula (Schultze-Blum), *Köln-Bild (Cologne Picture),* 1972
Oil and gold on wood, 88.7 x 129.7 cm
Donation Ludwig, 1976

Victor Vasarely, *Calota MC,* 1965–67
Tempera on canvas, 150 x 100 cm
Donation Ludwig, 1976

Maria-Helena Vieira da Silva, *Le Port (The Docks),* 1953
Oil on canvas, 97 x 131 cm
City of Cologne, 1962

Maurice de Vlaminck, *Stilleben mit Blumen und Früchten
(Still Life with Flowers and Fruit),* 1911
Oil on canvas, 60 x 73 cm
Donation Haubrich, 1946

Friedrich Vordemberge-Gildewart,
Komposition Nr. 122/1941 (Composition No. 122/1941), 1941
Oil on canvas, 60.5 x 80.5 cm
Collection Haubrich, 1953

Wolf Vostell, *Miss Amerika (Miss America),* 1968
Screen photo, varnish paint and silk screen on canvas,
200 x 120 cm
Donation Ludwig, 1976

Franz Erhard Walther, *Um Brutalität zu verstehen
(Vorschlag) (Towards an Understanding of Brutality),* 1967
4 boards with cloth cover, 190 x 19 cm
Donation Ludwig, 1976

Andy Warhol, *Do-it-yourself – Landscape,* 1962
Acrylic on canvas, 178 x 137 cm
Donation Ludwig, 1976

Andy Warhol, *129 Die in Jet-Plane Crash,* 1962
Acrylic on canvas, 254.5 x 182.5 cm
Donation Ludwig, 1976

Andy Warhol, *Red Race Riot,* 1963
Acrylic and Liquitex on canvas, 350 x 210 cm
Donation Ludwig, 1976

Andy Warhol, *Flowers,* 1964
Acrylic on canvas, 208 x 328 cm
Collection Ludwig, 1979

Tom Wesselmann, *Bathtub No. 3,* 1964
Oil on canvas, plastic, different objects, 213 x 270 x 45 cm
Donation Ludwig, 1976

Tom Wesselmann, *Landscape No. 2,* 1964
Paper, photo, oil paint, plastic, canvas, 193 x 239 cm
Donation Ludwig, 1976

Tom Wesselmann, *Great American Nude No. 98,* 1967
Oil on 5 canvas screens, 250 x 380 x 130 cm
Donation Ludwig, 1976

Fritz Winter, *Nächtlicher Regen (Nocturnal Rain),* 1952
Oil on canvas, 95.5 x 131.4 cm
Collection Haubrich, 1952

Wols (Wolfgang Alfred Otto Schulze-Battmann),
Les Voyelles (The Vowels), 1950
Oil on canvas, 61 x 46 cm
Donation Ludwig, 1976

Wols (Wolfgang Alfred Otto Schulze-Battmann),
Das blaue Phantom (Blue Phantom), 1951
Oil on canvas, 73 x 60 cm
City of Cologne, 1979

Index

Acknowledgements

© for the illustrations by the artists or their heirs at-law, or by the following:
Jankel Adler, Ernst Barlach, Max Beckmann, George Grosz, Käthe Kollwitz, Rune Mields, Hans Purrmann, Franz Radziwill, Renée Sintenis, Wolf Vostell by VG Bild-Kunst, Bonn, 1986; Arman, Pierre Bonnard, César, Salvador Dalí, Kees van Dongen, Max Ernst, Domenico Gnoli, Juan Gris, Fernand Léger, André Masson, Henri Matisse, Claude Monet, Francis Picabia, Pablo Picasso, Niki de Saint-Phalle, Victor Vasarely, Maurice de Vlaminck, Wols by VG Bild-Kunst, Bonn/SPADEM, Paris, 1986; Carl Andre, Öyvind Fahlström, Jasper Johns, Roy Lichtenstein, Robert Rauschenberg, James Rosenquist, Andy Warhol, Tom Wesselmann by VG Bild-Kunst, Bonn/VAGA, New York, N.Y., 1986; Carlo Carrá, Giorgio de Chirico, Gino Severini by VG Bild-Kunst, Bonn/SIAE, Rome, 1986; Karel Appel, Piet Mondrian by VG Bild-Kunst, Bonn/BEELDRECHT, Amsterdam, 1986; Paul Delvaux by VG Bild-Kunst, Bonn/SABAM, Brüssel, 1986; Bernhard Heisig, Wolfang Mattheuer by VG Bild-Kunst, Bonn/BFU, Berlin/GDR, 1986; Arnulf Rainer by VG Bild-Kunst, Bonn/VBK, Vienna, 1986; Josef Albers, Heinrich Campendonk, Lovis Corinth, Lyonel Feininger, Alexei von Javlensky, Paul Klee, Oskar Kokoschka, Otto Mueller, Karl Schmidt-Rottluff, Kurt Schwitters, Mark Tobey by COSMOPRESS, Geneva, 1986; Pierre Alechinsky, Hans Arp, Jean Bazaine, Georges Braque, Alexander Calder, Marc Chagall, Robert Delaunay, André Derain, Jean Dubuffet, Marcel Duchamp, Raymond Duchamp-Villon, James Ensor, Alberto Giacometti, Natalia Goncharova, Hans Hartung, Vassily Kandinsky, Yves Klein, František Kupka, Mikhail Larionov, Henri Laurens, Jacques Lipchitz, René Magritte, Alfred Manessier, Man Ray, Albert Marquet, Matta, Joan Miró, Martial Raysse, Germaine Richier, Jean-Paul Riopelle, Nicolas Schöffer, Pierre Soulages, Nicolas de Staël, Antoni Tàpies, Maria-Helena Vieira da Silva by ADAGP, Paris & COSMOPRESS, Geneva, 1986; Willi Baumeister by Archiv Baumeister, Stuttgart; Otto Dix by Otto Dix Stiftung, Vaduz; Erich Heckel by Nachlaß Erich Heckel, Hemmen-hofen; Ernst Ludwig Kirchner by Dr. Wolfgang and Ingeborg Henze, Campione d'Italia; Franz Marc by Galerie Stangl, München; Paula Modersohn-Becker by Paula Modersohn-Becker Stiftung, Bremen; Edvard Munch by Munch-Museet, Oslo; Emil Nolde by Nolde-Stiftung, Seebüll; Max Pechstein by Max Pechstein Archiv, Hamburg; Oskar Schlemmer by Familie Schlemmer, Nachlaß Oskar Schlemmer, Badenweiler; Boris Birger, Kasimir Malevich, Alexander Petrov, Nina Shilinskaya by VAAP, Moscow, 1986.